D1626174

# Intellectual Property — The New Law

# Intellectual Property — The New Law

## A Guide to the Copyright, Designs and Patents Act 1988

**Michael F Flint**
**Clive D Thorne**
**Alan P Williams**

London
BUTTERWORTHS
1989

| | |
|---|---|
| United Kingdom | Butterworth & Co (Publishers) Ltd, 88 Kingsway, LONDON WC2B 6AB and 4 Hill Street, EDINBURGH EH2 3JZ |
| Australia | Butterworths Pty Ltd, SYDNEY, MELBOURNE, BRISBANE, ADELAIDE, PERTH, CANBERRA and HOBART |
| Canada | Butterworths Canada Ltd, TORONTO and VANCOUVER |
| Ireland | Butterworth (Ireland) Ltd, DUBLIN |
| Malaysia | Malayan Law Journal Sdn Bhd, KUALA LUMPUR |
| New Zealand | Butterworths of New Zealand Ltd, WELLINGTON and AUCKLAND |
| Singapore | Butterworth & Co (Asia) Pte Ltd, SINGAPORE |
| USA | Butterworths Legal Publishers, ST PAUL, Minnesota, SEATTLE, Washington, BOSTON, Massachusetts, AUSTIN, Texas and D & S Publishers, CLEARWATER, Florida |

All rights reserved. No part of this publication may be reproduced or transmitted in any form or by any means (including photocopying and recording) without the written permission of the copyright holder except in accordance with the provisions of the Copyright Act 1956 (as amended) or under the terms of a licence issued by the Copyright Licensing Agency Ltd, 33-34 Alfred Place, London, England WC1E 7DP. The written permission of the copyright holder must also be obtained before any part of this publication is stored in a retrieval system of any nature. Applications for the copyright holder's written permission to reproduce, transmit or store in a retrieval system any part of this publication should be addressed to the publisher.

Warning: The doing of an unauthorised act in relation to a copyright work may result in both a civil claim for damages and criminal prosecution.

© Denton Hall Burgin & Warrens 1989

A CIP Catalogue record for this book is available from the British Library.

ISBN 0 406 503079

Typeset by Kerrypress, Luton
Printed by Mackays of Chatham plc

# Preface

This book does not deal with English intellectual property law generally, but only with the Copyright, Designs and Patents Act 1988. At the time of writing, none of the subsidiary legislation envisaged by the Act has been published, even in draft form, much less passed into law. The Act was passed on 15 November 1988. Only five sections are now in force. The rest of the Act (301 out of 306 sections) is expected to be brought into force during the course of 1989.

The Act completely replaces the existing copyright and designs law and the law relating to performers' protection. It makes relatively minor changes to trade mark and patent law.

The purpose of this book is to serve as a guide to the new legislation for legal practitioners and persons whose occupation requires a knowledge of copyright, performers' protection, design, trademark, and patent law. It does not pretend to be an academic analysis of the new law: that will no doubt follow in due course with the publication of new editions of the standard works on the subject.

However, until those new editions are published it is hoped that this book will prove to be a useful tool for those who have to advise on and use the new legislation, and that it will continue to be a valuable handbook for many years to come for those who have difficulty in finding room in their briefcases for the textbooks, containing as it does the complete text of the Act.

The book seeks to explain the new law, relate the new provisions to earlier legislation, and to international treaties and conventions, and to highlight those provisions in the Act which actually change the law. Because the whole approach to the drafting of the copyright and performers' protections Chapters of the Act is completely different from that adopted by the draftsmen of the Copyright Act 1956 and the Performers' Protection Acts 1958 to 1972, it is thought that this book may be more helpful than most books introducing amending legislation.

Chapters 1 to 5, parts of Chapter 6, Chapters 8 and 13 were written by Michael Flint, the rest of Chapter 6 and Chapters 7, 10, 11 and 12 by Alan Williams and Chapters 9 and 14 to 17 by Clive Thorne.

*Preface*

We would like to thank the partners of Denton Hall Burgin & Warrens for allowing us time to produce the work, the staff of Denton Hall Burgin & Warrens who aided its preparation and Butterworths for their efforts in facilitating prompt publication.

MFF
CDT
APW

January 1989

# Contents

# Table of Statutes

References in this Table to *Statutes* are to Halsbury's Statutes of England (Fourth Edition) showing the volume and page at which the annotated text of the Act may be found. References in the Table are to paragraph numbers. The Copyright, Designs and Patents Act 1988 is set out at pages 169–380

Chapter 1

# Introduction

**1.1** The Copyright Act 1911 was the first Copyright Act which covered the entire field of copyright and enabled the United Kingdom to ratify the Berne Convention as revised at Berlin on 13 November 1908. Between 1911 and 1956 there was no amending legislation, except for the Registered Designs Act 1949. The Dramatic and Musical Performers' Protection Act of 1925 did not, in fact, amend the 1911 Act, but introduced protection for performers (which was not in the nature of copyright protection) by making the infringement of performers' rights a criminal offence enforceable by a fine. The Copyright Act 1956, which came into force on 1 June 1957 and which was based upon the Gregory Report, enabled the United Kingdom to ratify the Berne Convention, as revised at Brussels on 26 June 1948. The Copyright Act 1956 was itself amended by the Copyright Act 1956 (Amendment) Act 1982, the Copyright (Amendment) Act 1983, the Criminal Justice Act 1982, the Cable and Broadcasting Act 1984 and the Copyright (Computer Software) Amendment Act 1985.

**1.2** In 1973, a departmental committee was set up under the chairmanship of Mr Justice Whitford to review the law of copyright designs. Its report, *Copyright and Designs Law* (Cmnd 6732), was published in 1977.

**1.3** In 1981, the Government published its Green Paper *Reform of the Law Relating to Copyright, Designs and Performers' Protection* (Cmnd 8302).

**1.4** Subsequently, in 1985, the Government published a further Green Paper entitled *The Recording and Rental of Audio and Video Copyright Material* (Cmnd 9445).

**1.5** The final paper to be produced before the Bill, which became the Copyright, Designs and Patents Act 1988 ('the 1988 Act'), was tabled before the House of Lords, was the White Paper, published in 1986 and entitled *Intellectual Property and Innovation* (Cmnd 9712). This White Paper dealt not only with copyright law but also with patent and trade mark law. Part 2 of the White Paper contained the Government's intentions for the reform of copyright law. The Bill which was tabled before the House of Lords was based upon most, but not all, of the White Paper proposals.

**1.6** One purpose of the 1988 Act is to enable the United Kingdom to ratify certain international conventions, which it is unable to do whilst the law is as set out in the Copyright Act 1956.

**1.7** The most important convention is the Berne Convention. The latest text of the Berne Convention is that which was revised in Paris in 1971. The 1988 Act brings United Kingdom law into line with the Paris Text by making the following changes:

(i) Under Section 48(1) of the 1956 Act, choreographic works were not protected unless they were reduced to writing. Section 3 of the 1988 Act protects choreographic works as dramatic works which need only to be 'recorded', but not necessarily in writing. This provision matches Article 2 of the Paris Text which only requires choreographic works to be 'fixed in some material form'.

(ii) Article 4 of the Paris Text demands that works of architecture erected in a Convention country must be protected. Because the erection of a building did not constitute publication under the 1956 Act, and the works of foreigners were not protected unless they were made by nationals of Convention countries or first published in a Convention country, the erection of a building designed by an architect who was not a national of a non-Convention country was not protected. Under the 1988 Act, section 175(3) provides that in the case of a work of architecture in the form of a building, construction of the building is to be treated as equivalent to publication of the work.

(iii) Article 7(2) of the Paris Text provides for a minimum term of copyright for a film of 50 years from first public showing or 50 years from making. Under the 1956 Act, section 13(3), a film was protected for 50 years from publication. The 1988 Act, section 13(1) provides that the term of copyright for a film is 50 years from when it was made or, if it was released during that period, 50 years from the end of the year in which it was released.

(iv) Article 15(2) of the Paris Text demands that the person whose name appears on the film 'in the usual manner' shall be presumed to be the maker unless the contrary is proved. There was no such presumption in the 1956 Act. The 1988 Act provides that when copies of a film as issued to the public bear a statement that a named person was the author or director of the film, that statement shall be presumed to be correct until the contrary is proved (section 105(2)(a)).

(v) Article 15 of the Berne Convention, as revised at Stockholm, requires Convention countries to allow designated authorities to sue in United Kingdom courts in respect of infringement of copyright in 'folklore'. There was no such provision in the 1956 Act, but section 169 of the 1988 Act introduces such a provision.

(vi) The 1956 Act did not contain any provisions protecting moral rights, except Section 43 which deals only with false attribution of authorship for a period of life plus 20 years. The Paris Text demands (Article 6 bis) that the Convention countries protect either the author's right of paternity or right of integrity for the copyright term of life plus 50 years. Chapter IV of the 1988 Act introduces full moral rights to British copyright law for the first time and complies with the Paris Text of the Berne Convention.

**1.8** The United Kingdom is a party to the Rome Convention 1961, but, as permitted by that Convention, made a special notification that for the broadcasts of foreign broadcasting organisations to be protected in the United Kingdom, they must have their headquarters in a contracting state and transmit from a contracting state. Section 156 of the 1988 Act provides that foreign broadcasts qualify for copyright protection if they satisfy one of the tests and, therefore, the United Kingdom will be able to withdraw its special notification under the Rome Convention.

**1.9** The United Kingdom is not a signatory to the 'Satellites' Convention 1974. By making the change referred to in the above paragraph, by defining a 'broadcast' in section 6 so as to include satellite transmissions intended for public reception and by including in the restricted acts applicable to broadcasts, the right to prevent the inclusion of broadcasts in cable programme services (section 16(1)(d)), the United Kingdom can now sign the Satellites Convention.

**1.10** The Act received Royal Assent on 15 November 1988. In June 1988 the Commission of the European Communities published a Green Paper, *Copyright and the Challenge of Technology — Copyright Issues Requiring Immediate Action.* The Green Paper makes recommendations for members to change their national copyright laws to deal with questions relating to piracy, the home copying of sound and audio-visual works, distribution and rental rights for sound and video recordings, the legal protection of computer programs, legal problems relating to the operations of data bases and the external aspects of copyright protection. The extent to which the 1988 Act meets these recommendations is discussed below, but in general, and subject to the actual wording of any directives that may be made by the EEC pursuant to the Green Paper, it would appear that the 1988 Act is not at variance with the recommendations in the Green Paper.

**1.11** The 1988 Act is divided into seven parts: Part I deals with copyright law, Part II with rights in performances, Part III with design right, Part IV with registered designs, Part V with patent agents and trade mark agents, and Part VI with patents, whilst Part VII contains various miscellaneous provisions. Part I of the Act is laid out in a different way from the 1956 Act. The 1956 Act dealt with each class of work in turn, setting out the applicable restricted acts, duration of copyright etc. The 1988 Act first defines all the copyright protected works, then deals with authorship and ownership, duration, rights and acts permitted in relation to copyright works. This approach and the drafting of the Act generally makes the Act more comprehensible than the 1956 Act and easier for the practitioner who needs to refer frequently to it, to find the relevant section.

**1.12** The 1988 Act does not amend the 1956 Act, which is repealed by the 1988 Act, but replaces it. The transitional provisions contained in Schedule

1 deal with matters relating to works created before the 1988 Act comes into force.

**1.13** The provisions of the Act relating to industrial designs follow the 1986 White Paper to a considerable extent. There are now three separate but distinct regimes for the protection of industrial designs: a totally new right akin to copyright called 'design right' covering functional shape and configuration; an enhanced Registered Designs Act 1949 covering non-function designs; and in the case of ornamentation and two-dimensional designs, copyright protection. The new 'design right', with its 'must-fit' and 'must-match' exceptions, seems to a large extent to exclude spare parts from protection.

**1.14** The Act makes small but significant amendments to patent and trade mark law including the establishment of a new status and privilege in discovery for patent and trade mark agents. Perhaps the most important of the amendments is the creation in section 300 of a new offence of fraudulently applying or using a trade mark. This is a move back to the offence of forging a trade mark contained in the Merchandise Marks Act 1887 and shortsightedly abolished by the Trade Descriptions Act 1968.

**1.15** Section 305 brought into effect on 15 November 1988, the date when the Act received Royal Assent, certain detailed provisions dealing with the filing of international patent applications and which amend sections 89 and 123 of the Patents Act 1977, and the provisions for the benefit of the Hospital for Sick Children (see paragraph 4.13).

Sections 293 and 294, dealing with licences of right in relation to old pharmaceutical patents, came into force on 16 January 1989.

The rest of the Act will be brought into force in whole or in part by statutory instrument.

Chapter 2

# Descriptions of work and related provisions

## Introduction

**2.1** Chapter I of Part I of the Act, after introductory provisions (sections 1 and 2), describes works which are entitled to copyright protection with related provisions (sections 3 to 8), sets out how the authorship of a work is to be determined and who is the first owner of the copyright in the work (sections 9 to 11) and the duration of copyright in each type of work (sections 12 to 15).

**2.2** Section 1 states that copyright is a property right which subsists, in accordance with Part I of the Act, in original literary, dramatic, musical or artistic works. It also subsists in sound recordings, films, broadcasts, cable programmes and the typographical arrangement of published editions. Copyright subsists in such works only if the requirements with respect to qualification set out in Chapter IX, are met.

### *Copyright as a property right*

**2.3** Copyright has always been treated as a property right and is part of that group of property rights known as intellectual property. However, this Act is the first Copyright Act actually to describe copyright as being a property right. It is, nevertheless, 'not a right to do anything, but to stop others from doing something' (Laddie, Prescott and Vitoria *Modern Law of Copyright* (2nd edn, 1987) p 1). In essence, the 1988 Act defines certain works in which protection exists and describes the rights of the owners of the copyright to prevent others from doing certain acts in relation to the work, with exceptions from those restricted acts.

### *Protection accorded only to defined works*

**2.4** Property right under copyright law subsists in the works set out in section 1(1). A work which does not fit within one of these descriptions is not entitled to copyright protection. This approach to copyright law is not followed in all countries by any means. The Berne Convention, Article

1 states that the countries to which the Convention applies constitute a Union for the protection of the rights of authors in their literary and artistic works. Article 2(1) defines the expression 'literary and artistic works' as including 'every production in the literary, scientific and artistic domain whatever may be the mode or form of its expression . . . .'. This is a far wider approach than that of the 1988 Act, which, in fact, adopts the same approach as the Copyright Acts of 1911 and 1956 in this regard. The Act contains definitions of each of the works protected (described in detail below) and if a work does not fit within the definition contained in the Act, then it will not be entitled to copyright protection even though it might be a 'production in the literary, scientific and artistic domain'.

### *No distinction between works and subject matters*

**2.5** The widest category of works is 'literary, dramatic, musical or artistic works'. These are defined in sections 3 and 4. The Copyright Act 1956 ('the 1956 Act') defined only these works as works and all other matters which were the subject of copyright protection were described as 'subject matters'. The reason for the distinction was that a 'subject matter' usually involves the incorporation in it of a literary, dramatic, musical or artistic work. Subject matters being sound recordings, films, broadcasts, cable programmes or typographical arrangements of published editions, in each case one of the works would have to be incorporated in order to produce the subject matter. The new Act makes construction and terminology of copyright law easier by rolling up the old subject matters with the old works and treating all categories as copyright works (section 1(2)).

Section 1(1)(b) includes, therefore, in the description of a copyright work, 'sound recordings, films, broadcasts or cable programmes'.

### *Literary, dramatic, musical and artistic works must be original*

**2.6** It will be noted that only literary, dramatic, musical or artistic works must be original in order to acquire copyright protection. The word 'original' has been the subject of a long line of judicial decisions. The most frequently cited decision is that of Peterson J in *University of London Press Ltd v University Tutorial Press Ltd* [1916] 2 Ch 601, in which the judge said:

> 'The word "original" does not in this connection mean that the word must be the expression of original or inventive thought. Copyright Acts are not concerned with the originality of ideas, but with the expression of thought, and, in the case of "literary work", with the expression of thought in print or writing. The originality which is required relates to the expression of the thought. But the Act [Copyright Act 1911] does not require that the expression must be in an original or novel form but that the work must not be copied from another work — that it should originate from the author.'

**2.7** Presumably the reason for the omission of the word 'original' in relation to works other than literary, dramatic, musical or artistic works, is due to the fact that the works listed in section 1(1)(b) and (c) incorporate other original works by their very nature — a sound recording will incorporate a literary or musical work, a film will incorporate a literary, musical and/or artistic work, etc. Sections 5(2), 6(5), 7(6), and 8(2) have the effect of making it clear that a copy or infringing version of one of these works or an earlier work of the same nature, does not itself require copyright protection.

### *Qualification for protection*

**2.8** Section 1(3) provides that even if a work comes within one of the descriptions of works set out in section 1(1)(a), (b) or (c), nevertheless it will not acquire copyright protection unless the requirements with respect to qualification for copyright protection are met. These requirements are set out in section 153 and the provisions referred to therein. They relate to the nationality of the author or the country where the work was first published or the broadcast or cable programme was transmitted. They are dealt with in detail in Chapter 12 below.

## Rights subsisting in copyright works

**2.9** Section 2(1) in effect outlines what ownership of copyright means — it is the exclusive right to do the acts set out in Chapter II of Part I of the Act, restricted by the copyright for the particular work in question. A copyright owner has no more wide-ranging rights than those set out in Chapter II. The copyright legislation of the United Kingdom has always followed this approach. Some countries express the right in more general terms. However, under UK copyright law, as re-enacted in this Act, a copyright owner cannot prevent someone doing something with a copyright work unless that action is within one of the acts restricted by the Act and is specified in Chapter II as a work of that description or such action constitutes a secondary infringement of copyright as set out in the same chapter. For example, the owner of the copyright in a painting cannot prevent the owner of the physical work of art exhibiting that work of art freely. The right to restrict exhibition is not one of the rights specified in Chapter II. Similarly, the owner of the copyright in a book cannot prevent that book being hired through a library, because the hiring of books is not an act restricted by Chapter II applicable to literary works.

### *Introduction of moral rights*

**2.10** Section 2(2) introduces the full panoply of moral rights into the United Kingdom copyright legislation for the first time. These are categorised as:

(i) the right to be identified as author or director;

(ii) the right to object to derogatory treatment of work; and

(iii) the right to privacy of certain photographs and films.

The Copyright Act 1956, section 43 gave to authors only the right to prevent some other person being attributed as the author of their works. The absence of moral rights provisions from UK copyright law had prevented the United Kingdom from ratifying the Paris Text of 1971 of the Berne Convention which required signatory States to provide protection for the moral rights of authors in literary, dramatic, musical and artistic works and films without discrimination between nationals and foreigners. The inclusion of the moral rights provisions contained in Chapter IV of Part I of the Act, will enable the United Kingdom to ratify the 1971 Paris Text of the Berne Convention.

Moral rights are dealt with in detail in Chapter 7 below.

**2.11** Sections 1 and 2 of the 1988 Act cover much the same ground as section 1 of the 1956 Act, in a more comprehensible and direct way. Section 1(1) of the 1956 Act covered the same ground as section 1(2) and (3) of the current Act cover. Section 1(2) of the 1956 Act compares to section 2(1) of the 1988 Act. Section 1(4) of the 1956 Act is covered by section 1(1) of the 1988 Act. Section 1(5) of the 1956 Act is covered by section 1(3), together with the provisions of section 148, of the 1988 Act. It may be that the approach of the draftsman to the 1988 Act will be found more logical and intelligible than the drafting of the 1956 Act.

## Descriptions of work and related provisions

**2.12** Sections 3 to 8 set out the descriptions of the works which are entitled to copyright protection. Bearing in mind that 'subject matters' as described in the 1956 Act are now described as 'works', the comparable sections in the 1956 Act were as follows:

| *Description of work* | *Section of 1956 Act* | *Section of 1988 Act* |
|---|---|---|
| Literary work | 48 | 3(1) |
| Dramatic work | 48 | 3(1) |
| Musical work | Not defined | 3(1) |
| Artistic work | 31, 48 | 4(1) |
| Sound recording | 12(9), 48 | 5(1) |
| Film | 13(10) | 5(1) |
| Broadcast | Television and sound broadcast defined in s 14(10) | 6(1) |
| Cable programme | 14A(11) (introduced by the Cable and Broadcasting Act 1984) | 7(1) |
| Published edition | Not defined | 8(1) |

## Literary works

**2.13** The 1956 Act did not attempt to give a full definition of 'literary work', but merely stated in section 48 that it included 'any written table or compilation'. The 1988 Act attempts a full definition (section 3(1)):

> **'any work, other than a dramatic or musical work, which is written, spoken or sung, and accordingly includes—**

(a) a table or compilation, and

(b) a computer program.'

It should first be noted that dramatic or musical works are expressly excluded from the definition. The 1956 Act was not specific in this regard. The distinction between literary and dramatic works is not of great importance. The restricted acts are, in general, the same for both types of work. The distinction is made because dramatic works are intended for performance whilst literary works are generally read. The importance of the new phraseology is to clarify the point that there cannot be a special class of composite copyright — a song cannot have a copyright in its own right. The music will be a musical work and the words either a dramatic work, if the words require acting or dancing for their proper representation, or a literary work, if they only require to be sung.

**2.14** The inclusion of tables or compilations and computer programs in the definition merely codifies existing case and statute law. Section 48(1) of the 1956 Act provided that a literary work 'includes any written table or compilation'.

The inclusion of a computer program in the definition of a literary work was introduced into the 1956 Act by the Copyright (Computer Software) Amendment Act 1985, although this Act was always intended to be temporary, pending a major revision of copyright law.

**2.15** It should be noted that a literary work does not need to possess aesthetic merit or literary style (*University of London Press Ltd v University Tutorial Press Ltd*). Football pools, lists of foxhounds, trade catalogues, examination papers, trade directories, railway timetables etc, have all been held to be literary works.

**2.16** It will be noted that there is no definition of a computer program. However, the additional inclusion of a 'table and computation' as a 'literary work' suggests that both individual computer programs as well as an assembly of programs constituting a software product are to be regarded as 'literary works'. It should also be noted that there are sections in the Act which relate specifically to computer programs and not to other forms of 'literary works'. These provisions include:

(a) the adaptation of a computer program (section 21(4));

(b) the rental of computer programs (section 18);

(c) dealings in devices designed to circumvent copyright protection when copies of a copyright work are issued to the public in an electronic form which is copy-protected (this provision would include computer programs) (section 296).

## Dramatic works

**2.17** 'Dramatic work' is defined in section 3(1) as including 'a work of dance or mime'. The definition of a dramatic work in the 1956 Act appeared in section 48(1) and was considerably longer:

> '"dramatic work" includes choreographic work or entertainment in dumb show if reduced to writing in the form in which the work or entertainment is to be presented, but does not include a cinematograph film, as distinct from a scenario or script for a cinematograph film.'

The reason for the change in description from choreographic work is that that expression implies resolution to written or other form. The word 'dance' does not have such an implication and, as is discussed below (paragraph 2.19), the Act seeks to relax the requirement as to the way in which copyright works are to be fixed to recognise changes in methods of fixation through videotape, film and other technical innovations. It is not clear why 'mime' has replaced 'entertainment in dumb show', except that mime is a word which is generally accepted nowadays to mean an entertainment in dumb show and may reflect the draftsman's desire to avoid unnecessary wording. The Concise Oxford Dictionary definition of 'mime' is 'simple farcical drama marked by mimicry; similar modern performance with gesture and usually without words'.

The words contained in the 1956 Act requiring the work to be reduced to writing are now covered by the provisions of section 3(2) and (3).

## Musical works

**2.18** 'Musical work' is defined in section 3(1) as follows:

> '"musical work" means a work consisting of music exclusive of any words or action intended to be sung, spoken or performed with the music.'

A musical work was not defined in the 1956 Act. There is no clear judicial definition of the expression. However, in *Redwood Music Ltd v B Feldman & Co Ltd* [1979] RPC 1 and *Redwood Music Ltd v Francis Day & Hunter Ltd* [1978] RPC 429, the court accepted, but did not hold, that a song could not be a musical work including the lyrics. The music was a musical work and the lyrics were a literary work. The new definition gives statutory effect to this position by expressly excluding from the definition, words or actions intended to be spoken or performed to the music. However, musical annotations or directions on a score are part of the musical work.

### *Recorded in writing etc*

**2.19** Section 3(2) provides that copyright does not subsist in a literary, dramatic or musical work unless and until it has been recorded in writing or otherwise. The 1956 Act dealt with this point in a somewhat elliptical manner by providing in section 49(4) that a work was not made until it was first reduced to writing or some other material form. The new Act therefore recognises that a work may be in existence before it acquires its copyright protection.

Possibly a more important result of this section is that works of dance or mime are now protected irrespective of the manner in which they are reduced to a material form. The 1956 Act, section 48(1) only protected them if they were reduced to writing. Accordingly, such works can now be protected once they have, for example, been filmed or recorded on videotape. This change brings United Kingdom legislation into line with the Paris Text of the Berne Convention, Article 2, paragraph 2, which requires only that works should be protected by being fixed in some material form (see Chapter 1, paragraph 1.6). 'Writing' is defined by section 178 as including any form of notation or code, whether by hand or otherwise and regardless of the method by which, or medium in or on which, it is recorded, and 'written' is to be construed accordingly.

**2.20** Section 3(3) provides that it is not necessary for the work to have been recorded for the purposes of subsection (2) by or with the permission of the author. The subsection also makes it clear that if it is not the author who records the work, copyright may nevertheless subsist in the record as distinct from the work recorded. Thus the reporter who takes down a speech in writing, may acquire copyright in his arrangement of the speech. Nevertheless, the copyright in the speech itself will belong to the speaker, if it is in fact entitled to copyright protection — by, for example, having previously been recorded in some form by the speaker.

## Artistic works

**2.21** Section 4 is simply a definition section defining 'artistic work'. Definitions of 'artistic work' were contained in sections 3(1) and 48 of the 1956 Act. The differences are slight.

**2.22** Section 4(1) divides artistic works into three categories:

(a) graphic works, photographs, sculptures or collages irrespective of artistic quality;

(b) works of architecture, being buildings or models for a building; and

(c) works of artistic craftsmanship.

Its approach is similar to that adopted in the 1956 Act except that in the 1956 Act the words used in the definition of 'artistic work' were then subject to further definition in the interpretation section, whereas the 1988 Act defines these words within the same section.

**2.23** Section 4(2) defines 'building', 'graphic work', 'photograph' and 'sculpture'.

'Building' is defined as including 'any fixed structure, and a part of a building or fixed structure'. The 1956 Act defined a building as including a structure, not limiting it to a fixed structure.

By including parts of a building or part of a fixed structure in the definition, a new extension to a building which is out of copyright will clearly now be entitled to copyright in its own right.

### *Graphic works*

**2.24** The expression 'graphic work' is a new one which did not appear in the 1956 Act definition of artistic works. It is defined as including:

(a) any painting, drawing, diagram, map, chart or plan; and

(b) any engraving, etching, lithograph, woodcut or similar work.

Section 3(1) of the 1956 Act included in the definition of artistic works, paintings, drawings and engravings. There were then separate definitions of drawings and engravings, which incorporated all the other words used within the definition of graphic work in the 1988 Act. In addition, 'print or similar work not being a photograph' was included. Presumably it is thought that the expression 'graphic work' is itself so wide that it must include prints and similar works. If the New Zealand decision in *Wham-O Manufacturing Co v Lincoln Industries* [1982] RPC 281 is right, then industrial moulds are still capable of protection as artistic works under the new Act.

### *Photographs*

**2.25** 'Photograph' is defined as meaning 'a recording of light or other radiation on any medium on which an image is produced or from which an image may by any means be produced and which is not part of a film'. The definition in section 48 of the 1956 Act was somewhat narrower and might well have been considered as being limited to conventional photographs taken using light-sensitive film. The new definition is wide enough to include, for example, holographic reproductions.

The final words of the definition carry forward the concept contained in the 1956 Act that a film is not a photograph and, therefore, as a film, does not obtain protection as an artistic work, but has its own protection as a separate category of work.

### *Sculptures*

**2.26** 'Sculpture' is defined as including a cast or model made for the purposes of sculpture and therefore is defined in exactly the same way as it was in section 48 of the 1956 Act.

### *Collages*

**2.27** It may be noted that there is no definition of 'collage'.

### *Works of artistic craftsmanship*

**2.28** Likewise, there is no definition of 'a work of artistic craftsmanship'. The 1956 Act provided that a work of artistic craftsmanship must be a work which did not fall within the definition of paintings, sculptures, etc or works of architecture. There is no similar limitation in the 1988 Act. Therefore, the case law on works of artistic craftsmanship must be used to determine the meaning of this expression. Like the 1956 Act, the 1988 Act draws a distinction between graphic works, photographs, sculptures or collages, as being works for which no artistic quality is required, to acquire copyright protection, whereas, in the case of artistic craftsmanship, such artistic quality is required unless the work falls within paragraphs (a) and (b) of section 4(1), as well as being a work of artistic craftsmanship. A leading case on works of artistic craftsmanship is *Hensher v Restawile Upholstery (Lancs) Ltd* [1976] AC 64, [1973] 3 All ER 414.

## Sound recordings

**2.29** Section 5(1) defines 'sound recording' and 'film'.

**2.30** The new definition of 'sound recording' is more detailed than that which appeared in section 12(9) of the the 1956 Act. It is defined as:

> '(a) a recording of sounds, from which the sounds may be reproduced, or
>
> (b) a recording of the whole or any part of a literary, dramatic or musical work, from which sounds reproducing the work or part may be produced,
>
> regardless of the medium on which the recording is made or the method by which the sounds are reproduced or produced.'

The 1956 Act defined 'sound recording' in section 12(9) and 'record' in section 48. It also defined 'reproduction' in section 48. There is no definition of 'record' in the 1988 Act because this word does not appear anywhere in the Act. The definition of 'recording' in Part II of the Act is not applicable to Part I of the Act.

It is presumably thought that the word 'reproduction' does not require definition as it has a clear enough meaning, but possibly the courts will refer to the 1956 Act should any doubt be cast upon the meaning of the word. However, the absence of a definition will widen rather than limit the meaning that was attributed to the word in the 1956 Act.

The first half of the definition covers sounds which are not recordings of literary, dramatic or musical works. This subparagraph would therefore give protection to a recording of, for example, birdsong or a steam engine.

Subparagraph (b) has been carefully drafted so as to exclude from protection a computer program on which a literary work has been recorded and which it is possible to play back so as to produce sound in the form of a meaningless noise to the human ear. It is not accorded copyright protection because, first, as it will not constitute a recording of sounds, it cannot come within subparagraph (a), and second, it will not be capable of producing sounds which reproduce a musical, literary or dramatic work as required under subparagraph (b).

The definition also makes it clear that a musical work which is composed electronically directly on to a recording medium, without the recording of sound having previously taken place, will itself create a sound recording in which copyright will subsist, as well as in the musical work in its own right.

***Film soundtracks are sound recordings***

**2.31** The 1956 Act excluded from the definition of a sound recording, the soundtrack associated with a cinematograph film. There is no longer any such exclusion.

## Films

**2.32** Section 5(1) defines 'film' as 'a recording on any medium from which a moving image may by any means be produced'. The 1956 Act defined film, using the expression 'cinematograph film', in section 13(10) in a rather more lengthy way. The new definition appears to achieve all that the 1956 Act definition achieved but the significant difference is that the soundtrack of the film is no longer protected as a film but as a sound recording.

***No copyright in copies of sound recordings and films***

**2.33** Section 5(2) provides that copyright does not subsist in a sound recording or film which is copied from a previous sound recording or film. This does not have the consequence, however, that because there is no copyright in the copies, they may be freely pirated as the infringement provisions, dealt with below, preclude this eventuality.

## Broadcasts

**2.34** Section 6 defines 'broadcast', and clarifies who is the person deemed to be making a broadcast and from where a broadcast is deemed to be made.

**2.35** Section 6(1) defines 'broadcast' as meaning:

> 'a transmission by wireless telegraphy of visual images, sounds or other information which—
>
> (a) is capable of being lawfully received by members of the public, or
>
> (b) is transmitted for presentation to members of the public;
>
> and references to broadcasting shall be construed accordingly.'

This is the first time that the word 'broadcast' has been defined for the purposes of copyright law. The meaning of the word has been examined by the courts on a number of occasions, but there was no clear decision as to its meaning prior to the introduction of this Act. However, it was generally assumed to mean transmissions by wireless telegraphy capable of being received by the public. Accordingly, the new definition does not significantly change the law. Doubts as to whether a transmission which was encrypted was a broadcast have been removed by section 6(2), which provides that an encrypted transmission is regarded as being lawfully received by members of the public, only if decoding equipment has been made available to members of the public by or with the authority of the person making the transmission or the person providing the contents of the transmission. Therefore, a transmission which is encrypted, but in respect of which decoders cannot be purchased or otherwise acquired lawfully by members of the public, will not be regarded as a broadcast.

The expression 'wireless telegraphy' means 'the sending of electro-magnetic energy over paths not provided by a material substance constructed or arranged for that purpose' (section 178). Wireless telegraphy does not, accordingly, include transmission by wire and, therefore, a cable transmission is excluded from the definition of a broadcast. It should be noted that the word 'lawfully' precludes the extension of the definition to transmissions which are 'pirate' broadcasts, ie broadcasts which are not authorised for reception under the Wireless Telegraphy Act 1949 or other similar legislation.

Under the 1956 Act, the only broadcasts that received copyright protection were those transmitted by the BBC or the Independent Broadcasting Authority and broadcasts by organisations of countries to which protection was extended by the Copyright (International Conventions) Order 1979.

### *Teletext transmissions protected as broadcasts*

**2.36** The words 'or other information' in the opening sentence of section 6(1) should be noted. They will accord protection to transmissions of teletext information or, for example, computer games or other computer information which may be transmitted for downloading into computers.

**2.37** Subparagraph (b) of section 6(1) deals with transmissions which are broadcasts for general reception, such as those of the IBA, the BBC and, in due course, the broadcasts of British Satellite Broadcasting plc, the franchisee of the UK direct broadcast satellite ('DBS') and other transmissions via satellites which are intended for reception by members of the public.

### *The maker of broadcasts*

**2.38** Section 6(3) provides that the person who makes a broadcast is the person transmitting the programme, if he has responsibility to any extent for its contents, and also the person providing the programme who makes, with the person transmitting it, the arrangements necessary for its transmission. 'Programme' is defined, in the context of broadcasting, as any item included in the broadcast.

Under the 1956 Act, because the IBA was the owner of the copyright and also the body transmitting the programme, the radio and television companies franchised by the IBA had no copyright ownership of their programmes. The effect of this subsection is, in the case of IBA broadcasts, to make both the IBA and the television and radio companies joint makers of the broadcast. The IBA has supervisory responsibility for the contents of the programming and also transmits the programme through its own transmitters. The television and radio companies supply the programme to the IBA for transmission.

On the other hand, in the case of satellite transmissions which are uplinked by British Telecom or another licensed UK telecommunications operator, only the company providing the programme will be the copyright owner of the broadcast, because the operator takes no responsibility for the contents of the programmes. If, however, the operator were, in any case, to seek to take some form of supervisory control over the programmes, it would become a joint copyright owner with the programme provider. The BBC, as both the provider of the programme and the owner of its own transmitters which takes responsibility for its own transmissions, continues, as under the earlier Act, to be a sole copyright owner. If an independent producer provided a programme to the BBC or an ITV contractor, that producer would not become a joint owner of the broadcast copyright, because only the BBC or the IBA would make the arrangements necessary for the transmission of the programme.

It should be noted that the words which effectively define a 'programme' so as to include any item in a broadcast, may have the effect of making a sub-contractor which, for example, televises live sporting events such as horse racing and transmits them via the transmitters of the IBA or the BBC, a co-owner.

### *Origin of satellite broadcasts*

**2.39** Section 6(4) provides that in the case of a satellite transmission, the place from which the signals carrying the broadcast are transmitted to the satellite, is the place from which the broadcast is made. The Cable and Broadcasting Act 1984 (Schedule 5, paragraph 6(7)) amended the 1956 Act to provide that a DBS broadcast originated in a place from which the signals were transmitted to the satellite.

The effect of section 6(4) is to extend this concept to all broadcasts caught by the definition in section 6(1), which is wide enough to include fixed satellite signals (FSS) as well as DBS signals. This approach is not necessarily one that will be adopted throughout the rest of Europe — the so-called 'Bogsch theory' predicates that the downlink from the satellite should be treated for copyright purposes as a separate broadcast act for the country of reception.

### *Reception of satellite broadcasts*

**2.40** Section 6(5) provides that references in Part I of the Act to the reception of a broadcast include reception of a broadcast relayed by means of a telecommunications system. 'Telecommunications system' is defined by section 178 as meaning 'a system for conveying visual images, sounds or other information by electronic means'. Section 6(5), together with this definition, is a simplified version of the provisions of section 48(4) of the 1956 Act. It is necessary, because in other parts of the Act there are references to the doing of various acts by 'reception of a broadcast' and the effect of this subsection is to include in such references the wire diffusion of broadcasts.

**2.41** Section 6(6) provides that copyright does not subsist in a broadcast infringing the copyright in another broadcast or in a cable programme.

## Cable programmes and cable programme services

**2.42** Section 7 defines 'cable programme service' and a number of related expressions. It also sets out exceptions to the definition. However, the Secretary of State is given the right to add or remove exceptions by statutory instrument. Copyright was accorded to cable programme services by amendments to the 1956 Act introduced by the Cable and Broadcasting Act 1984.

**2.43** It was notoriously difficult to comprehend the Cable and Broadcasting Act amendments, because not only was it necessary to refer to both the 1956 Act and the Cable and Broadcasting Act, but in addition it was necessary to refer to the Telecommunications Act 1984. The new Act obviates this necessity by defining and dealing with cable programmes and cable programme services without reference to other legislation.

**2.44** Section 7(1) defines 'cable programme' as 'any item included in a cable programme service'. Therefore, a cable programme is not limited to a full programme, but excerpts from programmes, newsbreaks and the like.

**2.45** The section 7(1) definition of 'cable programme service' is extensive and reference should be made to the text of the Act.

It should be noted that the words 'or other information' in the definition are wide enough to include such items as computer programs, which are not intelligible to the human eye or ear.

### *Microwave multiple distribution systems*

**2.46** A service which is sent by wireless telegraphy is excluded from the definition of a cable programme service. Thus, under the 1988 Act, Microwave Multiple Distribution Systems (MMDS) will not come within the definition of a cable programme service. MMDS is the system of transmitting microwave signals by terrestrial transmitters for domestic televison reception. However, it should be borne in mind that the Cable and Broadcasting Act 1984 is not amended in a similar manner, so that a MMDS system may require to be licensed under that Act, even though it has no copyright protection as a cable programme service.

### *Exceptions from the cable programme service definition*

**2.47** Section 7(2) sets out the five principal exceptions from the definition of 'cable programme service'. These can be summarised simply as follows:

(i) services which are essentially interactive;

(ii) closed user group business services;

(iii) domestic services;

(iv) non-business closed user group services such as hospitals etc;

(v) cable operators and broadcasters' in-house services.

Section 7(1)(a) differentiates between reception at two or more places which is simultaneous, or at different times. If the service is sent at different times, then in order to be a programme service, it must be sent in response to requests by different users. Accordingly, an interactive cable service whose subscribers can request specific programmes for individual reception, will come within the definition, in addition to the cable television services provided in the normal way to all subscribers for simultaneous reception. It should be noted that this subsection does not require the service to be made available to members of the public. Section 7(1)(b) provides that if the service does not fall within subsection (1)(a), then it must be for presentation to members of the public. It should also be noted that the definition in the Cable and Broadcasting Act which included a service presented 'to any group of persons' is no longer included. It is, however, doubtful whether this makes any difference in practice.

### *Interactive services*

**2.48** Section 7(2)(a) excepts from the definition of a cable programme service, a service or part of a service of which it is an essential feature that as an addition to the sending of information by the person providing the service, there will also be information sent on the same service for reception by the programme service provider. The expression 'part of a service' is important because it has the effect of excluding, inter alia, 'expert systems' which form part of a cable television operator's total service, whilst not excluding the rest of that service. An expert system is, for example, a data base which can be accessed, but which is also capable of receiving information.

An electronic mail-box system is not excluded by this subsection because the terminals of such systems are utilised *only* for the sending of material. However, it is arguable that such a system does not in any event come within the definition set out in section 7(1), because it is not intended for reception at two or more places, nor for presentation to members of the public.

Such services sent to two or more places might well fall within the definition, unless they are excluded by one of the other exceptions.

Section 7(2)(a) basically repeats the provisions of the Cable and Broadcasting Act, section 2(4).

### *Closed user group business services*

**2.49** Section 7(2)(b) effectively provides the same exception as section 6(3) of the Telecommunications Act 1984. To be excepted from the definition, a business service must be run only by the person carrying on the business; the information conveyed by the system must be for the purposes internal to the running of the business; it must not be made available to third parties; and it must not be connected to any other telecommunication system.

### *Domestic services*

**2.50** Section 7(2)(c) is similar to section 6(2) of the Telecommunications Act 1984. Domestic systems are excluded provided that they are run by an individual as distinct from a corporation; all the apparatus is under the individual's control; the information is intended to be conveyed solely for the domestic purposes of that individual; and the system is not connected to any other telecommunications system.

### *Non-business closed user group services*

**2.51** Section 7(2)(d) is similar to section 6(2)(b)(i) of the Telecommunications Act 1984, which exempts systems on a single set of premises in single occupation from the need to obtain a licence under that Act. Systems not requiring a licence under that Act did not come within the definition of a cable programme service in the Cable and Broadcasting Act and, therefore, did not acquire protection under the 1956 Act. To be excluded under section 7(2)(d) of the 1988 Act, the apparatus comprised in the system must be situated in or connected to premises which are in single occupation and must not be connected to any other system. Most importantly, however, where the cable programme service is operated as part of the amenities provided for residents or inmates of premises run as a *business*, then the exception does not apply and the service will constitute a cable programme service for the purpose of section 7(1). Services run by hotels, for example, are now within the definition; previously, they were excepted by section 48(3B) of the 1956 Act. Therefore, a hotel which relays a video to its guests will be running a cable programme service and will therefore need a licence from the copyright owner. It should be noted that the exception applies only where the premises are run as a business, so that hospitals which are part of the National Health Service, public universities, State schools etc can run such services without being deemed to run a cable programme service for the purposes of the Copyright Act.

### *'In-house' broadcast and cable programme services*

**2.52** Section 7(2)(e) also excludes services run only for the providers of broadcast or cable programme services. Therefore, the relay via a public switched network of a programme from a programme provider's studios to a cable television operator is not itself a cable programme service. Similarly, when television stations send by wire (as distinct by wireless telegraphy — see definitions) extracts of programmes to each other for the purpose only of viewing by executives of the stations, the sending of such signals will not constitute a cable programme service requiring a licence from the copyright owner.

### *Inclusion of cable programmes in cable programme services*

**2.53** Section 7(5) makes it clear that where there is a reference to the inclusion of a cable programme, or a work, in a cable programme service, the reference is to its transmission as part of the service. When there are references to a person including a cable programme or work in a cable programme service, the person referred to is the person who provides the service.

### *'Must carry' programmes excluded from protection*

**2.54** Section 7(6) excludes from copyright protection cable programmes which are included in cable programme services by the reception and immediate retransmission of a broadcast. The Cable and Broadcasting Act requires cable television operators to carry BBC and IBA programmes — the so called 'must carry' rule. Therefore, there is no separate copyright in these programmes where they are included in a cable programme service. This is a re-enactment of section 14A(ii) of the 1956 Act, as amended by the Cable and Broadcasting Act.

### *Infringing programmes excluded from protection*

**2.55** Also excluded, by section 7(6), are cable programmes which infringe — or to the extent that they infringe — the copyright in another cable programme or in a broadcast. Therefore, if a cable television operator includes in his cable programme service a broadcast for which he has no licence to relay, such as a pay television film channel, he has no copyright ownership or protection for that channel because no such copyright arises or vests in the cable television operator.

## Published editions

**2.56** Section 8(1) defines a 'published edition' as a 'published edition of the whole or any part of one or more literary, dramatic or musical works'. The definition applies only where the expression is used in the context of a typographical arrangement.

**2.57** Section 8(2) provides that copyright does not subsist in a typographical arrangement of a published edition to the extent that it reproduces the typographical arrangement of a previous edition. The same, virtually identical, words appear as the proviso to section 15(1) of the 1956 Act.

**2.58** The only significant difference in the wording between the 1988 Act and the 1956 Act is that the 1988 Act makes it quite clear that a published edition can mean a published edition of part of a literary, dramatic or musical work as distinct from the whole of such a work.

Chapter 3

# Authorship and ownership of copyright

## Introduction

**3.1** Sections 9, 10 and 11 deal with authorship and ownership of copyright. Section 9 defines 'author' and then sets out the person who shall be taken to be the author of each type of work. Section 10 deals with works of joint authorship and section 11 deals with the first ownership of copyright. The identification of the first author of a work is important not only to determine the ownership of the work, but also whether it qualifies for copyright. Chapter IX of Part I of the Act, which sets out the provisions for qualification for copyright protection, provides that copyright shall not subsist in a work unless certain qualifications are satisfied as regards the author (see paragraphs 12.4 to 12.7).

## Authorship generally

**3.2** Section 9(1) defines an 'author' in relation to a work as the person who creates it. There is no definition of 'author' in the 1956 Act, except in relation to photographs.

**3.3** Section 9(2) sets out the person who should be taken to be the author in the case of a sound recording, a film, broadcast, cable programme, and typographical arrangement of a published edition. Section 9(3) sets out the provisions as to who should be taken to be the author of a literary, dramatic, musical or artistic work which is computer-generated. There are no general principles as to who is the author of a literary, dramatic, musical or artistic work because Parliament did not consider it to be a difficult task to identify the author in the case of those works. There is a significant body of case law, however, in which the courts examined specific cases to identify who was the author of a particular literary, dramatic, musical or artistic work. The problem which the new Act does not seek to solve is that which arises when a copyright work has come into existence, which is based upon the idea of one person but which has been put into material form by another. The principle applied by the courts is to examine first what it is in which copyright exists: there is no copyright in ideas and therefore copyright will exist in the work which is first resolved into material form. The leading cases on the subject are *Walter v Lane* [1900] AC 539, considered in *Robertson v Lewis* [1976] RPC 169, and *Donoghue v Allied Newspapers Limited* [1938] Ch 106, [1937] 3 All ER 503. There is no reason to be believe that the wording of section 9 is such as to change the case law in this regard. However, section 3(3) of the 1988 Act (see paragraph 2.20) may have some impact in certain cases, such as the case of the shorthand writer who takes down a speech.

### *Authorship of sound recordings and films*

**3.4** Section 9(2)(a) provides that in the case of a sound recording or film, the person by whom the arrangements necessary for the making of the recording or film are undertaken, is the author.

So far as sound recordings are concerned, this is a significant change in the law from the 1956 Act. Under section 12(4) of that Act, the maker of a sound recording was entitled to the copyright in a recording. Under section 12(8), the maker of the recording was the person who owned the record at the time when the recording was made.

So far as films are concerned there is no change in the law — section 13(10) of the 1956 Act defined 'maker' in the same words as 'author' is defined in relation to a film by section 9 of the 1988 Act.

### *Authorship of broadcasts*

**3.5** Section 9(2)(b) provides that the author of a broadcast is the person making the broadcast. In the case of the reception and immediate retransmission of a broadcast, the author is the person making the broadcast which is retransmitted. In order to determine who is the person making the broadcast, it is necessary to refer to section 6(3) (see paragraph 2.38).

This is a significant change in the law: until the 1988 Act the only broadcasts entitled to copyright protection were those of the BBC, the IBA and those foreign broadcasts to which protection was extended by the Copyright (International Conventions) Order 1979.

### *Authorship of cable programme services*

**3.6** Section 9(2)(c) provides that the author of a cable programme service is the person providing the cable programme service. This repeats the provisions of section 14 A (3) of the 1956 Act (as amended by the Cable and Broadcasting Act 1984).

### *Authorship of typographical arrangements*

**3.7** Section 9(2)(d), by providing that the publisher is the author of a typographical arrangement of a published edition, repeats the provisions of section 15(2) of the 1956 Act.

### *Authorship of computer-generated works*

**3.8** Section 9(3) clarifies the position with regard to the authorship of computer-generated works, so far as literary, dramatic, musical or artistic works are concerned, by providing that the author is to be the person for whom the arrangements necessary for the creation of the work are undertaken — thereby equating computer-generated works to films and sound recordings so far as ownership is concerned.

'Computer-generated' is defined by section 178 as a work that is generated by computer in circumstances such that there is no human author of the work. The effect of section 9(3) is, therefore, to introduce into copyright law, for the first time, the concept of a separate copyright ownership for a work which is not created directly by a human being — where the originality, indeed, may be that of the computer itself. Until the passing of the 1988 Act it was generally considered that computers should be equated to typewriters when considering the ownership and copyright status generally of works produced by computers. For example, the directory that is produced by the input of a great many people and compiled by the use of a computer program without additional human aid might not have been entitled to copyright protection as a compilation on the grounds that there was no human authorship of the work. Computer-generated works prepared by means of computer analysis, for example, weather maps or directories, are now clearly subject to copyright protection.

## Unknown authorship

**3.9** The expression 'unknown authorship' is introduced by section 9(4) as applying to a work where the identity of none of the authors is known. Section 9(5) provides that the identity of an author is regarded as unknown if it is not possible for a person to ascertain his identity by reasonable enquiry. Once the author's identity is known, the work shall not subsequently be regarded as a work of unknown authorship. These provisions are very similar to those contained in section 11 of and Schedule 2 to the 1956 Act regarding unknown authorship.

## Joint authorship

**3.10** Section 10(1), by defining a work of joint authorship as that produced by the collaboration of two or more authors in which the contribution of each author is not distinct from that of the other author or authors, goes back to the terminology used in the 1911 Act. The 1956 Act, section 11(3) used the same wording except that the contribution in that case of each author had to be 'separate' from the contribution of the other author. There has been no reported judicial examination of the difference between the wording of the 1911 and 1956 Acts. The 1988 Act does not alter the position when authors of different kinds of works work together, for example, in such cases as the lyricist who works with a composer but neither contributes to the work of the other. In these cases, they are not considered as joint authors. Thus, a song consists of two separate works — a literary work as regards the lyrics and a musical work as regards the music.

**3.11** Section 10(2) provides that broadcasts shall be treated as works of joint authorship when more than one person is to be taken as making the broadcast — see paragraph 2.38, dealing with section 6(3).

**3.12** It should be noted that pursuant to section 10(3), wherever an author is referred to in the Act, the reference shall be construed in relation to a work of joint authorship as a reference to all the authors of the work.

## First ownership

**3.13** Section 11 deals with first ownership of copyright. By providing that the author of a work is the first owner of any copyright in it, it repeats the concept of the 1956 Act as regards ownership.

### *First ownership of works made in the course of employment*

**3.14** However, there is a significant change. Whereas both the 1956 Act (section 4(4)) and the 1988 Act (section 11(2)) provide that the first owner of literary, dramatic, musical or artistic works made by an employee in the course of his employment is the employer, there is now no limitation on the rights of first ownership of proprietors of newspapers, magazines etc. Section 4(2) of the 1956 Act limited the rights vesting in the employer in those cases to the right to publish in newspapers, magazines and similar periodicals.

It should also be noted that the wording of section 4(4) of the 1956 Act referred to 'a contract of service or apprenticeship', whereas section 11(2) of the 1988 Act speaks of works created 'in the course of his employment'.

But 'employed', 'employee', 'employer' and 'employment' are described in section 178 as referring to employment under a contract of service or of apprenticeship. There would not appear to be any substantive change in this regard.

### *Commissioned works of art*

**3.15** The provisions in section 4(3) of the 1956 Act, which accorded first ownership to persons commissioning the taking of photographs or the painting or drawing of a portrait or the making of an engraving, are not re-enacted. The first owner will be the photographer or the painter etc under the new Act, irrespective of how it was commissioned (unless the photographer, painter etc created the work in the course of his employment). Section 85 does, nonetheless, give certain moral rights to persons who, for private and domestic purposes, commission the taking of a photograph or the making of a film. But that section is concerned with according rights of privacy rather than copyright ownership.

## *Crown copyright excluded from first ownership provisions*

**3.16** The provisions of section 11 do not apply to Crown copyright, Parliamentary copyright or to the copyright owned by certain international organisations — see sections 163, 165 and 168 and paragraphs 12.16 to 12.24 below.

## *Transitional provisions as regards first ownership*

**3.17** Schedule 1, paragraph 11 provides that the question as to who was the first owner of copyright in an existing work is to be determined in accordance with the law in force at the time the work was made and not in accordance with the provisions of the 1988 Act, if made before that Act came into force. There is an important exception in the case of photographs, portraits, engravings etc commissioned prior to the commencement of the 1988 Act but made after the commencement of the 1988 Act — in those circumstances first ownership is to be determined in accordance with the provisions of the previous legislation. A similar exception applies in the case of sound recordings which have been commissioned. The provisions of section 12(4) of the 1956 Act would apply to recordings commissioned before the commencement of the 1988 Act so that the person commissioning the making of the sound recording will be the first owner.

# Chapter 4

# Duration of copyright

**4.1** Sections 12 to 15 deal with the duration of copyright in all kinds of works. Previously the provisions regarding duration of copyright appeared in the sections relating to particular works but now they are all to be found in these sections with minor exceptions.

## Literary, dramatic and musical works

**4.2** Section 12 deals with the copyright in literary, dramatic, musical or artistic works — there is no change in the provisions of the 1956 Act insofar as the period of copyright in these works continues to be 50 years from the end of the calendar year in which the author dies.

It is also the period of copyright specified by Article 7(1) of the Berne Convention.

**4.3** However, section 12 does contain some important changes from the 1956 Act. In the first place, under the 1956 Act the period of copyright related only to published works. A work that was first published many years after the death of the author enjoyed a copyright period of 50 years from the date of its publication. This is no longer the case. The copyright period will expire irrespective of the date of first publication.

Obviously there is a problem if the authorship of the work is not known and, therefore, there is no way to determine the end of the period of copyright by reference to the death of the author. Section 12(2) provides that copyright shall expire at the end of the period of 50 years from the end of the calendar year in which the work is first made available to the public. It should be noted that the concept of publication, which was that of issuing copies to the public (section 49(2) of the 1956 Act), for this purpose is replaced by section 12(2) to include performance in public, broadcasting and inclusion in cable programme services, as regards literary, dramatic or musical works; and exhibition in public or including the work in a film, broadcast or cable programme service as regards artistic works. Unauthorised acts are to be disregarded.

If a work is not made available to the public, it will continue to enjoy an indefinite copyright until it is made available to the public. However, section 57 contains provisions enabling works of unknown authorship to be published (see paragraph 6.36 below).

Computer programs are not protected by copyright from rental of copies to the public after 50 years from the end of the year when copies are first issued to the public (section 66(5) and paragraph 6.47 below).

### Photographs

**4.4** A further change effected by section 12 is to give to photographs the same copyright period as any other artistic works and not the limited period of 50 years under the 1956 Act.

### Computer-generated works

**4.5** Computer-generated literary, dramatic, musical or artistic works have a copyright period of 50 years from the end of the year in which the work was made — section 12(3).

### *Works of joint authorship*

**4.6** Section 12(4) deals with the period of copyright in works of joint authorship and basically re-enacts the provisions of the 1956 Act. In determining the commencement of the 50-year period for works of joint authorship, the date of death of the last of the authors to die is the relevant date.

As to works in joint Crown copyright, Parliamentary copyright or copyright of certain international organisations, see sections 163 to 166 and 168, which determine the period of duration of copyright for those works and not section 12.

## Sound recordings and films

**4.7** Section 13 sets out the duration of copyright in sound recordings and films. There are some significant changes from the 1956 legislation, although the basic period of copyright is still 50 years for both types of work.

Section 12(3) of the 1956 Act provided that the period of copyright in a sound recording was 50 years from the end of the calendar year in which the recording was first published. In the case of a film, the period of 50 years began when the film was registered (which is no longer applicable, the legislation regarding registration of films having been repealed); or, in the case of films which were not registered, the copyright period expired at the end of 50 years from the end of the calendar year in which the film was first published. The definition of publication, as mentioned above, was the issuing of copies to the public. Accordingly, a sound recording or film might have remained in copyright indefinitely because it was never published. The law has now been amended to bring it in line with the Paris Text of the Berne Convention, so that the copyright in sound recordings and films expires 50 years from the end of the calendar year in which they are made or, if released during that period, then 50 years from the end of the year in which they were released.

'Released' is defined in section 13(2) as meaning when first published, broadcast, or included in a cable programme service, in the case of both types of work. In the case of a film, or film soundtrack, released also means when the film is first shown in public. As in other cases, unauthorised acts are to be ignored in determining whether a work has been released.

'Publication' and related expressions (which include 'published') are defined in section 175(1) and, as regards films and sound recordings, means the issue of copies to the public, as in the 1956 Act. Section 176(4) expressly provides that the word 'published' does not mean the performance or broadcasting of works.

The courts have on numerous occasions considered what constitutes public performance and the reported cases should be referred to in construing the 1988 Act in this regard.

## Broadcasts and cable programmes

**4.8** Section 14 deals with the duration of copyright in broadcasts and cable programmes which is to be 50 years from the year in which the broadcasts were made, or the programme was included in the cable programme service. The section therefore re-enacts sections 14(2) and 14A(3) of the 1956 Act.

### *Repeat broadcasts and cable programmes*

**4.9** Section 14(2) re-enacts sections 14(3) and 14A(4) of the 1956 Act by providing that there will be copyright in a repeat broadcast or cable programme, which will expire at the same time as the copyright in the original broadcast or cable programme.

A repeat broadcast or cable programme is defined by section 14(3) as meaning a programme which is a repeat of a broadcast previously made, or of a cable programme previously included in a cable programme service. There was no definition of a 'repeat' in the 1956 Act, but the law has not changed in any way.

## Typographical arrangements

**4.10** Section 15 says that the duration of copyright in typographical arrangements of published editions is 25 years from the end of the calendar year in which the edition was first published. This re-enacts section 15(2) of the 1956 Act. 'Publication' is now defined in section 175.

## Transitional provisions

**4.11** The transitional provisions relating to the duration of copyright are to be found in Schedule 1, paragraph 12. The basic rule is that copyright will continue to subsist until the day on which it would have expired under the 1956 Act in relation to all works with certain exceptions. The principal exception relates to unpublished works, for which the general rule is that copyright will subsist until 50 years from the end of the year in which the copyright provisions of the 1988 Act come into force.

## Perpetual copyright under the 1775 Act

**4.12** The perpetual copyright conferred on universities and colleges by the Copyright Act 1775 expires 50 years from the end of the year in which the new copyright provisions come into force (Schedule 1, paragraph 13).

## Peter Pan and the Hospital for Sick Children

**4.13** Section 301 introduces a curious provision which entitles the Hospital for Sick Children, Great Ormond Street, to a right to continue to enjoy income from the exploitation of Sir James Barrie's *Peter Pan,* notwithstanding that copyright in that work expired on 31 December 1987. The details of the scheme, under which royalties are payable to the Hospital, are contained in Schedule 6. Royalties are payable in respect of any public performances, commercial publication, broadcasting or inclusion of the work in a cable programme service. No royalties are payable in respect of anything which could have been done without a copyright licence before 31 December 1987; nor are royalties payable in respect of anything done in pursuance of arrangements made before the passing of the 1988 Act. The royalty is to be determined by agreement or, failing agreement, by the Copyright Tribunal. The rights of the Hospital are not assignable and shall cease if the Hospital seeks to assign or change them.

Chapter 5

# Rights of copyright owners

**5.1** Chapter II of Part I of the 1988 Act deals with the acts restricted by copyright. In the 1956 Act, the restricted acts relating to a particular work or subject matter were to be found in the section dealing with that work or subject matter; in the new Act they are now grouped together in Chapter II. The Chapter begins by outlining the basic acts restricted by the copyright in all works and then elaborates on those restricted acts in later sections. Sections 22 to 26 deal with secondary infringment — infringement of copyright in a manner that does not constitute doing one of the acts restricted by the copyright. Finally section 27, the last section of Chapter II, deals with infringing copies.

## The restricted acts

**5.2** There are now five basic acts restricted by copyright which apply to all categories of works (section 16(1)):

(a) copying the work;

(b) issuing copies of the work to the public;

(c) performing, showing or playing the work in public;

(d) broadcasting the work or including it in a cable programme service;

(e) making an adaptation of the work or doing any of the other restricted acts in relation to an adaptation.

Section 16(2) provides that an infringing act is committed if a person does any of the acts restricted by the copyright without a licence from the copyright owner or authorises some other person to do such acts.

Although section 16(1) lists all the restricted acts, not all of the restricted acts are applicable to every category of work. In order to ascertain which restricted acts apply to which categories of works, it is necessary to look at the specific sections dealing with that restricted act. Thus, section 17 deals with copying; section 18 with issuing copies of the work to the public;

section 19 with performance; section 20 with broadcasting and the inclusion of works in cable programmes; and section 21 with adaptations of works.

### *Substantial part*

**5.3** Section 16(3) provides that references to the doing of a restricted act are to the doing of it in relation to the work as a whole or any substantial part of it. This is the 1988 version of section 49(1) of the 1956 Act. The expression 'substantial part' was used in both the 1911 and 1956 Acts and has been the subject of considerable judicial examination. The leading case is *Ravenscroft v Herbert* [1980] RPC 193. The essence of the decisions on the meaning of this expression is that quality, as much as quantity, is important in determining what is a substantial part.

Section 16(3) also provides that it is immaterial whether the restricted act is done directly or indirectly or whether any intervening acts themselves infringe the copyright. Thus copying an infringing copy, even without knowledge that the copy is an infringing copy, is a breach of copyright.

## Infringement by copying

**5.4** Section 17 deals with infringement of copyright by copying. It sets out the works to which it relates and clarifies certain acts which constitute copying in relation to certain works.

**5.5** Copying a work is an act restricted by the copyright in every description of copyright work. This was also the case under the 1956 Act.

### *Copying in relation to literary, dramatic and musical works*

**5.6** Section 17(2) deals with copying in relation to literary, dramatic, musical or artistic works. It means 'reproducing the work in any material form' and includes storing the work in any medium by electronic means. 'Electronic' is defined in section 178 as meaning actuated by electric, magnetic, electro-magnetic, electro-chemical or electro-mechanical energy; and 'in electronic form' means in a form usable only by electronic means.

These provisons are re-enactments of sections 2(5) and 3(5) of the 1956 Act as amended by the Copyright (Computer Software) Amendment Act 1985 and, as regards reproducing in any material form, of section 49(4) of that Act.

Section 17, together with section 9(3), would seem to meet the recommendation set out in paragraph 6.6.1 of the EEC Green Paper that legal action to protect the compilation of works within a data base should be available to copyright owners.

### *Copying in relation to artistic works*

**5.7** Section 17(3), which applies only to artistic works, provides that copying includes the making of a copy in three dimensions for two-dimensional works and vice versa. This was previously found in the definition of 'reproduction' in section 48 of the 1956 Act. Sections 51 to 53, dealing with copying of design documents for anything other than artistic works, should also be noted (see paragraphs 14.1 to 14.5).

### *Copying of single frames of a film*

**5.8** Section 17(4) puts into statutory form the decision in *Spelling Goldberg Productions Inc v BPC Publishing Ltd* [1981] RPC 280 that to make a photograph of part of an image which forms part of a film, broadcast or cable programme constitutes copying. Accordingly, making a photograph of a television screen showing a broadcast of a football game will infringe the copyright in the broadcast.

### *Copying of published editions*

**5.9** Section 17(5) provides that copying in relation to the typographical arrangement of a published edition means making a facsimile copy of the arrangement. 'Facsimile' is defined in section 178 as including a copy which is reduced or enlarged in scale.

## Issuing copies to the public

**5.10** Section 18 deals with the restricted act of issuing copies to the public — it applies to every description of work. It replaces the restricted act in the 1956 Act of publishing a work, which applied only to literary, dramatic, musical and artistic works.

**5.11** Section 18(2) provides that the issue to the public of copies of a work refers to the first act of putting the copies into circulation and not to any subsequent distribution, or hire, or loan of those particular copies. This subsection reverses the decision in *Infabrics Ltd v Jaytex Shirt Co* [1982] AC 1, [1981] 1 All ER 1057, HL, where it was held that the expression 'publishing the work', when used in the 1956 Act, referred to making available to the public copies of a work which was previously unpublished and that, therefore, sales or the issue of reproductions to the public (unless the first publication) were not included in the expression.

### *Exhaustion of rights*

**5.12** The doctrine of exhaustion of rights is not affected by this particular point, because it is made clear that when such a copy has been put into circulation, (subject to what is said below in relation to rental) there will be no breach of copyright in the further sale, hiring, distribution or loan of those copies.

Copies which have already been put into circulation can be imported into the UK for further distribution. However, copies which have not already been put into distribution outside the UK cannot be issued to the public without being in breach of this restricted act.

### *Rental of sound recordings, films and computer programs*

**5.13** There is a most important exception to the provisions of section 18(2). As regards sound recordings, films and computer programs, the restricted act of issuing copies to the public includes any rental of copies to the public. This is the first time that the concept of rental as a restricted act has been introduced into UK copyright legislation.

**5.14** 'Rental' is defined in section 178 as meaning any arrangement under which a copy of a work is made available for payment or in the course of a business for which payment is made, on terms that it will or may be returned.

**5.15** The wording is such that it will catch an arrangement under which a videotape (which is a film for the purposes of the Copyright Act) is sold on terms that the buyer can sell it back at a reduced price.

It should be noted that section 66 contains provisions for the Secretary of State to make orders providing for compulsory rental licences. This section is dealt with in paragraph 6.46 below.

### *Rental right recommended by the EEC Green Paper*

**5.16** Paragraphs 4.11.1 and 4.11.2 of the EEC Green Paper recommend that member States should introduce a right for authors of sound recordings and producers of videograms to authorise the commercial rental of their works. Thus section 18(2) meets this recommendation.

## Performance of works in public

**5.17** Section 19(1) deals with the restricted act of performance of a work in public and it applies only to literary, dramatic or musical works.

**5.18** Section 19(2) defines performance. The definition is to all intents and purposes the same as that contained in section 48(1) of the 1956 Act — it is a very wide definition intended to cover all present and future modes of performance that can be envisaged. It includes delivering lectures, addresses, speeches and sermons. It also includes 'any mode of visual or acoustic presentation', and the presentation by means of a sound recording, film, broadcast or cable programme of the work.

### *Playing or showing works in public*

**5.19** The section differentiates between the 'performance' of a work on the one hand and 'the playing or showing of a work in public' on the other. The latter, by section 19(3), is a restricted act applicable only to sound recordings, films, broadcasts or cable programmes. There are no definitions which deal with 'playing or showing a work in public'.

Although the approach is slightly different, the effect is much the same as that of the 1956 Act.

### *Liability for performing reception apparatus in public*

**5.20** Section 19(4) provides that when a breach of the restricted act of performing, playing or showing a work in public is committed by the use of apparatus for receiving visual images or sounds conveyed by electronic means (for example, by the use of a radio or television set), neither the performers, nor the radio station nor television station etc are to be liable for the infringement. The person controlling the operation of the apparatus by which the work is performed, played or shown in public will be liable — see also section 26 and paragraph 5.35 below. This provision re-enacts, in effect, section 49(5) of the 1956 Act. It is, however, worded in a manner that is wide enough to cover most technological innovations that can be conceived, except that it is limited to the reception of visual images or sounds by electronic means. 'Electronic' has a wide definition in section 178. However, it is possible that the use of light which is not actuated by electric energy would not be caught by the definition.

## Broadcasting and inclusion in cable programme services

**5.21** Section 20 deals with the restricted act of broadcasting or the inclusion of a work in a cable programme service — it applies to all categories of work other than the typographical arrangement of published editions.

## Adaptations

**5.22** Section 21 deals with the restricted act of making adaptations of works — it applies to literary, dramatic or musical works.

**5.23** Section 21(1) states that an adaptation is made when it is recorded, in writing or otherwise. Although 'recorded' is not defined in the Act ('writing' is defined in section 178), the wording is intended to be as wide as possible.
Section 21(2) accords protection to an adaptation itself by applying all the restricted acts to an adaptation.

**5.24** However, in the case of an infringement, the plaintiff would not have to show that the adaptation had been recorded at the time that the restricted act was done. Thus, if a performer improvised an adaptation of a piece of music which was copied by a member of the audience, the copyright in the adaptation would be infringed even though it had not yet been recorded with the licence of the performer.

**5.25** Section 21(3) defines adaptation in effectively the same manner as it is defined in section 2(6) of the 1956 Act. It means translations of all works, dramatic versions of non-dramatic works, non-dramatic versions of dramatic works, and comic strip versions of literary or dramatic works. In relation to musical works, an adaptation means an arrangement or transcription.

### *Adaptations to computer programs*

**5.26** Section 21(4) deals with adaptations to computer programs. A computer program is a literary work and is therefore entitled to protection against the doing of any of the restricted acts applicable to literary works. Section 9(4) defines 'translation', but only in relation to computer programs, as including a version of the program into which it is converted into or out of a computer language or code or into a different language or code otherwise than incidentally in the course of running a program. Therefore the consent of the owner of the copyright in a computer program is required to translate the program into a different computer language.

**5.27** Section 21(5), which provides that no inference should be drawn from section 21 as to what does or does not amount to copying, is intended to have the same effect as the final words of section 2(6) in the 1956 Act. It is, accordingly, clear that an adaptation can also amount to copying and can therefore be a breach of the restricted act of making copies.

## Transitional provisions relating to acts infringing copyright

**5.28** The transitional provisions relating to acts infringing copyright appear in Schedule 1, paragraphs 14 to 18 inclusive. Essentially, they provide that the provisions as to infringement contained in Chapters I and II of Part I of the 1988 Act apply only in relation to acts done after the commencement of the 1988 Act. In relation to acts done before that date, the provisions of the 1956 Act will continue to apply. The new restricted act of renting sound recordings, films or computer programs does not apply in relation to copies of those works acquired before the commencement of the 1988 Act, when the purpose of acquiring them was to rent the same.

## Secondary infringement of copyright

### *Importation*

**5.29** Section 22 is the first of the four sections dealing with secondary infringement and specifically deals with secondary infringement by importation into the UK of infringing copies. Section 27 defines and elaborates on the meaning of 'infringing copy' (see paragraphs 5.38 to 5.41). Copyright is infringed if the importer has no licence from the copyright owner. The importer will not be liable if he does not know, or has no reason to believe, that the article which he imports is an infringing copy. The section does not apply to importation for private and domestic use.

Whilst this section largely re-enacts sections 5(2) and 16(2) of the 1956 Act, there is an important change — under the 1956 Act, it was necessary to prove that the importer actually knew that it was an infringing copy. The addition of the words 'or has reason to believe is an infringing copy' will reduce the heavy burden of proof that was placed upon plaintiffs in infringement actions under the 1956 Act.

### *Possession or dealing*

**5.30** Section 23 sets out the provisions concerning infringement by possession in the course of business, sale, hiring, exhibiting in public, or distribution in the course of business by a person who knows or has reason to believe that the article is an infringing copy of a work. It essentially re-enacts the provisions of sections 5(3), 5(4), 16(3) and 16(4) of the 1956 Act. It applies to all categories of works. As in the case of section 22, this section also repeats the concept that an infringer is liable if he has reason to believe that the article is an infringing copy.

The important change introduced by this section is to provide that possession in the course of business can be an infringement. Comparable provisions were introduced by the Copyright Act 1956 (Amendment) Act 1982 and the Copyright (Computer Software) Amendment Act 1985, in that possession by way of trade of sound recordings, films and computer programs was a criminal offence if the person possessing them knew them to be infringing copies. The new civil remedy applies to possession of all types of infringing copyright material and, being a civil remedy, it is not limited to possession with a view to committing an act infringing the copyright.

### *Articles for making infringing copies*

**5.31** Section 24 deals with the manufacture, importation, possession, sale or hiring of articles which provide the means for making infringing copies. It only applies to such articles when they are specifically designed or adapted for making copies, so that an ordinary domestic video cassette recorder does not come within the section. Proof that the defendant knew or had reason to believe that the article was to be used to make infringing copies is necessary.

There was no comparable provision to section 24 in the 1956 Act, except that section 18 (which is not repeated in the new Act) gave copyright owners certain rights in respect of the conversion or detention by any person of any 'plates' used for making infringing copies.

Section 296, which creates a right of action by way of secondary infringement against persons who deal in devices designed to circumvent copy-protection, should also be referred to in this context (see paragraph 9.25).

The EEC Green Paper (paragraph 3.13.1) suggests that member States should take certain measures aimed to reduce home copying, which are principally aimed at digital audio recorders (DAT). The provisions of sections 24 and 296 go some way to meet these recommendations.

### *Transmission for copying purposes*

**5.32** Section 24(2) gives copyright owners a right against a person who transmits a work by means of a telecommunications system without the owners' licence if such person knows or has reason to believe that infringing copies of the work will be made by means of the reception of the transmission in the UK or elsewhere.

A 'telecommunications system' is defined by section 178 as meaning a system for conveying visual images, sounds or other information by an electronic means. Section 24(2) expressly excludes from the use of this expression in this subsection, transmission by broadcasting or inclusion in a cable programme service. The section therefore gives to copyright owners the right to prevent so-called 'downloading' without the licence of the copyright owner.

For example, if a film is transmitted without the licence of the copyright owner to a closed user group of subscribers by a television transmission, which, not being intended for reception by the public, does not constitute a broadcast when the purpose of such transmission is to enable subscribers to make copies of the film, there will be an infringement pursuant to this subsection.

### *Use of premises*

**5.33** Section 25 makes a person who gives permission to use a place of public entertainment for an infringing performance liable for the infringement, unless the person giving the permission believed on reasonable grounds that the performance would not infringe copyright. The section largely re-enacts section 5(5) and (6) of the 1956 Act. The principal changes are that there is now a positive test in that the person giving the permission is not liable if he believed that the performance would not infringe copyright, whereas in the 1956 Act it was a negative test in that he had to show that he was not aware or had no reasonable grounds for suspecting that there would be an infringement by the performance. Moreover, the provision that exempted the person giving permission from liability when permission was given gratuitously or for a nominal consideration, is now omitted.

### *Place of public entertainment*

**5.34** The expression 'place of public entertainment' is defined by section 25(2). It basically repeats section 5(6) of the 1956 Act without any change in meaning. It is wide enough to include not only obvious places such as concert halls, but also those which are occasionally used for public entertainment such as village halls and schools. Private houses which are not 'from time to time made available for hire' are excluded.

### *Supply of apparatus*

**5.35** Section 26 deals with liability for the provision of apparatus which is used for infringing performances of sound recordings, films and radio and television signals; of the occupier who gives permission for the use of such apparatus on his premises; and of the supplier of the sound recording or film which is played or shown in public. The wording of section 26(1)(c) — 'receiving visual images or sounds conveyed by electronic means' — which is primarily intended to catch infringing performances of broadcasts, is also wide enough to cover any new means of conveying visual images or sounds by electronic means not yet invented or available to the public.

Section 26(2) makes the supplier of the apparatus liable for the infringement subject to two conditions: (a) that he knew or had reason to believe that the apparatus was likely to be used to infringe copyright; and (b) that, in the case of apparatus whose normal use involves public performance, such as large video screens, background music systems and the like, he did not believe, on reasonable grounds, that it would be used so as to infringe copyright.

Condition (b) imposes a stricter liability on persons whose business is the provision of equipment used for public performance. Such persons should now take active steps to try to prevent use of the equipment they supply for performances which infringe copyright, by stating that, as part of the terms of the contract, it may be used only for the performance, playing or showing of works for which the hirer has a licence or for which no licence is required because the works are not in copyright. For example, the supplier of a background music system, which will be used to play music that can be heard by the public, should ensure that the occupier of the premises has licences from the appropriate collecting societies such as the Performing Rights Society or Phonographic Performance Ltd. The provisions of section 26(2) are new.

### *Occupier's liability*

**5.36** Section 26(3) makes the occupier of premises who gives permission for the apparatus to be brought onto the premises liable for infringement if, when giving permission, he knew or had reason to believe that the apparatus was likely to be so used as to infringe copyright. This subsection re-enacts section 48(6) of the 1956 Act. The only difference is that there is now a test of guilty knowledge which was not in the 1956 Act.

### *Supplier's liability*

**5.37** Under section 26(4), the supplier of a sound recording or film used to infringe copyright is liable for the infringement, subject to the same test of guilty knowledge. The liability extends even if infringement is by means of a copy made directly or indirectly from the copy which was supplied. Therefore, to lend someone a copy of a video tape so that the borrower may copy it and then perform it publicly without a licence would make the supplier of the first copy liable as well as the borrower.

## Infringing copies

**5.38** Section 27 defines and elaborates upon the definition of 'infringing copy'. Section 27(2) provides quite simply that an article is an infringing copy if its making constituted an infringement of the copyright of the work in question. This replaces section 18(3) of the 1956 Act, which said much the same thing but in a more complicated manner, by defining infringing copy separately in relation to different types of work and subject matters.

### *Infringing copies made abroad*

**5.39** Section 27(3) deals with infringing copies which have been made abroad. It replaces the final paragraph of section 18(3) and section 49(6) of the 1956 Act, provisions which have been the subject of judicial examination, particularly in *Infabrics Ltd v Jatex Ltd* (see paragraph 5.11) and *CBS United Kingdom Ltd v Charmdale Record Distributors Ltd* [1980] 2 All ER 807.

There are two branches to the subsection — first, the article has to have been either imported, or proposed to be imported, into the United Kingdom; second, the making of the article must have constituted an infringement of the copyright in the work or (most importantly) the making in the United Kingdom would have been a breach of an exclusive licence agreement relating to the work. It had been held in the above cases that the effect of the 1956 Act was that, if a copy of the work had been made outside the United Kingdom under licence from the copyright owner, it could be imported into the United Kingdom without becoming an infringing copy, notwithstanding the existence of an exclusive licence agreement for the United Kingdom granted to a third party. The new wording effectively reverses those decisions in this regard.

Thus, articles lawfully made outside the United Kingdom cannot be imported without the consent of the exclusive licensee for the United Kingdom. However, in considering this subsection, section 27(5) should be borne in mind, which provides that, notwithstanding subsection (3), articles which can be imported lawfully into the United Kingdom by virtue of any enforceable Community right within the meaning of section 2(1) of the European Communities Act 1972, will not be infringing copies. Pursuant to decisions of the European Court of Justice (*Deutsche Grammophon v Metro-SB-Grossmarkte* [1971] ECR 487 and *Musik-Vertrieb Membran v GEMA* [1981] ECR 147), articles lawfully made in one member State of the European Community can be freely moved to or from other member States without the consent of the copyright owner or his exclusive licensees, notwithstanding that such movement, in the absence of the provisions of the Treaty of Rome as applied by the European Court of Justice, would have constituted a breach of copyright in a member State.

### *Presumptions*

**5.40** Section 27(4) sets out the presumption that once it has been proved that an article is a copy of a copyright work and that copyright subsists or has at any time subsisted in the work, then, unless the contrary can be proved, the article is presumed to have been made at the time when copyright subsists in the work. This is a simplified version of section 20(4) of the 1956 Act, which applied only to literary, dramatic, musical or artistic works and which required that a name purporting to be that of a publisher must appear on copies of the work as first published. The presumption set out in this subsection applies to all classes of work.

### *Cross-references to permitted copying sections of the Act*

**5.41** Section 27(6) provides that copies of works made pursuant to the provisions of the Act which permit copying in certain circumstances, will nevertheless constitute infringing copies if used for purposes other than those envisaged by the specific provisions of the Act. These include such copies as those made by educational establishments and librarians, or for the purposes of advertising artistic works, or for the purposes of broadcasting or inclusion in cable programme services, or under statutory licence for reprographic copying or works in electronic form which have been purchased. The relevant sections are sections 32(5), 35(3), 36(5), 37(3)(b), 56(2), 63(2), 68(4) and 141.

### *Transitional provisions relating to infringing copies*

**5.42** The transitional provisions dealing with infringing copies are set out in Schedule 1, paragraph 14(3). They provide in effect that, when the infringing copy was made before the commencement of the 1988 Act, then the earlier law shall apply: the 1911 Act or the 1956 Act depending on the date the article was made.

Chapter 6

# Acts permitted in relation to copyright works

**6.1** Chapter III of Part I of the Act sets out the acts which may be done in relation to copyright works, ie, the exceptions to the restricted acts. After the introductory section (section 28), the following sections deal with exceptions relating to the matters in the second column:

| *Section* | *Exception relevant to* |
|---|---|
| 29 to 31 | General |
| 32 to 36 | Education |
| 37 to 44 | Libraries and archives |
| 45 to 50 | Public administration |
| 51 to 53 | Designs |
| 54 to 55 | Typefaces |
| 56 | Works in electronic form |
| 57 to 65 | Miscellaneous: literary, dramatic, musical and artistic works |
| 66 to 67 | Miscellaneous: sound recordings, films and computer programs |
| 68 to 75 | Miscellaneous: broadcasts and cable programmes |
| 76 | Adaptations |

**6.2** Section 28 contains provisions to ensure that, in construing the Act, it is clear that any reference to a work, without a specific description of that copyright work in Chapter III, is a reference to a work of any description. The provisions of the Chapter are not to be treated as restricting the scope of the acts restricted by copyright, and are to be construed independently of each other.

## Fair dealing

**6.3** The first of the exceptions to be dealt with is fair dealing. This is covered by sections 29 and 30. The expression 'fair dealing' is not defined in the Act, nor was it in the 1956 Act. It was thought that it would be impossible to devise a general formula which would be appropriate in all cases and that unfairness, either to copyright owners or to users, would inevitably result.

Section 16(3) provides that the doing of an act restricted by the copyright in a work without an appropriate licence constitutes an infringement in relation only to the whole or a substantial part of the work (see paragraph 6.3 above). Fair dealing extends to the doing of an act in relation to a part of a work which may be a substantial part. It is permitted only for the purposes of private study, research, criticism, review and news reporting.

To constitute fair dealing, the usage must be compatible with fair practice, or with a use that is not so substantial that it extends beyond that which is justified for the purpose. Thus, to reproduce a photograph of a painting in the pages of a magazine accompanying a criticism of the artist's works would be fair dealing, whereas to reproduce a full size copy of the painting in poster form would normally not constitute fair dealing. One test is whether the usage interferes with normal exploitation of the work — in which event it would not constitute fair dealing.

### *Fair dealing for research or private study*

**6.4** Section 29(1) provides that fair dealing, for the purposes of research or private study, with a literary, dramatic, musical or artistic work, does not infringe the copyright in the work, or in the typographical arrangement of the work in the case of a published edition.

Section 29(1) is virtually a repetition of the equivalent sections of the 1956 Act (section 6(1) as regards literary, dramatic and musical works and section 9(1) as regards artistic works), except fair dealing is permitted not only in respect of literary, dramatic and musical works, but also in respect of typographical arrangements of those works. Accordingly, a student making a reprographic copy of a reasonable part of a literary work which is contained in a published edition will not constitute a breach of the copyright in either the work or the typographical arrangement.

Section 29(2) permits fair dealing for the purposes of research and private study with typographical arrangements of published editions of works, whether or not such works are themselves the subject of copying protection.

Section 29(3) deals with copying by a person other than a researcher or student. Subsection (3)(a), which deals with copying by librarians, provides that there is no fair dealing if the copying would not be permitted under section 38 or 39 by virtue of regulations made under section 40 (see paragraphs 6.13 to 6.15). Sections 38 and 39 deal with the right of librarians to supply copies of articles from periodicals and parts of published works. As regards copying by persons other than librarians, there will be no fair dealing if the person doing the copying knows or has reason to believe that it will result in copies of substantially the same material being provided to more than one person, at substantially the same time and for substantially the same purpose. The purpose of section 29(3) is to reconcile the fair dealing provisions with the provisions relating to copying by librarians set out in sections 38 and 39.

It should be noted that no acknowledgment is required in the case of fair dealing for research or private study, even though research may lead to the publication of research papers.

### *Fair dealing for criticism, review and reporting*

**6.5** Section 30 deals with fair dealing for criticism, review and the reporting of current events. These exceptions were dealt with in the 1956 Act in section 6(2) and (3). Under the 1956 Act, fair dealing for these purposes was applicable only to literary, dramatic or musical works. Fair dealing for such purposes now extends to all categories of copyright work. The new Act extends criticism and review fair dealing not only to works, but also to performances of works. Accordingly, the inclusion of a film clip in a television programme reviewing, for example, new films, will not need the consent of the copyright owner or licensee of the film, provided that there is a sufficient acknowledgement. The requirement that fair dealing for both types of purposes must be accompanied by a sufficient acknowledgment is perpetuated, except that no acknowledgment is required in connection with the reporting of current events by means of sound recordings, films, broadcasts or cable programmes. There is an important exception, however, to this exemption in section 30(3) for the purpose of reporting current events — it does not apply to photographs, because news photographs have, in many cases, unique value which might be seriously eroded by publication for the reporting of current events.

'Sufficient acknowledgment' is defined in section 78. The acknowledgment must identify the work in question both by title (or other description) and the author. No acknowledgment is required in the case of anonymous works, or unpublished works, where it is not possible to ascertain the identity of the author. This expression was defined in section 6(10) of the 1956 Act and it only differs from the definition therein in that the latter contained no exception for unpublished works.

### *Incidental inclusion of works in sound recordings, films, broadcasts and cable programmes*

**6.6** Section 31 provides that copyright in all types of work is not infringed by its incidental inclusion in an artistic work, sound recording, film, broadcast or cable programme. Section 9(5) of the 1956 Act contained a similar provision with regard to the inclusion of artistic works only in films or television broadcasts. Section 31(2) permits the playing, showing, broadcasting or inclusion in a cable programmes service of anything whose making was not an infringement of the copyright because of such incidental inclusion. However, section 31(3) provides that a musical work, words spoken or sung with music, or so much of a sound recording, broadcast or cable programme as includes a musical work or words of a song, is not to be regarded as incidentally included in another work, if it has been deliberately so included. Therefore, there will be an infringement of copyright if, for example, music playing on a radio is deliberately included on the soundtrack of a film. If, on the other hand, whilst filming an exterior sequence, music is recorded on the soundtrack which incidentally happens to be performed within earshot but is not under the control of the maker of the film, there will be no infringement of the copyright in that music. The distinction between a musical work and words spoken or sung with music is necessary because the lyrics of a song are a literary work and not part of the musical work.

## Education

**6.7** Section 32(1) permits (where the copying is done in the course of instruction or preparation for instruction) the copying of a literary, dramatic, musical or artistic work by a person giving or receiving instruction. This restates section 41(1)(a) of the 1956 Act and, as before, the copying may not be done by a reprographic process. Subsection (2) is new: it permits copying by a person (giving or receiving instruction) of a sound recording, film, broadcast or cable programme in the course of, or of preparation for, instruction. The copying of any underlying work is permitted under subsection (1)

Subsection (3) permits copying of a work for the purposes of an examination, whether setting the questions or answering them. This does not extend subsection (4) to the making of a reprographic copy of a musical work for use by an examination candidate in performing the work.

Subsection (5) makes any subsequent dealing with a copy, made in accordance with the foregoing sections, an infringing dealing. 'Dealing' means selling, letting for hire, offering or exposing for sale or hire.

### *Anthologies for educational use*

**6.8** Restating section 6(6) of the 1956 Act, section 33(1) permits the inclusion of a short passage from a published literary or dramatic work in a collection intended (and so described in its title and advertisements) for use in educational establishments where the collection consists mainly of public domain material. This does not apply to taking material from a work which is itself intended for use in educational establishments. No more than two excerpts from copyright works by the same author (published by the same publisher over any period of five years) may be so used. Subsection (3) defines 'excerpts from works by the same author' and subsection (4) extends use to 'any use for the educational purposes' so allowing use in, for example, a student's house.

### *Performing, playing or showing work in the course of activities of educational establishment*

**6.9** Section 34(1) provides that the performance of a literary, dramatic or musical work before, for example, a school audience (as defined) is not a public performance where done by a teacher or pupil (or by anyone there for the purposes of instruction) in the course of the activities of the establishment. Subsection (2) provides that it is not a playing or showing of a work in public to show a film or perform a sound recording before an audience at an educational establishment for the purposes of instruction. Subsection (3) provides that it is not enough to be a parent to be 'directly connected' with the activities. If parents attend a school play, therefore, copyright clearance is probably necessary for the performance. A school disco (at which no parents or other members of the public are present) is not necessarily a public performance but is not specifically excluded from being so by this section.

### *Recordings by educational establishments of broadcasts and cable programmes*

**6.10** Section 35(1) permits a recording to be made at an educational establishment for the educational purposes of the establishment but this does not apply (subsection (2)) to the extent that there is a certified licensing scheme under section 143. Subsection (3) provides that any subsequent use of the copy will probably be an infringing use.

### *Reprographic copying by educational establishments*

**6.11** Section 36(1) permits educational reprographic copying of passages from published literary, dramatic or musical works of up to one per cent in any calendar quarter. Subsection (3) prohibits such copying if a licence is available for such copying and the person making the copies knew or ought to have been aware of that fact. Subsection (4) effectively ensures that such licences cannot be for less than one per cent of a work per quarter, and subsection (5) prohibits further dealing with the copy.

## Libraries and archives

**6.12** Section 37(1) defines a prescribed library or archive. Subsection (2) permits a librarian or archivist, when copying, to rely on a signed declaration unless he is aware that it is false; the subsection provides that copies may not be supplied unless a signed declaration is obtained. Subsection (3) makes a declarant who supplies false particulars liable him or herself for infringement of copyright.

### *Articles in periodicals*

**6.13** Section 38(1) permits the librarian of a prescribed library, complying with the prescribed conditions, to make copies of articles in a periodical without infringing copyright. Subsection (2) sets out what the relevant prescribed conditions must, as a minimum, include.

### *Parts of published works*

**6.14** By section 40, the librarian of a prescribed library may, if the conditions are complied with, copy part of a literary, dramatic or musical work (other than an article in a periodical) without infringing any copyright in the work. Subsection (2) lists the the prescribed conditions.

### *Restriction on production of multiple copies*

**6.15** The regulations prescribed under sections 38 and 39 must contain provisions requiring a librarian to be satisfied that the request for a copy is 'not related to any similar requirement of another person'. Subsection

(2) sets out what the regulations may also provide. Thus, for example, the supply of a single copy to each member of a class is not permitted.

### *Supply of copies to other libraries*

**6.16** Section 41(1) permits swapping between prescribed libraries of copies of an article in a periodical, or the whole or part of a published edition of a literary, dramatic or musical work, unless the librarian knows (or could by reasonable enquiry ascertain) the identity of a person entitled to authorise the copying.

### *Replacement copies*

**6.17** Under section 42, a librarian or archivist may, subject to following the prescribed conditions, make a copy from any item in the permanent collection of a library or archive to preserve it, or replace an item that has been lost in another permanent collection. Such copying is limited to cases where it is not reasonably practicable to purchase a replacement.

### *Unpublished works*

**6.18** Under section 43, on following the prescribed conditions, a librarian or archivist may copy the whole or part of an unpublished literary dramatic or musical work unless the copyright owner has prohibited copying *and* the librarian or archivist ought to have been aware of the fact. Subsection (3) sets out what the prescribed conditions must include.

### *Copies as condition of export*

**6.19** Section 44 provides that it is not infringement of copyright to copy an article of cultural or historical importance which cannot lawfully be exported from the UK unless a copy is made and deposited in an appropriate library or archive.

## Exceptions for public administration purposes

**6.20** Sections 45 to 50 deal with acts permitted in relation to copyright works for the purposes of public administration. Similar provisions appeared in the 1956 Act but were distributed amongst various sections.

**6.21** Section 45(1) provides that copyright is not infringed by anything done for the purposes of Parliamentary or judicial proceedings. Under section 45(2), there is no copyright prohibition upon the reporting of the proceedings, but the copying of published reports of such proceedings (such as Hansard and the law reports) must be authorised by the copyright owners. The provisions of the section apply to all types of work and to all restricted acts.

Section 46 contains similar provisions applicable to Royal Commissions or statutory inquiries. In addition, the copyright in works or material from them which is contained in reports of such proceedings, is not infringed by the publication of reports of the proceedings (section 46(3)). There was no comparable exception in the 1956 Act.

Section 46(4) defines 'Royal Commission' as including a Commission appointed for Northern Ireland under Her Majesty's prerogative powers. 'Statutory inquiry' is defined as meaning 'an inquiry held or investigation conducted in pursuance of a power or duty conferred by or under an enactment'. For example, an investigation conducted by the Office of Fair Trading or by the Office of the Director-General of Telecommunications would constitute a statutory inquiry.

### *Copying material open to public inspection*

**6.22** Section 47 contains extensive provisions permitting the copying and issuing of copies to the public of material open to public inspection or on official registers. There are limitations on what can be published and in general it requires the authority of the 'appropriate person'.

**6.23** Under section 47(1), the material must be:

(a) open to public inspection pursuant to a statutory requirement. 'Statutory requirement' is defined as meaning a requirement imposed by provisions made by or under an enactment (section 47(6)); or

(b) on a statutory register.

The literary copyright in such material is not infringed by copying provided that:

(a) it contains factual information; and

(b) it is copied with the authority of the appropriate person; and

(c) copies are not issued to the public.

**6.24** Under section 47(2), the material must be open to public inspection pursuant to a statutory requirement, but unlike section 47(1) it does not apply to material on a statutory register.

Copyright in such material is not infringed by copying or issuing to the public copies of the material, provided that:

(a) the authority of the appropriate person has been obtained; and

(b) the purpose of the copying or publication is to enable it to be inspected at a more convenient time or place or otherwise for facilitating the exercise of any right for the purpose of which the statutory requirement is imposed.

**6.25** Under section 47(3), the material must satisfy either of conditions (a) or (b) (set out in paragraph 6.23) of section 47(1) and in addition it must be material which contains information about matters of general scientific, technical, commercial or economic interest.

Copyright in such material is not infringed by copying or issuing to the public copies of the materials provided that:

(a) the authority of the appropriate person has been obtained; and

(b) the purpose is that of disseminating the information.

This subsection would apply, for example, to patent specifications filed at the Patent Office.

'Appropriate person' is defined by section 47(6) as meaning the person required to make the material open to public inspection or to the person maintaining a statutory register.

**6.26** Section 47(4) provides that the Secretary of State may make an order requiring copies to be marked as the order specifies so as to avoid abuse of sections 47(1) to (3).

**6.27** Section 47(5) provides that the Secretary of State may by order extend the application of subsections (1) to (3) to material made open to public inspection by international organisations or persons who have functions in the United Kingdom under international agreement or to registers maintained by international organisations.

The orders made under this section must be made by statutory instrument subject to annulment by either House of Parliament.

## *Material communicated to the Crown*

**6.28** Section 48 deals with material communicated to the Crown. It applies only to literary, dramatic, musical and artistic works. First, the material must have been communicated to the Crown in the course of public business. It must have been communicated with the licence of the copyright owner. The document or other material thing embodying the work must be in the the custody or control of the Crown. 'Public business' is defined as any activity carried on by the Crown. The Crown is permitted under the conditions set out in the section to copy and to issue copies of such a work to the public. The conditions are:

(a) the copying or publication must be for the purpose for which the work was communicated to the Crown or for any related purpose which could reasonably have been anticipated by the copyright owner;

(b) the work may not be one which has previously been published except by virtue of section 48.

Subsection (5) provides that the section is subject to any agreement to the contrary between the Crown and the copyright owner. One must therefore wonder why it was necessary to introduce the section in the first place.

### *Copying of public records*

**6.29** Section 49 permits the copying of material comprised in public records within the meaning of the Public Records Act 1958, the Public Records (Scotland) Act 1937 and the Public Records Act (Northern Ireland) 1923. The material must be open to public inspection. It is necessary to obtain the authority of the officer appointed under the Act. This section is a re-enactment of section 42 of the 1956 Act. It should be noted that unlike the provisions of section 47, copying under section 49 can be for any purpose.

**6.30** Section 50 makes it clear that where the doing of a particular act is specifically authorised by Act of Parliament, whenever passed, then the doing of that Act shall not infringe copyright; but the section is not to be construed as excluding any defence of statutory authority.

The word 'specifically' should be noted; a general authorisation is not sufficient.

*Note*: Sections 51 to 53 are dealt with in paragraphs 14.1 to 14.5.

## Typefaces

**6.31** Section 54(1) allows the use of a typeface in the ordinary course of printing and provides that even use of an infringing typeface is not an infringement. Nevertheless, where persons make, import, possess or deal with equipment for printing in a particular typeface, then, notwithstanding subsection (1), the copyright owner in the typeface can obtain remedies, viz under section 24 (secondary infringement), sections 99 and 100 (order for delivery up and right of seizure), section 107(2) (offence of making or possessing such an article), and section 108 (order for delivery up in criminal proceedings).

'Dealing with' has the same meaning as elsewhere in this Act.

### *Equipment for reproducing a typeface*

**6.32** Section 55 applies where equipment specifically intended to produce material in a typeface has been marketed with the licence of a copyright owner. The copyright in a typeface lasts for 25 years from the end of the year in which the first article was marketed and thereafter the artistic work may be copied by making further equipment. 'Marketed' means sold, let, hire or offered or exposed for sale or hire, in the UK or elsewhere.

## Exceptions for works in electronic form

**6.33** Section 56 deals with the exceptions from the restricted acts applicable to works in electronic form.

'In electronic form' is defined by section 178 as meaning 'in a form usable only by electronic means'. 'Electronic' is also defined by section 178. A computer program is a work in electronic form.

**6.34** Copies of works in electronic form may be copied if they have been purchased on terms which expressly or impliedly allow the purchaser to copy the work or adapt it in connection with his use of it. In order to use a computer program, it is normally necessary to copy all or part of it, and thus there is an implied or express term on purchase permitting the purchaser to copy or adapt it.

Section 56(2) to 56(4) are interesting in that they give transferees from the purchaser the benefit of the terms of the licence under which the purchaser acquired the copy.

By section 56(2), transferees from the purchaser are permitted to do anything which the purchaser is allowed to do, provided that there were no express terms on the original sale to the purchaser which:

(a) prohibited the transfer of the copy by the purchaser, imposed obligations which continue after transfer, prohibited the assignment of any licence or terminated any licence on a transfer, or

(b) provide for the terms on which a transferee may do the things which the purchaser was permitted to do.

These provisions apply where the original purchased copy is no longer usable and a further copy is transferred in its place, and also to subsequent transfers. However, any copies or adaptations made by the purchaser which he does not transfer, are to be treated as infringing copies after the transfer. Thus, the purchaser of a computer program who is not prohibited by express terms from selling the program or otherwise transferring it to another person, may not do anything with the copies which he made while the program was in his possession which would be in breach of any of the restricted acts relating to computer programs.

## Acts permitted in relation to literary, dramatic, musical and artistic works

**6.35** Sections 57 to 65 deal with acts which are permitted in relation to literary, dramatic, musical and artistic works. They deal with anonymous or pseudonymous works, notes of spoken words, public readings, scientific abstracts, recordings of folksongs, artistic works on public display, advertisements of sales of artistic works, making of subsequent works by the same artist and reconstruction of buildings.

### *Anonymous or pseudonymous works*

**6.36** Section 57 deals with anonymous or pseudonymous works. It will be recalled that section 12(2) accords to literary, dramatic, musical and artistic works of unknown authorship a period of copyright of 50 years from the year in which such work is first made available to the public. Section 9(4) and 9(5) define works of unknown authorship and explain what is meant by 'unknown' in relation to the author of a work. Comparable but less comprehensive provisions appeared in Schedule 2 to the 1956 Act.

Section 57 applies whether or not the work has been published but in practice will be largely applicable in cases of unpublished works. Copyright in such literary, dramatic, musical or artistic works is not infringed if it has not been possible on reasonable enquiry to ascertain the identity of the author and it is reasonable to assume that the copyright has expired or the author died 50 years or more before the beginning of the year in which the act which would otherwise be an infringement, is done. It also provides that there is no infringement if this is the situation at the time when arrangements were made for the act to be done. This will recover the situation that would arise if arrangements were made to film or televise literary, dramatic, musical or artistic works at a time when the identity of the author were not known and could not by reasonable enquiry be ascertained, but were discovered before the film had completed shooting. The section does not apply to Crown copyright or to copyright vested in international organisations. There are also provisions in subsection (3) relating to works of joint authorship, so that it is necessary to show that it was impossible to ascertain the identify of any of the authors for the section to apply.

### *Use of notes or recordings of spoken words*

**6.37** Section 58 deals with the use of notes or recordings of spoken words made for the purpose of reporting current events, or of broadcasting or including in any cable programme service the whole or part of the work. It is not an infringement of the literary copyright in the spoken words to use them for such purposes, subject to the following conditions:

(a) the record must be a direct record and not taken from a previous record, broadcast or cable programme;

(b) the making of the record must not have been prohibited by the speaker;

(c) if copyright already existed in the work (ie the spoken words) the record must not infringe its copyright;

(d) the use to be made of the record must not be prohibited by the speaker or copyright owner before the record is made; and

(e) the use must be by or with the authority of persons lawfully in possession of the record.

These provisions are new and use copyright law to protect the privacy of speakers by enabling them to prevent publication of a speech where they have expressly requested that it should not be taken down or recorded or made the subject of a public report.

### *Public reading or recitation*

**6.38** Section 59 effectively repeats section 6(5) of the 1956 Act in permitting the reading or recitation in public of reasonable extracts of published literary or dramatic works, when accompanied by a sufficient acknowledgment (as defined in section 178). Section 59(2) extends this exception to permit the making of sound recordings, broadcasts or the inclusion in cable programme services of such readings or recitations 'provided that the recording, broadcast or cable programme consists mainly of material in relation to which it is not necessary to rely on [section 59(1)]'. On the basis that 'mainly' means more than 50 per cent, it would appear that up to 50 per cent of a television broadcast could consist of the reading of a reasonable extract without requiring permission from the copyright owner of the literary or dramatic work in question. 'Reasonable extract' is not defined in the Act and although the same wording appeared in both the 1911 and 1956 Acts, it does not appear to have been considered by the courts.

The extension of the right to broadcasting reverses the proviso to section 6(5) in the 1956 Act.

### *Abstracts of scientific or technical articles*

**6.39** Section 60 provides that where abstracts of scientific or technical articles are published in association with an article in a periodical, there will be no copyright infringement either of the abstract or of the article, if copies of the abstract are made or issued to the public. The only exception is if there is a licensing scheme under section 143 providing for the grant of licences (see paragraphs 10.73 to 10.77). This is a new provision — no comparable provision appeared in the 1956 Act.

### *Recording of folksongs*

**6.40** Section 61 permits the making of sound recordings of folksongs for archival purposes without infringing the literary and musical copyright in the words and music. Section 61(2) effectively defines a 'folksong' as being a song with words that are unpublished and of unknown authorship. A sound recording of a performance of such a song may be made only for the purpose of including it in an archive maintained by a designated body. The making of the recording will not infringe the words as a literary work or the music as a musical work. It is, however, a condition that the making of the recording does not infringe any other copyright and is not prohibited by any performer. If, therefore, the words of a folksong used music which is in copyright, the section would not apply to permit the unlicensed recording of the music.

Subject to meeting the conditions to be prescribed in an order to be made by the Secretary of State, copies of the sound recording may be made and supplied by the archivist for purposes of research and private study. Not more than one copy is to be furnished to any one person. 'Designated', as regards the archive, means designated by the Secretary of State, who is only permitted to designate bodies when he is satisfied that they are not established or conducted for profit. There was no comparable provision in the 1956 Act.

### *Representation of artistic works on public display*

**6.41** Section 62 deals with buildings, sculptures, models and/or buildings and works of artistic craftsmanship situated in public places or in premises open to the public.

The making of graphic works, photographs or films, or broadcasting or including visual images of such works in cable programme services do not infringe the copyright in such work. Furthermore, the graphic works, photographs, films etc may be broadcast or included in cable programme services.

The section effectively repeats section 9(3) and (4) of the 1956 Act. 'Graphic works' is defined in section 178 (see paragraph 2.24).

### *Advertisement of sale of artistic works*

**6.42** Section 63 introduces a new concept to UK copyright law by permitting persons to copy or issue copies to the public of artistic works for the purpose of advertising the sale of these works. This avoids the need for someone who is selling, for example, a painting in which he does not own the copyright from having to trace the copyright owner and obtain his permission to reproduce the work in a sales catalogue.

If the copy is 'dealt with' for any other purpose, it will be treated as an infringing copy. 'Dealt with' is defined as meaning 'sold, or let for hire, offered or exposed for sale or hire exhibited in public or distributed' (section 63(2)). Thus, art sales catalogues cannot subsequently be sold without the consent of the copyright owners of the pictures reproduced in them.

### *Making of subsequent works by the same artist*

**6.43** Section 64 follows section 9(9) of the 1956 Act. The wording is rather more succinct but the effect is the same in that it permits authors of artistic works to copy other works of their own, of which they are no longer the copyright owners, provided they do not repeat or imitate the main design of the early work.

### *Reconstruction of buildings*

**6.44** Section 65 is the equivalent to section 9(10) of the 1956 Act in that it permits the reconstruction of a building without infringing the copyright in the building or the drawings under which the original building was constructed.

## Acts permitted in relation to sound recordings, films and computer programs

**6.45** Sections 66 and 67 deal with acts permitted in relation to sound recordings, films, and computer programs without infringing the copyright therein. They are rental (under certain conditions) and playing of sound recordings for the purposes of clubs, societies etc.

### *Rental of sound recordings, films and computer programs*

**6.46** Section 66 lays down the provisions whereby the Secretary of State may make an order for what is, in effect, a statutory licence for the rental of sound recordings, films or computer programs. Section 18(2) provides that the restricted act of issuing copies to the public of sound recordings, films and computer programs includes rental of copies to the public.

If the Secretary of State makes such an order, then the works that are the subject of the order are to be treated as licensed by the copyright owner, subject only to the payment of such a reasonable royalty or other payment as may be agreed or determined in default of agreement by the copyright tribunal. The terms of the order may vary according to the work, the copies rented, the renter or circumstances of the rental (section 66(3)).

No such order shall apply if there is a licensing scheme certified for the purposes of this section under section 143 (see paragraphs 10.73 to 10.77).

This is an entirely new provision. The only provision in the 1956 Act which could be compared to it was the statutory licence for recording of musical works contained in section 8. Apart from the fact that that section dealt with only musical works, it differed from the present provisions in that it laid down in some detail the terms of the statutory licence and how it should be obtained. The provisions of section 8 of the 1956 Act have now been repealed.

### *Computer program rental after 50 years*

**6.47** Section 66(5) permits the rental of computer programs before the copyright period of the life of the author plus 50 years has expired — they can be rented after 50 years from the end of the year in which copies were first issued to the public in an electronic form. No payment to the author is required. Effectively, therefore, there is a different period of copyright as regards rental of computer programs.

### *Playing of sound recordings for purposes of clubs, societies etc*

**6.48** Section 67 permits the playing of sound recordings by clubs, societies and other organisations subject to the following conditions:

(a) that the organisation is not established or conducted for profit; and

(b) that the proceeds of any charge for omission must be applied for the purposes of the organisation.

The full wording of the condition to the effect that the organisation must not be conducted for profit could give rise to difficulties because the organisation must show that its main objects are charitable, but it does not need to be registered as a charity, and if not charitable, must be concerned with the advancement of religion, education or social welfare. These conditions are very wide and most non-profit making organisations would be able to comply with them.

This section re-enacts section 12(7)(b) of the 1956 Act. It should be noted that the other exception contained in that subsection which permitted sound recordings to be heard in public where persons reside or sleep as part of the amenities provided for their residents, has not been re-enacted. It should also be noted that this exception is applicable only to sound recordings and not to musical or any other works.

## Acts permitted in relation to broadcasts and cable programmes

**6.49** Sections 68 to 75 deal with the exceptions to the restricted acts applicable to broadcast and cable programmes. These include incidental recording for broadcast and cable programmes, recordings for supervision and control for time-shifting, photographs of broadcasts, free public showing, retransmission of broadcasts in cable programmes, provision of sub-titled copies and recording for archival purposes.

### *The ephemeral right*

**6.50** Section 68 is the re-enactment of the so called 'ephemeral right' provisions contained in section 6(7) of the 1956 Act, with the difference that it makes the ephemeral right a statutory licence rather than an exception. Where a broadcaster or cable programme service operator has a licence to broadcast or include in a cable programme service a work of any kind other than a broadcast, cable programme or typographical arrangement, he may make copies of the work provided they are not used for any other purpose and are destroyed within 28 days of first being used. If they are used for any other purpose or kept beyond the 28 day-period, the copies are treated as infringing copies. Section 6(7) of the 1956 Act was limited to literary, dramatic or musical works. The ephemeral right is permitted by Article 11(3) of the Berne Convention and Article 15(1) of the Rome Convention. It should be noted that the section is so worded that it does not allow copies permitted to be made under its provisions to be networked.

### *Recording for purposes of supervision and control*

**6.51** Section 69 contains provisions entitling the BBC, television and radio stations licensed by the IBA and cable programme operators licensed by the Cable Authority, to make copies of their programmes and to retain them, in order to supervise and control their programmes as regards the BBC, and, as regards the other persons, in order to comply with requirements of the IBA or the Cable Authority. The Cable Authority and the IBA are also given the right to make copies for the purpose of maintaining supervision and control over programmes. Until the passing of the Act, television radio stations and cable programme operators had been obliged, as part of the terms of the licences from copyright owners, to obtain the rights to make and retain copies of programmes to comply with their obligations to the IBA and the Cable Authority.

### *Recording for purposes of time-shifting*

**6.52** Section 70 deals with the problem of recording for purposes of time-shifting. 'Time shifting' is not defined in the Act, and indeed the section does not use the expression, except in the side note. The section permits the making, for private and domestic use only, of recordings or broadcasts or cable programmes solely for the purpose of enabling them to be viewed or listened to at a more convenient time. There is no infringement of the broadcast cable programme or any work included therein. There is no restriction on how long the recordings may be retained.

Article 9(2) of the Berne Convention provides that:

> 'It shall be a matter for legislation in the countries of the Union to permit the reproduction of such works in certain special cases, provided that such reproduction does not conflict with the normal exploitation of the work and does not unreasonably prejudice the legitimate interests of the author.'

Accordingly, the UK Government may have difficulty in ratifying the Paris Text of the Berne Convention, unless it can show that section 70 is a special case and that the section comes within the two provisos to Article 9(2). There is no provision in the Act for remuneration for the author for recording for private and domestic use, whether by way of a levy on audio or video cassettes or in any other manner. It is generally accepted that the intention of Article 9(2) is that there should be compulsory licences in fields in which works are normally exploited — and the effect of section 70 is to create a compulsory licence.

However, as regards broadcasts, sound recordings and the rights of performers, the Rome Convention for the protection of performers, producers of programmes and broadcasting organisations permits exceptions to the protection against unauthorised fixation in respect of private use, so that section 70 will not cause difficulties as regards that Convention. In any event, sections 14 and 14A of the 1956 Act permitted the making of copies of broadcasts and cable programmes for private purposes.

### *Photographs of television broadcasts or cable programmes*

**6.53** Section 71 permits the making of photographs of television broadcasts and cable programmes, but they can only be made for private and domestic use.

### *Free public showing or playing of broadcast or cable programmes*

**6.54** Section 72, which deals with the free public showing or playing of broadcast or cable programmes, is a re-enactment of sections 14 and 14A of the 1956 Act. Public performance of broadcasts or cable programmes where audiences have not paid for admission, is permitted. There are no significant changes from the earlier provisions, except that sound broadcasts are now accorded the same treatment as television broadcasts.

### *Reception and retransmission of broadcasts in cable programme services*

**6.55** Section 73 deals with the reception and retransmission of broadcasts in cable programme services and is included in order to enable cable programme operators to comply with their 'must carry' obligations under section 13(1) of the Cable and Broadcasting Act 1984: the Cable Authority can and does require the BBC and certain ITV programmes to be included in cable services. Section 73 is largely a re-enactment of section 14(8A) of the 1956 Act.

There is, however, an important addition — broadcasts made for reception in the area in which the cable programme service is provided may be included in the cable programme service without copyright infringement of the broadcast or the work included in the broadcast, provided that they are not satellite transmissions or encrypted transmissions. It should be borne in mind that 'broadcast' is now defined far more widely than under the 1956 Act and includes transmissions not only of the BBC and IBA but also of other organisations (see paragraph 2.35 above). Direct broadcast satellite transmissions must, however, be included in cable programme services if they are so required by the Cable Authority, notwithstanding the provision quoted above from section 73(2)(b), because they would fall within section 73(2)(a), the paragraphs (a) and (b) being in the alternative.

### *Provision of sub-titled copies of broadcasts or cable programmes*

**6.56** Section 74 permits a body, designated for the purpose by the Secretary of State, to make copies of television broadcasts of cable programmes and to issue them to the public with sub-titles for the benefit of deaf persons or persons who are hard of hearing or otherwise handicapped. No copyright licences are required by such designated body from the copyright owners of the broadcast cable programmes or works included in them.

### *Recording for archival purposes*

**6.57** Section 75 deals with recording for archival purposes. A body designated by the Secretary of State may make copies of broadcasts or cable programmes of a class of programme designated by the Secretary of State and place the same in an archive maintained by it without infringing the copyright in the broadcast, the cable programme, or any work included in it.

'Designated' means designated by an order made by a statutory instrument. The Secretary for State may not designate a body unless he is satisfied that it is not established or conducted for profit.

## Acts permitted in relation to adaptations

**6.58** Section 76 clarifies the position with regard to the doing of acts which are permitted by Chapter III of Part I of the Act (sections 28 to 75) in relation to an adaptation. The doing of such acts will not infringe the copyright in the literary, dramatic or musical work from which the adaptation has been made. 'Adaptation' is defined in section 21(3).

## Transitional provisions

**6.59** The transitional provisions regarding Chapter III of Part I are contained in Schedule 1, paragraphs 15 to 18. The paragraphs should be referred to for their detailed provisions, but essentially they operate as follows.

Section 57, dealing with anonymous or pseudonymous works, takes effect in relation to all existing works, with the exception of photographs and works enjoying perpetual copyright.

Section 7(6) to (8) of the 1956 Act continue to apply in relation to existing works as regards the copying of unpublished works in libraries etc, publication of such copies and the broadcasting, performance etc of material so published.

Paragraphs 17 and 18 of Schedule 1 deal with works made before 1 July 1912 and do not confer on such works additional rights under the new Act, any more than such works were granted any new rights under the 1956 Act. Accordingly, such pre-1911 Act works only enjoy the copyright rights that they enjoyed before the 1911 Act came into force.

Chapter 7

# Moral rights

## Introduction

**7.1** In civil law, the 'droit moral' (or moral right) is the right of an author to have his creation respected. Any abuse of that right may give rise to a cause of action. An author has a wide range of perpetual and inalienable rights in respect of his creation, and it seems that they include the right to be given credit; the right not to have the work changed, and perhaps to require that it is maintained in good condition; the exclusive right to authorise publication; and the right to withdraw the work and revise it.

The right is not a property right; it is part of an author's personality. The droit moral can easily be distinguished from the economic rights. According to Brian Lewis, 'in practice, the courts rarely come to the aid of an author who has parted with his financial rights and seeks an injunction solely to enforce his droit moral. There is only one case in which it has done so against the assignee of such rights. The most it will usually do is to award damages for the harm done to the author's reputation and the sum in question will be relatively minor. As however it is usually easy for an author to find a young briefless avocat eager for a chance to prove his metal for remarkably small fees, actions for an injunction are not infrequent and can be time-consuming and expensive, as the publisher or producer defendant who is at risk will probably brief a senior, more expensive member of the bar' (*The Droit Moral in French Law* (1981) 12 EIPR in 1983).

Common law does not have such respect for creativity. It recognises that there are economic rights to be bargained and dealt with, but it recognises artistic integrity only with reluctance. One example is section 43 of the 1956 Act which 'is more apt to protect a person to whom authorship is falsely attributed than an author whose authorship is not acknowledged' (*The Whitford Report* (Cmnd 6732, 1977) p 17); outside copyright law, the law of defamation and of passing-off provide further examples. Section 43 of the 1956 Act, however, gives protection for only 20 years post mortem auctoris, whilst Article 6 of the Paris Text of the Berne Convention requires life plus 50 years.

## *1956 Act position*

**7.2** Section 43 of the 1956 Act was the statutory culmination of a development in the law which many say had its first recognisable beginnings in the case of *Archbold v Sweet* ((1832) 5 Ca&P 219, [1832] 172 ER 947; see also *Ridge v English Illustrated Magazine* [1911–16] Macg Cop Cas 91), where the plaintiff, a barrister, complained successfully that the third edition of a book (of which Mr Archbold was the author and in which he sold the copyright to the defendant), which he had declined to edit, was full of errors and injured his reputation.

Another case is that of *Joseph v National Magazine Co Ltd* [1959] 1 Ch 14, where an author successfully obtained damages when he complained about proposed alterations to his article on jade and the magazine published the amended article without giving the author credit. The court's rationale was that the author had lost the advantage of having a signed article published in the magazine. The court declined to order specific performance.

## *Origins of the moral right*

**7.3** According to Charles Clark, 'the origins of moral rights as part of copyright law lie in the historical imbalance of bargaining power between creator and entrepreneurs. The nineteenth century laissez-faire view of contractual freedom in England and in most common law countries left their whole relationship at law to the terms of their contract for the transfer of economic rights of property with such comfort for the preservation of the moral rights of reputation as the author might find outside contract in the field of tort, eg defamation, injurious falsehood or passing off' (*Moral Rights,* also published in *Publishing Agreements* (Unwin Hyman, 1988)).

The Berne Convention first tried to come to terms with the issue in the Rome Text of 1928, which incorporated two moral rights, those of paternity and of integrity. The Brussels Text of 1948 made it clear that reputation could also be prejudiced by actions other than distortion, mutilation or modification. The Stockholm Text added in 1967 that the moral right granted under Berne should endure 'at least until the expiry of the economic rights' (Paris Text).

## *Whitford*

**7.4** But it was not until the Paris Text that the enforcement of moral rights was made an integral part of Berne. (The Stockholm Text of Berne states at paragraph 1: 'Independently of the author's economic rights, and even after the transfer of the said rights, the author shall have the right to claim authorship of the work, and to object to any distortion, mutilation or other modification of, or other derogatory action in relation to the said work, which would be prejudicial to his honour or reputation.') The UK is presently not a signatory to the Paris Text for this reason. It is arguable that the UK has been in breach of its treaty obligations even under the Stockholm Text. This issue was just touched on in the case of *Frisby v BBC* [1967] 2 All ER 106 (where the complaint was about the removal by the BBC of two — claimed to be the key to the whole — words from a line in a play being made by the BBC), but the issue was decided on the construction of the Screenwriters' Guild agreement with the BBC and the contract between Frisby and the BBC.

Whitford (Cmnd 6732) approved the general philosophy of the moral rights protected by the Paris Text and said (p 18):

> 'Although the Berne Convention limits our freedom of action this is the price we pay for joining in a multi-national agreement with some 60 other countries and thus giving our authors, composers, artists and film makers the enormous benefit of copyright protection in all those countries without formality, merely by virtue of their having created a work.'

**7.5** Whitford made no provision for other moral rights, such as the droit de divulgation (the right to control circulation of a work before its completion for publication); the droit de suite (the right to follow the economic success of the work); the right of withdrawal after publication of a work of which its author no longer approves; or the right of access (mainly by artists to their paintings after sale).

### *White Paper*

**7.6** The Government White Paper (Cmnd 9712, 1986) provides:

> '19.2 The Berne Convention distinguishes between an author's economic rights and his moral rights the former enabling him to earn money, the latter protecting his reputation. The moral rights specified in the Convention are:
>
> (a) the right to claim authorship of the work, eg by being named as author; and
>
> (b) the right to object to any distortions of the work which are prejudicial to his honour or reputation.
>
> In the United Kingdom, moral rights are at present provided to some extent by copyright law, which contains certain provisions regarding false attribution of authorship, and to some extent by the common law in the form of the laws of contract, passing off and defamation. Whitford cast some doubt on whether the law satisfies the Brussels Text of Berne. Whether or not these doubts are justified, amendment of the law will be necessary to comply with the Paris Text of the Berne Convention which requires member States to protect some at least of the moral rights, at least until the expiry of the copyright.
>
> 19.3 As foreshadowed in the 1981 Green Paper [*Reform of the Law relating to Copyright, Designs and Performers' Protection* (Cmnd 8302, 1981)] the Government proposes to legislate for moral rights as follows:
>
> '(a) authors will be given the right to claim authorship and to object to distortion, but not to modification of a work to which they could not reasonably refuse consent;
>
> (b) these moral rights will be independent of the economic rights, and will be exercisable only by the author. After his death they may be exercised by the person who inherits the copyright or, if the author no longer owns

the copyright at his death, by the person to whom he had bequeathed them. An author will be able to waive his moral rights, and such waiver will override any inheritance or bequest; and

(c) moral rights will apply for the duration of the copyright.'

## The new position

**7.7** It may well be that in civil law jurisdictions droit moral is more honoured in rhetoric than in practice, but what will be the position in the UK? The provision for moral rights is to be found in Chapter IV of Part I of the Act, sections 77 to 89. They are the right to be identified as author or director; the rights to object to derogatory treatment of the work, and to false attribution of work; and the right to privacy of certain photographs and films.

## Right to be identified (or paternity right)

**7.8** Section 77 defines the circumstances in which the author, or director of a film, has a right to be identified as such. The author (and wherever used in this part of text the word 'author' means the creator) of a copyright literary, dramatic, musical or artistic work, and the director of a copyright film, has the right to be identified as the author or director of the work in the circumstances mentioned below; but the right is not infringed unless it has been asserted in the terms of section 78 (see below) and a court is required by section 78(5), when considering remedies, to take account of any delay in asserting the right.

### *Literary and dramatic works (but not lyrics)*

**7.9** By section 77(2), the author of a literary or dramatic work (but not of lyrics) must be identified whenever the work or any adaptation is:

(i) published commercially or performed in public;

(ii) broadcast or included in a cable programme service; or

(iii) copies of a film, or sound recording, including the work are issued to the public.

### *Musical works (and lyrics)*

**7.10** By section 77(3), the author of a musical work, and of lyrics, has the right to be identified whenever:

(i) a work is published commercially;

(ii) a sound recording is issued to the public;

(iii) a soundtrack including the work is issued to the public; or

(iv) a film embodying the soundtrack is shown to the public.

This right extends to adaptations.

## *Adaptation*

**7.11** 'Adaptation' as used here, of course, bears the meaning given to it in section 21(3), and thus includes the stage play of the book, a translation, an agreement or transcription etc.

## *Artistic works*

**7.12** By section 77(4), the author of an artistic work must be identified where the work:

(i) is published commercially or exhibited in public or included in a broadcast or cable programme; or

(ii) is included in a film which is shown in public or copies of which are issued to the public.

In the case of a work of architecture in the form of a building, or a sculpture or a work of artistic craftsmanship, the right applies if a graphic work representing it, or a photograph of it, is issued to the public.

## *Works of architecture*

**7.13** By section 77(5), the architect of a building has the right to be identified on it (or on the first where more than one is constructed to the same design). The identification must be visible to persons entering or approaching the building.

## *Identification*

**7.14** Section 77(6) provides that the director of a film must be identified whenever the film is shown in public, broadcast or included in a cable programme service, or whenever copies of the film are issued to the public.

In the case of a performance, the identification must be such that a person seeing or hearing the performance will notice it.

In the case of copies of a work issued to the public, the author or the director must be so identified (either in or on the copy) so that his identity is brought to the notice of the purchaser.

In each case the identification must be clear and reasonably prominent.

## *Form of identification*

**7.15** By section 77(8), where an author or director uses a pseudonym, then that form must be used; otherwise any reasonable form of identification must be used, except where a particular form is specified, in which case that form must be used.

**7.16** Section 77(9) provides for exceptions to the right (as to which, see section 79).

## Assertion

**7.17** Section 78 requires that the paternity right must be asserted before it can be infringed.

**7.18** By section 78(2), the paternity right may be asserted generally or in relation to any specified act or description of acts. If the assertion is made in an assignment of the copyright, then a statement to that effect may be included. Alternatively, the assertion may be made by written instrument signed by the person asserting the right.

It appears that a personal assertion is needed and that, for example, collective assertion by a trade union on behalf of its members, or an assertion by an agent on behalf of his author, is not possible. But presumably a duly appointed attorney could effectively assert the right on behalf of his appointor.

### *Public exhibition of artistic works*

**7.19** Section 78(3)(a) provides that the right may be asserted as regards public exhibition of an artistic work, by the author ensuring that, when he parts with possession of the original or a copy made by him, he is identified on it or on a frame or mount 'or other thing to which it is attached'.

Section 78(3)(b) allows the author or other *first* owner of copyright to assert his right by including an assertion in the licence by which he authorises the making of copies.

It should be noted that the wording of the section does not exclude other ways of asserting the right. It is submitted that any other form of assertion would have to be at least as good in terms of giving notice to the world.

As regards fixing an identification on the frame or mount of an artistic work, it should be noted that if the work becomes detached from the frame or mount, the right has nevertheless been asserted and that the assertion does not fall away with the frame. It will be advisable to include a warranty in future documents of acquisition of an artistic work to the effect that an assertion has, or has not, been made in respect of that work. If in doubt, steps should always be taken to ensure that the author is identified in any public exhibition of the work.

The right, once asserted, follows on to any copy made of the original work.

This does not seem to be a major problem in relation to well-known works of art because it may be assumed that owners will want to have the author's name affixed. Problems will arise with regard to lesser works of art and everyday works of art such as an illustration or a cheap statuette bought, for example, in a tourist shop, if such works are subsequently exhibited in public. No definition of this term is provided by the Act but cf 'publication', which is defined in section 175.

# COPYRIGHT LAW IN THE UNITED KINGDOM AND THE RIGHTS OF PERFORMERS, AUTHORS AND COMPOSERS IN EUROPE

## Supplementary Information

*British Leyland Motor Corporation Limited v. Armstrong Patents Company Limited*

The House of Lords upheld the appeal of Armstrong Patents Co. Ltd. from the judgment of the Court of Appeal (*The Times* 28.2.1986, see para. 518). The majority (Lord Scarman, Lord Edmund-Davies, Lord Bridge of Harwich and Lord Templeman) held that the car owner's right of repair prevailed, and that consequently British Leyland (BL) could not exercise their copyright in the drawings concerned to prevent the copying of the exhaust pipes by Armstrong Patents Co. Ltd. The owner of a car has the right to keep it in running order. In some circumstances the enforcement of the manufacturer's copyright in spare parts drawings must yield to the maintenance of a supply of parts to sustain the owner's right of repair (Lord Bridge of Harwich). If a patent or a registered design were involved, other considerations would arise, but that was not the case here, nor did the principle of implied licence apply. The principle that a grantor cannot derogate from his grant by using property retained by him so as to render property granted by him unfit for the purpose for which the grant was made applied, and BL could not exercise their copyright so as to prevent the car being repaired by replacement of the exhaust pipe (Lord Templeman). The majority did not consider that there should be a departure from decisions in previous cases (including *L.B. (Plastics) Ltd. v. Swish Products Ltd.*, see paras. 239, 516) establishing that the protection afforded by copyright to a drawing could be used to prevent the reproduction of a functional object depicted in a drawing, though Lord Scarman and Lord Templeman considered that Parliament did not intend that copyright should be used in this way. Lord Griffiths also allowed the appeal, but on different grounds.

The House of Lords did not disturb the Court of Appeal's finding that copyright in artistic works incorporating "functional" designs was not affected by s. 10 of the Copyright Act 1956 (see para. 920), so that (subject to the law as to acts not constituting infringement of copyright, see above and Chapter 6) the position in this connection is still as outlined in para. 921. The previous cases concerning implied licence to repair (see para. 432), para. 518 and references in the text to the *British Leyland* cases (see Table III) must be read in the light of the House of Lords decision summarised in this note.

*Additional notes:*

A White Paper setting out the Government's proposals for legislation concerning copyright (and other matters) was published on 15 April 1986 (*Intellectual Property and Innovation,* Cmnd. 9712): these proposals will be analysed in the first annual supplement to this work (cf. p. xcvi). For summary note, see overleaf.

In *Armstrad* (see p. cvii), the Court of Appeal held that marketing the machines did not constitute authorisation of infringement, but declined to make the declaration sought (*The Times* 30.10.1985 and cf. paras. 503, 530). The Court of Appeal dismissed the appeals in *Merlet* (*The Times* 6.11.1985, see para. 517) and (stating the relevant principles) in *Faccenda Chicken* (*The Times* 11.12.1985, see para. 758).

Footnote 30 of Chapter 5 refers to para. 530. *Photocopying and the law* (see para. 647) has been withdrawn: as to photocopying, see now *Reprographic Copying of Books and Journals* (British Copyright Council, 1985); the current allowable limits for criticism or review quotations should be checked with the copyright owner, publisher or organization concerned. As to Table V, see S.I. 1985/1777, 1985-88, and as to para. 904, S.I. 1985/784.

21 April 1986

## White Paper, April 1986 (Cmnd. 9712)

*Proposed legislation*

The following is a brief summary of the main provisions of the proposed legislation on designs, copyright and performers' protection (not including the proposals concerning patents etc.). The first bracketed reference number is to the White Paper Chapter, the second to the relevant *Copyright Law in the United Kingdom* paragraph.

**A** An "unregistered design right" to be introduced for the protection of original designs against copying, to apply to both functional and aesthetic designs (3) (934). Unauthorised reproduction for sale etc., importation etc. to be infringements. Protection for 10 years following first marketing: manufacturing licences in last 5 years. *British Leyland* spare parts exemption not to apply, but there will be a limited exemption for repair by the owner, himself or by contract. If design unregistrable under 1949 Act, right dependent on certain criteria. **B** *Registered Designs Act* 1949 to be restricted to genuinely aesthetic designs, and term of protection extended to 25 years (3) (914-21, 908). **C** Introduction of blank tape levy (not applicable to video tape), payable by manufacturers and first trader importers: levy maximum of 10 per cent of total retail sales value of particular medium (6) (1310-11). **D** Compulsory licensing system covering recording by educational establishments of broadcast or cabled video material (7) (509, 556). **E** Any collecting society operating photocopying licensing scheme will be obliged to include in scheme a provision to indemnify licensees (8). **F** Licensing of multiple copying by educational institutions to be introduced (8). **G** Exceptions: (a) related multiple copy library production to be excluded from exception of s. 7 (8) (643), (b) fair dealing exceptions to be extended to cover published edition copyright (8) (643), (c) research and private study exception of ss. 6,7 will not include copying for commercial research (8) (640), (d) judicial proceeding exception to be extended to published edition and sound recording copyrights (8) (638, 634), (e) exceptions to be introduced to cover copying of public inspection documents, statutory copying obligation, library copying of unpublished works, documents for export (8), (f) broadcasters' ephemeral recording rights to be extended (8) (611), (g) exceptions of s. 40 (1) (2) to be extended to other broadcasters (10) (540). **H** Provisions of 1985 (Computer Software) Act to be retained: clarification that copyright subsists in works fixed in any form from which they can in principle be reproduced, and that reproduction rights extend to copying by fixing a work on any medium from which the work can in principle be reproduced (9) (205). **I** Repeals and abolitions: (a) s. 48(3B), cable programme incidental service (10) (534, 631), (b) s. 8, statutory recording licence (11) (646), (c) conversion damages (12) (722, 729), (d) s. 12 (7)(a), sound recording amenity use (13) (634). See also M below. **J** Lawfully receivable fixed satellite service (FSS) transmissions to count as broadcasting and to be protected: retransmitting of FSS transmissions to be under copyright regime (10) (115, 535). **K** Civil and criminal remedies to be strengthened (12) (701 ff.). **L** Apparatus suppliers to be liable as contributory infringers in certain cases (13) (530). **M** Duration of protection: (a) unlimited term and perpetual copyrights to be abolished (15) (303, 104), (b) amendment of protection terms of anonymous and pseudonymous works, photographs, films, sound recordings and Crown copyright (15) (303, 317, 316, 310). **N** Authorship and ownership of copyright: amendments concerning joint authorship, photographs, Crown copyright, Parliamentary material (16) (401 ff.). **O** Jurisdiction of Tribunal to be extended (18) (445). **P** Moral rights to be introduced (19) (743). **Q** Measures to be introduced to conform to Paris Act of Berne Convention (15,19) (306, 237). **R** Performers' protection: civil and criminal remedies to be strengthened; variety artists to be protected (14) (783 ff.).

© J.A.L. Sterling 1986

### *Notice of assertion*

**7.20** By section 78(4)(a), all persons who subsequently obtain title through the original assignment (whether or not they have notice) will be bound by the assertion.

By section 78(4)(b), in the case of an assertion by instrument in writing, only persons to whose notice the assertion is brought will be bound by it.

By section 78(4)(c), an assertion under section 78(3)(a) (identification attached to a work of art) will bind anyone into whose hands the original or copy comes, whether or not the identification is still present or visible and, it is submitted, whether or not the new owner could (even after reasonable care) have decided that the assertion was once there and subsequently removed.

By section 78(4)(d), an assertion under section 78(3)(b) (assertion in licence) will bind the licensee and anyone into whose hands a licensed copy of the work comes, whether or not he has notice of the assertion.

## Exceptions

**7.21** Because of the complications that would arise if the identification right was applicable to every work or every occasion, section 79 provides exceptions.

**7.22** Basically, no right of paternity applies to a computer program, the design of a typeface or any computer-generated work (defined in section 178).

### *Employees*

**7.23** By section 79(3), the right does not apply where the copyright in the work originally vested in an employer, but to the extent only that the dealing with the work is done with the authority of the copyright owner.

This exception was introduced as a Government amendment to the original Bill when it accepted the argument that the right would otherwise impose too great a burden on employers and infringe upon normal commercial and business practices. It is not clear, however, what the position is if the dealing is done *without* the authority of the copyright owner. Presumably in such circumstances the right will be enforceable by the author (or director) if he did not waive his right in his contract with the employer. The right is not assignable, so the employer cannot exercise it.

Subject to what the contract may say, presumably the author (or director) may *consent* to the dealing even if the employer does not. This would still leave the employer with his remedies under copyright.

### *Copyright*

**7.24** Section 79(4)(a) sets out those exceptions which reflect situations where copyright itself would not be infringed, for example:

(i) fair dealing exceptions in respect of the reporting of current events in a sound recording, film, broadcast or cable programme (reflecting section 30) (but not, note, in any newspaper or magazine or in any hard copy re-publication of the sound recording, film etc). It was felt by the Government that to allow the right to be exercised in any of the above circumstances would effectively reinstate the 'sufficient acknowledgment' requirement which section 30(2) excludes for reasons of the practical difficulties involved;

(ii) exceptions where the work is incidentally included in an artistic work, sound recording, film, broadcast, or cable programme so that, for example, an architect cannot require credit in a film simply because the building he designed appears in the background in a film (section 31). But if the subject of the film were architects or buildings and the building featured in the film, then appropriate credit would have to be given;

(iii) in respect of exam questions, an exam candidate does not have to identify the authors of works he quotes (although he may get better marks if he does!) (section 32(3));

(iv) there is no right of paternity in respect of literary works quoted in the written judgment of a court (section 45). It should be noted that this exception applies not only to the use of that work for reporting current events, but also so that any work made for that purpose is excluded, however it is used.

**7.25** Subsections (4)(e), (f), (g) and (h) set out further exceptions.

**7.26** Section 79(5) disapplies the right from any work made for the purpose of reporting current events.

### *Journalism; works of reference*

**7.27** Section 79(6) excludes the right in relation to publication in:

(a) a newspaper, magazine or similar periodical; or

(b) an encyclopaedia, dictionary, yearbook or other collective work of reference,

of any literary, dramatic, musical or artistic work *made for the purposes of such publication* or supplied with the author's consent for such purposes.

It was felt that, for example, there are so many contributors in some collective works (defined in section 178) that it would be impractical or inappropriate to identify them all; in works of joint authorship it may not only be impossible to distinguish different authors' contributions, but there may also be heavy editing where the work is required to follow a specific house style. Newspaper editors did not like the idea of a possible injunction and even the loss of an entire edition, if a journalist could exercise his right in respect of the smallest paragraph of a contribution.

### *Crown/Parliamentary copyright*

**7.28** Not surprisingly the right does not apply (section 79(7)) to a work in which Crown or Parliamentary copyright subsists, or to a work in which copyright originally vested in an international organisation, unless the author or director was previously identified in published copies of the work.

## Right to object to derogatory treatment of work (or right of integrity)

**7.29** By section 80, the author of a copyright literary, dramatic, musical or artistic work, and the author of a copyright film, has the right in specific circumstances not to have his work subjected to derogatory treatment.

### *'Treatment' and 'derogatory'*

**7.30** Section 80(2) defines treatment as 'any addition to or deletion from or alteration to or adaptation of the work', other than:

(i) a translation; or

(ii) an arrangement or transcription of a musical work involving no more than a change of key or register.

The treatment of a work is derogatory if it amounts to 'distortion or mutilation of the work or is otherwise prejudicial to the honour or reputation of the author or director'.

### *Infringement*

**7.31** The right is infringed in the following circumstances:

*(1) subsection (3):* in respect of a literary, dramatic or musical work, by anyone who:

(i) publishes a derogatory treatment of the work commercially, performs it in public or broadcasts or includes it in a cable programme service; or

(ii) issues to the public copies of a film or sound recording of, or including a derogatory treatment of, the work.

*(2) subsection (4):* in respect of an artistic work, by anyone who does any of the following to a derogatory treatment of the work:

(i) publishes it commercially;

(ii) exhibits it in public;

(iii) broadcasts, or includes a visual image of it in a cable programme service;

(iv) shows in public a film including a visual image of it, or issues to the public copies of such a film; or

(v) in the case of a work of architecture in the form of a model for a building, or a sculpture or a work of artistic craftsmanship, issues to the public copies of a graphic work representing, or of a photograph of, it.

*(3) subsection (6):* by a person who:

(i) shows a derogatory treatment of a film in public, broadcasts or includes it in a cable programme service; or

(ii) issues to the public copies of a derogatory treatment of the film; the right applies also to the accompanying film soundtrack.

**7.32** Section 80(5) disapplies the right in respect of a building, but where the architect is identified on the building and the building is the subject of derogatory treatment, the architect has the right to require his identification to be removed.

**7.33** Section 80(7) extends the right to the treatment of parts of the work resulting from a previous treatment by a person other than the author or director only if those parts are, or are likely to be, attributed to, or regarded as, the work of the author or director.

**7.34** Section 80(8) provides for certain exceptions to, and qualifications of, the right (see sections 81 and 82 respectively).

## Exceptions to the right of integrity

**7.35** By section 81, the right of integrity does not apply to a computer program, to a computer-generated work (defined in section 178), or to any work made for the purpose of reporting current events.

Nor does it apply to the publication of a literary, dramatic, musical or artistic work made for, or supplied with the consent of the author for the purposes of such publication, where the publication is in:

(i) a newspaper, magazine or periodical;

(ii) an encyclopaedia, dictionary, yearbook or other collective work of reference.

The right does not apply in respect of any subsequent exploitation elsewhere of such a work without any modification of the published version.

It should be noted that this reference to subsequent exploitation is unique to section 81 and is not present in section 79.

## Qualification of the right of integrity

**7.36** Section 82 qualifies the right in respect of works:

(i) in which copyright originally invested in the employer;

(ii) in which Crown or Parliamentary copyrights subsists; or

(iii) where the copyright originally vested in an international organisation.

**7.37** The right does not apply in relation to anything done to such works by or with the authority of the copyright owner unless the author or director

(i) is identified at the time of the relevant act; or

(ii) had previously been identified in or on published copies of the work and, where in such a case the right does apply, it is not infringed if there is a sufficient disclaimer.

### *Sufficient disclaimer*

**7.38** Section 82(3) defines 'sufficient disclaimer' as a reasonably clear and prominent statement, made at the time of the relevant act and along with the identification of the author, that the work has been subjected to treatment to which the author or director has not consented.

## Infringement by possession or dealing

**7.39** Section 83 provides that the right is infringed by a person who:

(i) possesses in the course of business;

(ii) sells or lets for hire or offer;

(iii) exposes for sale or hire;

(iv) in the course of a business, exhibits in public or distributes; or

(v) distributes other than in the course of a business so as to affect prejudicially the honour or reputation of the author or director,

any article which is and which he knows, or has reason to believe, to be an infringing article.

### *Infringing article*

**7.40** By section 83(2), an 'infringing' article is a work, or a copy of a work, which has been subjected to derogatory treatment and has been, or is likely to be, the subject of any of the acts mentioned in section 80 in circumstances infringing the right of integrity.

## False attribution of work

**7.41** By section 84, a person has the right in the circumstances mentioned in this section not to have a literary, dramatic, musical or artistic work falsely attributed to him as author and not to have a film falsely attributed to him as director. 'Attribution' means a statement, whether expressed or implied, as to who is the author or director.

### *Infringement*

**7.42** The right is infringed in the following circumstances:

*(1) subsection (2):* by a person who:

(i) issues to the public copies of a work; or

(ii) exhibits in public an artistic work or a copy of an artistic work,

in or on which there is a false attribution.

*(2) subsection (3):* by a person who:

(i) performs a literary, dramatic or musical work in public, broadcasts it or includes it in a cable programme service as being the work of a person; or

(ii) shows a film in public, broadcasts it or includes it in a cable programme service as being directed by a person,

knowing or having reason to believe that the attribution is false.

*(3) subsection (4):* by the issue to the public, or the public display, of material containing a false attribution in connection with any of the acts mentioned in subsection (2) or (3).

*(4) subsection (5):* by a person who in the course of business:

(i) possesses, or deals with, a copy of a work in or on which there is a false attribution; or

(ii) in the case of an artistic work, possesses or deals with the work itself when there is a false attribution in or on it,

knowing or having reason to believe that there is such an attribution *and* that it is false.

*(5) subsection (6):* in an artistic work by a person who in the course of a business:

(i) deals with a work which has been altered after the author parted with possession of it as being the unaltered work of the author; or

(ii) deals with a copy of such a work as being a copy of the unaltered work of the author,

knowing or having reason to believe that that is not the case.

*(6) subsection (8):* where contrary to the fact:

(i) a literary, dramatic or musical work is falsely represented as being an *adaptation* of a work of a person; or

(ii) a *copy* of an artistic work is falsely represented as being a copy made by the author.

**7.43** 'Dealing' means selling or letting for hire, offering or exposing for sale or hire, exhibiting in public or distributing.

## Right to privacy of certain photographs and films

**7.44** Now that the copyright in a photograph belongs to the maker of the photograph rather than to the owner of the film, it is even more important that protection should be afforded to persons of whom photographs are taken in certain private and domestic situations. Thus, section 85 provides that a person who commissions a photograph, or the making of a film for private and domestic purposes, has, where copyright subsists in the resulting work, the right not to have:

(a) copies of the work issued to the public;

(b) the work exhibited or shown in public; or

(c) the work broadcast or included in a cable programme service;

and anyone who does or authorises the doing of any of the foregoing infringes that right.

### *Exceptions to right of privacy*

**7.45** Section 85(2) provides certain exceptions where the doing of an act would not infringe copyright in the work. These exceptions are:

(a) incidental inclusion of the work in an artistic work, film, broadcast or cable programme (section 31);

(b) Parliamentary and judicial proceedings (section 45);

(c) Royal Commissions and statutory inquiries (section 46);

(d) acts done under statutory authority (section 50);

(e) anonymous or pseudononymous works: acts permitted on assumptions as to expiry of copyright or death of author (section 57).

## Duration of rights

**7.46** The right to be identified as author or director, the right to object to derogatory treatment and the right to the privacy of certain photographs and films continue to subsist so long as copyright subsists in the work.

The right as to false attribution continues until 20 years after a person's death.

## Consent and waiver

**7.47** By section 87, a person may *consent* to the doing of any of the restricted acts and he may *waive* his right by instrument in writing.

**7.48** Section 87(3) provides that a waiver may relate to a specific work or to works of a specified description or to works generally, and to existing or future works, and may be conditional or unconditional and may be expressed to be subject to revocation. If the waiver is made in favour of the owner or prospective owner of the copyright in the work or works to which it relates, it shall be presumed to extend to his licensees and successors in title unless a contrary intention is expressed.

**7.49** Section 87(4) provides that the general law of contract or estoppel in relation to an informal waiver or other transaction continues to apply. An interesting question which arises is whether consideration is required for the enforcement of a waiver.

It seems that the inclusion in subsection (3)(b) of the words 'and may be expressed to be subject to revocation' implies that gratuitous but unqualified waivers are binding. Further, a waiver not expressed to be subject to revocation is apparently irrevocable. Section 95(4) makes a consent or waiver given by the author binding on his estate and persons deriving title following his death. It is submitted that a waiver does not require consideration before it is binding on the giver thereof.

## Joint works

**7.50** By section 88, the right to be identified as author or director is, in the case of a work of joint authorship, a right of each joint author to be identified as a joint author, which must be asserted by each joint author in relation to himself.

**7.51** By section 88(2), the right to object to derogatory treatment of a work is a right of each joint author, and his right is satisfied if he consents to the treatment in question.

**7.52** A waiver by one joint author does not affect the rights of the other joint author(s) (section 88(3)).

**7.53** By section 88(4), the right of false attribution is infringed by any false statement as to the authorship of a work of joint authorship and by the false attribution of joint authorship in relation to a work of sole authorship; and such a false attribution infringes the right of every person to whom authorship of any description is, rightly or wrongly, attributed.

**7.54** The above applies in relation to a film which is 'jointly directed' if it is made by the collaboration of two or more directors and their contributions are not distinct from each other.

**7.55** By section 88(6), each person who commissioned the making is entitled to the right to privacy of certain photographs and films so that the right of each is satisfied if he consents to the act in question and a waiver by one does not affect the rights of the others.

**7.56** The right to be identified as author or director and the right to privacy of certain photographs and films apply in relation to the whole or any *substantial* part of a work (section 89(1)).

**7.57** The right to object to derogatory treatment and to false attribution apply in relation to the *whole or any part* of a work (section 82(2)).

## Moral rights not assignable

**7.58** Section 94 provides that moral rights are not assignable. By section 95(1), on the death of the person entitled to the right of paternity, the right of integrity and the right to privacy, the rights pass by will as may be specifically directed or, if there is no direction, the rights pass to the person to whom the copyright passes and otherwise are exercisable by the personal representatives.

**7.59** However, section 95(2) provides that where a bequest is limited so as to apply:

(i) to one or more but not all of the things the copyright owner has the exclusive right to do or authorise; or

(ii) to part but not to the whole of the period for which the copyright is to subsist,

any right which passes with the copyright by virtue of subsection (1) is correspondingly divided.

**7.60** Where the right becomes exercisable by more than one person, it may in the case of the right to identification be asserted by any of them; in the case of the right to integrity or to privacy, the right is exercisable by each of them and is satisfied in relation to any of them if he consented to the treatment or act in question; and any waiver of the right in accordance with section 87 by one of such persons does not affect the rights of the other(s).

**7.61** Section 95(4) provides that a consent or waiver previously given or made binds any person to whom the right passes by virtue of subsection (1).

**7.62** Section 95(5) provides that any infringement, after a person's death, of the right of false attribution is actionable by his personal representatives.

**7.63** By section 95(6), any damages recovered by personal representatives will devolve as part of the estate as if the right of action had subsisted and been vested in the person immediately before his death.

## Transitional provisions — Schedule 1

**7.64** Paragraph 22 of Schedule 1 provides that there can be no infringement of any moral right by reason of an act done before commencement of the Act, but of course section 43 of the 1956 Act continues to apply in respect of all acts done up to commencement.

It is not clear what the position is with regard to a repetition of an act *after* commencement: for instance, a book published before commencement, then (a) re-issued and (b) re-published after commencement. Arguably, moral rights may then be infringed.

### *Paternity and integrity*

**7.65** An author of a literary, dramatic, musical or artistic work must survive until commencement of the Act to obtain his paternity and integrity rights.

There are no paternity or integrity rights in a film made before commencement. The survival of the directors is not relevant. 'Made' means completed — see paragraph 1(3) of Schedule 1.

**7.66** The rights of paternity and integrity do not apply in respect of existing literary, dramatic, musical and artistic works (where the author has survived the commencement). 'Existing' again means completed before commencement.

Where copyright first vested in the author, the rights do not apply to anything which, by virtue of an assignment made or licence granted before commencement, may be done without infringing copyright. Thus, where an author enters into a publishing agreement *before* commencement, these new rights do not apply to any use of an existing work, pursuant to the publishing agreement.

Where copyright first vested elsewhere than in the author (for example, in an employer), the rights do not apply to anything done by or with the licence of the copyright owner.

**7.67** Where the work is not completed by commencement, moral rights may be enforced notwithstanding the existence of a prior licence or assignment.

**7.68** The rights of paternity and integrity are not enforceable in respect of anything done (at any time) pursuant to section 8 of the 1956 Act (statutory recording licence). It should be noted that in certain circumstances the statutory recording licence can continue for up to a year beyond commencement.

**7.69** The right to privacy of certain photographs and films does not apply to photographs *taken* or films *made* before commencement. It will apply to photographs or films commissioned before commencement but not taken or made until afterwards.

Chapter 8

# Dealings with rights in copyright works

**8.1** Sections 90 to 93 deal with assignments, licences and testamentary dispositions of copyright works. Sections 94 and 95 deal with the transmission of moral rights.

## Assignments and licences

**8.2** Section 90 repeats, with very little change, section 36 of the 1956 Act, providing that copyright is transmissible by assignment, testamentary disposition or by operation of law, as personal or moveable property. However, the provisions which deal with partial assignments are changed. Under the 1956 Act an assignment could be limited so as to apply to some but not all of the countries in relation to which the owner of the copyright has exclusive rights. Partial assignments now must be limited only in relation to the restricted acts and to part of the copyright period. The reason for the change is that, unlike the 1956 Act, the new Act does not provide for UK copyright to extend beyond the United Kingdom.

There is no change in the provision that assignments of copyright must be in writing. Licences, as distinct from assignments, are not required to be in writing. Section 176(1) provides that the requirement that an assignment must be in writing is satisfied by the affixation of its seal. This does not mean that an assignment by a company is effective only if under seal, but rather seeks to clarify the position that sealing as well as signature by a director or other authorised officer will be sufficient to satisfy section 90(3).

Section 90(3) virtually repeats section 36(4) of the 1956 Act in providing that licences granted by copyright owners are binding on their successors in title who have actual or constructive notice of the licence.

## Prospective ownership of copyright

**8.3** Section 91 effectively repeats section 37 of the 1956 Act in permitting the assignment of future copyright. There is virtually no change in the wording. It is somewhat more succinct and easier to construe. Section 91(2) defines 'future copyright' and 'prospective owner' in much the same way as they are defined in the 1956 Act. Section 91(3) provides that licences granted by prospective owners of copyright are binding on successors in title to their interest.

The only substantive change is the removal of the restriction on the assignment of future copyright in television broadcasts. The 1956 Act, Schedule 5, limited the right of the only possible owners of copyright in television broadcasts under that Act, the BBC and the IBA, to assign future copyright to one organisation each.

## Exclusive licences

**8.4** Section 92 defines 'exclusive licence' using much the same wording as section 19(9) of the 1956 Act. An exclusive licence must be in writing signed by the copyright owner. An exclusive licensee has the same rights against a successor in title who is bound by the licence, by virtue of having actual or contractual notice of its existence, as he has against the person granting the licence.

## Copyright passing under will with unpublished works

**8.5** Section 93 deals with copyright passing under wills with unpublished works. Under this section (which repeats, with one change, section 38 of the 1956 Act), where a document or other material thing is bequeathed, unless a contrary indication is indicated in the testator's will, bequests shall be construed as including the copyright in the work incorporated in the material thing. The changes in the new Act apply these provisions not only to manuscripts of literary, dramatic or musical works, but also to other material things embodying literary, dramatic, musical and artistic works and sound recordings or films. In every case, it is a condition that the work must not have been published before the death of the testator. This is an exception to the general rule that copyright does not pass with the sale or other disposition of a material object, such as a painting or film.

## Transitional provisions

### *Assignments and licences*

**8.6** The transitional provisions concerning assignments and licences are to be found in paragraphs 25 to 28 of Schedule 1 to the Act.

Documents made or events occurring before the commencement of the 1988 Act (ie under the 1911 or 1956 Act) shall have the corresponding operation in the work under the 1988 Act. Expressions used in such documents are to be construed in accordance with their effect immediately before commencement (paragraph 25 of Schedule 1).

The provisions of section 91(1) of the 1988 Act and of section 37(2) of the 1956 Act, dealing with the assignment of future copyright, are not to have any retrospective effect. Therefore, assignments of future copyright made before 1 June 1957 will continue to be ineffective.

### *Reversionary copyright*

**8.7** Paragraph 27(1) of Schedule 1 preserves the reversionary copyright provisions of the 1911 Act in respect of assignments and grants of interests in literary, dramatic, musical or artistic works made between the passing of the 1911 Act and 1 June 1957 — such assignments and grants are effective only until the expiration of 25 years from the death of the author when the rights granted revert to his estate. However, paragraph 27(2) provides that the copyright expectant on the termination of the 25-year period may, after commencement, be assigned by the author in his lifetime. In the absence of such an assignment, the rights devolve on his personal representatives on his death. Paragraph 27(3) provides that nothing in the Schedule will affect prior assignments of the reversionary interest or of the copyright after the reversionary interest has fallen in.

The exception from the reversionary copyright provisions of collective works and the definition of collective works, that originally appeared in the 1911 Act, are maintained without change.

### *Pre-1911 Act assignments*

**8.8** Paragraph 28 continues the transitional provisions of the 1956 Act relating to assignments and grants made before 1 July 1912, beyond the commencement of the 1988 Act, in that they have the corresponding operation in relation to copyright under the 1988 Act.

### *Pre-1956 Act bequests*

**8.9** Paragraph 30 of Schedule 1 provides that section 93 of the 1988 Act, under which copyright passes under wills with unpublished works (see paragraph 8.5 above) does not apply where the testator died before 1 June 1957 and, in the case of a testator who died after that date but before commencement, it applies only to an original document embodying a work. The reason for this provision is that section 93 of the 1988 Act applies not only to documents, but also to other material things which are the subject of a bequest, whereas section 38 of the 1956 Act applied only to manuscripts.

Chapter 9

# Remedies for infringement

## Infringement actionable

**9.1** Section 96 restates the fundamental principle previously existing in section 17(1) of the Copyright Act 1956 that an infringement of copyright is actionable by the copyright owner and that relief by way of damages, injunctions, accounts or otherwise is available to a plaintiff as in the case of the infringement of any other property right.

## Limited defence of innocence

**9.2** Section 97(1) sets out a limited defence of innocence to a damages claim. If it is shown by the defendant at the time of the infringement that he 'did not know and had no reason to believe' the subsistence of copyright, the plaintiff is not entitled to an award of damages against him. This provision is expressed to be without prejudice to any other remedy such as injunctive relief or an account of profits. The wording of this section is somewhat different from the equivalent section 17(2) of the 1956 Act which required the defendant to have 'no reasonable grounds for suspecting' the subsistence of copyright. The defence is therefore now arguably wider than existed under the 1956 Act.

### Additional damages

**9.3** Section 97(2) retains with amendment the provisions for statutory additional damages for flagrant infringement that were previously set out in section 17(3) of the 1956 Act. Under section 17(3) the court had to be satisfied, in addition to the tests of flagrancy and accrued benefit to the infringer, that 'effective relief would not otherwise be available'. Under the new section, the court has a discretion to award 'such additional damages as the justice of the case may require', having regard to all the circumstances and in particular to:

(i) the flagrancy of the infringement; and

(ii) any benefit accruing to the defendant by reason of the infringement.

Section 97(2) leaves unresolved the question of whether exemplary damages at common law under the *Rookes v Barnard* principle are capable of being awarded as well as additional damages under the section. There is no reason to assume that the decision of Ungoed-Thomas J in *Beloff v Pressdram Ltd* [1973] RPC 765 to the effect that exemplary damages for copyright infringement cannot be awarded except under the Act, does not remain good law, although the point was left open by Sir Robert Megarry V-C in *Lady Anne Tennant v Associated Newspapers Ltd* [1979] FSR 298.

## Limited defence if licence of right available

**9.4** Section 98 creates a limited defence to infringement in proceedings for infringement of copyright in respect of which a licence of right is available under section 144 as a result of a Monopolies and Mergers Commission report. The defendant must undertake to take a licence of right by agreement or as settled by the Copyright Tribunal. If these conditions are satisfied, no injunctive relief or order for delivery up may be granted and the amount recoverable by way of damages or an account of profits is not deemed to exceed double the amount which would have been payable if the licence had been granted. Section 98(3) adds the qualification that the remedies available in respect of an infringement committed before licences of right were available remain unaffected.

## Order for delivery up

**9.5** Section 99 places the copyright owner's rights to delivery up of infringing copies on a statutory basis. Section 18 of the 1956 Act embodied the concept of the infringer converting the copyright owner's rights in infringing copies to his own use. As well as leading to the much criticised and now repealed remedy of conversion damages, the concept of conversion enabled delivery up of infringing copies. This was put on a statutory footing by the Torts (Interference with Goods) Act 1977. The 1988 Act does not resurrect the notion of conversion of infringing copies, so it has become necessary for the remedy of delivery up to have a separate statutory basis.

**9.6** The effect of section 99 is to enable the copyright owner to apply to the court for an order that the infringing copy or article be delivered up to him or such other person as the court may direct. The court is empowered to entertain such an application:

(i) where a person has an infringing copy of a work in his possession, custody or control in the course of a business; or

(ii) where a person has in his possession, custody or control an article specifically designed or adapted for making copies of a particular copyright, knowing or having reason to believe that it has been or is to be used to make infringing copies.

It should be noted specifically that the power to seek delivery up of an infringing copy can only be exercised against an infringer acting in the course of business. An order for delivery up cannot be made more than six years after the infringing copy or article was made (see further section 113). The person to whom delivery up is made must hold the infringing copy or article pending an order for disposal under section 114.

## Right of seizure

**9.7** Section 100 creates a novel right for the copyright owner to seize infringing copies. The section is to some extent less draconian than originally proposed. It was the subject of considerable criticism as a self-help Anton Piller order which would lead inexorably to breaches of the peace. In its final form, the section provides that the copyright owner or a person authorised by him may seize an infringing copy from premises (which are deemed to include land, buildings, movable structures, vehicles, vessels, aircraft and hovercraft) and detain the copy provided that the following conditions are satisfied:

(i) the infringing copy is found exposed or otherwise immediately available for sale or hire;

(ii) the copyright owner would be entitled to apply for a delivery-up order under section 99;

(iii) the power is subject to any court order under section 114 as to the disposal of the infringing copy or other article;

(iv) before anything is seized, notice of the time and place of the proposed seizure must be given to a local police station;

(v) a person exercising the right of seizure may enter premises to which the public have access;

(vi) a person exercising the right of seizure may not seize anything in the possession, custody or control of a person at his permanent or regular place of business;

(vii) a person exercising the right of seizure may not use any force; and

(viii) at the time when anything is seized there shall be left at the place where it was seized a notice in the prescribed form containing the prescribed particulars as to the person by whom or on whose authority the seizure is made and the grounds on which it is made (the form of notice is to be governed by statutory instrument).

## Rights and remedies of an exclusive licensee

**9.8** Section 101 has the effect of simplifying the rights of an exclusive licensee compared to the corresponding previous provision found in section 19 of the 1956 Act. Section 101(1) provides that an exclusive licensee has (other than against the copyright owner) the same rights and remedies in respect of matters occurring after the grant of the licence as if the licence had been an assignment. No attempt is made in the section to specify an exclusive licensee's rights and remedies. Instead, section 101(2) provides that his rights and remedies 'are concurrent' with those of the copyright owner; and references in the relevant provisions of Part I of the Act to the copyright owner shall be construed accordingly. This section must procedurally be considered together with section 102.

Section 101(3), which replaces section 19(4) of the 1956 Act, makes it clear that when an action is brought by an exclusive licensee pursuant to the rights given to him by section 101, the defendant to the action 'may avail himself of any defence which would have been available to him if the action had been brought by the copyright owner'.

### *Exclusive licensee — exercise of concurrent rights*

**9.9** Section 102 corresponds to section 19(3) of the 1956 Act and deals with the circumstances in which there is an action for infringement of copyright brought by either the copyright owner or the exclusive licensee in respect of which they have concurrent rights of action.

Section 102(1) provides that either of them may not without leave of the court proceed with the action unless the other is joined as a party, whether as plaintiff or added as a defendant.

If either of them is added as a defendant, he is not liable for any costs in the action unless he (actively) takes part in the proceedings (section 102(2)). Nor do the requirements of section 102(1) affect the granting of interlocutory relief to the copyright owner or exclusive licensee alone (section 102(3)). Examples of cases in which leave of the court was given to enable the action to proceed without joining either the copyright owner or the exclusive licensee include *Warwick Film Productions Ltd v Eisinger* [1972] RPC 587 and *Bodley Head Ltd v Alec Flegon* [1972] RPC 587. The test would appear to be whether or not the other party is readily available to be joined to the action.

Section 102(4) is a new subsection applying to actions for infringement relating wholly or partly to an infringement in which the copyright owner and an exclusive licensee have or had concurrent rights of action and whether or not they are both parties to the action. In such cases, the following directions as to remedies are provided:

(a) in assessing damages, the court shall take into account the terms of the licence and 'any pecuniary remedy' already awarded or available in respect of the infringement;

(b) no account of profits shall be directed if an award of damages, or an account of profits has been directed in favour of the other of them in respect of the infringement; and

(c) if an account of profits is directed, the court shall apportion the profits between them as the court considers just, subject to any agreement between them.

Section 102(5) requires the copyright owner to 'notify' any exclusive licensee having concurrent rights:

(a) before applying for an order for delivery up under section 99;

(b) on exercising the right of seizure under section 100.

The exclusive licensee may apply to the court for an order under section 99 or to prohibit the exercise of the right of seizure under section 99. The court may then make such order as it thinks fit 'having regard to the terms of the licence'.

## Remedies for the infringement of moral rights

**9.10** Section 103 provides the statutory basis for a remedy for the infringement of moral rights. By section 103(1), an infringement is expressed to be actionable as a breach of statutory duty owed to the person entitled to the right.

**9.11** Section 77 creates an express right in favour of an author of a copyright literary, dramatic, musical or artistic work and the director of a copyright film not to have the work 'subjected to derogatory treatment'. This right is, by section 103(2), enforceable by means of an injunction provided the court considers it an 'adequate remedy in the circumstances'. An injunction cannot be awarded if a disclaimer is given in such terms and in such manner as approved by the court.

## Copyright presumptions

**9.12** Sections 104 to 106 set out the rebuttable presumptions applying to different categories of copyright work. They follow loosely similar provisions previously contained in section 20 of the 1956 Act, which in practice worked reasonably well (see, for example, *Warwick Film Productions Ltd v Eisinger* [1969] 1 Ch 508).

### *Literary, dramatic, musical and artistic works*

**9.13** (a) By section 104, where a name purporting to be that of the author appeared on copies of the work as published or on the work when it was made:

(i) the name shall be presumed to be the name of the author of the work; and

(ii) the work shall be presumed to have been made outside the course of the author's employment, outside Crown copyright, outside Parliamentary copyright or outside copyright vesting in certain international organisations (section 104(2)).

This presumption also applies in relation to each alleged author in a work alleged to be one of joint authorship (section 104(3)).

(b) Where the name of the purported author does not appear but:

(i) the work qualifies for protection under section 155 as a result of the country of first publication; and

(ii) a name purporting to be that of the publisher appeared on the work as first published

the person whose name appeared shall be presumed to have been the copyright owner at the time of publication (section 104(4)).

(c) If the author of the work is dead or his identity cannot be ascertained by reasonable inquiry, it shall be presumed that the work is original and the plaintiff's allegations as to first publication are correct (section 104(5)).

## *Sound recordings and films*

**9.14** (a) By section 105, where copies of the recording as issued to the public bear a label or other mark stating:

(i) that a named person was the owner of copyright in the recording at the date of issue of copies; or

(ii) that the recording was first published in a specified year or in a specified country,

the label or mark shall be admissible as evidence of the facts stated (section 105(1)).

(b) Where copies of the film as issued to the public bear a statement:

(i) that a named person was the author or director of the film;

(ii) that a named person was the owner of copyright in the film at the date of issue of the copies;

(iii) that the film was first published in a specified year or specified country,

the statement shall be admissible as evidence of the facts stated (section 105(2)).

Section 105(3) establishes that the presumptions also apply in proceedings relating to an infringement alleged to have occurred before the date on which the copies were issued to the public.

## *Computer programs*

**9.15** Where copies of the computer program are issued to the public in electronic form bearing a statement:

(a) that a named person was the owner of copyright in the program at the date of issue of the copies; or

(b) that the program was first published in a specified country or that copies of it were first issued to the public in electronic form in a specified year,

the statement shall be admissible as evidence of the facts stated.

### *Crown copyright*

**9.16** Section 106 applies in proceedings involving a literary, dramatic or musical work in which Crown copyright subsists. A statement on printed copies of the work of the year in which the work was first published commercially is admissible in evidence of that fact.

**9.17** It should be noted that the presumptions do not apply to proceedings for a criminal offence under section 107 (section 107(6)).

## Criminal offences

**9.18** Section 107 consolidates, with amendment, the offences created by section 21 of the 1956 Act, as well as the 'video piracy' offences created by the Copyright Act 1956 (Amendment) Act 1982 and the Copyright (Amendment) Act 1983 amendments to the 1956 Act. Section 107 embraces all 'copyright works' within the Act. The offences created by the section broadly relate to 'dealing' in an article which the defendant knows or has reason to believe is an infringing copy. The acts prohibited are:

(a) making for sale or hire;

(b) importing into the United Kingdom otherwise than for private and domestic use;

(c) possessing in the course of a business with a view to committing any infringing act;

(d) in the course of a business:

  (i) selling or letting for hire;

  (ii) offering or exposing for sale or hire;

  (iii) exhibiting in public;

  (iv) distributing;

(e) distributing otherwise than in the course of a business to such an extent as to affect prejudicially the owner of the copyright.

A new offence is created by section 107(2) so that a person who makes or possesses an article 'specifically designed or adapted for making copies of a particular copyright work' and knows or has reason to believe that it is used to make infringing copies for sale or hire or for use in the course of a business, commits an offence. It is probable that this offence is designed to replace section 21(3) of the 1956 Act, which created an offence of making or possessing a plate. The new offence is wider, embracing 'any article'. This was prompted by the growth of counterfeiting and technically advanced forms of copying.

It should be noted that all offences under section 107 require a heavy degree of mens rea as to knowledge of the existence of copyright. At the time of the passage of the Copyright Act 1956 (Amendment) Act 1982 it was widely believed that such a burden of proof on the prosecution might forestall the effectiveness of the Act. This has not been the case and the amended section 21 proved a successful weapon against video piracy. Now similar provisions cover all types of copyright work.

**9.19** Section 107(3) is based upon section 21(5) of the 1956 Act, whereby the causing of a literary, dramatic or musical work to be shown in public was an offence if the defendant knew that copyright subsisted in the work and the performance constituted an infringement. The new subsection adds to the offence the playing or showing in public of a sound recording or film and expressly excludes from liability for the offence the reception of a broadcast or cable programme.

### *Penalties*

**9.20** The penalties for the offences under section 107 are set out in the following table.

| *Offence* | *Section* | *Mode of trial* |
|---|---|---|
| Making for sale or hire | 107(1)(a) | Indictable and summary |
| Importing into the United Kingdom | 107(1)(b) | Indictable and summary |
| Possessing in the course of a business | 107(1)(c) | Summary only |
| In the course of business: | 107(1)(d) | |
| selling or letting for hire | 107(1)(d)(i) | Summary only |
| offering or exposing | 107(1)(d)(ii) | Summary only |
| exhibiting in public | 107(1)(d)(iii) | Summary only |
| distributing | 107(1)(d)(iv) | Indictable and summary |
| Distributing to affect prejudicially the owner of copyright | 107(1)(e) | Indictable and summary |
| Making or possessing an article designed to make copies | 107(2) | Summary only |
| Public performance of a copyright work | 107(3) | Summary only |

Offences triable summarily *and* on indictment have a maximum penalty of six months' imprisonment or a fine not exceeding the statutory maximum on summary conviction, and on indictment, an unlimited fine or up to two years' imprisonment or both.

Offences triable only summarily have a maximum penalty of six months' imprisonment or a fine up to level 5 on the standard scale or both.

### *Delivery up of infringing copies in criminal proceedings*

**9.21** Section 108 gives power to the criminal courts in which proceedings are brought for offences under section 107 to order delivery up of infringing copies. This is an elaboration on the powers of destruction and delivery up formerly contained in section 21(9) of the 1956 Act. The new section provides that the court before which proceedings are brought against a person for an offence under section 107 may, if satisfied that at the time of his arrest or charge:

(a) he had in his possession, custody or control in the course of a business an infringing copy of a copyright work; or

(b) he had in his possession, custody or control an article specifically designed or adapted for making copies of a particular copyright work, knowing or having reason to believe that it had been, or was to be, used to make infringing copies,

order that the infringing copy or article be delivered up to the copyright owner or to such other person as the court may direct.

It is significant that in order for the power to deliver up to be exercised there is no requirement for a conviction. All that is required is that the defendant should be arrested or charged and that at the time of his arrest or charge he has in his possession, custody or control infringing copies or an instrument for infringement. It should also be noted that the infringing copy must be possessed by the defendant in the course of a business. This is not a requirement for the possession of instruments of infringement. In the latter case, the prosecution must show that the defendant knew or had reason to believe that the article in question 'had been or was to be used to make infringing copies'. It is also significant that the benefit of the order for delivery up can be directed both to the copyright owner or to another person. This clearly gives a wide discretion to the criminal courts and it may be that the criminal courts will now become battlegrounds for establishing both title to copyright and rights in infringing articles.

Section 108(2) defines when a person shall be treated as charged with an offence.

Section 108(3) makes it clear that an order for delivery up under section 108(1) may be made by the court of its own motion or on the application of the prosecutor and may also be made whether or not the defendant is convicted of the offence under section 107. An appeal lies to the Crown Court against an order being made by a magistrates' court.

Section 108(5) provides that a person to whom an infringing copy or other article is delivered up in pursuance of section 108 shall retain it pending a decision whether to make a disposal order under section 114.

### *Search warrants*

**9.22** Section 109 gives to magistrates power, upon being satisfied by information on oath given by a constable that there are reasonable grounds that an offence under section 103(1)(a), (b), (d)(iv) or (e) has been or is about to be committed in any premises and that there is evidence that such an offence has been or is about to be committed in those premises, to issue a warrant authorising a constable to enter and search the premises using such reasonable force as is necessary. By section 109(3), a warrant may authorise persons to accompany any constable executing the warrant. This would presumably permit the copyright owner to enter with the constable for the purposes of identifying evidence of infringing articles. In executing a warrant, a constable may seize an article if he reasonably believes that it is evidence that an offence under section 107(1) has been or is about to be committed. It should be noted that the power of seizure is not limited in the same way as the power to obtain a warrant. For the purposes of the section, 'premises' includes land, buildings, moveable structures, vehicles, vessels, aircraft and hovercraft. There is no express power for a trading standards officer to apply for a search warrant, although in practice there would appear to be nothing to prevent the trading standards officer accompanying the police constable executing the warrant. Regrettably, past experience has shown little enthusiasm for the police authorities and trading standards authorities to work in conjunction in the enforcement of intellectual property offences.

### *Corporate liability for offences under section 107*

**9.23** Section 110 is an important section designed to remove the corporate veil in respect of offences under section 103 and to create a statutory liability for directors and officers over and above their common law liability (see *Tesco Supermarkets Ltd v Nattrass* [1972] AC 153). The section provides that where an offence under section 107 is committed by a body corporate and is proved to have been committed with the 'consent or connivance' of a director, manager, secretary or other similar officer of the company or a person purporting to act in any such capacity, he as well as the body corporate is guilty of the offence. The decision to include 'manager' in the section may well give rise to a dispute as to the meaning of the term, especially if it is alleged that a defendant is 'purporting to act' as 'manager'.

## Provision for preventing importation of infringing copies

**9.24** Sections 111 and 112 replace the little used and relatively ineffective provisions of section 22 of the 1956 Act. The new provisions should also be considered in the context of the powers given to the Customs and Excise by the recent EEC Directive 3842/86, which lays down measures to prohibit the free circulation of counterfeit goods within the EEC.

The scheme of the sections is that the owner of the copyright in a published literary, dramatic or musical work may give written notice to the Customs and Excise setting out:

(a) that he is the owner of the copyright in the work; and

(b) that he requests the Customs and Excise for a specified period to treat as prohibited goods printed copies of the work which are infringing copies.

During the currency of the notice, the importation of goods to which the notice relates, otherwise than by a person for his private and domestic use, is prohibited. There is no other penalty against an importer other than forfeiture of the goods. Section 111(2) provides that the period specified in the notice shall not exceed five years nor extend beyond the subsistence of copyright. Section 111(3), which is a new subsection, gives a similar right to the owner of a copyright in a sound recording or film, save that the copyright owner is obliged to give details of the time and place at which the infringing copies of the work are expected to arrive in the United Kingdom.

Section 112 enables the Customs and Excise to make regulations prescribing the form in which notice is to be given under section 111 and requiring a person giving notice to furnish the Customs and Excise with such evidence as may be specified in regulations, either on giving notice or when the goods are imported or at both those times but also to comply with such other conditions as may be specified in the regulations. By section 112(2), the regulations may require the payment of fees, the giving of security and an indemnity to the Customs and Excise against third party liability or expense by the copyright owner. Section 112(4) requires the regulations to be made by statutory instrument. There are a number of differences between the new powers and those contained in section 22 of the 1956 Act. In particular, the power to treat as prohibited goods (in respect of literary, dramatic and musical works) relates to all printed copies of the work which are infringing copies. This simplifies the previous somewhat tortuous definition of an infringing copy contained in section 22(2) of the 1956 Act. The addition of express provisions in relation to sound recordings and films is to be welcomed. This was a recommendation of the Whitford Committee (paragraph 725). It is perhaps unjustified that the copyright owner in a sound recording or film has the additional burden of having to give notice as to when and where the infringing recording or film is expected to arrive in the United Kingdom.

## Devices designed to circumvent copy-protection

**9.25** Section 296 creates a right of action by way of secondary infringement against a person who deals in devices 'specifically designed or adapted to circumvent a form of copy-protection' or 'publishes information intended to enable or assist persons to circumvent a form of copy-protection'. The section applies only where copies of a copyright work are issued to the public, by or with the licence of the copyright owner 'in an electronic form which is copy-protected'. The section therefore applies to protect software products, perhaps contained on disk or tape, which contain devices designed to prevent unauthorised copying or use. The section is aimed at devices such as 'bit copiers', which are especially designed to circumvent protective devices. Because the tort created by the section is a tort of secondary infringement, the defendant must know or have reason to believe that the device in question will be used to make infringing copies. The acts prohibited by section 296(2) give to 'a person issuing copies of the copyright work to the public' the same rights as a copyright owner in respect of an infringement of copyright. These rights are deemed to include, by section 296(3), the right to seek orders for delivery up of the devices. The forms of copy-protection safeguarded are defined by section 296(4) as including 'any device or means intended to prevent or restrict copying of a work or to impair the quality of copies made'. It is provided by section 296(6) that the copyright presumptions contained in sections 104 to 106 apply and that the withdrawal of the privilege against self-incrimination contained in section 72 of the Supreme Court Act 1981 applies to proceedings under section 296.

### *Fraudulent reception of transmissions*

**9.26** Section 297 creates an offence whereby a person who dishonestly receives a programme included in a broadcasting or cable programme service with intent to avoid payment of 'any charge applicable to the reception of the programme' commits a summary offence with a penalty of a fine not exceeding level 5 on the standard scale. The section has the effect of extending the offences already existing in sections 53 and 54 of the Cable and Broadcasting Act 1984 and is designed to prevent the evasion of payment for the reception of broadcasting services including satellite and cable programme services. Section 297(2) makes provision for the offence to be committed by a body corporate and creates a personal liability on the officers of the body corporate if the offence is committed with the consent or connivance of 'a director, manager, secretary or other similar officer of the body corporate.'

### *Rights and remedies in respect of apparatus for the unauthorised reception of transmissions*

**9.27** Section 298 creates civil remedies in favour of a person who:

(a) makes charges for the reception of programmes included in a broadcasting or cable programme service provided from a place in the United Kingdom; or

(b) sends encrypted transmissions of any other description from a place in the United Kingdom.

Such a person is given by section 298(2) the same rights and remedies as a copyright owner in respect of infringement against a person who makes, imports or sells or lets for hire any apparatus or device designed or adapted to enable or assist persons to receive programmes without payment, for example, equipment for 'hacking into a cable network' or 'publishes any information which is calculated to enable or assist persons to receive the programmes or other transmissions when they are not entitled to do so'. The section is similar to section 296 and, like that section, gives the same rights of delivery up and seizure as are contained in sections 99 and 100.

It also withdraws the privilege against self-incrimination contained in section 72 of the Supreme Court Act 1981. By section 298(5), the limited defence of section 97(1) is deemed to apply to section 298 (but does not apply to section 296).

### *Supplementary provisions as to fraudulent reception*

**9.28** Section 299 provides that sections 297 and 298 may by Order in Council be made to apply in relation to programmes included in broadcasting or cable services provided from a country outside the United Kingdom and in relation to programmes and encrypted transmissions sent from a country outside the United Kingdom. This power is subject to section 299(2), which requires that there is 'adequate protection in that country to persons making charges for programmes included in broadcasting or cable programme services provided from the United Kingdom'. It therefore creates a requirement of reciprocity. Section 299(4) makes it clear that sections 297 and 298 apply to 'feeder' services supplied to broadcasting services or cable programme services, whether they consist of sound or visual images. This subsection is the equivalent of section 53(2)(c) of the Cable and Broadcasting Act 1984.

## Transitional provisions in relation to remedies for infringement

**9.29** Schedule 1, paragraphs 31 to 33 provide as follows:

(1) *additional damages:* section 17(3) of the 1956 Act will continue to apply in relation to infringements committed before commencement of the Act (paragraph 31(1));

(2) *conversion damages:* section 18 of the 1956 Act will not apply after commencement of the Act except in relation to proceedings *begun* before the commencement of the Act (paragraph 31(2));

(3) *delivery up:* the powers created by section 99 apply to infringing copies and other articles made before or after commencement of the Act (paragraph 31(2));

(4) *rights of seizure:* the powers created by section 100 apply to infringing copies and other articles made before or after commencement of the Act (paragraph 31(2));

(5) *presumptions:* the new presumptions created by sections 104 to 106 apply only in proceedings under the 1988 Act; otherwise section 20 of the 1956 Act applies (paragraph 31(4));

(6) *exclusive licensees:* section 19 of the 1956 Act continues to apply in relation to infringements committed before the commencement date (paragraph 31(3));

(7) *criminal provisions:* section 21 of the 1956 Act continues to apply in relation to acts done before the commencement date, and thereafter section 107 applies (paragraph 33(1)).

Chapter 10

# Copyright licensing

## Introduction

**10.1** Lord Mansfield said:

> 'We must take care to guard against two extremes equally prejudicial; the one, that men of ability, who have employed their time for the service of their community, may not be deprived of their just merits, and the reward of their ingenuity and labour; the other, that the world may not be deprived of improvements, nor the progress of the arts be retarded.' (*Sayer v Moore* (1785))

Collective copyright licensing has flourished since section 23 of the 1956 Act set up the Performing Rights Tribunal to hear disputes between licensing bodies and persons (or organisations claiming to be representative of them) requiring licences. Such licensing goes back before then; the Performing Rights Society was set up in 1914 and the Phonographic Performance Ltd (representing record companies) and the Mechanical Copyright Protection Society (representing composers and publishers) followed afterwards.

**10.2** Copinger notes that 'from the point of view of (authors) and owners of . . . copyright the system has great advantages, in that no individual (author or owner) can in practice, secure adequate protection for his work, or deal with the very large number of persons and bodies desirous of exploiting such works' (Copinger and Skone *James on Copyright* (12th edn, 1980)). Copinger goes on to say that the public has an equal advantage, since licences can be obtained from a single organisation.

**10.3** However, the Government was concerned about the monopoly power so created, hence the establishment of the PRT, which had conduct of only three rights: the performance in public or the broadcast or diffusion of a literary dramatic or musical work or any adaptation; the performance in public of a sound recording; and public broadcasting. Many had felt for some time that the Tribunal's powers were too limited and the Government has taken this opportunity to set up a body, renamed the Copyright Tribunal, with much broader powers (see Chapter 11).

**10.4** The White Paper (Cmnd 9712) enthusiastically endorsed the Copyright Licensing Agency (CLA)/Local Authority Agreement relating to copying from books, periodicals and journals in schools and colleges. The Government thought this was welcome evidence that it was justified in its view that satisfactory contractual arrangements were possible under the existing law, but that, since collecting societies were effectively monopolies, it would in general be desirable to provide an arbitration mechanism in order to settle disagreements; jurisdiction is awarded to the Copyright Tribunal.

**10.5** To ensure that educational establishments were able to make copies of broadcasts and cable programmes and also multiple photocopies of very small proportions of any copyright work for group instruction, such establishments are permitted by sections 35 and 36 respectively to copy broadcasts and cable programmes in their entirety and to copy not more than 1 per cent of any work in each quarter of the year until such time as, or to the extent that, licences are available authorising the copying in question and, in the case of reprographic copying, the person making the copies knew or ought to have been aware of that fact (see paragraphs 6.10 and 6.11).

**10.6** Chapter VII of Part I therefore provides a framework for licensing schemes, licensing bodies and licences. Together with Chapter VIII, it represents a restatement and expansion of the provisions of the 1956 Act. It represents an expansion to the extent that the new Copyright Tribunal may turn out to be less of a tribunal of appeal restraining excesses of monopoly power and more of a detailed regulatory body overseeing something uncomfortably close to statutory licensing.

**10.7** According to Charles Clark and Colin Hadley:

> 'the task of reconciling the interests of those — authors and their business partners, publishers — who create copyright works with the interests of those — students, teachers, researchers, people in the professions and in business — who *use* copyright works through copying them is still with us. It may nicely turn out, in the long perspective of history, that the moment of the technology totally changed the context of reproduction, that is the invention of the Xerox machine, which opened the doors to massive infringement of the rights of creators, was also the moment of the technology of reconciliation, that is the invention of the computer, which opened the doors to control of and reward for that massive infringement. Photocopying machinery has made individual control of the creators' rights of reproduction impossible, so that collective control and rewards through collecting societies has become not just desirable, but necessary, and that collective control and reward depend on the capacities of the computer to absorb, record and distribute.' (Charles Clark and Colin Hadley *Collective Administration of Literary Works, Principles and Practice: the British Experience* (1988))

**10.8** The same authors say that there are indications that in the advanced national economies of Western Europe, approximately 200 copy pages per head of population would be a reasonable estimate of annual use of copyright works. In the UK, the State school system uses approximately 90 million copy pages of copyright works per year. The role of collective administration of rights in literary works is not therefore peripheral to the copyright system.

It is rapidly becoming the copyright system's central strategy for literary works in reconciling creator and user interests.

**10.9** It was the Whitford Report (Cmnd 6732) which suggested the most likely solution to the photocopying problem — a collective administration system for copying rights organised by the rights owners themselves. From that suggestion came the Wolfenden Committee, comprised of representatives of authors, societies and publishers' associations. This was followed by the de Freitas Committee, which eventually gave birth to the Copyright Licensing Agency Limited, in 1983. Whitford, in Chapter 4 of his Report, concentrated on reprography. Conscious of the UK's obligations under the international copyright Conventions (UCC and Berne), he proposed a flexible system of blanket licensing to cater for all user requirements for facsimile copies but no compulsory licence to publish. To encourage copyright owners to set up schemes, he said that reprographic reproduction should not be an infringement unless and until a blanket licensing scheme was in place. All negotiations between collecting societies and users should be subject, in the case of a dispute, to appeal to a Copyright Tribunal. Once a scheme was in operation, the present latitude for making single copies (sections 6 and 7 of the 1956 Act) should cease, even for the making, by the student himself, of copies.

**10.10** Article 9.1 of the Paris Text of the Berne Convention provides that authors shall have the exclusive right of authorising the reproduction of their protected works in any manner or form. Article 9.2, however, allows countries to permit the reproduction of works in certain special cases, provided that the reproduction does not conflict with normal exploitation of the work and does not unreasonably prejudice the legitimate interests of the author. The Universal Copyright Convention also allows exceptions which do not conflict with the spirit and provisions of the Convention and which offer a 'reasonable degree of effective protection'.

**10.11** The 1981 Green Paper (Cmnd 8302) rejected both the statutory approach to blanket licensing and the abolition of fair dealing and library exceptions in relation to photocopying. The Government considered that students and libraries should not be discouraged from using the modern technological tool of the photocopier for copying which is for manifestly fair dealing purposes.

> 'The difficulty of enforcing individual copyrights in the face of the ubiquitous photocopier makes blanket licensing the appropriate solution in most cases . . . the Government considers that copyright owners should not in general be obliged to join blanket licensing schemes and should in general retain their exclusive rights. It does, however, consider that a derogation from this principle is justified to ensure that the educational sector is not unreasonably denied photocopying licences.'

### *Collective licensing*

**10.12** Chapter VII of Part I builds on the foundation laid by the 1956

Act. 'Licensing scheme' is the new name for 'licence scheme' and 'licences' now fall within the newly named Copyright Tribunal's jurisdiction.

**10.13** A *licensing scheme* is the same as the old licence scheme in the 1956 Act and, by section 116, is a scheme setting out:

> '(a) the classes of case in which the operator of the scheme, or the person on whose behalf he acts, is willing to grant copyright licences, and
>
> (b) the terms on which licences would be granted in those classes of case.'

**10.14** A *licensing body* means a society or other organisation which has as its main object, or one of its main objects, the negotiation or granting of copyright licences covering works of more than one author. This includes not only the main collecting societies but also, for example, a music publisher, if licensing was (which it could be) one of its main objects.

**10.15** A copyright *licence* means a licence to do or authorise the doing of any act restricted by copyright.

**10.16** Chapter VII does not apply to licences or licensing schemes covering a single collective work or collective work of which the authors are the same or works made by, or by employees of, or commissioned by, a single individual firm, company or group of companies.

**10.17** A licence under a licensing scheme — a scheme licence — is something offered to the world in general and anyone who complies with the terms will be entitled to a licence.

A non-scheme licence is one which is restricted to an individual user or group of users.

## References and applications with respect to licensing schemes

**10.18** The provisions set out in sections 118 to 123 apply to:

(a) licensing schemes operated by licensing bodies which cover literary, dramatic or musical works of more than one author in respect of licences for—

  (i) copying the work;
  (ii) performing, playing or showing the work in public;
  (iii) broadcasting the work or including it in a cable programme service;

(b) all licensing schemes in relation to the copyright in a sound recording (other than a film soundtrack when accompanying a film) broadcast or cable programme or the typographical arrangement of published editions; and

(c) all licensing schemes in relation to the copyright in sound recordings, films or computer programs so far as they relate to licences for the rental of copies to the public.

**10.19** It should be noted that whilst a licensing scheme operated by an individual publisher (rather than a collecting society) would only be covered where the publisher could demonstrate that the granting of licences was one of its main objects, a licensing scheme operated by a record company would be covered since, restating the 1956 Act position, it is not a requirement that licensing schemes for sound recording copyrights should be operated by licensing bodies.

**10.20** The Tribunal has no jurisdiction over a scheme covering the works of one author of literary, dramatic, musical or artistic works or films, but it does have jurisdiction in such circumstances over sound recordings, broadcasts or cable programmes.

### *Reference of proposed licensing scheme to the Tribunal*

**10.21** Section 118 permits the terms of a licensing scheme proposed to be operated by a licensing body to be referred to the Tribunal by an organisation claiming to be representative of potential users.

This will allow a scheme in negotiation to be referred to the Tribunal, for example, where the potential users consider it unlikely that agreement will be reached.

The Tribunal may decline to entertain the reference for instance because it considers that negotiations are in too early a stage and that no sensible order could be made. But if it agrees to do so then, having considered the matter referred it must make such order, either confirming or varying the proposed scheme, (either generally or so far as it relates to cases of the description to which the reference relates) as the Tribunal (in its own discretion) may determine to be reasonable in the circumstances. The Tribunal's order may, or may not, be limited for a particular period of time.

### *Reference of a licensing scheme to the Tribunal*

**10.22** Section 119 (corresponding broadly to section 25(1) and (5) to (7) of the 1956 Act) permits a dispute arising in relation to a licensing scheme in operation to be referred to a Tribunal by:

'(a) a person claiming that he requires a licence in the case of a description to which the scheme applies, or

(b) an organisation claiming to be representative of such persons.'

This covers reference of a scheme in its entirety where a potential user does not accept the terms or charges as a whole. Disputes over the specific operation of a scheme, for example, over the grant of a specific licence for a specific venue or a specific occasion, are covered by section 121.

**10.23** Section 119(2) provides that the existing scheme will remain in operation until proceedings on the reference are concluded.

**10.24** By section 119(3) and (4), the Tribunal can make such order effective for such period of time as it considers to be reasonable.

### *Further reference of a scheme*

**10.25** Where the Tribunal's order following a previous reference of the scheme remains in force the operator or a potential user claiming that he requires a licence, may re-refer the scheme (so far as it relates to cases of the same description) on certain conditions.

**10.26** Section 120(2) limits the re-referral of a scheme (otherwise than with the special leave of the Tribunal) within twelve months from the date of the previous order or, if the order was made so as to be in force for fifteen months or less then, until the last three months before the expiry of the order.

**10.27** By section 120(3), a scheme referred to the Tribunal under this section remains in operation until proceedings on the reference are concluded. By section 120(4) and (5), the Tribunal, having considered the reference, may make such order for such period of time as it considers reasonable in the circumstances.

Corresponding broadly to section 26 of the 1956 Act, this section gives an operator or a user the right to apply to the Tribunal to vary the terms of an existing order where, for example, circumstances have changed, or a royalty variation is required.

### *Application for licence under licensing scheme*

**10.28** A person may apply to the Tribunal where he claims, in a case covered by a licensing scheme, that the operator has refused to grant him a licence or has failed to do so within a reasonable time of being asked.

**10.29** By section 121(2), a person may also apply to the Tribunal where he claims, in a case excluded from a licensing scheme, that the operator has either refused to grant him a licence or has failed to do so within a reasonable period of time and that in the circumstances it is unreasonable that a licence should not be granted; or has proposed terms for a licence which are unreasonable.

**10.30** Section 121(3) defines those cases which are to be regarded as excluded from a licensing scheme. These are if:

> '(a) the scheme provides for the grant of licences subject to terms excepting matters from the licence and the case falls within such an exception, or
> (b) the case is so similar to those in which licences are granted under the scheme that it is unreasonable that it should not be dealt with in the same way.'

By section 121(4) and (5), the Tribunal may make such order for such period of time as it considers reasonable.

It is suggested that the Tribunal will face difficulties in those cases where, because the operator does not have the rights, the case falls within an exception to a scheme. The CLA, for instance, in its standard licence excepts certain works and classes of work because certain copyright owners did not want their works to be included in a collective licensing scheme. The Tribunal cannot order the CLA to include such works (because the CLA does not have the rights) and has no jurisdiction (on this wording anyway) to require the copyright owners to include their works within the scheme.

### *Application for review*

**10.31** By section 122, equating to section 27A of the 1956 Act, where the Tribunal has made an order under section 121 that a person is entitled to a licence under a licensing scheme, the operator of the scheme or the original applicant may apply to the Tribunal to review its order. However, by section 122(2), an application may not be made except with special leave of the Tribunal within twelve months from the date of the order, or of the decision on a previous application, or if the order was made so as to be in force for fifteen months or less or, as a result of the decision on a previous application under this section, is due to expire within fifteen months of that decision, until the last three months before the expiry date.

By section 122(3), the Tribunal shall on an application for review confirm or vary its order as it determines.

### *Licensing scheme: effect of Tribunal's order*

**10.32** By section 123, equating to section 29 of the 1956 Act, where a licensing scheme has been confirmed or varied by the Copyright Tribunal under section 118, 119 or 120, it shall be in force for so long as the order remains in force.

**10.33** By section 123(2), where, whilst an order is in force, a person either pays to the operator of the scheme any charges payable or, where the amount cannot be ascertained, gives an undertaking to pay when ascertained, and complies with the other terms applicable to such a licence, then he is in the same position as the holder of a licence granted by the owner of the copyright.

**10.34** Except where the Tribunal's order under sections 119 or 120 *reduces* the charges payable for licences, the order may be retrospective but not to a date earlier than the date of reference or the date the scheme came into effect.

**10.35** Section 123(4) provides that an order of the Tribunal under section 119 or 120 made with respect to a scheme which is certified for any purpose under section 143, has effect (so far as it reduces the charges payable for licences) from the date on which the *reference* was made (ignoring, for these purposes, the date of the order).

**10.36** Where an order is made under section 121, then on the same basis as in section 123(2), the person in whose favour the order is made is also considered to have the benefit of a licence from the copyright owner.

## Licences

**10.37** Sections 124 to 128 apply to the rules relating to licences (other than pursuant to a licensing scheme) issued by licensing bodies covering (except in respect of sound recordings) the works of more than one author.

**10.38** The relevant licences are those relating to copyright in literary, dramatic, musical or artistic works or films (or film soundtracks when accompanying a film) which cover works of more than one author so far as they authorise (i) copying the work, (ii) performing, playing or showing the work in public or (iii) broadcasting the work or including it in a cable programme service; and copyright in a sound recording other than a film soundtrack when accompanying a film broadcast or cable programme, or the typographical arrangement of a published edition; and copyright in sound recordings, films or computer programs where they relate to the rental of copies to the public. These sections contain equivalent provision for licences as sections 118 to 123 apply to licensing schemes. Only licences granted by a licensing body are covered. The provisions are very similar to those contained in sections 118 to 123, but the draftsman decided, for reasons of clarity, to set them out separately. The main objects of a *licensing body* must include a provision that the body is entitled to represent the works of more than one author (section 116(2)).

### *Reference of proposed licence*

**10.39** Section 125 permits a prospective licensee to refer the terms of a proposed licence to the Tribunal, which may decide whether it wishes to entertain the reference; if it decides to do so then it may make such order confirming or varying the terms as it considers to be reasonable in the circumstances for such period of time as it decides.

### *Reference of expiring licence*

**10.40** Section 126 allows a licensee, within the last three months before expiry, to apply to the Tribunal that it is unreasonable that the licence should expire by effluxion of time or as a result of notice given by the licensing body.

**10.41** If a reference is made to the Tribunal, the licence remains in operation until the Tribunal has made its order.

### *Application for review*

**10.42** Section 127 permits either body to apply for a review of the Tribunal's order but, except with special leave, not within twelve months from the order or, if the order was expressed to be in force for fifteen months or less, until the last three months before the expiry date. The Tribunal may make such order as it sees fit.

### *Effect of order*

**10.43** By section 128, a person entitled to the benefit of an order is, as long as the order remains in force and provided he pays the charges and complies with the terms, regarded as being in the same position, so far as infringement of copyright is concerned, as if he had at all material times been the holder of a licence from the copyright owner.

**10.44** Section 128(2) permits the benefit of the order to be assigned, provided that neither the order nor the original licence prohibit assignment.

**10.45** Section 128(3) permits an order, so far as it varies charges, to be backdated to the date of the reference or the date of the licence.

### *Unreasonable discrimination*

**10.46** By section 129, the Tribunal is obliged to have regard in determining what is reasonable on a reference or application in respect either of a scheme or a licence, to:

> 'the availability of other schemes or the granting of other licences; and the terms of those schemes or licences.'

The Tribunal is required to ensure that there is no unreasonable discrimination between licensees. This section carries into the 1988 Act the same criterion as set out in the 1956 Act. The Tribunal may look at all similar schemes or licences.

### *Reprographic licences*

**10.47** By section 130, in respect of reprographic rights licensing, the Tribunal must consider:

> '(a) the extent to which published editions of the works in question are otherwise available,
>
> (b) the proportion of the work to be copied, and
>
> (c) the nature of the use to which the copies are likely to be put.'

If a book were currently in print, photocopying of it could compete with sales. A teacher may wish to copy extracts from several books because the purchase of sufficient copies of *all* the books for each member of the class was outside the school's purchasing budget.

### *Recording for educational purposes*

**10.48** By section 131, the Tribunal, in respect of licences for the recording by or on behalf of educational establishments of broadcast or cable programmes which include copyright works, or the making of copies of such recordings for educational purposes, must consider, when it decides what charges should be paid, the extent to which the copyright owners have already received or are entitled to receive, payment for the inclusion of their works in the broadcast or programme.

The White Paper (paragraph 18.14) foreshadowed this provision. Educational television programmes would probably have been made on the basis that broadcasting fees would be the sole revenue source.

**10.49** In respect of licences for sound recordings, films, broadcasts or cable programmes which are or may include any entertainment or other event, section 132 requires the Tribunal to have regard to the conditions imposed by the promoters of the entertainment or other event. The Tribunal is not entitled to hold a refusal or failure to grant a licence to be unreasonable if it could not have been granted consistently with those conditions but the Tribunal is not required to have regard to any such conditions so far as they (a) purport to regulate the charges, or (b) relate to payments to be made to the promoters for the grant of facilities for making the recording, film, broadcast or cable programme. This is a broader re-enactment of section 29(4) of the 1956 Act. Now included are sound recordings, films and cable programmes (and not only broadcasts).

**10.50** By section 133, in considering what charges should be paid for a licence on a reference or application relating to licences for the rental to the public of copies of sound recordings, films or computer programs, the Tribunal must take into account any reasonable payments which the owner of the copyright is liable to make in consequence of the granting of the licence.

The 1961 Rome Convention gives performers and record companies the right to get 'equitable remuneration' from the broadcasting and public performance of commercial records containing their performances.

Members are entitled to make their own provisions as to how this right is put into effect. The UK has chosen to require performers to look only to the record company (and not to the broadcaster) for their share. Record companies pay 20 per cent of their 'broadcasting revenues' to their artists; 12½ per cent is paid to the Musicians Union for musicians whose contributions cannot be identified.

In a recent High Court case, *AIRC v PPL and the MU* (1986), Harman J ruled that 'it cannot be proper to take into account what is reasonable . . . the ways in which one party voluntarily or under the compulsion of a trades union, chooses to spend its money'.

A later Tribunal decision (unappealed) concluded that a reasonable royalty could be negotiated with the Musicians Union.

This section clarifies the position and now allows the Tribunal to take into account 'all *reasonable* payments which the copyright owner is liable to make' (section 133(2)).

### *'Must carry'*

**10.51** Section 134 applies to licences to include a literary, dramatic, musical or artistic work or sound recording or film in a broadcast or cable programme service where the first transmission is immediately retransmitted.

Where the further transmission is to the same area as the first, the Tribunal has to consider what payment the owner has already received which might have adequately remunerated him; where the further transmission is to an area outside that to which the first transmission was made, the Tribunal has to ignore the further transmission in calculating the payments for the first transmission (except where it is satisfied that the cable authority had a duty to secure inclusion of the broadcast in the cable programme service when the Tribunal must ensure that the charges payable for licences to the first transmission adequately reflect that fact).

The intentions of this section are to avoid double charging in respect of what is in effect a single transmission; ensure the Tribunal take into account the fact that rights owners have already been remunerated for the retransmission; and ensure that copyright owners are remunerated as a consequence of 'must carry' provisions.

**10.52** Section 135 emphasises the Tribunal's obligation to have regard to all relevant considerations, not just to those listed above.

## Implied indemnity

**10.53** Section 136 implies in every relevant scheme or (where granted by a licensing body) licence an undertaking by the operator or the licensing body to indemnify the licensee against any liability incurred by the licensee in infringing copyright in circumstances within the apparent scope of the licence.

The relevant schemes or licences are those for licensing reprographic copying of published literary, dramatic, musical or artistic works, or the typographical arrangement of published editions, where the scheme or licence does not specify the works to which they apply with such particularity as to enable licensees to determine whether a work falls within the scheme or licence by inspection of the scheme or licence and the work.

**10.54** The indemnity covers liability to pay costs reasonably incurred by a licensee in connection with actual or contemplated proceedings against him but the licence or scheme may contain reasonable provision allowing the operator or licensing body to defend the claim or to take over the conduct of proceedings.

### *Apparent scope*

**10.55** A case is deemed to be within the apparent scope of a licence, and thus covered by the indemnity, if:

> '(a) it is not apparent from inspection of the licence and the work that it does not fall within the description of works to which the licence applies; and
> (b) the licence does not expressly provide that it does not extend to copyright of the description infringed.'

## Extension of coverage of scheme or licence

**10.56** In the case of a scheme or licence authorising the making by or on behalf of educational establishments (for the purposes of instruction) of reprographic copies of published literary, dramatic, musical or artistic works or of the typographical arrangement of published editions, section 137 (complementing section 36) allows the Secretary of State, where he considers that:

> '(a) works of a description similar to those covered by the scheme or licence are unreasonably excluded from it, and
> (b) making them subject to the scheme or licence would not conflict with the normal exploitation of the works or unreasonably prejudice the legitimate interests of the copyright owners',

to order that the scheme or licence must be extended to those works. He must give notice of his proposal to the copyright owners, the licensing body in question and such other persons or organisations as he thinks fit. (Article 9(2) of the Berne Convention requires that the legitimate interests of the copyright owner must not be unreasonably prejudiced and that the normal exploitation of a work must not be interfered with.)

**10.57** The notice must inform the persons of their right to make written or oral representations about the proposal within six months from the date of the notice and, before making an order, the Secretary of State must take into account any representations made to him and such other matters as appear (to him) relevant.

## Application to vary or discharge

**10.58** Section 138 allows the owner of copyright in a work in respect of which an order under the preceding section is in force to apply, giving reasons, to the Secretary of State for variation or discharge. The Secretary of State cannot, in the absence of exceptional circumstances, entertain any application within two years of the original order.

**10.59** If the Secretary of State does not confirm the order forthwith, then he must give notice of the application to the licensing body in question and such other persons as he sees fit, such notice again informing the persons of their right within two months to make representations. In considering the application, the Secretary of State will take into account the reasons for the application, and any representations made to him and such other matters as are relevant and then he may make such order as he thinks fit, confirming or discharging the original order or varying it so as to exclude works from it.

**10.60** Section 139 gives to the owner of the copyright in the work which is the subject of an order under section 137 (order extending coverage of scheme or licence) the right to appeal to the Tribunal, which may confirm or discharge or vary the order, so as to exclude works from it, as it thinks fit, having regard to the considerations mentioned in section 137(2).

The Tribunal has power to confirm or discharge the order or make any other order provided it is one that the Secretary of State could have made. The appeal must be brought within six weeks or such further period as the Tribunal allows.

The Secretary of State's order under sections 137 and 138 cannot come into effect for six weeks or, if an appeal is duly brought, until the appeal proceedings are disposed of or withdrawn. If the appeal is brought late, then any decision of the Tribunal will not affect the validity of anything done in reliance on the order before the Tribunal's decision takes effect.

## New scheme or licence

**10.61** By section 140, in connection with the making by or on behalf of educational establishments for the purposes of instruction of reprographic copies of (a) published literary dramatic musical or artistic works, or (b) the typographical arrangements of published editions, if the Secretary of State considers that any works are not covered by an existing licensing scheme or general licence and that he cannot, pursuant to section 137, extend the coverage of the scheme or licence, then he may set up an enquiry into whether a new scheme or general licence is required.

**10.62** The Secretary of State will set up the procedures to be followed in relation to such an enquiry. As a minimum, such procedures must provide for notice to be given to the relevant persons and for the making of representations. Any interested party may make representations also.

**10.63** The person appointed by the Secretary of State to hold the enquiry may not recommend the making of a new provision unless he is satisfied (a) that it would be of advantage to educational establishments, and (b) that making the additional works subject to a licensing scheme or licence would not conflict with the normal exploitation of the works or unreasonably prejudice the legitimate interests of the copyright owners.

**10.64** If the person does recommend the making of new provision then he must specify any terms (other than terms as to charges payable) on which authorisation under the new provision should be available.

### *General licence*

**10.65** In this (and the next section) 'general licence' means a licence granted by a licensing body which covers *all works* of the description to which it applies.

### *Statutory licence*

**10.66** Section 141 permits the Secretary of State, within one year of the making of a recommendation under section 140, to provide to the extent that the recommendation has not been followed, a royalty-free statutory licence for such works on such terms as he thinks fit.

**10.67** The recommendation shall be regarded as having been followed if in respect of any educational establishment:

(a) a certified licensing scheme has been established; or

(b) a general licence has been—

  (i) granted to or for its benefit; or
  (ii) referred by or on behalf of that establishment to the Tribunal under section 125; or
  (iii) offered to or for the benefit of that establishment and refused without such a reference.

For the meaning of 'certified licensing scheme' see section 143.

**10.68** Where the Secretary of State establishes a statutory licence, any existing licence will cease to have effect to the extent that it is more restricted or more onerous than the statutory licence.

**10.69** The statutory licence *must* be royalty-free, but the Secretary of State may include such other terms as were contained in the recommendation or as he sees fit.

**10.70** The Secretary of State's order may prohibit further dealing with a copy made in accordance with the statutory licence. 'Dealt with' means sold or let for hire, offered or exposed for sale or hire or exhibited in public.

**10.71** A statutory licence may not come into force for at least six months and may, within the framework of the terms of the recommendation, be varied from time to time.

## Rental royalty

**10.72** Section 142 gives the Tribunal jurisdiction to settle the royalty or other sum payable for the rental of sound recordings, films and computer programs. An application may be made by a copyright owner or a person claiming to be licensed by him. The Tribunal may make such order as it sees fit and either party may appeal to vary the order, but not within twelve months of the original order.

## Certification

**10.73** Part I of the 1988 Act contains a number of provisions allowing reproduction of copyright works in the absence of a certified scheme.

Section 143 requires the Secretary of State to certify a licensing scheme on the application of a person operating or proposing to operate it and for the purposes of:

(i) educational recording of broadcasts or cable programmes (section 35);

(ii) abstracts of scientific or technical articles (section 60);

(iii) the rental of sound recordings, films or computer programs (section 66);

(iv) subtitled copies of broadcasts or cable programmes for people who are deaf or hard of hearing (section 74); or

(v) reprographic copying of published works by educational establishments (section 141).

**10.74** The Secretary of State must certify the scheme if he is satisfied that (a) it enables the works to which it relates to be identified with sufficient certainty by persons likely to require licences, and (b) sets out clearly the charges (if any) payable and other terms on which licences will be granted.

**10.75** The scheme cannot come into operation earlier than (a) eight weeks after the date of the order, or (b) if subject to a reference of a proposed scheme to the Tribunal, when the Tribunal's order comes into force or the reference is withdrawn.

**10.76** A certified scheme may not be varied except subject to an order of the Secretary of State, who must vary it where the variation has been ordered by the Tribunal under section 118, 119 or 120 and who may revoke an order if the scheme ceases to be operated or is no longer operated according to its terms.

## Monopolies and mergers

**10.77** By section 144, the powers conferred by Part I of Schedule 8 to the Fair Trading Act 1973 are extended in certain circumstances to include power to cancel or modify conditions in licences or to provide that licences shall be available as of right. The Tribunal has power to settle the terms of a licence available pursuant to this section, but a Minister is entitled to exercise the powers available only if he is satisfied that this will not contravene any copyright convention to which the UK is a party.

Chapter 11

# Copyright Tribunal

## The Tribunal

**11.1** Section 145 (recognising its extended jurisdiction) renames the Performing Rights Tribunal, established under section 23 of the 1956 Act, and provides that it will consist of the chairman and two deputy chairmen (who must be a barrister, advocate or solicitor of not less than seven years' standing or who must have held judicial office) appointed by the Lord Chancellor, with between two and eight ordinary members appointed by the Secretary of State. Under section 23(2) of the 1956 Act, there was provision only for a chairman and two to four ordinary members.

### *Membership*

**11.2** Section 146 sets out the basis on which members hold and vacate office, and also that on which a person can be replaced during illness or other absence. This restates the existing law. In a new provision, the Lord Chancellor is required to exercise his powers in consultation with the Lord Advocate.

### *Financial*

**11.3** Section 147 provides for remuneration and for the appointment of staff to service the Tribunal. The cost of the Tribunal (subject to approval by the Treasury) comes out of money provided by Parliament.

### *Constitution*

**11.4** Section 148 sets the quorum, which must be at least three, of whom one must be the chairman or deputy chairman; decisions are by majority vote, with the chairman having a casting vote. If the chairman is unable to continue, then he will choose a substitute from among the members to take his place and a suitably qualified (ie eligible for appointment as deputy chairman) person to advise members on questions of law.

## Jurisdiction

**11.5** Section 149 sets out the jurisdiction of the Tribunal, which is to hear and determine proceedings under:

'(a) section 118, 119 or 120 (reference of licensing scheme);

(b) section 121 or 122 (application with respect to entitlement to licence under licensing scheme);

(c) section 125, 126 or 127 (reference or application with respect to licensing by licensing body);

(d) section 139 (appeal against order as to coverage of licensing scheme or licence);

(e) section 142 (application to settle royalty or other sum payable for rental of sound recording, film or computer program);

(f) section 144(4) (application to settle terms of copyright licence available as a right);

(g) section 190 (application to give consent for purposes of Part II on behalf of performer); and

(h) paragraph 5 of Schedule 6 (determination of royalty or other remuneration to be paid to trustees for the Hospital for Sick Children).'

The first three cases correspond broadly to section 24(1) of the 1956 Act; the remainder are new cases for reference to the Tribunal.

### *Power to make rules*

**11.6** Section 150 allows the Lord Chancellor, again after consultation with the Lord Advocate, to draw up the rules for the Tribunal and set the fees (with the approval of the Treasury). Subsection (3) sets out what provision must be made by the rules, ie that the Tribunal must be satisfied that an organisation making a reference under section 118, 119 or 120 is reasonably representative of the class of persons it claims to represent and requiring the Tribunal to give adequate notice to those concerned and allow them to state this case. The rules, which are made by statutory instrument, may also make provision for such matters as appeals.

### *Costs, proof of order etc*

**11.7** Section 151(1) allows the Tribunal to order costs and to tax (or settle the manner in which the costs are to be taxed). Subsection (2) provides that a document, purporting to be a copy (certified by the chairman) of an order of the Tribunal, shall be sufficient evidence of the order unless the contrary is proved. In Scotland evidence may be taken from witnesses under oath.

This section restates paragraphs 5, 7 and 8 of Schedule 4 to the 1956 Act.

## Appeals

**11.8** Section 152 permits an appeal on a point of law to the High Court or Court of Session. Provision will be made for time limits, and may be made for permitting the suspension of Tribunal orders whilst an appeal is pending, for modifying an order whilst an appeal is pending and for the publication of notices so that persons affected by any suspension are aware of the suspension.

## Transitional provisions

**11.9** Paragraph 34 of Schedule 1 permits the Lord Chancellor (after consulting the Lord Advocate) to make such provisions (by way of statutory instrument) as he deems appropriate with regard to pending proceedings.

Chapter 12

# Qualification for and extent of copyright protection

**12.1** The provisions of this Chapter restate in one place the provisions as to qualification which were spread out across the 1956 Act. The provisions substantially re-enact the existing law.

## Subsistence

**12.2** Section 153 provides that copyright subsists in a work only where the qualification requirements are satisfied as regards:

(a) the author (see section 154);

(b) the country in which the work was first published (see section 155); or

(c) in the case of a broadcast or cable programme, the country from which the broadcast was made or the cable programme was sent (see section 156).

Once the requirements are met, copyright does not cease to subsist as a result of any subsequent event.

**12.3** The position is different for Crown and Parliamentary copyright and for copyright subsisting in certain international organisations (see sections 163 to 166 and 168 respectively).

### *Qualifying person*

**12.4** Section 154 provides that an author is a qualifying person if at the material time he was:

(a) a British citizen, a British Dependent Territory citizen, a British National (Overseas), a British Overseas citizen, a British subject or a British protected person within the meaning of the British Nationality Act 1981;

(b) an individual domiciled or resident in the UK or another country to which the relevant provisions of this Part extend; or

(c) a body incorporated under the law of a part of the UK or of another country to which the Act extends.

**12.5** If the Act is applied to another country, then an author is a qualified person if he was a citizen or subject of or an individual domiciled or resident in, or a body incorporated under the law of, that country.

**12.6** A work of joint authorship qualifies, if at the material time any of the authors satisfies the above requirements. In such a case, only those authors who satisfy these requirements are taken into account for the purposes of:

(a) first ownership;

(b) duration of copyright; and

(c) anonymous or pseudonymous works.

### *Material time*

**12.7** By section 154(4), 'material time' in relation to literary, dramatic, musical or artistic work is as follows:

(i) in the case of an unpublished work, when the work was made, or otherwise a substantial part of that period;

(ii) in the case of a published work, when the work was first published or, if the author had died before that time, immediately before his death;

(iii) in relation to a sound recording or film, when it was made;

(iv) in relation to a broadcast, when the broadcast was made;

(v) in relation to a cable programme, when it was included in a cable programme service; and

(vi) in relation to a typographical arrangement, when the edition was first published.

### *First publication*

**12.8** By section 155, a literary, dramatic, musical or artistic work, a sound recording or a film or the typographical arrangement of a published edition qualifies for copyright protection if it is first published either in the UK or in another country to which the Act extends or is applied.

'Simultaneous publication', ie within the previous 30 days, in one country does not prevent publication in another being first publication.

### *Broadcasts and cable programmes*

**12.9** By section 156, a broadcast qualifies for copyright protection if it is made from, and a cable programme qualifies if it sent from, a place in the UK or another country to which the Act extends or is applied.

## Extent and application

**12.10** By section 157, the Act *extends* to England, Wales, Scotland and Northern Ireland. The Act may by Order in Council be extended to the Channel Islands, the Isle of Man or any colony, subject to such exceptions and modifications as may be specified. Section 158 provides for the position where a country ceases to be a colony. There are immediate requirements for reciprocity of protection and a limitation of Crown and Parliamentary copyright.

**12.11** By section 159 the Act may, by Order in Council, be *applied* to countries to which it does not extend if satisfactory provision has been or will be made under the law of that country giving adequate reciprocal protection. Section 160 gives authority for Her Majesty by Order in Council to withdraw rights in respect of authors connected with that country.

**12.12** Section 161 extends this Part of the Act to UK territorial waters and to things done in the UK sector of the continental shelf on a structure or vessel which is present there for purposes directly connected with the exploration of the sea bed or subsoil or the exploitation of their natural resources. Section 162 applies this part of the Act to things done on a British ship, aircraft or hovercraft.

### *Transitional provisions*

**12.13** Paragraph 35 of Schedule 1 provides that every work in which copyright subsisted under the 1956 Act immediately before commencement is deemed to satisfy the requirements of Part I of the Act as to qualification for copyright protection.

**12.14** Paragraph 36 contains provisions relating to the staying in force of the 1911 and 1956 Acts where relevant and for Orders in Council to regulate the coming into force of the Act.

**12.15** Paragraphs 38 and 39 provide that the Act does not apply to anything done before commencement in territorial waters or the UK section of the continental shelf or on British ships, aircraft and hovercraft.

## Crown copyright

**12.16** Crown copyright applies to a work made by an officer or servant of the Crown in the course of his duties. Such work qualifies for copyright protection without reference to any other qualification; Her Majesty is the first owner of that copyright.

Crown copyright remains Crown copyright whether or not the work is subsequently assigned to another person.

**12.17** Crown copyright in a literary, dramatic, musical or artistic work continues to subsist for 125 years from the end of the calendar year in which the work was made or, if the work is published commercially (defined in section 175(2)), before the end of the period of 75 years from the end of that calendar year, for 50 years from the end of the calendar year in which it was first so published.

**12.18** Section 163(4) provides that, in the case of joint authorship, Crown copyright applies only to the contribution to the whole of the author who is an officer or servant of the Crown.

Crown copyright is subsumed by Parliamentary copyright.

**12.19** Section 164 provides that Her Majesty is entitled to copyright in every Act of Parliament or Measure of the General Synod of the Church of England. Such copyright subsists for 50 years from the end of the year in which, for example, Royal Assent was given.

## Parliamentary copyright

**12.20** Section 165 creates a new copyright, Parliamentary copyright, which applies to a work made by or under the direction or control of either House of Parliament. (Subsection (4) defines works made by or under the control of Parliament; it should be noted that a work commissioned by Parliament is not necessarily made under its direction or control.) The ordinary requirements for qualification do not apply.

### *Duration*

**12.21** Parliamentary copyright continues for 50 years from the end of the year in which the work was made.

Section 165(7) applies the section to works made under the direction or control of the legislative body of a country to which this Part of the Act extends.

Section 166 provides that copyright in every Bill introduced into Parliament belongs to one or both of the Houses of Parliament. Parliamentary copyright in a Bill ceases on Royal Assent or on withdrawal or rejection unless it remains possible for it to be presented for Royal Assent in that session.

**12.22** Section 167 gives to each House of Parliament the legal capacity of a body corporate, not affected by prorogation or dissolution. The functions of the House of Commons as copyright owner may be exercised by the Speaker (or by the Chairman or Deputy Chairman of Ways and Means) and continue following dissolution of Parliament until a new appointment is made.

The functions of the House of Lords are exercised by the Clerk of Parliaments (or by the Clerk Assistant or Reading Clerk).

**12.23** Legal proceedings must be brought by or against the House of Commons in the name of the Speaker of the House of Commons and, for the House of Lords, in the name of the Clerk of the Parliaments.

## International organisations

**12.24** Section 168, restating section 33 of the 1956 Act, provides that where an original literary, dramatic, musical or artistic work is made by an officer or employee of, or is published by, an international organisation to which this section applies, ie one to which Her Majesty has by Order in Council declared that it should apply, and does not otherwise qualify for copyright protection, then copyright nevertheless subsists in the work and the international organisation is first owner of the copyright. An international organisation is deemed to have the legal capacity of a body corporate.

This recognises the UK's obligations under the UCC and provides protection where sections 154 and 155 do not already do so.

### *Duration*

**12.25** Copyright will subsist for 50 years from the end of the calendar year in which the work was made or for such longer period as may be specified.

### *Transitional provisions*

**12.26** Paragraphs 40 and 41 of Schedule 1 contain provisions relating to the coming into effect of Crown copyright and its duration and will repay careful study.

Paragraph 43 provides that Parliamentary copyright adheres to existing unpublished literary, dramatic, musical or artistic works but not otherwise to existing works.

Parliamentary copyright does not apply to public, private or personal bills introduced, published, deposited or given a first reading as indicated.

Paragraph 44 sets out the circumstances in which copyright vests in certain international organisations.

## Folklore

**12.27** Section 169 deems that copyright subsists in an unpublished literary, dramatic, musical or artistic work of unknown authorship if there is evidence that the author was a qualifying individual by connection with a country outside the UK. This assumption applies until the contrary is proved.

If in any other country a body is appointed to protect and enforce copyright in such works, then that body may be designated, by Order in Council, for the purposes of this section and such a body is thereafter recognised in the UK as having authority to do anything which it is empowered to do under the law of its country (other than assign copyright) and it may bring proceedings in its own name.

By subsection (6), the section does not apply if there has been an assignment of the copyright in the work by the author of which notice has been given to the designated body. Nothing in the section affects the validity of an assignment of copyright made or licence granted by the author or person lawfully claiming under him.

This section recognises Article 15(4) of the Paris Text of the Berne Convention requiring member States to enforce copyright in folklore.

## Savings

**12.28** Section 171 saves the right or privileges of any person under any other enactment, the right or privileges of the Crown, the right or privileges of Parliament, the right of the Crown to use or deal with articles forfeited and the operation of any rule of equity relating to breaches of trust or confidence.

Section 172 restates and amends the 1956 Act. It is expressly provided that any provision of this Part of the Act which corresponds to a provision of the previous law shall not be construed as departing from the previous law merely because of a change of expression.

Section 172(3) provides that decisions under the 1956 Act may be referred to in order to establish whether the Act departs from the previous law, or otherwise for establishing the true construction of the Act.

## 'Educational establishment'

**12.29** 'Educational establishment' is defined in section 174. It means any school or any other educational establishment specified by order of the Secretary of State. The Secretary of State may extend the provisions to teachers who are employed by an LEA to give instruction outside an educational establishment to pupils who are unable to attend an educational establishment.

'Teacher' and 'pupil' include respectively any person who gives and any person who receives instruction.

## 'Publication' and 'commercial publication'

**12.30** Section 175 contains specific definitions of 'publication' and 'commercial publication'. 'Publication' means the issue to the public of copies of the work. 'Commercial publication' is a new concept in copyright law — it is narrower than publication and requires that copies issued to the public must have been made in advance of the receipt of orders. One of the effects of this, for example, is to cover the publishing operations of

HMSO but to rule out publication by issue of photocopies to the public by the Public Record Office.

Construction of a building is treated as equivalent to publication of a work.

The following do not constitute publication (or commercial publication):

(a) in the case of a literary, dramatic, or musical work:
   - (i) the performance of the work; or
   - (ii) the broadcasting of the work or its inclusion in a cable programme service (otherwise than for the purposes of an electronic retrieval system);

(b) in the case of an artistic work:
   - (i) the exhibition of the work
   - (ii) the issue to the public of a graphic work representing, or of photographs of, a work of architecture in the form of a building or a model for a building, a sculpture or a work of artistic craftsmanship;
   - (iii) the issue to the public of copies of a film including the work; or
   - (iv) the broadcasting of the work or its inclusion in a cable programme service (otherwise than for the purposes of an electronic retrieval system);

(c) in the case of a sound recording of a film;
   - (i) the work being played or shown in public; or
   - (ii) the broadcasting of the work or its inclusion in a cable programme service.

**12.31** Publication is not effected where it is merely colourable and not intended to satisfy the reasonable requirements of the public. No account is to be taken for the purposes of this section of any unauthorised act.

## Signature by body corporate

**12.32** Section 176 provides that certain documents are effective only if 'signed' and describes how a body corporate is to sign a document. Following general company law principles, it is possible for an individual to sign a document on behalf of a company.

Subsection (1) provides that the requirement is *also* satisfied in the case of a body corporate if it affixes its seal to the document.

Subsection (2) deals with those circumstances where a document must be signed *by a person* to be effective, ie a document containing an assertion of a paternity right or waiver of moral rights. A body corporate will satisfy the requirement of *signature* if an individual signs on its behalf or if it affixes its seal.

Section 177 applies certain definitions to Scotland. Section 178 sets out a series of minor definitions. Section 179 contains an index of defined expressions.

Chapter 13

# Rights in performances and performers' protection

## Introduction

**13.1** Part II of the Act, which deals with rights in performances, replaces the Performers' Protection Acts 1958 to 1972. The protection given to performers by those Acts was to make certain unauthorised acts connected with performances of literary, dramatic, musical or artistic works criminal offences punishable by fines and/or imprisonment. No civil remedies were accorded to performers either by those Acts or by the Copyright Act 1956. In a line of cases including *RCA v Pollard* [1983] Ch 135, [1982] 3 All ER 771, it was held that the performers' protection legislation did not give to performers a civil right of action against bootleggers who made unauthorised copies of their works; nor were bootleggers liable to record companies, who had exclusive recording contracts with performers, whose works were the subject of a 'bootlegged' recording. Bootlegging is the practice of making an unauthorised recording of an artist's live performance at, for example, a concert.

Although Whitford did not recommend that performers should enjoy civil remedies in respect of bootleg recordings, the White Paper (Cmnd 9712, 1986) did so recommend. Accordingly, Part II of the Act now contains provisions giving not only performers, but also persons who have exclusive recording rights with performers, civil remedies against bootleggers.

**13.2** The provisions of the Performers' Protection Acts are largely re-enacted but the penalties and criminal procedure are now made consistent with those in the copyright field.

**13.3** The test of guilty knowledge in respect of criminal offences under Part II has modified the tests that were contained in the Performers' Protection Acts to bring them in line with changes proposed generally in regard to copyright offences (see Chapter 9 above).

**13.4** Also in line with the copyright provisions of the Act, the courts are given discretion to order the destruction of illicit sound recordings, films and equipment specifically adapted for the purpose of producing such recordings and films.

## Definitions of 'performance' and 'recording'

**13.5** Section 180 (the first section of Part II) begins, in subsection (1), by outlining the fact that Part II confers rights on performers by requiring their consent to the exploitation of their performances and on persons having recording rights in relation to a performance.

Section 180(2) defines 'performance' and 'recording' for the purposes of Part II. It should be noted that the definition of 'performance' contained in section 19(2) of the Act does not apply to Part II any more than the section 180 definition applies for the purposes of Part I of the Act. Similarly, the section 180 definition of 'recording' is not applicable to Part I.

The Dramatic and Musical Performers' Protection Act 1958, as amended by the Performers Protection Act 1963, defines 'performance of a dramatic or musical work' as 'the performance of any actors, singers, musicians, dancers or other persons who act, sing, deliver, declaim, play in or otherwise perform literary, dramatic, musical or artistic works'. The new definition does not rely upon the nature of the work which is performed — although it will have much the same effect. 'Performance' means:

'(a) a dramatic performance (which includes dance and mime),
(b) a musical performance,
(c) a reading or recitation of a literary work, or
(d) a performance of a variety act or any similar presentation,

which is, or so far as it is, a live performance given by one or more individuals.'

The performance of artistic works is presumably omitted on the grounds that, to the extent that they can be performed, they will constitute a dramatic performance: 'dramatic work' includes dance or mime (section 3(1)). Most performance art, to the extent that it qualifies for copyright protection, will come under the heading of mime.

By removing the requirement that the performance must be of a category of copyright work, the definition will apply to a performance of a work which has not acquired copyright because it has not previously been recorded, in writing or otherwise (see section 3(2)). Section 180(2)(d) gives effect to the intention expressed in the White Paper to extend protection to performances by variety artists, such as jugglers and acrobats, who do not normally perform literary, dramatic, musical or artistic works.

'Recording' is defined as meaning, in relation to a performance, a film or sound recording:

'(a) made directly from the live performance,
(b) made from the broadcast of, or cable programme including, the performance, or
(c) made, directly or indirectly, from another recording of the performance.'

A recording, for the purposes of Part II, therefore encompasses both films and phonograms. It also extends to sound recordings or films, which are copies of other 'recordings' of the performance.

### *Acts done before commencement*

**13.6** Section 180(3) is effectively a transitional provision, in that it provides that the rights conferred under Part II of the Act apply to performances which took place before the commencement of the Act, but no act done before commencement or in pursuance of arrangements made before commencement shall be regarded as infringing these rights. Therefore, there will be no civil remedies available against a bootlegger for the making of an unauthorised recording before the commencement of the Act, but he could be sued for dealing with that recording after the commencement of the Act.

### *Rights under Part II independent of copyright*

**13.7** Section 180(4) makes it clear that the rights conferred by Part II stand alone and are not in any way dependent on the copyright or moral rights in the works used in the performance or of recordings or broadcasts made of the performance.

## Qualifying performances

**13.8** Section 181 deals with the conditions as to the citizenship and residence of a performer and the place of the performance for a performance to become a 'qualifying performance'. A performance is a qualifying performance only if it is given by a qualifying individual or takes place in a qualifying country. Section 206 defines a 'qualifying country' as the United Kingdom, another member State of the EEC or a country designated by an order made under section 208 of the Act. The effect of sections 206 and 208 is that countries will be designated under section 206 only if they provide reciprocal protection, either pursuant to a convention relating to performers' rights to which the United Kingdom is also a party, or the Government is satisfied that there is adequate protection for British performances.

The Dramatic and Musical Performers' Protection Act 1958 was amended by the Performers' Protection Act 1963 so as to enable effect to be given to the Rome Convention of 1961; it contained similar provisions with regard to the country of qualification.

A 'qualifying person' is defined in section 206(1) as meaning an individual or a body corporate or any other body having legal personality which is formed under UK law, or that of another qualifying country, and which has a place of business at which a substantial business activity is carried on in such country. Section 206(3) provides that no account should be taken in dealings in goods outside the qualifying country in determining whether a substantial business is carried on there.

Section 206(1) defines 'qualifying individual' as a citizen of, or subject of, or an individual resident in, a qualifying country. Section 206(2) provides that as regards the UK, the qualifying individual must be a British citizen. As regards the colonies of the UK, a qualifying individual must be a British Dependent Territories' citizen.

## Infringement by recording, live transmission and use of recordings

**13.9** Sections 182 to 184 set out the ways in which a performer's rights are infringed. They do not vary from the provisions in this regard of the Performers' Protection Acts. Section 182 provides that the making without the performer's consent of recordings (which, it will be recalled, includes films) and broadcasting live or including live performances in cable programme services without consent, infringes the performer's rights. The performer's rights are not infringed by the making of a recording without consent for private or domestic use. A performer who considers that he will suffer by the making of private recordings must protect himself by other means, such as prohibiting recording equipment being used at concerts. Section 183 deals with the public performance, broadcasting or inclusion in a cable programme service of a recording of a qualifying performance made without the performer's consent.

It is a defence to section 182 to show that at the time of the infringement the defendant believed on reasonable grounds that the performer had given his consent. It is a defence to section 183 to show that the defendant neither knew nor had reason to believe that the recording was made without consent.

### *Importing, possessing, or dealing with illicit recordings*

**13.10** Section 184 deals with infringement of a performer's rights by importing, possessing for business purposes or dealing with illicit recordings without the performer's consent.

It is necessary to show that the person against whom the infringement of importation of, possession of for business and dealing with illicit recordings is alleged, knew or had reason to believe that the recording was illicit. A further defence is available under section 184(2) — the defendant can limit the damages claimed against him to an amount not exceeding a reasonable claim in respect of the act complained of if he can show that he innocently acquired the illicit recording. 'Innocently acquired' means that the person acquiring the recording did not know, and had no reason to believe, that it was an illicit recording.

It will be noted that the words 'which he knows or has reason to believe. . . .' are the same as those used in sections 22 to 26 of Part I of the Act, dealing with secondary infringement.

'Illicit recording' is defined in section 197 and, for the purposes of sections 182 to 184, means a recording made otherwise than for private purposes, without the performer's consent.

A further defence in respect of the making of recordings and the importation of, possession of and dealing with illicit recordings, is for the defendant to show that the act complained of was for private and domestic use and not in the course of business. A similar defence was available under the Performers' Protection Acts.

## Rights of persons having recording rights

**13.11** Sections 185 to 188 deal with the rights of persons having exclusive recording contracts with a performer.

### *Exclusive recording contract*

**13.12** Section 185(1) defines 'exclusive recording contract' in a straightforward manner as a contract between a performer and another person under which that other person is entitled to the exclusion of other persons (including the performer) to make recordings of one or more of his performances with a view to their commercial exploitation.

### *Person having recording rights*

**13.13** A 'person having recording rights' is defined by section 185(2) as being a person who is a party to or has the benefit of an exclusive recording contract or to whom the benefit of such contract has been assigned. Such a person must also be a qualifying person.

**13.14** Section 185(3) deals with the case when the person having recording rights is not a qualifying person by allowing his licensees or assignees of such licensees who are qualifying persons, to be regarded as the person having recording rights. Thus, an American record company (assuming that the USA is not a qualifying country) having an exclusive recording contract, will not itself have the benefit of the protection of this Part of the Act, but such benefit will be acquired by persons licensed by the record company to make recordings with a view to their commercial exploitation. 'With a view to their commercial exploitation' means with a view to the recordings being sold or let for hire or shown or played in public (section 185(4)).

**13.15** Sections 186, 187 and 188 are equivalent to sections 182, 183 and 184 in respect of persons having recording rights, in that they give the same rights to such persons as the earlier sections give to performers, with the same qualifications and defences available to the persons against whom actions for infringement are brought. Accordingly, section 186 provides that consent is required for the recording of the performance when the performer is subject to an exclusive contract; section 187 provides that it is an infringement of recording rights to use a recording made without such consent and section 188 provides that it is an infringement of recording rights to import, possess or deal with illicit recordings.

Under those sections, the consent is required either of the person having recording rights, or of the performer. Therefore, even though a performer might cause a breach of his exclusive recording contract by giving the consent, the person having recording rights will have no cause for action against the person who makes the recording, performs it, broadcasts it, imports it or deals with it.

## Acts permitted notwithstanding Part II

**13.16** Section 189 introduces the provisions of Schedule 2, which specifies acts which may be done notwithstanding the rights conferred by Part II of the Act, being acts which correspond broadly to certain of those specified in Chapter III (sections 28 to 75) of Part I of the Act (see Chapter 6 above).

Accordingly, all the exceptions to the restricted acts which can be translated to relate to performers' rights and the rights of persons having recording rights, are introduced by virtue of the provisions of Schedule 2.

## Power of Tribunal to give consent on behalf of performer

**13.17** Section 190 gives the Copyright Tribunal the right to consent to the making of a recording of a performance from a previous recording when the identity of the performer cannot be traced or a performer unreasonably withholds his consent.

Section 190(4) and (5) lay down the rules that the Tribunal must follow in deciding whether a performer has unreasonably withheld his consent. The performer must disclose his reasons for refusing consent. The Tribunal may not give consent unless it is satisfied that the performer's reasons include the protection of a legitimate interest of the performer. The Tribunal is empowered to make such order as it thinks fit as to the payment of consideration for the consent being given (section 190(2)).

## Duration of rights conferred by Part II

**13.18** Section 191 provides that the period of the rights conferred is 50 years from the end of the calendar year in which the performance takes place.

**13.19** Section 192 provides that the rights conferred on performers and persons having recording rights are not assignable or transmittable subject to the exceptions set out in section 192(2). This subsection permits the performer to pass the rights to such person as he may by testamentary disposition specifically direct and, failing such direction, the rights are exercisable by his personal representatives.

**13.20** Section 193 provides that consent may be given, not only for specific performance, but also for past and future performances. However, there is no provision comparable to that in section 7(a) of the Dramatic and Musical Performers' Protection Act 1958, under which the consent could be given in writing by a person who represented that he was authorised by the performers to give it on their behalf. A conductor would frequently give consent on behalf of the members of an orchestra. It will now be necessary to obtain individual consents. However, under section 193(2), a person having recording rights in a performance is bound by the consents given by the performer as if he had given the consent himself.

## Infringement actionable as breach of a statutory duty

**13.21** Section 194 provides that an infringement is actionable as a breach of statutory duty. It had been held in a number of cases, including *RCA v Pollard* (see paragraph 13.1) that under the old legislation, no civil suit could be brought against an infringer on the grounds of breach of statutory duty.

## Order for delivery up

**13.22** Section 195 makes provision for orders to be made by the court for the delivery up of illicit recordings to the persons having performers' rights or recording rights. Such order may only be made against the person who has the illicit recordings in his possession, custody or control in the course of a business.

## Right to seize illicit recordings

**13.23** Section 196 gives persons who would be entitled to apply for an order under section 195, the right themselves to seize and detain illicit recordings of performances which are exposed or are immediately available for sale or hire. The conditions which must be satisfied before such rights are exercised are the giving of notice of the intended seizure to the local police station; a limitation on the place where they may be seized to places where the public have access; no use of force; and the leaving of a notice in a prescribed form at the place where the seizure is made. In addition, and importantly, nothing may be seized which is in the possession, custody or control of the person at his permanent or regular place of business. Therefore, a seizure could be made from a casual street trader but not from a market stall holder who has a regular position in the market. Premises for the purposes of seizure is defined widely and includes vessels, aircraft and hovercraft (section 196(5)).

## Meaning of 'illicit recording'

**13.24** By section 197, an 'illicit recording' is one which:

(a) is a recording of the whole or a substantial part of a performance;

(b) is not made for private purposes;

(c) for the purposes of a performer's rights, is made without the performer's consent;

(d) for the purposes of the rights of a person having recording rights, is made without the consent of either such person or the performer.

## Offences

**13.25** Sections 198 to 205 set out the provisions regarding criminal liability for making, dealing with, or using illicit recordings. Offences are committed by doing the same acts as those which give rise to civil liability. The defences are similar.

The penalties include fines and imprisonment or both and delivery up of illicit recordings. Section 202 provides that where an offence is committed by a body corporate and is proved to have been committed with the consent or connivance of a director, manager, secretary or other similar officer of the body, those persons as well as the body corporate are guilty of the offence and are liable to be proceeded against.

### *Limitation on period for remedy of delivery up*

**13.26** Section 203 contains a limitation period in respect of remedies for delivery up — six years in the case of both civil and criminal proceedings from the date when the illicit recording was made. There are, however, certain exceptions set out in section 203(2) to the limitation period in the case of civil proceedings.

### *Order as to disposal of illicit recording*

**13.27** Section 204 provides for orders to be made as to the disposal of illicit recordings — the person having performers' rights or recording rights in relation to a performance, may apply to the court to have the illicit recordings delivered to him or destroyed or otherwise dealt with as the court may think fit, or for an application that no such order should be made. If no such order is made, then the person from whom the recording was seized may be entitled to have it returned to him.

### *Jurisdiction of county court*

**13.28** Section 205 gives to county courts jurisdiction to entertain proceedings to make orders for the delivery up of illicit recordings and as to their disposal, where the value of the recordings does not exceed the county court limit for actions in tort.

**13.29** Section 206 defines 'qualifying country', 'qualifying individual' and 'qualifying person'.

## Countries to which Part II extends

**13.30** Part II, by section 207, extends to England and Wales, Scotland and Northern Ireland.

### *Countries enjoying reciprocal protection*

**13.31** Section 208 provides that, by order in council, a 'Convention country', or a country which makes provision under its law giving adequate protection for British performances, may be designated as enjoying reciprocal protection under Part II.

A 'Convention country' is one which is a party to a Convention relating to performers' rights to which the United Kingdom is also a party.

### *Territorial waters, ships etc*

**13.32** Sections 209 and 210 provide that for the purposes of Part II the territorial waters and structures on the continental shelf of the United Kingdom and also British ships, aircraft and hovercraft shall be treated as part of the United Kingdom.

**13.33** Sections 211 and 212 deal with interpretation. They should be specifically referred to, although most of the expressions used in Part II such as broadcast, cable programme, film, literary work, published and sound recording, bear the same meaning as that attributed to them by Part I of the Act.

## Chapter 14

# Design right

### The old scheme of design protection

**14.1** The history of the old scheme of design copyright protection is well set out in the speeches of Lords Bridge of Harwich, Templeman and Griffiths in *British Leyland v Armstrong* [1986] 1 AC 577.

The combined effect of section 10 of the 1956 Act and the Design Copyright Act 1968, despite the much-praised dissenting speech of Lord Griffiths, was finally approved by the majority of the House of Lords in *British Leyland v Armstrong*. It gave a period of protection of 50 years plus life for functional designs. The rationale behind the protection was that 3-dimensional articles could be regarded as infringements of the original draughtsman's drawings, which were themselves original artistic works. In addition to a very lengthy period of protection, infringement of functional designs gave rise to other ramifications over the period of protection such as liability for additional damages under section 17(3) of the 1956 Act, possible criminal offences under section 21 of the 1956 Act and, most serious of all, liability for conversion damages under section 18 of the 1956 Act.

This extreme protection given to functional designs had to be contrasted with the more limited protection given to designs with 'eye appeal', which could only be protected on the assumption that they were registrable under the Registered Designs Act 1949, for a period of fifteen years from the date of first marketing under the law of artistic copyright and for three consecutive periods of five years (ie a maximum of fifteen years) under the Registered Designs Act 1949.

Not surprisingly, and despite successful efforts at enforcing the 50-year period of protection (see, for example, *LB Plastics v Swish Products Ltd* [1979] RPC 551), the higher courts, as a matter of policy, have recently attempted to reduce the efficacy of the 50-year plus life period of functional design protection. This was demonstrated by the spare parts exception approved by the majority of the House of Lords in *British Leyland* and by the refusal of the Privy Council in *Interlego AG v Tyco Industries Inc* [1988] 3 WLR 678 to extend originality to re-draws of industrial designs containing visually insignificant amendments.

## The new scheme of design protection

**14.2** Broadly, the scheme of the Act in relation to industrial designs is as follows:

(a) a new unregistered property right called 'design right' protecting original non-commonplace designs of the shape or configuration of articles against copying. Although the design right bears resemblance to copyright protection, it is a statutory right quite separate from the law of artistic copyright. Design right is intended to last until ten years after first marketing subject to an overall fifteen-year limit from creation of the design;

(b) an amended Registered Designs Act, with the period of protection increased from a maximum of 15 to 25 years;

(c) the retention of copyright protection for designs of articles which are themselves designed as artistic works and which are exploited industrially, with a 25-year period of protection after first marketing;

(d) the retention of a 50-year plus life period of copyright protection for artistic works *not* exploited industrially.

### *The interaction of copyright and design right*

**14.3** Section 51(1) provides that it is not an infringement of any copyright in:

(a) a design document; or

(b) a model recording or embodying a design or anything other than an artistic work or a typeface,

to make an article to the design or to copy an article made to the design.

The effect of this important section is to abolish copyright protection for design documents or models. However, the section leaves untouched copyright protection for 2-dimensional patterns or ornaments applied to industrially produced articles and for 3-dimensional designs of articles which are themselves artistic works. For the purposes of construing section 51, 'design' is defined as 'the design of any aspect of the shape or configuration (whether internal or external) of the whole or part of an article *other than surface decoration*'. 'Design document' is defined as any record of a design whether in the form of a drawing, a written description, a photograph, data stored in a computer or otherwise. It should be noted that 'surface decoration' is excluded from section 51. It would therefore still be an infringement of artistic copyright to copy such surface decoration. An example might be a decorative scroll. It should also be noted that, by section 51(2), it is not an infringement of copyright to issue to the public or include in a film, broadcast or cable programme service, anything the making of which was by virtue of section 51(1) not an infringement of copyright. An example might include the reproduction of an otherwise infringing article in an advertising broadcast.

### *Exploitation of designs derived from artistic works*

**14.4** Section 52 governs the effect of the exploitation of artistic works which have been exploited by or with the licence of the copyright owner. It would include, for example, the exploitation of a work of sculpture where articles made to that design by industrial process have been marketed in the United Kingdom or elsewhere, for example, models of a sculpture. The section provides that after the end of a period of 25 years from the end of the calendar year in which such articles are first marketed, the work may be copied without infringing copyright in the work, ie the copyright period is limited to 25 years. Section 52(3) governs the circumstances where only part of an artistic work is exploited in this way and provides that the 25-year period of protection applies only in relation to that part.

Section 52(4) gives to the Secretary of State for Trade and Industry power to make provision by statutory instrument as to the circumstances in which an article or any description of article is to be regarded for the purposes of the section as made by an industrial process and excluding from the operation of the section such articles of a primarily literary or artistic character as he thinks fit. Section 52(6) defines 'the marketing of an article' for the purposes of the section as referring to the article 'being sold or let for hire or offered or exposed for sale or hire'.

### *Interaction of copyright and registered designs*

**14.5** This section is designed to ensure that there is no infringement of artistic copyright in a 'corresponding design' by anything done in pursuance of an assignment or licence granted by the proprietor of a registered design who relies in good faith on the registration. 'Corresponding design' is defined by section 53(2) as a design within the meaning of the Registered Designs Act 1949 which, if applied to an article, would be treated as a copy of the artistic work. This provision was necessary because registered designs may constitute artistic works protectable by copyright in accordance with section 52.

## Definition of 'design right'

**14.6** Section 213(1) defines 'design right' as 'a property right which subsists in accordance with Part III of the Act in an original design'. For this Part of the Act only, 'design' is defined as 'the design of any aspect of the shape or configuration (whether internal or external) of the whole or part of an article'. It should be stressed that design right is not intended to protect ornamentation. Design right subsists only where the design is a design of an article. The design need not have eye-appeal and can be both functional or aesthetic.

**14.7** 'Original' is not defined. Section 213(4), however, provides a negative exclusion to the effect that a design is not 'original' if it is 'commonplace in the design field in question at the time of its creation', ie excluding mundane designs from protection. This subsection was much criticised during the passage of the Act through Parliament as constituting a recipe for complex litigation as to originality which would be determined largely by expert evidence. Whether or not a design is 'commonplace', is an objective test which can be determined only by expert evidence. Whether or not the test is workable in respect of an unregistered right, is a matter for contention. The Act does not state whether the tests for 'originality' in the copyright sense retain value in respect of design right, although the intention would appear to be that they do.

**14.8** Section 213(3) specifies the circumstances in which design right does *not* subsist. These are:

(a) a method or principle of construction. This excludes matters which are properly protectable under patent law;

(b) features of shape or configuration of an article which —

  (i) enable the article to be connected to or placed in around or against another article so that either article may perform its function (eg connecting parts), or

  (ii) are dependent upon the appearance of another article on which the article is intended by the designer to form an integral part (eg body panels); or

(c) surface decoration.

**14.9** Exceptions (b)(i) and (ii) have become known as the 'fit' and 'match' exceptions. Within the context of design right, they represent the equivalent of the 'spare parts exception' as propounded by the House of Lords in *British Leyland v Armstrong* [1986] 1 AC 577. There is no post-*British Leyland* case law on the interpretation of the spare parts exception and in any event the exception would probably have had to have been decided as to whether the infringing article constituted a genuine spare part. In the case of design right this is not necessary. It is perhaps a pity that, unlike the 'spare parts exception', the new test is not based upon an exception from infringement. However, the test to be applied is now purely statutory, ie do the features of shape or configuration enable the article to be connected to another article so that either article may perform its function, or are other features of shape or configuration dependent upon the appearance of the article of which that article is intended by the designer to form an integral part. In both cases, it is probable that expert evidence will be required to enable the tests to be applied and in the case of the 'match' expection it is probable that the evidence of the designer may be of crucial importance. In passing it should be noted that the Privy Council in *Interlego AG v Tyco Industries Inc* [1988] 3 WLR 678 obtained considerable asistance from the evidence of the designer in deciding whether the design of the Lego bricks in that case was a design capable of registeration under the Registered Designs Act 1949. The general effect of the exceptions is that if there is no design freedom because of the need to 'fit' or to 'match', there is no design right protection. Surface decoration such as ornamentation is excluded from design right. It may be capable of protection as an artistic work or under the Registered Designs Act.

**14.10** Design right does not come into existence unless and until the design has been recorded in a design document or an article has been made to the design (section 213(6)).

### *Ownership of design right*

**14.11** The first owner of any design right is defined by section 215(1) as the 'designer' of the design provided that it was not created in pursuance of a commission or in the course of employment. In the case of a commission, the person commissioning the design is regarded as the first owner and, in the case of a design created by an employee in the course of his employment, his employer is regarded as the owner of any design right. If the design qualifies for design right protection by the first marketing of articles made to the design, the ownership provisions are governed by section 220.

**14.12** 'Designer' is defined by section 214(1) as the person 'who creates the design'. Section 214(2) makes provision for the increasingly common computer-generated design and provides that 'a person by whom the arrangements are necessary for the creation of a design are undertaken shall be taken to be designer'. This is an unsatisfactory definition. It is by no means clear what 'arrangements' are required. Further 'arrangements' may be put in hand by a number of people. Does that mean that they are all to be regarded as joint designer? It may well be that a corporate body could be regarded as a designer.

### *Duration of design right*

**14.13** By section 216, the term of design right protection is limited to the shorter of:

(a) a term of fifteen years from the end of the year in which the design was first recorded in a material form; *or*

(b) a term of ten years from the end of the year in which articles made to the design were first marketed, provided that the articles are first marketed within five years from the end of the year in which articles are made to that design.

In practice, it is probable that protection will normally end ten years after articles made to the design are first marketed. The overall fifteen-year limit is designed to avoid the possibility of a perpetual period of design right protection.

Section 216(2) provides that marketing includes marketing anywhere in the World by or with the licence of the design right owner.

## Qualification for design right protection

**14.14** Under section 217, a design qualifies for design right protection in three different ways:

(a) if the designer is a qualified person, under section 218;

(b) if the commissioner of the design (or employer in the case of a design prepared in the course of employment) is a qualified person, under section 219;

(c) if neither section 218 nor section 219 is applicable, if the first marketing of articles made to the design is by a qualified person and takes place in the United Kingdom or in a country to which the provisions of the Act are extended by order under section 255 or in a member State of the European Economic Community, or in a designated 'reciprocal protection' country, under section 256.

### *Qualification by reference to designer*

**14.15** This provision can apply only to a design which is not created in pursuance of a commission or in the course of employment. The designer must be a qualifying individual as defined in section 217(1) or, in the case of a computer-generated design, a 'qualifying person' as defined under section 217(1). In the case of a joint design, protection is acquired if any of the designers is a qualifying individual or, in the case of a computer-generated design, a qualifying person.

### *Qualifying individuals and persons*

**14.16** A 'qualifying individual' is defined as a citizen or subject of, or a person who is habitually resident in, a qualifying country. A 'qualifying person' is defined as a qualifying individual or a body corporate or other body having legal personality which is formed under the law of a part of the United Kingdom or another qualifying country and has a place of business in any qualifying country at which substantial business activity is carried on. The term also includes the Crown and the government of any other qualifying country. By section 217(3), a 'qualifying country' is defined as:

(a) the United Kingdom;

(b) a country to which the Act is extended to by virtue of an order made under section 255;

(c) another member State of the European Economic Community; or

(d) a country designated under an order made pursuant to section 256 giving that country reciprocal protection for the purposes of defining a 'qualifying person'.

Section 217(5) makes it clear that in deciding whether substantial activity is carried on at a place of business in any country, no account shall be taken of dealings in goods which are at all material times outside that country.

### *Qualification by reference to a commission or employment*

**14.17** Section 219(1) provides that a design qualifies for design right protection if it is created in pursuance of a commission from a qualifying person or in the course of employment with a qualifying person. Joint commissions or joint employment are governed by section 219(2) which enable protection to exist if any of the commissioners or employers is a qualifying person. By section 219(3), if a design is jointly commissioned or created in the course of joint employment only those commissioners or employers who are qualifying persons are entitled to the benefit of design right under section 215(2) and (3).

### *Qualification by reference to first marketing*

**14.18** This section deals with designs which do not otherwise qualify for protection by reference to the designer. By section 220(1), if a design does not qualify for protection under section 218 or 219, protection will exist if the first marketing of articles made to the design:

(a) is by a qualifying person who is exclusively authorised to put such articles on the market in the United Kingdom; and

(b) takes place in the United Kingdom, another country to which the Act is extended to by virtue of an order under section 255 or another member State of the European Economic Community.

If the first marketing of articles made to the design is undertaken jointly by two or more persons, section 220(2) provides that the design qualifies for protection if any of those persons is a qualifying person exclusively authorised to put such articles on the market in the United Kingdom. Section 220(4) defines 'exclusively authorised' as authorisation by the person who would have been first owner of design right as designer, commissioner of the design or employer of the designer if he had been a qualifying person (or by a person lawfully claiming under such a person) and exclusivity which is capable of being enforced by legal proceedings in the United Kingdom.

It is clear from section 263(2) that the required acts of 'marketing' must be real, intended to satisfy the 'reasonable requirements of the public' and not be merely 'colourable' in order to comply with the provisions of the section.

### *Residual power to make further provision for qualification*

**14.19** By section 221, enabling power exists for orders in council to be made by statutory instrument to provide for design right protection to be extended 'with a view to fulfilling an international obligation of the United Kingdom'.

### *Dealings with design right*

**14.20** It is intended that design right can be exploited and dealt in like any other property. Section 222 provides that design right is capable of transmission by way of assignment, by testamentary deposition and by operation of law as personal or movable property. Section 221(2) makes it clear that there may be a partial transmission of design right in respect of some of the rights of the design right owner and in respect of part of the period of subsistence of the right. An assignment of design right must be in writing signed by or on behalf of the assignor. Section 222(4) provides that a licence granted by the owner of design right is binding on every successor entitled to his interest in the right except a purchaser in good faith for valuable consideration and without notice of the licence or a person deriving title from such a purchaser.

### *Future design right*

**14.21** Section 223 governs the position in relation to the whole or partial assignment of 'future design right', ie design right which is yet to be. Future design right is defined as design right 'which will or may come into existence in respect of a future design or class of designs or on the occurrence of a future event'. Upon the future design right coming into existence the assignee of the future design right or other person claiming under him is expressed to be entitled as against all other persons to require the right to be vested in him. A licence granted by a prospective owner of design right is expressed to be binding on every successor in title except a purchaser in good faith for valuable consideration and without notice of the licence or a person deriving title from such a purchaser.

### *Ownership of a design right which is a registered design*

**14.22** Section 224 deals with the circumstances in which a design in which design right subsists, is also a registered design. It creates a presumption in the absence of contrary agreement that an assignment of the registered design rights shall also be taken to include an assignment of design right.

## Primary infringement of design right

**14.23** The rights of the owner of design right, although akin to the rights of a copyright owner, are somewhat different, especially in relation to the meaning of 'infringement'. It should also be noted that the 'lay infringement' test embodied in section 9(8) of the 1956 Act no longer has any role in the context of design right. The primary right of the owner of design right is set out in section 226(1) as follows:

> 'The exclusive right in the United Kingdom to reproduce the design for commercial purposes:
>
> (a) by making articles to that design, or

(b) by making a design document recording the design for the purpose of enabling such articles to be made.'

It is significant that the right is restricted to 'commercial purposes', which is defined in section 263(3) as being done 'with a view to the article in question being sold or hired in the course of a business'. Reproduction for other (private) purposes is not an infringement of design right.

**14.24** The definition of reproduction is set out in section 226(2) so that the making of articles to the design means copying (independent creation is thus excepted) the design so as to produce articles 'exactly or substantially to that design'. It is arguable that the use of the words 'exactly or substantially' means that the degree of infringement must be high and possess a strong degree of visual similarity. This is something the courts were edging towards under the law of design copyright (see, for example, *Rose v Beckett* (1988) 2 July, unreported, Whitford J, but approved in *Interlego AG v Tyco Industries Inc* [1988] 3 WLR 678). Design right is expressed by section 226(3) to be infringed by a person who, without the licence of the design right owner, does, or authorises another to do, anything which by virtue of the section is the exclusive right of the design right owner. The act of infringement encompasses authorisation. There is no definition of 'authorises'. Assistance on the meaning of this is arguably obtainable from the copyright 'authorisation' cases. The leading authority on the meaning of 'authorisation' is now *CBS Songs Ltd v Amstrad Consumer Electronics plc* [1988] 2 All ER 484.

**14.25** Section 226(4) deals with the assembly of a kit so that design right is also infringed by a person who, without the licence of the design right owner, does or authorises another to do either of the exclusive rights, of the design right owner in relation to a kit. A kit is defined as a 'complete or substantially complete' set of components intended to be assembled into an article (made to the design).

**14.26** The law of design copyright recognised a concept of indirect infringement so that it was possible to have an infringement of design drawings even though the drawings had never been seen by the infringer (see, for example, *British Leyland v Armstrong* [1986] 1 AC 577). This concept is embodied in section 226(5), which indicates that a reproduction may be 'direct or indirect and it is immaterial whether any intervening acts themselves infringe the design right'.

## Secondary infringement

**14.27** Section 227(1) creates secondary infringement in respect of a person who, without the licence of the design right owner:

(a) imports into the United Kingdom for commercial purposes; or

(b) has in his possession for commercial purposes; or

(c) sells, lets for hire or offers or exposes for sale or hire, in the course of a business, an article which is and which he knows or has reason to believe is an infringing article.

As with section 5(2) of the 1956 Act, objective knowledge is a requirement of liability under this section. Section 227(2) establishes liability for secondary infringement in relation to any of the acts set out in section 227(1) in relation to a kit.

It should be noted that there is no infringement if the restricted acts are undertaken for non-commercial purposes. 'Commercial purposes' is defined by section 263(3).

## Definition of 'infringing article'

**14.28** An infringing article is defined by section 228. The section provides that an article is an infringing article if 'its making to that design was an infringement of design right in the design'. Section 228(3) states that an article is also an infringing article if:

'(a) it has been or is proposed to be imported into the United Kingdom, and

(b) its making to that design in the United Kingdom would have been an infringement of design right in the design or a breach of an exclusive licence agreement relating to the design.'

Section 228(4) creates a presumption to the effect that if it is shown that an article is made to a design in which design right subsists or has subsisted at any time, the article was made at a time when design right subsisted. Section 228(5) excludes from section 228(3) articles which may lawfully be imported into the United Kingdom by virtue of any enforceable European Community right. The European Court of Justice has held that where an article has been marketed in a member State with the consent of a rights' owner, importation cannot be prevented. A design document, even though its making was or would have been an infringement of design right, is not regarded as an 'infringing article'. Thus only actual articles infringe.

## Remedies for infringement

**14.29** By section 229(1), an infringement of design right is actionable by the design right owner. Section 229(2) states that in an action for infringement of design right all such relief by way of damages, injunctions, accounts or otherwise is available to the plaintiff as is available in respect of the infringement of any other property right. Section 229(3) creates the equivalent of section 17(3) of the 1956 Act by enabling a court to award 'such additional damages as the justice of the case may require'. In so doing the court must have regard to all the circumstances and in particular to the flagrancy of the infringement and any benefit accruing to the defendant by reason of the infringement. This provision is subject to the limited defence of innocent infringement which is set out in section 233.

### *Delivery up of infringing articles*

**14.30** Section 230 gives the owner of the design right entitlement to an order that the infringing article be forfeited and delivered up to him. This arises in circumstances where a defendant has in his possession, custody or control for commercial purposes an infringing article or has in his possession, custody or control anything specifically designed or adapted for making articles to a particular design, provided that he knows or has reason to believe that it has been or is to be used to make an infringing article. An order under section 230 cannot be made unless the court makes an order or it appears to the court that there are grounds for making an order for the disposal of infringing articles under section 231. In any event an application for an order for delivery up may not be made after the end of the period of six years from the date on which 'the article or thing in question' was made. If during the whole or any part of that six-year period the design right owner is under a disability or is prevented by fraud or concealment from discovering the facts entitling him to apply for an order under section 230, the period of time is extended to six years from the date on which he ceased to be under a disability or could with reasonable diligence have discovered the facts. By section 230(6), a person to whom an infringing article is delivered up pursuant to an order under section 231 is required to retain the article pending the making of an order for disposal or a decision not to make an order for disposal under section 231.

### *Orders as to the disposal of infringing articles*

**14.31** Section 231 enables an application to be made to the court for an order that an infringing 'article or other thing' that has been delivered up in pursuance of an order under section 230 shall be:

(a) forfeited to the design right owner; or

(b) destroyed or otherwise dealt with as the court may think fit.

**14.32** In considering whether or not to make any order, the court is required by section 231(2) to consider whether other remedies are available which would be adequate to compensate the design right owner and to protect his interests. If there is more than one person interested in an 'article or other thing', the court is required by section 231(4) to make such order as it thinks just and is empowered to direct that the object be sold or otherwise dealt with and the proceeds divided. If, on the other hand, the court decides no order should be made under section 231, the person in whose possession custody or control the 'article or other thing' was before being delivered up or seized is entitled to its return. Section 231(3) provides that rules of court are to be made as to service of notice on persons having an interest in the article or thing and such person is entitled to appear in proceedings under the section, whether or not he was served with the notice and to appeal against any order made under the section. A county court may entertain jurisdiction for proceedings under sections 230 and 231 where the value of the infringing articles and other things in question does not exceed the county court limit. The jurisdiction of the High Court is, nevertheless, preserved by section 232(3).

## *Defence of innocent infringement of design right*

**14.33** Section 233 creates a limited defence of innocent infringement of design right in respect of both primary and secondary infringement. In the case of primary infringement, if it is shown that at the time of the infringement the defendant did not know, and had no reason to believe, that design right subsisted in the design to which the action relates, the plaintiff is not entitled to damages, although he is entitled to other remedies including injunctions and orders for delivery up and disposal. In the case of secondary infringement, if a defendant is able to show that the infringing article was innocently acquired by him or a predecessor in title, the only available remedy against him is damages not exceeding a reasonable royalty in respect of the act complained of. This means that traders who have innocently acquired infringing articles are able to dispose of that stock on paying a reasonable royalty after they are put on notice that the articles infringe. Section 233(3) defines 'innocently acquired' as meaning that the person acquiring the article did not know and had no reason to believe that it was an infringing article.

## *Rights and remedies of the exclusive licensee*

**14.34** Section 234 makes provision for an exclusive licensee to have, except against the design right owner, the same rights and remedies in respect of matters occurring after the grant of the licence as if the licence had been an assignment of rights. The section gives exclusive licensees the same rights and remedies in respect of infringement as the design right owner whether alone or concurrently. Section 234(2) ensures that an exclusive licensee's rights and remedies are concurrent with those of the design right owner, whilst section 234(3) enables a defendant to an action brought by an exclusive licensee to avail himself of any defence which would have been available if the action had been brought by the design right owner. In exercising concurrent rights of action, neither the design right owner nor the exclusive licensee may, without leave of the court, proceed with the action, unless the other is joined as a plaintiff or added as a defendant (section 235). If a design right owner or exclusive licensee is added as a defendant pursuant to section 235(1), he is not liable for any costs in the action unless he takes part in the proceedings. Section 235(1) and (2) do not, however, affect the granting of interlocutory relief on the application of either the design right owner or an exclusive licensee. In an action for infringement of the design right in respect of which the design right owner and exclusive licensee have concurrent rights of action, the court in assessing damages is required to take into account the terms of the licence and any pecuniary remedy or any awarded or available to either the design right owner or the licensee in respect of the infringement. No account of profits is available if an award of damages has been made, or an account of profits had been directed, in favour of either the design right owner or an exclusive licensee and, if an account is directed, the court is obliged to apportion the profits 'as the court considers just', subject to any agreement between the design right owner and the exclusive licensee.

## Exceptions to the rights of design right owners

### *Infringement of copyright*

**14.35** Section 236 preserves the exclusivity of remedies for infringement of design right and infringement of copyright by providing that where copyright subsists in a work which consists of or includes a design in which design right subsists, there is no infringement of design right in the design if anything is done which is an infringement of copyright in the work. The section is complementary to section 51(1).

### *Licences of right*

**14.36** With the object of encouraging industrial competition, licences of right to perform acts restricted by design right are available as of right during the final five-year term of protection. 'Any person' is entitled by section 237 to a licence in the last five years of the term of design right to do anything which would otherwise infringe the design right. By section 237(2), in default of agreement between the design right owner and licensee, the terms of the licence are to be settled by the Comptroller-General of Patents, Designs and Trademarks. A residual power rests with the Secretary of State under section 237(3) to exclude the licence of right provisions if it is necessary to do so in order to comply with an international obligation or to secure or maintain reciprocal protection for British designs in other countries. Such orders are to be made by statutory instrument. It is understood that this power was specifically designed to deal with European Council Directive 87/54/EEC on the protection of the design of semiconductor integrated circuits, which requires that the ten-year period of protection remains undiluted by an automatic licence of right.

### *Licences of right in the public interest*

**14.37** By section 238(1), if the Monopolies and Mergers Commission reports that conditions in licences of right or a refusal of a design right owner to grant licences on reasonable terms may be expected to operate or have operated against the public interest, the Commission is expressed to have powers (originally stemming from Part I of Schedule 8 to the Fair Trading Act 1973) to cancel or modify those conditions and, instead or in addition, to require that licences in respect of the design right shall be available as of right. In default of agreement, the terms of such licence are to be settled by the Comptroller-General of Patents, Designs and Trademarks. This section follows the pattern of section 51 of the Patents Act 1977.

### *Undertaking to take licence of right in infringement proceedings*

**14.38** Section 239 limits the available remedies in cases where a licence of right is available but not negotiated by the licensee. In proceedings for infringement of design right in a design in any respect of which a licence is available as of right under section 237 or 238, provided the defendant undertakes to take a licence on terms as may be agreed (or, in default of agreement, settled by the Comptroller-General of Patents, Designs and Trademarks), no injunction may be granted against the defendant, no order for delivery up shall be made under section 230 and the amount recoverable by way of damages or an account of profits shall not exceed double the amount which would have been payable by the defendant as licensee if such a licence on those terms had been granted before the earliest infringement. Section 239(2) enables an undertaking to take a licence to be given at any time before a final order in the proceedings without any admission of liability. The section does not affect the available remedies in relation to a infringement committed before licences of right were available.

### *Crown use of designs*

**14.39** Section 240 creates an exception to design right protection in relation to the use of designs protected by design right by the Crown. A government department or a person authorised in writing by government department may, without infringing the design right owner:

(a) do anything for the purpose of supplying articles for the services of the Crown; or

(b) dispose of articles no longer required for the services of the Crown.

The services of the Crown are defined as limited to the defence of the realm, health service purposes and foreign defence purposes. Section 240(5) defines 'Crown use' in relation to a design as the doing of anything by virtue of this section which would otherwise be an infringement of design right in the design. The effect of this 'Crown immunity' against design right infringement is further extended by section 240(6) so that the authority of any government department in respect of Crown use may be given to a person either before or after the use of the design. A person acquiring anything sold in the exercise of section 240 and any person claiming under him is also protected from infringement and may deal with the design as if the design right were held on behalf of the Crown (and did not infringe).

### *Agreement on Crown use*

**14.40** Section 241 provides the procedure for setting the terms for Crown use and sets out a procedure whereby the government department concerned shall as soon as practicable notify the design right owner of and give him such information as to the extent of the use that the design right owner may from time to time require. This procedure does not apply if it appears to the government department that it would be contrary to the public interest or if the identity of the design right owner is unable to be ascertained on reasonable enquiry. Section 241(2) provides that the terms of Crown use shall be as are agreed, either before or after the use, between the government department concerned and the design right owner subject to the approval of the Treasury or, in default of agreement, as are determined by the court. If the identity of the design right owner cannot be ascertained on reasonable inquiry, the government department may apply to the court, which is empowered to order that no royalty or other sum shall be payable in respect of Crown use until the owner agrees terms with the department or refers the matter to the court for determination (section 241(3)).

### *Rights of third parties in the case of Crown use*

**14.41** Section 242(1) nullifies the provision of any licence assignment or agreement made between the design right owner or anyone deriving title from him and any person other than a government department in relation to Crown use of a design or any act incidental to Crown use, insofar as they can:

(a) restrict or regulate anything done in relation to the design or the use of any model document or other information relating to it; or

(b) provide for the making of payments in respect of such use deemed not to be an infringement of copyright.

Section 242(2) provides that the provisions of section 242(1) are not to be taken as authorising the disclosure of models, documents or information in contravention of the licence, assignment or agreement. Section 242(3) provides that if an exclusive licence is in force in respect of the design and if the licence was granted for royalties, any agreement between the design right owner and the government department under section 241 requires the consent of the licensee, and the licensee is entitled to recover from the design right owner a proportion of the payment for Crown use as may be agreed between them or, in default of agreement, as determined by the court. If an exclusive licence was granted otherwise than for royalties, section 241 is deemed to apply. In the case of assignment of the design right to the design right owner, section 242(2) provides for the provision of payment for Crown use between the design right owner and the assignor.

### *Crown use — compensation for loss of profit*

**14.42** If Crown use is made of a design, the government department is required to pay, under section 243, compensation to the design right owner or the exclusive licensee (if there is an enforceable exclusive licence) any loss resulting from the design right owner or exclusive licensee not being awarded a contract to supply articles made to the design. Section 243(5) sets out guidelines for the determination of the compensation for loss of profit.

### *Provision for Crown use during a period of emergency*

**14.43** This section extends the powers of Crown use created by section 240 during a period of emergency so that the power to do any act which would otherwise be an infringement of design right is no longer an infringement if it is done for any purpose which appears to the government department concerned necessary or expedient for the purposes set out in section 244(1)(a) to (g). A period of emergency is defined by section 244(3) as a period declared to be so by order in council to be laid before and approved by resolution of each Houses of Parliament.

### *Residual power to create exceptions to design right*

**14.44** Residual powers to create further exceptions to infringements of design right are given to the Secretary of State under section 245(1) if it appears to him necessary in order to:

(a) comply with an international obligation of the United Kingdom; or

(b) secure or maintain reciprocal protection for British designs in other countries.

The power is required to be exercised by statutory instrument but an order made by statutory instrument may make different provision for different descriptions of design or article. This section was prompted by European Council Directive 87/54/EEC on the protection of the topography of semiconductor integrated services and which requires an exception for processes of reverse engineering peculiar to semiconductor circuits.

## Jurisdiction of the Comptroller-General of Patents, Designs and Trade Marks and of the court in relation to design right

### *Jurisdiction of the Comptroller-General of Patents, Designs and Trade Marks*

**14.45** Section 246 gives jurisdiction to the Comptroller-General upon reference by a party to a dispute in relation to:

(a) subsistence of design right;

(b) the term of design right; or

(c) the identity of the person in whom design right first vested.

It is provided by section 246(2) that the Comptroller-General's decision on the reference is binding on the parties to the dispute. Other courts or tribunals are only given jurisdiction in respect of:

(a) a reference or appeal from the Comptroller-General;

(b) infringement or other proceedings in which the issue arises incidentally, or

(c) proceedings brought with the agreement of the parties or the leave of the Comptroller-General.

Section 246(3) gives the Comptroller-General jurisdiction to decide any incidental question of fact or law arising in the course of a reference under section 246.

Under section 251(1), the Comptroller-General may at any time order the whole proceedings or any question or issue (whether of fact or law) to be referred, on such terms as he may direct to the High Court. He may also make such an order if the parties to the proceedings agree that he should do so. By section 251(3), the court may exercise any power available to the Comptroller-General in relation to the matter referred to it and may also, following its determination, refer any matter back to the Comptroller-General. Appeal from any decision of the Comptroller-General in proceedings before him under section 246 lies to the High Court. It can be seen that, although the Comptroller-General has exclusive jurisdiction, it is open to the parties to agree that the Comptroller-General shall refer the proceedings or any question or issue in the proceedings to the High Court.

### *Jurisdiction of the Comptroller-General in relation to licences of right*

**14.46** Section 247 gives the Comptroller-General jurisdiction to settle the terms of licences of right. A person requiring a licence of right pursuant to section 237 (licences available in the last five years of design right) or pursuant to an order under section 238 (licences available in the public interest following a report of the Monopolies and Mergers Commission) may apply to the Comptroller-General to settle the terms of the licence. An application for the settlement of the terms of the licence available in the last five years of design right may not be made earlier than one year before the earliest date on which the licence may take effect (section 247(2)). The terms of the licence settled by the Comptroller-General enable a licensee (in the case of a section 237 licence) to do everything which would be an infringement of the design right in the absence of a licence and (in the case of a section 238 licence) everything in respect of which a licence is so available. Provision is made by section 247(4) for a statutory instrument setting out the factors to which the Comptroller-General is required to have regard in settling the licence terms. By section 247(6), a section 237 licence has effect on the earliest date on which the licence may take effect if the application is made before that date and in all other cases from the date on which the application was made to the Comptroller-General.

**14.47** If the applicant for a licence of right is unable on reasonable enquiry to discover the identity of the design right owner, the Comptroller-General may, in settling the terms of the licence, order that it shall be free of any obligation as to royalties or other payments (section 248). However, in this case, the design right owner may apply to the Comptroller-General to vary the terms of the licence with effect from the date on which his application is made. If it subsequently transpires that the licence was not available as of right and the terms of the licence are settled by the Comptroller-General, section 248(4) provides that the licensee shall not be liable in damages for or for an account of profits in respect of anything done before he was aware of any claim by the design right owner. By section 249, an appeal lies from the decision of the Comptroller-General under section 247 or 248 to the Appeal Tribunal constituted under section 28 of the Registered Designs Act 1949.

***Procedures before the Comptroller-General of Patents, Designs and Trade Marks***

**14.48** The Secretary of State is empowered by section 250(1) to make rules governing the procedures to be followed in proceedings before him. The rules may make provision for prescribed forms; fees to be paid; the rectification of procedural irregularities; the mode of giving evidence, compelling the attendance of witnesses and discovery of and production of documents; the appointment of advisers to assist the Comptroller-General; prescribing time limits; empowering the Comptroller-General to award costs and to direct how, to what party and from what parties, costs are to be paid. The rules are to be made by statutory instrument.

## Threatening an infringement of design right

**14.49** Section 253 creates a new tort of groundlessly threatening another person with proceedings for infringement of design right by section 253(1). A person aggrieved by the threats may bring an action claiming:

(a) a declaration to the affect that the threats are unjustifiable;

(b) an injunction against the continuance of threats;

(c) damages in respect of any loss which the person threatened has sustained by the threats.

By section 253(2), the plaintiff bears the burden of proof that the threats were made and that he is a person aggrieved by them. If he succeeds in doing this, he is entitled to the relief claimed, unless the defendant is able to show that the acts in respect of which proceedings were threatened did constitute, or if done would have constituted, an infringement of the design right concerned. Section 253(3) excludes from the tort threats of infringement alleged to consist of 'making or importing anything'. The mere notification that a design is protected by design right is deemed by section 253(4) not to constitute a threat of proceedings for the purposes of the section. The introduction of this provision is clearly designed to bring the law of design right into line with the similar provision of threatening patent infringement contained in section 70 of the Patents Act 1977. It should be noted that the plaintiff need not be the person threatened. It could be his customers.

## Limitation on licensee of right not to claim in connection with design right owner

**14.50** Under section 254, a licensee of right (pursuant to section 237 or 238) shall not, without the consent of the design right owner, apply to goods which he is marketing or proposes to market in reliance on that licence, a trade description indicating that he is the licensee of the design right owner or use any trade description in an advertisement in relation to such goods. A contravention of this section is actionable by the design right owner. The section is designed to limit the right of the licensee of right to promote himself by relying upon good will belonging to the design right owner.

Although section 254(3) gives 'trade description' and 'advertisement' the same meaning as in the Trade Descriptions Act 1968, it would seem that normally there would not be criminal liability under the 1968 Act where, in contravention of section 254, a licensee of right described himself as the licensee of the design right owner.

## Extent of operation of Part III (design right provisions)

**14.51** By section 255, the design right provisions of the Act are expressed to extend to England, Wales, Scotland and Northern Ireland, although provision is available by section 255(2) for the relevant part of the Act to be extended by Order in Council to any of the Channel Islands, the Isle of Man or any Colony (this might include Hong Kong). Section 255(4) enables the legislature of a country to which provisions in this Part of the Act have been extended to modify or add to the provisions as the legislature may consider necessary to adapt provisions to the circumstances of that country, but not to deny design right protection in a case where it would otherwise exist.

**14.52** By section 256, if it appears that the law of a country provides adequate protection for British designs, an order in council may designate that country as one enjoying reciprocal protection under Part III of the Act or, if adequate protection exists only for certain classes of British design, only for designs applied to those classes of article. An example is the USA, which at present only protects the designs of semiconductor integrated circuit microchips.

### *Territorial waters*

**14.53** Section 257 ensures that design right protection is available in UK territorial waters and on specified vessels and structures exploring the UK continental shelf.

## Transitional provisions in relation to design right

**14.54** Schedule 1, paragraphs 19 to 20 provide as follows:

(1) The exclusion of copyright protection in section 51 does not apply for a period of ten years after commencement date in relation to a design recorded or embodied in a design document or model before the commencement date (paragraph 19(1)).

(2) During the ten-year period, the licence of right provisions (sections 237 to 239) apply in relation to copyright as in relation to design right. The availability of a licence of right during the last five years of the ten-year period from commencement date (paragraphs 19(2) and (3)).

(3) The right to seize infringing copies contained in section 100 will not apply to anything to which it would not apply if the design in question had been first recorded or embodied in a design document or model after commencement date (paragraph 19(8)).

Chapter 15

# Registered designs

## Major amendments to the Registered Designs Act 1949

**15.1** Part IV makes major amendments to the Registered Designs Act 1949 which take into account the new importance given to that Act by the extension of the period of duration of designs registrable under the Act from a total period of 15 years to a total period of 25 years. By section 272, the 1949 Act is further amended in accordance with Schedule 3, which contains minor amendments and amendments consequential upon the provisions of sections 265 to 271. The full amended text of the Registered Designs Act 1949 is set out in Schedule 4 to the Act.

### *Amended definition of registerable designs*

**15.2** Section 265 creates a new definition of designs registrable under the Registered Designs Act 1949. The old definition of 'design', meaning features of shape, configuration, pattern or ornament applied to an article by any industrial process, is retained. The main amendment relates to that part of the definition which stated that designs could only be registered if they were features which were 'judged solely by the eye' and were not features 'dictated solely by function'. The old definition gave rise to considerable difficulties of interpretation (see further *Amp v Utilux* [1970] RPC 397; *Interlego AG v Tyco Industries Inc* [1988] 3 WLR 678; and the dicta of Lord Bridge in *British Leyland v Armstrong* [1986] AC 577 at 618). The new provision simply requires designs to include 'features which in the finished article appeal to and are judged by the eye'.

The main differences between the new definition and the previous definition are as follows:

(a) The separate exclusion in section 1(1)(b)(i) of features of shape and configuration of an article 'dictated solely by the function which the article has to perform', from the definition of 'design'.

(b) The introduction of an exclusion from the definition of 'design' by section 1(1)(b)(ii) of features of shape or configuration which are 'dependent upon the appearance of another article of which the article is intended by the author of the design to form an integral part'. The effect of this provision is to create a 'must match' exception in relation to registered designs consistent with the similar provision in section 213 (3)(b)(ii) in relation to design right.

(c) Simplification of section 1(2), which originally provided that a design shall not be registered unless it is 'new or original'. The requirement of novelty alone is retained (this was recently considered by the Privy Council in *Interlego AG v Tyco Industries Inc* supra), but in a positive form so that 'a design which is new' may be registered in respect of any article or set of articles specified in the application. Section 1(4) of the amended Act provides that a design shall not be regarded as 'new' if it is the same as a design:
   (i) registered in respect of the same or any other article in pursuance of a prior application; or
   (ii) published in the United Kingdom in respect of the same or any other article before the date of the application, or if it differs from such a design only in immaterial details or in features which are variants commonly used in the trade.

(d) New section 1(3) provides a further limitation on registrability. It adds to the definition of 'eye appeal' in section 1(1) by providing that a design shall not be registered in respect of an article 'if the appearance of the article is not material, that is, if aesthetic considerations are not normally taken into account to a material extent by persons acquiring or using articles of that description, and would not be so taken into account if the design were to be applied to the article'. This subsection stresses the importance of 'aesthetic considerations'. It is arguable that it will add considerably to the burden of assessing whether a design is registerable and require the giving of expert evidence as to the existence of 'aesthetic considerations' when registrability is in dispute.

**15.3** Section 265(2) provides that the amendments to section 1 do not apply in relation to applications for registration made before the commencement of Part IV of the 1988 Act.

### *Applications for registration made before commencement of the Act*

**15.4** The transitional section 266 provides that, where a design is registered under the Registered Designs Act 1949 in pursuance of an application for registration made after 12 January 1988 and before the commencement of Part IV of the Act, but which could not have been registered under section 1 of the 1949 Act, as amended by section 265, the right in the registered design expires ten years after the commencement of Part IV of the Act (if it does not in any event expire earlier). Any person after the commencement of Part IV is entitled as of right to a licence to do anything which would otherwise infringe the right in the registered design. The section creates a form of licence of right which by section 266(2), in default of agreement, is to be settled by the registrar on an application by the person requiring the licence. The terms settled by the registrar shall authorise the licensee to do everything which would otherwise be an infringement of the right in the registered design. Provision is also made by section 266(3) for the registrar to take into account such factors as may be prescribed by statutory instrument.

### *Authorship and ownership of designs*

**15.5** Section 267 is designed to rationalise section 2 of the Registered Designs Act 1949 so as to make it commensurate with the equivalent design right provisions. Section 2 is amended to provide that the author of a design should be treated as the 'original proprietor of the design', subject to the following provisions:

(a) where a design is created in pursuance of a commission for money or money's worth, the person commissioning the design is to be treated as the original proprietor (section 2(1A))

(b) where a design is created by an employee in the course of his employment, his employer is to be treated as the original proprietor of the design (section 2(1B)).

The 'author' of a design is defined by section 267(3) as the person who creates it. Provision is also made by the creation of a new section 2(4) providing that in the case of a computer-generated design in circumstances such that there is no human author, the person by whom the arrangements necessary for the creation of the design are made should be taken to be the author. It is provided by section 267(4) that the amendments to section 2 of the 1949 Act do not apply in relation to an application for registration made before the commencement of Part IV of the Act.

### *Rights given by registration of designs*

**15.6** Section 268 makes considerable amendments to section 7 of the Registered Designs Act 1949 in relation to the rights given by registration of a registered design. The registered proprietor has the exclusive right:

(a) to make or import—

  (i) for sale or hire, or

  (ii) for use for the purposes of trade or business; or

(b) to sell hire or offer or expose for sale or hire,

an article in respect of which the design is registered and to which that design or a design not substantially different from it has been applied

Section 7(2) provides that it is an infringement to do anything without the licence of the registered proprietor, which by section 7(1) is the exclusive right of the proprietor. The exclusive right is also infringed, under section 7(3), by making anything or enabling any article to be made in respect of which the design is registered and to which the design or a design not substantially different from it has been applied, however, without the licence of the registered proprietor.

**15.7** Section 7(4) creates additional similar infringements in relation to a kit infringement as if they were done in relation to an assembled article. A 'kit' is defined as a complete or substantially complete set of components intended to be assembled into an article. Section 7(6) excludes from infringement the reproduction of a feature of the design which by section 1(1)(b) is left out of account in determining whether the design is registerable. Section 7(5) provides that no proceedings are to be taken in respect of an infringement committed before the date upon which the certificate of registration of the design is granted. The amendments to section 7 do not apply in relation to the designs registered in pursuance to an application made before the commencement of Part IV of the Act.

### *Duration of right in registered designs*

**15.8** Section 8 of the Registered Designs Act 1949 is amended by section 269 so that the original right in a registered design subsisting in the first instance for a period of five years from the date of registration may be extended for a second, third, fourth and fifth period of five years (ie to a maximum of 25 years) by applying to the registrar for an extension and paying the prescribed renewal fee. Provision is made by section 8(4) for a period of grace of six months following the expiration of each period of five years for a late application for extension of the registration to be made upon payment of the prescribed renewal fee and any prescribed additional fee. If this is done, there is no detriment to the proprietor of the registered design. By section 8A, provision is provided for restoration of the rights in a registered design if the design has lapsed. The effect of such a restoration is set out in section 8B. If anything is done under or in relation to the right during the period between expiry and restoration, it shall be treated as valid.

### *Public interest licence of right*

**15.9** Section 270 adds a new section 11A to the Registered Designs Act 1949. Where a report of the Monopolies and Mergers Commission contains anti-competitive conclusions (as defined), the appropriate Minister may apply to the registrar 'to take action under section 11A'. By section 11A(3) and upon an application under section 11A, if it appears to the registrar that the matters specified in the Commission report include:

(a) conditions in licences granted in respect of a registered design by its proprietor restricting the use of the design by the licensee or the right of the proprietor to grant other licences; or

(b) a refusal by the proprietor of a registered design to grant licences on reasonable terms,

the registrar may by order cancel or modify any such addition or make an entry in the register to the fact that licences of right in respect of the design are to be available. In default of agreement, the terms of such licence are to be settled by the registrar and the licence has effect from the date upon which the application to him was made.

This is clearly a corresponding provision to section 238 in relation to public interest licences of right in respect of design right.

If, in proceedings for infringement of the right in a registered design in respect of which a licence of right is available under section 11A, the defendant undertakes to take a licence on agreed terms or as settled by the registrar, no injunction shall be granted against him and the amount recoverable by way of damages or on account of profits shall not exceed double the amount which would have been payable by him as licensee if a licence on those terms had been granted before the earliest infringement. An undertaking to take a licence may be given at any time before a final order in the proceedings, without any admission of liability. Section 11B(3) provides that nothing in the section affects the remedies available in respect of an infringement committed before licences of right were available.

### *Compensation for Crown use*

**15.10** Section 271 amends Schedule 1 to the Registered Designs Act 1949 by creating a new paragraph 2A providing for government departments in the circumstances provided for to pay compensation to the registered proprietor or an exclusive licensee for any loss resulting from his not being awarded a contract to supply articles to which the design is applied.

Chapter 16

# Patents

**16.1** Sections 274 to 281 of Part V make specific provisions in relation to patent agents. Part VI makes specific amendments to patent law including the creation of a patents county court, and restricts the provision of licences of right in respect of certain old pharmaceutical patents originally granted under the Patents Act 1949.

## Patent agents and patent attorneys

**16.2** Section 274 abolishes the so-called 'patent agents'' monopoly in proceedings before the Patent Office and defines the business of a patent agent as carrying on the business of acting as agent for others for the purpose of:

(a) applying for or obtaining patents in the United Kingdom or elsewhere; or

(b) conducting proceedings before the Comptroller-General for Patents, Designs and Trade Marks relating to applications for, or otherwise in connection with, patents.

The section does not affect any restriction under the European Patent Convention in relation to European patents. Article 134 of the European Patent Convention provides that representation before the European Patent Office can be undertaken only by those on a maintained list.

**16.3** By section 275(1), the Secretary of State for Trade and Industry may make rules requiring the maintenance of a register of patent agents. This already existed under section 123(2) of the Patents Act 1977. By section 275(2), the rules may contain provision for the payment of prescribed fees, erasure from the register of patent agents, or the suspension of a person's registration. The rules may delegate the keeping of the register to another person and may confer on that person power to make regulations with respect to payment of fees other matters regulated by the rules and other functions including disciplinary functions.

**16.4** Section 276 limits the categories of persons entitled to describe themselves as patent agents and in particular an individual or partnership shall not carry on a business or describe itself as a 'patent agent' or 'patent attorney' unless they are registered patent agents or the partnership satisfies other prescribed conditions. Section 276(6) creates an offence for contravention of section 276, prescribing with a penalty on summary conviction consisting of a fine not exceeding level 5. An exclusion exists under section 278 so that a solicitor or a firm of solicitors may be described as 'patent attorney' or 'patent attorneys' respectively.

**16.5** By section 277, the term 'European patent attorney' or 'European patent agent' can be used by any individual, partnership or body corporate who are on the list of professional representatives maintained by the European Patent Office in pursuance of the European Patent Convention.

**16.6** By section 279, the Secretary of State for Trade and Industry may make rules prescribing the conditions to be satisfied for the purposes of section 276 in relation to a partnership or a body corporate where the partners or directors are not all qualified 'patent agents' persons under section 276. The rules may prescribe conditions as to the proportion of directors who must be qualified patent agents and impose requirements as to their identification in professional advertisements, circulars or letters and the manner in which a partnership or body corporate is to organise its affairs so as to secure the qualified persons (who are defined as registered patent agents or on the list of professional representatives maintained by the European Patent Office) exercises a sufficient degree of control over the activities of unqualified persons.

## Privileged communications with patent agents

**16.7** Section 280 replaces sections 104 and 105 of the Patents Act 1977 and applies to communications 'as to any matter relating to the protection of an invention, design, technical information, trade mark or service mark, or as to any matter involving passing off':

(a) between a person and his patent agent; or

(b) for the purpose of obtaining or in response to a request for information which a person is seeking for the purpose of instructing his patent agent.

The section provides that the same privilege from disclosure in legal proceedings in England, Wales or Northern Ireland exists in respect of such communications as between a person and his solicitor or for the purpose of obtaining or in response to a request for information which a person seeks for the purpose of instructing his solicitor. Section 280(3) provides an equivalent privilege in Scottish legal proceedings.

## Patents county courts

**16.8** Sections 287 to 292 set out the framework for a county court jurisdiction over patents and designs in England and Wales. Section 287 provides that the Lord Chancellor may by order made by statutory instrument designate any county court as a patents county court and confer on it a jurisdiction to hear and determine such descriptions of proceedings:

(a) relating to patents or designs; or

(b) ancillary or arising out of the same subject matter as proceedings relating to patents or designs, as may be specified in the order.

**16.9** This provision is intended to place a greater burden on county courts in respect to the resolution of disputes involving patents or designs. It is envisaged by section 288 that an order in council may provide financial limits for proceedings within the special jurisdiction of a patents county court. When a plaintiff had a cause of action for more than the financial limit, he is able under section 288 to abandon the excess part of his claim and give the patents county court jurisdiction to hear and determine the action, although the plaintiff may still not recover more than the financial limit imposed.

**16.10** If the parties agree, by means of a signed memorandum, that a patents county court shall have jurisdiction in any proceedings, the patents county court will be entitled to hear and determine the proceedings notwithstanding any financial limit. By section 289(2), and having regard to the financial position of the parties, the High Court may order the transfer of proceedings from the High Court to a patents county court or, if the proceedings have already begun in the county court, refrain from ordering a transfer to the High Court, notwithstanding that the proceedings are likely to raise an important question of fact or law.

**16.11** By section 290, if an action is commenced in the High Court which could have been commenced in a patents county court and in which the plaintiff recovers less than the prescribed amount of the county court limit, he is not entitled to recover costs over and above the county court scale. This is subject to the discretion of the High Court (set out in section 290(4)) to order payment of costs on the High Court scale if it is satisfied 'that there was sufficient reason for bringing the action in the High Court'.

### *Proceedings in patents county courts*

**16.12** By section 291, the Lord Chancellor is given power to nominate a person entitled to sit as county court judge designated in a patents county court as a 'patents judge' (he would presumably be a circuit judge). Provision is made for county court rules to secure, so far as is practical and appropriate, that proceedings within the jurisdiction of a patents county court are dealt with by the patents judge, and that the patents judge, rather than a registrar or other officer of the court deals with interlocutory matters in the proceedings. Section 291(3) enables county court rules to make provision for scientific advisers or assessors to assist the court and a new power to order the Patent Office to inquire and to report on any question of fact or opinion.

### *Rights of registered patent agents in patents county court*

**16.13** Section 292 provides that a registered patent agent may do, in or in connection with proceedings in a patents county court, anything which a solicitor is able to do other than prepare a deed. A registered patent agent is therefore given a right of audience in the patents county court. The Lord Chancellor is given power, to be exercised by regulations, to impose conditions and restrictions as to the rights of registered patent agents in the patents county court. Provisions in section 292 are designed to place registered patent agents on the same footing as solicitors in patents county courts, including giving the court the same power to enforce an undertaking given by a registered patent agent and to provide scales of costs to be paid to patent agents.

## Limitation on licences of right in respect of pharmaceutical patents

**16.14** The effect of section 293 is to allow owners of patents for medicinal products or any other products specified by Ministerial order to be removed from the licence of right provisions in Schedule 1 to the Patents Act 1977.

Section 293 amends paragraph 4(2)(c) of Schedule 1 to the 1977 Act to make licences of right no longer available in the extended four-year term of certain 1949 Act patents. Under the Patents Act 1949, patents expired after sixteen years. The provisions of Schedule 1 to the Patents Act 1977 extended the term to twenty years' protection contained in that Act retrospectively to existing 1949 patents, but subject to 'licences of right' in respect of the additional four years of protection. The amendment in paragraph 4(2)(c), as set out in section 293, creates a new paragraph 4A to Schedule 1 to the 1977 Act, which excepts 'pharmaceutical use' from the extension term of the patent created by the 1977 Act. 'Pharmaceutical use' is defined as including use as a medicinal product within the meaning of the Medicines Act 1968. Licences of right are therefore no longer available during the additional four-year term for pharmaceutical patents obtained under the 1949 Act.

## Time for application for settlement of licence of right terms

**16.15** Section 294 amends Schedule 1 to the Patents Act 1977 by adding a new paragraph 4B. It gives a statutory basis to the practice of the Comptroller-General not to deal with applications to settle licence of right terms more than one year before the patent becomes subject to a licence of right.

## Patents amendments generally

**16.16** By section 295, additional minor amendments to the Patents Act 1949 and the Patents Act 1977 are set out in Schedule 5.

Chapter 17

# Trade marks

## Trade mark agents

**17.1** Sections 282 to 284 are designed to govern the registration of a body of 'registered trade mark agents' and to provide privilege for communications with registered trade mark agents.

**17.2** Section 282 establishes the basis for a register of trade mark agents and provides that the Secretary of State for Trade and Industry may make rules requiring the keeping of a register of persons 'who act as agent for others for the purpose of applying for or obtaining the registration of trade marks'. A 'registered trade mark agent' means a person whose name is entered on the register kept under section 282.

**17.3** Rules created by statutory instrument may contain provisions regulating the registration of registered trade mark agents and including the provision for the payment of fees, erasure from the register or the suspension of a persons registration. The rules may also delegate the keeping of the register to another person (presumably the Institute of Trade Mark Agents) and confer on that person the power to make regulations with regard to fees and disciplinary functions.

**17.4** Section 283 provides that an individual who is not a registered trade mark agent shall not:

(a) commercially carry on a business (otherwise than in partnership) under any name or description which contains the words 'registered trade mark agent'; or

(b) in the course of a business, describe or hold himself out or permit himself to be described or held out as a 'registered trade mark agent'.

Similar provisions are provided for partnerships and bodies corporate describing themselves or holding themselves out as registered trade mark agents. The Secretary of State is empowered to make rules prescribing the conditions to be satisfied in relation to a mixed partnership or body corporate where not all the partners or directors are registered trade mark agents. Section 283(6) creates an offence for a breach of section 283 with a fine on summary conviction not exceeding level 5 on the standard scale.

## Privilege of communications of registered trade mark agents

**17.5** Section 284 is designed to amend the law following the decision in *Re Dormeuil Trademark* [1983] RPC 131, where the court held that a trade mark agent does not enjoy the same legal professional privilege as a patent agent and his communications with his clients are available for disclosure on discovery. Section 284 provides that privilege attaches in relation to communications as to any matter relating to the protection of any design, trade mark or service mark, or as to any matter involving passing off, and also to any communication passing between a person and his trade mark agent or for the purpose of obtaining, or in response to, a request for information which a person is seeking for the purpose of instructing his trade mark agent, as it would mutatis mutandis in respect of a solicitor.

## Fraudulent application or use of a trade mark

**17.6** Section 300 makes amendments to section 58 of the Trade Marks Act 1938 which are designed to strengthen the criminal law of trade mark infringement in relation to product counterfeiting. To a large extent, the amendments were accepted at the instigation of the Anti-Counterfeiting Group. The Trade Marks Act 1938 is amended by the creation of an offence of the fraudulent use or application of a registered trade mark.

**17.7** A new section 58A of the Trade Marks Act 1938 provides that it is an offence for a person:

(a) to apply a mark identical to or nearly resembling a registered trade mark to goods, or to material used or intended to be used for labelling packaging or advertising goods; or

(b) to sell or let for hire or offer or expose for sale or hire or distribute—
   (i) goods bearing such a mark, or
   (ii) material bearing such a mark which is used or intended to be used for labelling, packaging or advertising goods; or

(c) to use material bearing such a mark in the course of a business for labelling packaging or advertising goods; or

(d) to possess in the course of a business goods or materials bearing such a mark with a view to doing any of the things mentioned in paragraphs (a) to (c),

when he is not entitled to use the mark in relation to the goods in question and the goods are not connected in the course of trade with a person who is so entitled.

It can be seen that the offence is wide and covers a number of acts including the application of a mark to goods and to packaging, the sale or offer for sale of goods or material bearing the false trade mark and to use material bearing the mark for labelling packaging or promotional purposes.

**17.8** It is also an offence under section 58A(2) to possess in the course of a business goods or material bearing a mark identical to or nearly resembling a registered trade mark with a view to enabling or assisting another person to do any of the things mentioned in (a) to (c) above, knowing or having reason to believe that the other person is not entitled to use the mark in relation to the goods in question and that the goods are not connected in the course of trade with a person who is so entitled. This new subsection creates a form of secondary infringement.

**17.9** Section 58A(3) provides a defence so that an offence is only committed if the defendant:

(a) acts with a view to gain for himself or another or with intent to cause loss to another; and

(b) intends that the goods in question should be accepted as connected in the course of trade with a person entitled to use the mark in question.

It is a defence by a person *charged* with an offence under (a) to (d) to show that he believed on reasonable grounds that he was entitled to use the mark in relation to the goods in question. This qualification is intended to ensure that 'civil' trade mark infringement is not caught by the offence.

**17.10** Section 58A(4) sets out the penalties: on summary conviction to imprisonment for a term not exceeding six months or a fine not exceeding the statutory maximum or both; and on conviction on indictment to a fine that is potentially unlimited or imprisonment for a term not exceeding ten years or both. The offence is therefore 'arrestable' within the Police and Criminal Evidence Act 1984, enabling the use of police powers of search without warrant.

**17.11** By section 58A(5), where an offence committed by a body corporate is proved to have been committed with the consent or connivance of a director, manager, secretary or other similar officer of the body or a person purporting to act in any such capacity, he as well as the body corporate is guilty of the offence.

## Delivery up of offending goods

**17.12** Section 300 creates provision for the forfeiture of offending goods and material and also other infringing goods in respect of which no charges were brought or convictions secured. It adds a new section 58B to the Trade Marks Act 1938, under which the criminal court by which a person is convicted of an offence under section 58A may, if satisfied at the time of the defendant's arrest *or charge* that he had in his possession, custody or control:

(a) goods or material in respect of which the offence was committed; or

(b) goods of the same description as those in respect of which the offence was committed or materials similar to those in respect of which the offence was committed, bearing a mark identical to or nearly resembling that in relation to which the offence was committed,

order the goods or material to be delivered up to such person as the court may direct.

**17.13** By section 58B(5), the person to whom the goods or material are delivered up is obliged to retain then pending the making of an order for disposal under section 58C.

**17.14** For the purposes of section 58, a person is treated as charged with an offence when he is orally charged or is served with a summons or indictment.

**17.15** Under section 58C, where goods or material have been delivered up by order under section 58B, an application may be made to the court for an order that they be destroyed or forfeited to such person as the court may think fit. Provision is to be made by rules of court as to the service of notice on persons having an interest in the goods or material and any such person is entitled to appear in proceedings for an order under the section and to appeal against any order made. If an appeal is made, the order is expressed not to take effect until the end of the period from which notice of an appeal may be given or until the final determination or abandonment of the appeal. A person with an interest in goods or material includes any person in whose favour an order could be made under the similar provisions in section 114, 204 or 231 of the 1988 Act. Proceedings for an order for disposal may be brought in the county court provided the value of the goods or material in question does not exceed the county court limit. The jurisdiction of the High Court is expressly not affected.

**17.16** In order to enforce the offence under section 58A, section 58C provides that enforcement of section 58A falls within the functions of trading standards officers and that their powers contained in the Trade Descriptions Act 1968, including the power to make test purchases (section 27), the power to enter the premises and inspect and seize goods and documents (section 28) apply.

# THE COPYRIGHT, DESIGNS AND PATENTS ACT 1988

(c 48)

## ARRANGEMENT OF SECTIONS

### PART I
### COPYRIGHT

### CHAPTER I
### SUBSISTENCE, OWNERSHIP AND DURATION OF COPYRIGHT

*Introductory*



*Descriptions of work and related provisions*



*Authorship and ownership of copyright*



*Duration of copyright*



### CHAPTER II
### RIGHTS OF COPYRIGHT OWNER



*Secondary infringement of copyright*



*Infringing copies*

## CHAPTER III

## ACTS PERMITTED IN RELATION TO COPYRIGHT WORKS

*Introductory*

28 Introductory provisions

*General*

29 Research and private study
30 Criticism, review and news reporting
31 Incidental inclusion of copyright material

*Education*

32 Things done for purposes of instruction or examination
33 Anthologies for educational use
34 Performing, playing or showing work in course of activities of educational establishment
35 Recording by educational establishments of broadcasts and cable programmes
36 Reprographic copying by educational establishments of passages from published works

*Libraries and archives*

37 Libraries and archives: introductory
38 Copying by librarians: articles in periodicals
39 Copying by librarians: parts of published works
40 Restriction on production of multiple copies of the same material
41 Copying by librarians: supply of copies to other libraries
42 Copying by librarians or archivists: replacement copies of works
43 Copying by librarians or archivists: certain unpublished works
44 Copy of work required to be made as condition of export

*Public administration*

45 Parliamentary and judicial proceedings
46 Royal Commissions and statutory inquiries
47 Material open to public inspection or on official register
48 Material communicated to the Crown in the course of public business
49 Public records
50 Acts done under statutory authority

*Designs*

51 Design documents and models
52 Effect of exploitation of design derived from artistic work
53 Things done in reliance on registration of design

*Typefaces*

54 Use of typeface in ordinary course of printing
55 Articles for producing material in particular typeface

*Works in electronic form*

56 Transfers of copies of works in electronic form

*Miscellaneous: literary, dramatic, musical and artistic works*

57 Anonymous or pseudonymous works: acts permitted on assumptions as to expiry of copyright or death of author
58 Use of notes or recordings of spoken words in certain cases
59 Public reading or recitation
60 Abstracts of scientific or technical articles
61 Recordings of folksongs
62 Representation of certain artistic works on public display
63 Advertisement of sale of artistic work
64 Making of subsequent works by same artist
65 Reconstruction of buildings

## CHAPTER VI

## REMEDIES FOR INFRINGEMENT

*Rights and remedies of copyright owner*

96 Infringement actionable by copyright owner
97 Provisions as to damages in infringement action
98 Undertaking to take licence of right in infringement proceedings
99 Order for delivery up
100 Right to seize infringing copies and other articles

*Rights and remedies of exclusive licensee*

101 Rights and remedies of exclusive licensee
102 Exercise of concurrent rights

*Remedies for infringement of moral rights*

103 Remedies for infringement of moral rights

*Presumptions*

104 Presumptions relevant to literary, dramatic, musical and artistic works
105 Presumptions relevant to sound recordings, films and computer programs
106 Presumptions relevant to works subject to Crown copyright

*Offences*

107 Criminal liability for making or dealing with infringing articles, &c
108 Order for delivery up in criminal proceedings
109 Search warrants
110 Offence by body corporate: liability of officers

*Provision for preventing importation of infringing copies*

111 Infringing copies may be treated as prohibited goods
112 Power of Commissioners of Customs and Excise to make regulations

*Supplementary*

113 Period after which remedy of delivery up not available
114 Order as to disposal of infringing copy or other article
115 Jurisdiction of county court and sheriff court

## CHAPTER VII

## COPYRIGHT LICENSING

*Licensing schemes and licensing bodies*

116 Licensing schemes and licensing bodies

*References and applications with respect to licensing schemes*

117 Licensing schemes to which ss 118 to 123 apply
118 Reference of proposed licensing scheme to tribunal
119 Reference of licensing scheme to tribunal
120 Further reference of scheme to tribunal
121 Application for grant of licence in connection with licensing scheme
122 Application for review of order as to entitlement to licence
123 Effect of order of tribunal as to licensing scheme

*References and applications with respect to licensing by licensing bodies*

124 Licences to which ss 125 to 128 apply
125 Reference to tribunal of proposed licence
126 Reference to tribunal of expiring licence
127 Application for review of order as to licence
128 Effect of order of tribunal as to licence

*Factors to be taken into account in certain classes of case*

129 General considerations: unreasonable discrimination
130 Licences for reprographic copying
131 Licences for educational establishments in respect of works included in broadcasts or cable programmes
132 Licences to reflect conditions imposed by promoters of events
133 Licences to reflect payments in respect of underlying rights
134 Licences in respect of works included in re-transmissions
135 Mention of specific matters not to exclude other relevant considerations

*Implied indemnity in schemes or licences for reprographic copying*

136 Implied indemnity in certain schemes and licences for reprographic copying

*Reprographic copying by educational establishments*

137 Power to extend coverage of scheme or licence
138 Variation or discharge of order extending scheme or licence
139 Appeals against orders
140 Inquiry whether new scheme or general licence required
141 Statutory licence where recommendation not implemented

*Royalty or other sum payable for rental of certain works*

142 Royalty or other sum payable for rental of sound recording, film or computer program

*Certification of licensing schemes*

143 Certification of licensing schemes

*Powers exercisable in consequence of competition report*

144 Powers exercisable in consequence of report of Monopolies and Mergers Commission

## CHAPTER VIII

## THE COPYRIGHT TRIBUNAL

*The tribunal*

145 The Copyright Tribunal
146 Membership of the tribunal
147 Financial provisions
148 Constitution for purposes of proceedings

*Jurisdiction and procedure*

149 Jurisdiction of the tribunal
150 General power to make rules
151 Costs, proof of orders, &c

*Appeals*

152 Appeal to the court on point of law

## CHAPTER IX

## QUALIFICATION FOR AND EXTENT OF COPYRIGHT PROTECTION

*Qualification for copyright protection*

153 Qualification for copyright protection
154 Qualification by reference to author
155 Qualification by reference to country of first publication
156 Qualification by reference to place of transmission

*Extent and application of this Part*

157 Countries to which this Part extends
158 Countries ceasing to be colonies

*Supplementary*



CHAPTER X

MISCELLANEOUS AND GENERAL

*Crown and Parliamentary copyright*



*Other miscellaneous provisions*



*Transitional provisions and savings*



*Interpretation*



PART II

RIGHTS IN PERFORMANCES

*Introductory*



*Performers' rights*



*Rights of person having recording rights*



*Exceptions to rights conferred*

*An Act to restate the law of copyright, with amendments; to make fresh provision as to the rights of performers and others in performances; to confer a design right in original designs; to amend the Registered Designs Act 1949; to make provision with respect to patent agents and trade mark agents; to confer patents and designs jurisdiction on certain county courts; to amend the law of patents; to make provision with respect to devices designed to circumvent copy-protection of works in electronic form; to make fresh provision penalising the fraudulent reception of transmissions; to make the fraudulent application or use of a trade mark an offence; to make provision for the benefit of the Hospital for Sick Children, Great Ormond Street, London; to enable financial assistance to be given to certain international bodies; and for connected purposes* [15 November 1988]

# PART I

# COPYRIGHT

## CHAPTER I

## SUBSISTENCE, OWNERSHIP AND DURATION OF COPYRIGHT

*Introductory*

### 1 Copyright and copyright works

(1) Copyright is a property right which subsists in accordance with this Part in the following descriptions of work—

(*a*) original literary, dramatic, musical or artistic works,
(*b*) sound recordings, films, broadcasts or cable programmes, and
(*c*) the typographical arrangement of published editions.

(2) In this Part "copyright work" means a work of any of those descriptions in which copyright subsists.

(3) Copyright does not subsist in a work unless the requirements of this Part with respect to qualification for copyright protection are met (see section 153 and the provisions referred to there).

### 2 Rights subsisting in copyright works

(1) The owner of the copyright in a work of any description has the exclusive right to do the acts specified in Chapter II as the acts restricted by the copyright in a work of that description.

(2) In relation to certain descriptions of copyright work the following rights conferred by Chapter IV (moral rights) subsist in favour of the author, director or commissioner of the work, whether or not he is the owner of the copyright—

(*a*) section 77 (right to be identified as author or director),
(*b*) section 80 (right to object to derogatory treatment of work), and
(*c*) section 85 (right to privacy of certain photographs and films).

*Descriptions of work and related provisions*

### 3 Literary, dramatic and musical works

(1) In this Part—

"literary work" means any work, other than a dramatic or musical work, which is written, spoken or sung, and accordingly includes—

(*a*) a table or compilation, and
(*b*) a computer program;

"dramatic work" includes a work of dance or mime; and

"musical work" means a work consisting of music, exclusive of any words or action intended to be sung, spoken or performed with the music.

(2) Copyright does not subsist in a literary, dramatic or musical work unless and until it is recorded, in writing or otherwise; and references in this Part to the time at which such a work is made are to the time at which it is so recorded.

(3) It is immaterial for the purposes of subsection (2) whether the work is recorded by or with the permission of the author; and where it is not recorded by the author, nothing in that subsection affects the question whether copyright subsists in the record as distinct from the work recorded.

**4 Artistic works**

(1) In this Part "artistic work" means—

(*a*) a graphic work, photograph, sculpture or collage, irrespective of artistic quality,
(*b*) a work of architecture being a building or a model for a building, or
(*c*) a work of artistic craftsmanship.

(2) In this Part—

"building" includes any fixed structure, and a part of a building or fixed structure;

"graphic work" includes—

(*a*) any painting, drawing, diagram, map, chart or plan, and
(*b*) any engraving, etching, lithograph, woodcut or similar work;

"photograph" means a recording of light or other radiation on any medium on which an image is produced or from which an image may by any means be produced, and which is not part of a film;

"sculpture" includes a cast or model made for purposes of sculpture.

**5 Sound recordings and films**

(1) In this Part—

"sound recording" means—

(*a*) a recording of sounds, from which the sounds may be reproduced, or
(*b*) a recording of the whole or any part of a literary, dramatic or musical work, from which sounds reproducing the work or part may be produced,

regardless of the medium on which the recording is made or the method by which the sounds are reproduced or produced; and

"film" means a recording on any medium from which a moving image may by any means be produced.

(2) Copyright does not subsist in a sound recording or film which is, or to the extent that it is, a copy taken from a previous sound recording or film.

**6 Broadcasts**

(1) In this Part a "broadcast" means a transmission by wireless telegraphy of visual images, sounds or other information which—

(*a*) is capable of being lawfully received by members of the public, or
(*b*) is transmitted for presentation to members of the public;

and references to broadcasting shall be construed accordingly.

(2) An encrypted transmission shall be regarded as capable of being lawfully received by members of the public only if decoding equipment has been made available to members of the public by or with the authority of the person making the transmission or the person providing the contents of the transmission.

(3) References in this Part to the person making a broadcast, broadcasting a work, or including a work in a broadcast are—

(*a*) to the person transmitting the programme, if he has responsibility to any extent for its contents, and (*b*) to any person providing the programme who makes with the person transmitting it the arrangements necessary for its transmission;

and references in this Part to a programme, in the context of broadcasting, are to any item included in a broadcast.

(4) For the purposes of this Part the place from which a broadcast is made is, in the case of a satellite transmission, the place from which the signals carrying the broadcast are transmitted to the satellite.

(5) References in this Part to the reception of a broadcast include reception of a broadcast relayed by means of a telecommunications system.

(6) Copyright does not subsist in a broadcast which infringes, or to the extent that it infringes, the copyright in another broadcast or in a cable programme.

**7 Cable programmes**

(1) In this Part—

"cable programme" means any item included in a cable programme service; and

"cable programme service" means a service which consists wholly or mainly in sending visual images, sounds or other information by means of a telecommunications system, otherwise than by wireless telegraphy, for reception—

(*a*) at two or more places (whether for simultaneous reception or at different times in response to requests by different users), or

(*b*) for presentation to members of the public,

and which is not, or so far as it is not, excepted by or under the following provisions of this section.

(2) The following are excepted from the definition of "cable programme service"—

(*a*) a service or part of a service of which it is an essential feature that while visual images, sounds or other information are being conveyed by the person providing the service there will or may be sent from each place of reception, by means of the same system or (as the case may be) the same part of it, information (other than signals sent for the operation or control of the service) for reception by the person providing the service or other persons receiving it;

(*b*) a service run for the purposes of a business where—

(i) no person except the person carrying on the business is concerned in the control of the apparatus comprised in the system,

(ii) the visual images, sounds or other information are conveyed by the system solely for purposes internal to the running of the business and not by way of rendering a service or providing amenities for others, and

(iii) the system is not connected to any other telecommunications system;

(*c*) a service run by a single individual where—

(i) all the apparatus comprised in the system is under his control,

(ii) the visual images, sounds or other information conveyed by the system are conveyed solely for domestic purposes of his, and

(iii) the system is not connected to any other telecommunications system;

(*d*) services where—

(i) all the apparatus comprised in the system is situated in, or connects, premises which are in single occupation, and

(ii) the system is not connected to any other telecommunications system,

other than services operated as part of the amenities provided for residents or inmates of premises run as a business;

(*e*) services which are, or to the extent that they are, run for persons providing broadcasting or cable programme services or providing programmes for such services.

(3) The Secretary of State may by order amend subsection (2) so as to add or remove exceptions, subject to such transitional provision as appears to him to be appropriate.

(4) An order shall be made by statutory instrument; and no order shall be made unless a draft of it has been laid before and approved by resolution of each House of Parliament.

(5) References in this Part to the inclusion of a cable programme or work in a cable programme service are to its transmission as part of the service; and references to the person including it are to the person providing the service.

(6) Copyright does not subsist in a cable programme—

(*a*) if it is included in a cable programme service by reception and immediate re-transmission of a broadcast, or

(*b*) if it infringes, or to the extent that it infringes, the copyright in another cable programme or in a broadcast.

### 8 Published editions

(1) In this Part "published edition", in the context of copyright in the typographical arrangement of a published edition, means a published edition of the whole or any part of one or more literary, dramatic or musical works.

(2) Copyright does not subsist in the typographical arrangement of a published edition if, or to the extent that, it reproduces the typographical arrangement of a previous edition.

## *Authorship and ownership of copyright*

### 9 Authorship of work

(1) In this Part "author", in relation to a work, means the person who creates it.

(2) That person shall be taken to be—

(*a*) in the case of a sound recording or film, the person by whom the arrangements necessary for the making of the recording or film are undertaken;

(*b*) in the case of a broadcast, the person making the broadcast (see section 6(3)) or, in the case of a broadcast which relays another broadcast by reception and immediate re-transmission, the person making that other broadcast;

(*c*) in the case of a cable programme, the person providing the cable programme service in which the programme is included;

(*d*) in the case of the typographical arrangement of a published edition, the publisher.

(3) In the case of a literary, dramatic, musical or artistic work which is computer-generated, the author shall be taken to be the person by whom the arrangements necessary for the creation of the work are undertaken.

(4) For the purposes of this Part a work is of "unknown authorship" if the identity of the author is unknown or, in the case of a work of joint authorship, if the identity of none of the authors is known.

(5) For the purposes of this Part the identity of an author shall be regarded as unknown if it is not possible for a person to ascertain his identity by reasonable inquiry; but if his identity is once known it shall not subsequently be regarded as unknown.

### 10 Works of joint authorship

(1) In this Part a "work of joint authorship" means a work produced by the collaboration of two or more authors in which the contribution of each author is not distinct from that of the other author or authors.

(2) A broadcast shall be treated as a work of joint authorship in any case where more than one person is to be taken as making the broadcast (see section 6(3)).

(3) References in this Part to the author of a work shall, except as otherwise provided, be construed in relation to a work of joint authorship as references to all the authors of the work.

### 11 First ownership of copyright

(1) The author of a work is the first owner of any copyright in it, subject to the following provisions.

(2) Where a literary, dramatic, musical or artistic work is made by an employee in the course of his employment, his employer is the first owner of any copyright in the work subject to any agreement to the contrary.

(3) This section does not apply to Crown copyright or Parliamentary copyright (see sections 163 and 165) or to copyright which subsists by virtue of section 168 (copyright of certain international organisations).

*Duration of copyright*

### 12 Duration of copyright in literary, dramatic, musical or artistic works

(1) Copyright in a literary, dramatic, musical or artistic work expires at the end of the period of 50 years from the end of the calendar year in which the author dies, subject to the following provisions of this section.

(2) If the work is of unknown authorship, copyright expires at the end of the period of 50 years from the end of the calendar year in which it is first made available to the public; and subsection (1) does not apply if the identity of the author becomes known after the end of that period.

For this purpose making available to the public includes—

(*a*) in the case of a literary, dramatic or musical work—

(i) performance in public, or
(ii) being broadcast or included in a cable programme service;

(*b*) in the case of an artistic work—

(i) exhibition in public,
(ii) a film including the work being shown in public, or
(iii) being included in a broadcast or cable programme service;

but in determining generally for the purposes of this subsection whether a work has been made available to the public no account shall be taken of any unauthorised act.

(3) If the work is computer-generated neither of the above provisions applies and copyright expires at the end of the period of 50 years from the end of the calendar year in which the work was made.

(4) In relation to a work of joint authorship—

(*a*) the reference in subsection (1) to the death of the author shall be construed—

(i) if the identity of all the authors is known, as a reference to the death of the last of them to die, and

(ii) if the identity of one or more of the authors is known and the identity of one or more others is not, as a reference to the death of the last of the authors whose identity is known; and

(*b*) the reference in subsection (2) to the identity of the author becoming known shall be construed as a reference to the identity of any of the authors becoming known.

(5) This section does not apply to Crown copyright or Parliamentary copyright (see sections 163 to 166) or to copyright which subsists by virtue of section 168 (copyright of certain international organisations).

**13 Duration of copyright in sound recordings and films**

(1) Copyright in a sound recording or film expires—

(*a*) at the end of the period of 50 years from the end of the calendar year in which it is made, or

(*b*) if it is released before the end of that period, 50 years from the end of the calendar year in which it is released.

(2) A sound recording or film is "released" when—

(*a*) it is first published, broadcast or included in a cable programme service, or

(*b*) in the case of a film or film sound-track, the film is first shown in public;

but in determining whether a work has been released no account shall be taken of any unauthorised act.

**14 Duration of copyright in broadcasts and cable programmes**

(1) Copyright in a broadcast or cable programme expires at the end of the period of 50 years from the end of the calendar year in which the broadcast was made or the programme was included in a cable programme service.

(2) Copyright in a repeat broadcast or cable programme expires at the same time as the copyright in the original broadcast or cable programme; and accordingly no copyright arises in respect of a repeat broadcast or cable programme which is broadcast or included in a cable programme service after the expiry of the copyright in the original broadcast or cable programme.

(3) A repeat broadcast or cable programme means one which is a repeat either of a broadcast previously made or of a cable programme previously included in a cable programme service.

**15 Duration of copyright in typographical arrangement of published editions**

Copyright in the typographical arrangement of a published edition expires at the end of the period of 25 years from the end of the calendar year in which the edition was first published.

## CHAPTER II

## RIGHTS OF COPYRIGHT OWNER

*The acts restricted by copyright*

**16 The acts restricted by copyright in a work**

(1) The owner of the copyright in a work has, in accordance with the following provisions of this Chapter, the exclusive right to do the following acts in the United Kingdom—

(*a*) to copy the work (see section 17);
(*b*) to issue copies of the work to the public (see section 18);
(*c*) to perform, show or play the work in public (see section 19);
(*d*) to broadcast the work or include it in a cable programme service (see section 20);
(*e*) to make an adaptation of the work or do any of the above in relation to an adaptation (see section 21);

and those acts are referred to in this Part as the "acts restricted by the copyright".

(2) Copyright in a work is infringed by a person who without the licence of the copyright owner does, or authorises another to do, any of the acts restricted by the copyright.

(3) References in this Part to the doing of an act restricted by the copyright in a work are to the doing of it—

(*a*) in relation to the work as a whole or any substantial part of it, and
(*b*) either directly or indirectly;

and it is immaterial whether any intervening acts themselves infringe copyright.

(4) This Chapter has effect subject to—

(*a*) the provisions of Chapter III (acts permitted in relation to copyright works), and
(*b*) the provisions of Chapter VII (provisions with respect to copyright licensing).

**17 Infringement of copyright by copying**

(1) The copying of the work is an act restricted by the copyright in every description of copyright work; and references in this Part to copying and copies shall be construed as follows.

(2) Copying in relation to a literary, dramatic, musical or artistic work means reproducing the work in any material form.

This includes storing the work in any medium by electronic means.

(3) In relation to an artistic work copying includes the making of a copy in three dimensions of a two-dimensional work and the making of a copy in two dimensions of a three-dimensional work.

(4) Copying in relation to a film, television broadcast or cable programme includes making a photograph of the whole or any substantial part of any image forming part of the film, broadcast or cable programme.

(5) Copying in relation to the typographical arrangement of a published edition means making a facsimile copy of the arrangement.

(6) Copying in relation to any description of work includes the making of copies which are transient or are incidental to some other use of the work.

**18 Infringement by issue of copies to the public**

(1) The issue to the public of copies of the work is an act restricted by the copyright in every description of copyright work.

(2) References in this Part to the issue to the public of copies of a work are to the act of putting into circulation copies not previously put into circulation, in the United Kingdom or elsewhere, and not to—

(*a*) any subsequent distribution, sale, hiring or loan of those copies, or
(*b*) any subsequent importation of those copies into the United Kingdom;

except that in relation to sound recordings, films and computer programs the restricted act of issuing copies to the public includes any rental of copies to the public.

**19 Infringement by performance, showing or playing of work in public**

(1) The performance of the work in public is an act restricted by the copyright in a literary, dramatic or musical work.

(2) In this Part "performance", in relation to a work—

(*a*) includes delivery in the case of lectures, addresses, speeches and sermons, and

(*b*) in general, includes any mode of visual or acoustic presentation, including presentation by means of a sound recording, film, broadcast or cable programme of the work.

(3) The playing or showing of the work in public is an act restricted by the copyright in a sound recording, film, broadcast or cable programme.

(4) Where copyright in a work is infringed by its being performed, played or shown in public by means of apparatus for receiving visual images or sounds conveyed by electronic means, the person by whom the visual images or sounds are sent, and in the case of a performance the performers, shall not be regarded as responsible for the infringement.

**20 Infringement by broadcasting or inclusion in a cable programme service**

The broadcasting of the work or its inclusion in a cable programme service is an act restricted by the copyright in—

(*a*) a literary, dramatic, musical or artistic work,
(*b*) a sound recording or film, or
(*c*) a broadcast or cable programme.

**21 Infringement by making adaptation or act done in relation to adaptation**

(1) The making of an adaptation of the work is an act restricted by the copyright in a literary, dramatic or musical work.

For this purpose an adaptation is made when it is recorded, in writing or otherwise.

(2) The doing of any of the acts specified in sections 17 to 20, or subsection (1) above, in relation to an adaptation of the work is also an act restricted by the copyright in a literary, dramatic or musical work.

For this purpose it is immaterial whether the adaptation has been recorded, in writing or otherwise, at the time the act is done.

(3) In this Part "adaptation"—

(*a*) in relation to a literary or dramatic work, means—

(i) a translation of the work;
(ii) a version of a dramatic work in which it is converted into a non-dramatic work or, as the case may be, of a non-dramatic work in which it is converted into a dramatic work;
(iii) a version of the work in which the story or action is conveyed wholly or mainly by means of pictures in a form suitable for reproduction in a book, or in a newspaper, magazine or similar periodical;

(*b*) in relation to a musical work, means an arrangement or transcription of the work.

(4) In relation to a computer program a "translation" includes a version of the

program in which it is converted into or out of a computer language or code or into a different computer language or code, otherwise than incidentally in the course of running the program.

(5) No inference shall be drawn from this section as to what does or does not amount to copying a work.

*Secondary infringement of copyright*

**22 Secondary infringement: importing infringing copy**

The copyright in a work is infringed by a person who, without the licence of the copyright owner, imports into the United Kingdom, otherwise than for his private and domestic use, an article which is, and which he knows or has reason to believe is, an infringing copy of the work.

**23 Secondary infringement: possessing or dealing with infringing copy**

The copyright in a work is infringed by a person who, without the licence of the copyright owner—

(*a*) possesses in the course of a business,
(*b*) sells or lets for hire, or offers or exposes for sale or hire,
(*c*) in the course of a business exhibits in public or distributes, or
(*d*) distributes otherwise than in the course of a business to such an extent as to affect prejudicially the owner of the copyright,

an article which is, and which he knows or has reason to believe is, an infringing copy of the work.

**24 Secondary infringement: providing means for making infringing copies**

(1) Copyright in a work is infringed by a person who, without the licence of the copyright owner—

(*a*) makes,
(*b*) imports into the United Kingdom,
(*c*) possesses in the course of a business, or
(*d*) sells or lets for hire, or offers or exposes for sale or hire,

an article specifically designed or adapted for making copies of that work, knowing or having reason to believe that it is to be used to make infringing copies.

(2) Copyright in a work is infringed by a person who without the licence of the copyright owner transmits the work by means of a telecommunications system (otherwise than by broadcasting or inclusion in a cable programme service), knowing or having reason to believe that infringing copies of the work will be made by means of the reception of the transmission in the United Kingdom or elsewhere.

**25 Secondary infringement: permitting use of premises for infringing performance**

(1) Where the copyright in a literary, dramatic or musical work is infringed by a performance at a place of public entertainment, any person who gave permission for that place to be used for the performance is also liable for the infringement unless when he gave permission he believed on reasonable grounds that the performance would not infringe copyright.

(2) In this section "place of public entertainment" includes premises which are occupied mainly for other purposes but are from time to time made available for hire for the purposes of public entertainment.

### 26 Secondary infringement: provision of apparatus for infringing performance, &c

(1) Where copyright in a work is infringed by a public performance of the work, or by the playing or showing of the work in public, by means of apparatus for—

(*a*) playing sound recordings,
(*b*) showing films, or
(*c*) receiving visual images or sounds conveyed by electronic means,

the following persons are also liable for the infringement.

(2) A person who supplied the apparatus, or any substantial part of it, is liable for the infringement if when he supplied the apparatus or part—

(*a*) he knew or had reason to believe that the apparatus was likely to be so used as to infringe copyright, or
(*b*) in the case of apparatus whose normal use involves a public performance, playing or showing, he did not believe on reasonable grounds that it would not be so used as to infringe copyright.

(3) An occupier of premises who gave permission for the apparatus to be brought onto the premises is liable for the infringement if when he gave permission he knew or had reason to believe that the apparatus was likely to be so used as to infringe copyright.

(4) A person who supplied a copy of a sound recording or film used to infringe copyright is liable for the infringement if when he supplied it he knew or had reason to believe that what he supplied, or a copy made directly or indirectly from it, was likely to be so used as to infringe copyright.

*Infringing copies*

### 27 Meaning of "infringing copy"

(1) In this Part "infringing copy", in relation to a copyright work, shall be construed in accordance with this section.

(2) An article is an infringing copy if its making constituted an infringement of the copyright in the work in question.

(3) An article is also an infringing copy if—

(*a*) it has been or is proposed to be imported into the United Kingdom, and
(*b*) its making in the United Kingdom would have constituted an infringement of the copyright in the work in question, or a breach of an exclusive licence agreement relating to that work.

(4) Where in any proceedings the question arises whether an article is an infringing copy and it is shown—

(*a*) that the article is a copy of the work, and
(*b*) that copyright subsists in the work or has subsisted at any time,

it shall be presumed until the contrary is proved that the article was made at a time when copyright subsisted in the work.

(5) Nothing in subsection (3) shall be construed as applying to an article which may lawfully be imported into the United Kingdom by virtue of any enforceable Community right within the meaning of section 2(1) of the European Communities Act 1972.

(6) In this Part "infringing copy" includes a copy falling to be treated as an infringing copy by virtue of any of the following provisions—

section 32(5) (copies made for purposes of instruction or examination),

section 35(3) (recordings made by educational establishments for educational purposes),
section 36(5) (reprographic copying by educational establishments for purposes of instruction),
section 37(3)(*b*) (copies made by librarian or archivist in reliance on false declaration),
section 56(2) (further copies, adaptations, &c of work in electronic form retained on transfer of principal copy),
section 63(2) (copies made for purpose of advertising artistic work for sale),
section 68(4) (copies made for purpose of broadcast or cable programme), or
any provision of an order under section 141 (statutory licence for certain reprographic copying by educational establishments).

## CHAPTER III

## ACTS PERMITTED IN RELATION TO COPYRIGHT WORKS

### *Introductory*

#### 28 Introductory provisions

(1) The provisions of this Chapter specify acts which may be done in relation to copyright works notwithstanding the subsistence of copyright; they relate only to the question of infringement of copyright and do not affect any other right or obligation restricting the doing of any of the specified acts.

(2) Where it is provided by this Chapter that an act does not infringe copyright, or may be done without infringing copyright, and no particular description of copyright work is mentioned, the act in question does not infringe the copyright in a work of any description.

(3) No inference shall be drawn from the description of any act which may by virtue of this Chapter be done without infringing copyright as to the scope of the acts restricted by the copyright in any description of work.

(4) The provisions of this Chapter are to be construed independently of each other, so that the fact that an act does not fall within one provision does not mean that it is not covered by another provision.

### *General*

#### 29 Research and private study

(1) Fair dealing with a literary, dramatic, musical or artistic work for the purposes of research or private study does not infringe any copyright in the work or, in the case of a published edition, in the typographical arrangement.

(2) Fair dealing with the typographical arrangement of a published edition for the purposes mentioned in subsection (1) does not infringe any copyright in the arrangement.

(3) Copying by a person other than the researcher or student himself is not fair dealing if—

(*a*) in the case of a librarian, or a person acting on behalf of a librarian, he does anything which regulations under section 40 would not permit to be done under section 38 or 39 (articles or parts of published works: restriction on multiple copies of same material), or

(*b*) in any other case, the person doing the copying knows or has reason to believe that it will result in copies of substantially the same material being provided to more than one person at substantially the same time and for substantially the same purpose.

**30 Criticism, review and news reporting**

(1) Fair dealing with a work for the purpose of criticism or review, of that or another work or of a performance of a work, does not infringe any copyright in the work provided that it is accompanied by a sufficient acknowledgement.

(2) Fair dealing with a work (other than a photograph) for the purpose of reporting current events does not infringe any copyright in the work provided that (subject to subsection (3)) it is accompanied by a sufficient acknowledgement.

(3) No acknowledgement is required in connection with the reporting of current events by means of a sound recording, film, broadcast or cable programme.

**31 Incidental inclusion of copyright material**

(1) Copyright in a work is not infringed by its incidental inclusion in an artistic work, sound recording, film, broadcast or cable programme.

(2) Nor is the copyright infringed by the issue to the public of copies, or the playing, showing, broadcasting or inclusion in a cable programme service, of anything whose making was, by virtue of subsection (1), not an infringement of the copyright.

(3) A musical work, words spoken or sung with music, or so much of a sound recording, broadcast or cable programme as includes a musical work or such words, shall not be regarded as incidentally included in another work if it is deliberately included.

*Education*

**32 Things done for purposes of instruction or examination**

(1) Copyright in a literary, dramatic, musical or artistic work is not infringed by its being copied in the course of instruction or of preparation for instruction, provided the copying—

(*a*) is done by a person giving or receiving instruction, and
(*b*) is not by means of a reprographic process.

(2) Copyright in a sound recording, film, broadcast or cable programme is not infringed by its being copied by making a film or film sound-track in the course of instruction, or of preparation for instruction, in the making of films or film sound-tracks, provided the copying is done by a person giving or receiving instruction.

(3) Copyright is not infringed by anything done for the purposes of an examination by way of setting the questions, communicating the questions to the candidates or answering the questions.

(4) Subsection (3) does not extend to the making of a reprographic copy of a musical work for use by an examination candidate in performing the work.

(5) Where a copy which would otherwise be an infringing copy is made in accordance with this section but is subsequently dealt with, it shall be treated as an infringing copy for the purpose of that dealing, and if that dealing infringes copyright for all subsequent purposes.

For this purpose "dealt with" means sold or let for hire or offered or exposed for sale or hire.

**33 Anthologies for educational use**

(1) The inclusion of a short passage from a published literary or dramatic work in a collection which—

(*a*) is intended for use in educational establishments and is so described in its title, and in any advertisements issued by or on behalf of the publisher, and
(*b*) consists mainly of material in which no copyright subsists,

does not infringe the copyright in the work if the work itself is not intended for use in such establishments and the inclusion is accompanied by a sufficient acknowledgement.

(2) Subsection (1) does not authorise the inclusion of more than two excerpts from copyright works by the same author in collections published by the same publisher over any period of five years.

(3) In relation to any given passage the reference in subsection (2) to excerpts from works by the same author—

(*a*) shall be taken to include excerpts from works by him in collaboration with another, and
(*b*) if the passage in question is from such a work, shall be taken to include excerpts from works by any of the authors, whether alone or in collaboration with another.

(4) References in this section to the use of a work in an educational establishment are to any use for the educational purposes of such an establishment.

**34 Performing, playing or showing work in course of activities of educational establishment**

(1) The performance of a literary, dramatic or musical work before an audience consisting of teachers and pupils at an educational establishment and other persons directly connected with the activities of the establishment—

(*a*) by a teacher or pupil in the course of the activities of the establishment, or
(*b*) at the establishment by any person for the purposes of instruction,

is not a public performance for the purposes of infringement of copyright.

(2) The playing or showing of a sound recording, film, broadcast or cable programme before such an audience at an educational establishment for the purposes of instruction is not a playing or showing of the work in public for the purposes of infringement of copyright.

(3) A person is not for this purpose directly connected with the activities of the educational establishment simply because he is the parent of a pupil at the establishment.

**35 Recording by educational establishments of broadcasts and cable programmes**

(1) A recording of a broadcast or cable programme, or a copy of such a recording, may be made by or on behalf of an educational establishment for the educational purposes of that establishment without thereby infringing the copyright in the broadcast or cable programme, or in any work included in it.

(2) This section does not apply if or to the extent that there is a licensing scheme certified for the purposes of this section under section 143 providing for the grant of licences.

(3) Where a copy which would otherwise be an infringing copy is made in accordance with this section but is subsequently dealt with, it shall be treated as an infringing copy for the purposes of that dealing, and if that dealing infringes copyright for all subsequent purposes.

For this purpose "dealt with" means sold or let for hire or offered or exposed for sale or hire.

**36 Reprographic copying by educational establishments of passages from published works**

(1) Reprographic copies of passages from published literary, dramatic or musical works may, to the extent permitted by this section, be made by or on behalf of an educational establishment for the purposes of instruction without infringing any copyright in the work, or in the typographical arrangement.

(2) Not more than one per cent. of any work may be copied by or on behalf of an establishment by virtue of this section in any quarter, that is, in any period 1st January to 31st March, 1st April to 30th June, 1st July to 30th September or 1st October to 31st December.

(3) Copying is not authorised by this section if, or to the extent that, licences are available authorising the copying in question and the person making the copies knew or ought to have been aware of that fact.

(4) The terms of a licence granted to an educational establishment authorising the reprographic copying for the purposes of instruction of passages from published literary, dramatic or musical works are of no effect so far as they purport to restrict the proportion of a work which may be copied (whether on payment or free of charge) to less than that which would be permitted under this section.

(5) Where a copy which would otherwise be an infringing copy is made in accordance with this section but is subsequently dealt with, it shall be treated as an infringing copy for the purposes of that dealing, and if that dealing infringes copyright for all subsequent purposes.

For this purpose "dealt with" means sold or let for hire or offered or exposed for sale or hire.

*Libraries and archives*

**37 Libraries and archives: introductory**

(1) In sections 38 to 43 (copying by librarians and archivists)—

(*a*) references in any provision to a prescribed library or archive are to a library or archive of a description prescribed for the purposes of that provision by regulations made by the Secretary of State; and

(*b*) references in any provision to the prescribed conditions are to the conditions so prescribed.

(2) The regulations may provide that, where a librarian or archivist is required to be satisfied as to any matter before making or supplying a copy of a work—

(*a*) he may rely on a signed declaration as to that matter by the person requesting the copy, unless he is aware that it is false in a material particular, and

(*b*) in such cases as may be prescribed, he shall not make or supply a copy in the absence of a signed declaration in such form as may be prescribed.

(3) Where a person requesting a copy makes a declaration which is false in a material particular and is supplied with a copy which would have been an infringing copy if made by him—

(*a*) he is liable for infringement of copyright as if he had made the copy himself, and

(*b*) the copy shall be treated as an infringing copy.

(4) The regulations may make different provision for different descriptions of libraries or archives and for different purposes.

(5) Regulations shall be made by statutory instrument which shall be subject to annulment in pursuance of a resolution of either House of Parliament.

(6) References in this section, and in sections 38 to 43, to the librarian or archivist include a person acting on his behalf.

**38 Copying by librarians: articles in periodicals**

(1) The librarian of a prescribed library may, if the prescribed conditions are complied with, make and supply a copy of an article in a periodical without infringing any copyright in the text, in any illustrations accompanying the text or in the typographical arrangement.

(2) The prescribed conditions shall include the following—

(*a*) that copies are supplied only to persons satisfying the librarian that they require them for purposes of research or private study, and will not use them for any other purpose;

(*b*) that no person is furnished with more than one copy of the same article or with copies of more than one article contained in the same issue of a periodical; and

(*c*) that persons to whom copies are supplied are required to pay for them a sum not less than the cost (including a contribution to the general expenses of the library) attributable to their production.

**39 Copying by librarians: parts of published works**

(1) The librarian of a prescribed library may, if the prescribed conditions are complied with, make and supply from a published edition a copy of part of a literary, dramatic or musical work (other than an article in a periodical) without infringing any copyright in the work, in any illustrations accompanying the work or in the typographical arrangement.

(2) The prescribed conditions shall include the following—

(*a*) that copies are supplied only to persons satisfying the librarian that they require them for purposes of research or private study, and will not use them for any other purpose;

(*b*) that no person is furnished with more than one copy of the same material or with a copy of more than a reasonable proportion of any work; and

(*c*) that persons to whom copies are supplied are required to pay for them a sum not less than the cost (including a contribution to the general expenses of the library) attributable to their production.

**40 Restriction on production of multiple copies of the same material**

(1) Regulations for the purposes of sections 38 and 39 (copying by librarian of article or part of published work) shall contain provision to the effect that a copy shall be supplied only to a person satisfying the librarian that his requirement is not related to any similar requirement of another person.

(2) The regulations may provide—

(*a*) that requirements shall be regarded as similar if the requirements are for copies of substantially the same material at substantially the same time and for substantially the same purpose; and

(*b*) that requirements of persons shall be regarded as related if those persons receive instruction to which the material is relevant at the same time and place.

**41 Copying by librarians: supply of copies to other libraries**

(1) The librarian of a prescribed library may, if the prescribed conditions are complied with, make and supply to another prescribed library a copy of—

(*a*) an article in a periodical, or
(*b*) the whole or part of a published edition of a literary, dramatic or musical work,

without infringing any copyright in the text of the article or, as the case may be, in the work, in any illustrations accompanying it or in the typographical arrangement.

(2) Subsection (1)(*b*) does not apply if at the time the copy is made the librarian making it knows, or could by reasonable inquiry ascertain, the name and address of a person entitled to authorise the making of the copy.

**42 Copying by librarians or archivists: replacement copies of works**

(1) The librarian or archivist of a prescribed library or archive may, if the prescribed conditions are complied with, make a copy from any item in the permanent collection of the library or archive—

(*a*) in order to preserve or replace that item by placing the copy in its permanent collection in addition to or in place of it, or
(*b*) in order to replace in the permanent collection of another prescribed library or archive an item which has been lost, destroyed or damaged,

without infringing the copyright in any literary, dramatic or musical work, in any illustrations accompanying such a work or, in the case of a published edition, in the typographical arrangement.

(2) The prescribed conditions shall include provision for restricting the making of copies to cases where it is not reasonably practicable to purchase a copy of the item in question to fulfil that purpose.

**43 Copying by librarians or archivists: certain unpublished works**

(1) The librarian or archivist of a prescribed library or archive may, if the prescribed conditions are complied with, make and supply a copy of the whole or part of a literary, dramatic or musical work from a document in the library or archive without infringing any copyright in the work or any illustrations accompanying it.

(2) This section does not apply if—

(*a*) the work had been published before the document was deposited in the library or archive, or
(*b*) the copyright owner has prohibited copying of the work,

and at the time the copy is made the librarian or archivist making it is, or ought to be, aware of that fact.

(3) The prescribed conditions shall include the following—

(*a*) that copies are supplied only to persons satisfying the librarian or archivist that they require them for purposes of research or private study and will not use them for any other purpose;
(*b*) that no person is furnished with more than one copy of the same material; and
(*c*) that persons to whom copies are supplied are required to pay for them a sum not less than the cost (including a contribution to the general expenses of the library or archive) attributable to their production.

**44 Copy of work required to be made as condition of export**

If an article of cultural or historical importance or interest cannot lawfully be exported from the United Kingdom unless a copy of it is made and deposited in an appropriate library or archive, it is not an infringement of copyright to make that copy.

*Public administration*

**45 Parliamentary and judicial proceedings**

(1) Copyright is not infringed by anything done for the purposes of parliamentary or judicial proceedings.

(2) Copyright is not infringed by anything done for the purposes of reporting such proceedings; but this shall not be construed as authorising the copying of a work which is itself a published report of the proceedings.

**46 Royal Commissions and statutory inquiries**

(1) Copyright is not infringed by anything done for the purposes of the proceedings of a Royal Commission or statutory inquiry.

(2) Copyright is not infringed by anything done for the purpose of reporting any such proceedings held in public; but this shall not be construed as authorising the copying of a work which is itself a published report of the proceedings.

(3) Copyright in a work is not infringed by the issue to the public of copies of the report of a Royal Commission or statutory inquiry containing the work or material from it.

(4) In this section—

"Royal Commission" includes a Commission appointed for Northern Ireland by the Secretary of State in pursuance of the prerogative powers of Her Majesty delegated to him under section 7(2) of the Northern Ireland Constitution Act 1973; and

"statutory inquiry" means an inquiry held or investigation conducted in pursuance of a duty imposed or power conferred by or under an enactment.

**47 Material open to public inspection or on official register**

(1) Where material is open to public inspection pursuant to a statutory requirement, or is on a statutory register, any copyright in the material as a literary work is not infringed by the copying of so much of the material as contains factual information of any description, by or with the authority of the appropriate person, for a purpose which does not involve the issuing of copies to the public.

(2) Where material is open to public inspection pursuant to a statutory requirement, copyright is not infringed by the copying or issuing to the public of copies of the material, by or with the authority of the appropriate person, for the purpose of enabling the material to be inspected at a more convenient time or place or otherwise facilitating the exercise of any right for the purpose of which the requirement is imposed.

(3) Where material which is open to public inspection pursuant to a statutory requirement, or which is on a statutory register, contains information about matters of general scientific, technical, commercial or economic interest, copyright is not infringed by the copying or issuing to the public of copies of the material, by or with the authority of the appropriate person, for the purpose of disseminating that information.

(4) The Secretary of State may by order provide that subsection (1), (2) or (3) shall, in such cases as may be specified in the order, apply only to copies marked in such manner as may be so specified.

(5) The Secretary of State may by order provide that subsections (1) to (3) apply, to such extent and with such modifications as may be specified in the order—

(*a*) to material made open to public inspection by—

(i) an international organisation specified in the order, or

(ii) a person so specified who has functions in the United Kingdom under an international agreement to which the United Kingdom is party, or

(*b*) to a register maintained by an international organisation specified in the order,

as they apply in relation to material open to public inspection pursuant to a statutory requirement or to a statutory register.

(6) In this section—

"appropriate person" means the person required to make the material open to public inspection or, as the case may be, the person maintaining the register;

"statutory register" means a register maintained in pursuance of a statutory requirement; and

"statutory requirement" means a requirement imposed by provision made by or under an enactment.

(7) An order under this section shall be made by statutory instrument which shall be subject to annulment in pursuance of a resolution of either House of Parliament.

### 48 Material communicated to the Crown in the course of public business

(1) This section applies where a literary, dramatic, musical or artistic work has in the course of public business been communicated to the Crown for any purpose, by or with the licence of the copyright owner and a document or other material thing recording or embodying the work is owned by or in the custody or control of the Crown.

(2) The Crown may, for the purpose for which the work was communicated to it, or any related purpose which could reasonably have been anticipated by the copyright owner, copy the work and issue copies of the work to the public without infringing any copyright in the work.

(3) The Crown may not copy a work, or issue copies of a work to the public, by virtue of this section if the work has previously been published otherwise than by virtue of this section.

(4) In subsection (1) "public business" includes any activity carried on by the Crown.

(5) This section has effect subject to any agreement to the contrary between the Crown and the copyright owner.

### 49 Public records

Material which is comprised in public records within the meaning of the Public Records Act 1958, the Public Records (Scotland) Act 1937 or the Public Records Act (Northern Ireland) 1923 which are open to public inspection in pursuance of that Act, may be copied, and a copy may be supplied to any person, by or with the authority of any officer appointed under that Act, without infringement of copyright.

### 50 Acts done under statutory authority

(1) Where the doing of a particular act is specifically authorised by an Act of Parliament, whenever passed, then, unless the Act provides otherwise, the doing of that act does not infringe copyright.

(2) Subsection (1) applies in relation to an enactment contained in Northern Ireland legislation as it applies in relation to an Act of Parliament.

(3) Nothing in this section shall be construed as excluding any defence of statutory authority otherwise available under or by virtue of any enactment.

*Designs*

**51 Design documents and models**

(1) It is not an infringement of any copyright in a design document or model recording or embodying a design for anything other than an artistic work or a typeface to make an article to the design or to copy an article made to the design.

(2) Nor is it an infringement of the copyright to issue to the public, or include in a film, broadcast or cable programme service, anything the making of which was, by virtue of subsection (1), not an infringement of that copyright.

(3) In this section—

"design" means the design of any aspect of the shape or configuration (whether internal or external) of the whole or part of an article, other than surface decoration; and

"design document" means any record of a design, whether in the form of a drawing, a written description, a photograph, data stored in a computer or otherwise.

**52 Effect of exploitation of design derived from artistic work**

(1) This section applies where an artistic work has been exploited, by or with the licence of the copyright owner, by—

(*a*) making by an industrial process articles falling to be treated for the purposes of this Part as copies of the work, and

(*b*) marketing such articles, in the United Kingdom or elsewhere.

(2) After the end of the period of 25 years from the end of the calendar year in which such articles are first marketed, the work may be copied by making articles of any description, or doing anything for the purpose of making articles of any description, and anything may be done in relation to articles so made, without infringing copyright in the work.

(3) Where only part of an artistic work is exploited as mentioned in subsection (1), subsection (2) applies only in relation to that part.

(4) The Secretary of State may by order make provision—

(*a*) as to the circumstances in which an article, or any description of article, is to be regarded for the purposes of this section as made by an industrial process;

(*b*) excluding from the operation of this section such articles of a primarily literary or artistic character as he thinks fit.

(5) An order shall be made by statutory instrument which shall be subject to annulment in pursuance of a resolution of either House of Parliament.

(6) In this section—

(*a*) references to articles do not include films; and

(*b*) references to the marketing of an article are to its being sold or let for hire or offered or exposed for sale or hire.

**53 Things done in reliance on registration of design**

(1) The copyright in an artistic work is not infringed by anything done—

(*a*) in pursuance of an assignment or licence made or granted by a person registered under the Registered Designs Act 1949 as the proprietor of a corresponding design, and (*b*) in good faith in reliance on the registration and without notice of any proceedings for the cancellation of the registration or for rectifying the relevant entry in the register of designs;

and this is so notwithstanding that the person registered as the proprietor was not the proprietor of the design for the purposes of the 1949 Act.

(2) In subsection (1) a "corresponding design", in relation to an artistic work, means a design within the meaning of the 1949 Act which if applied to an article would produce something which would be treated for the purposes of this Part as a copy of the artistic work.

*Typefaces*

### 54 Use of typeface in ordinary course of printing

(1) It is not an infringement of copyright in an artistic work consisting of the design of a typeface—

(*a*) to use the typeface in the ordinary course of typing, composing text, typesetting or printing,
(*b*) to possess an article for the purpose of such use, or
(*c*) to do anything in relation to material produced by such use;

and this is so notwithstanding that an article is used which is an infringing copy of the work.

(2) However, the following provisions of this Part apply in relation to persons making, importing or dealing with articles specifically designed or adapted for producing material in a particular typeface, or possessing such articles for the purpose of dealing with them, as if the production of material as mentioned in subsection (1) did infringe copyright in the artistic work consisting of the design of the typeface—

section 24 (secondary infringement: making, importing, possessing or dealing with article for making infringing copy),
sections 99 and 100 (order for delivery up and right of seizure),
section 107(2) (offence of making or possessing such an article), and
section 108 (order for delivery up in criminal proceedings).

(3) The references in subsection (2) to "dealing with" an article are to selling, letting for hire, or offering or exposing for sale or hire, exhibiting in public, or distributing.

### 55 Articles for producing material in particular typeface

(1) This section applies to the copyright in an artistic work consisting of the design of a typeface where articles specifically designed or adapted for producing material in that typeface have been marketed by or with the licence of the copyright owner.

(2) After the period of 25 years from the end of the calendar year in which the first such articles are marketed, the work may be copied by making further such articles, or doing anything for the purpose of making such articles, and anything may be done in relation to articles so made, without infringing copyright in the work.

(3) In subsection (1) "marketed" means sold, let for hire or offered or exposed for sale or hire, in the United Kingdom or elsewhere.

*Works in electronic form*

### 56 Transfers of copies of works in electronic form

(1) This section applies where a copy of a work in electronic form has been purchased on terms which, expressly or impliedly or by virtue of any rule of law, allow the purchaser to copy the work, or to adapt it or make copies of an adaptation, in connection with his use of it.

(2) If there are no express terms—

(*a*) prohibiting the transfer of the copy by the purchaser, imposing obligations which continue after a transfer, prohibiting the assignment of any licence or terminating any licence on a transfer, or

(*b*) providing for the terms on which a transferee may do the things which the purchaser was permitted to do,

anything which the purchaser was allowed to do may also be done without infringement of copyright by a transferee; but any copy, adaptation or copy of an adaptation made by the purchaser which is not also transferred shall be treated as an infringing copy for all purposes after the transfer.

(3) The same applies where the original purchased copy is no longer usable and what is transferred is a further copy used in its place.

(4) The above provisions also apply on a subsequent transfer, with the substitution for references in subsection (2) to the purchaser of references to the subsequent transferor.

*Miscellaneous: literary, dramatic, musical and artistic works*

### 57 Anonymous or pseudonymous works: acts permitted on assumptions as to expiry of copyright or death of author

(1) Copyright in a literary, dramatic, musical or artistic work is not infringed by an act done at a time when, or in pursuance of arrangements made at a time when—

(*a*) it is not possible by reasonable inquiry to ascertain the identity of the author, and

(*b*) it is reasonable to assume—

(i) that copyright has expired, or

(ii) that the author died 50 years or more before the beginning of the calendar year in which the act is done or the arrangements are made.

(2) Subsection (1)(*b*)(ii) does not apply in relation to—

(*a*) a work in which Crown copyright subsists, or

(*b*) a work in which copyright originally vested in an international organisation by virtue of section 168 and in respect of which an Order under that section specifies a copyright period longer than 50 years.

(3) In relation to a work of joint authorship—

(*a*) the reference in subsection (1) to its being possible to ascertain the identity of the author shall be construed as a reference to its being possible to ascertain the identity of any of the authors, and

(*b*) the reference in subsection (1)(*b*)(ii) to the author having died shall be construed as a reference to all the authors having died.

### 58 Use of notes or recordings of spoken words in certain cases

(1) Where a record of spoken words is made, in writing or otherwise, for the purpose—

(*a*) of reporting current events, or
(*b*) of broadcasting or including in a cable programme service the whole or part of the work,

it is not an infringement of any copyright in the words as a literary work to use the record or material taken from it (or to copy the record, or any such material, and use the copy) for that purpose, provided the following conditions are met.

(2) The conditions are that—

(*a*) the record is a direct record of the spoken words and is not taken from a previous record or from a broadcast or cable programme;
(*b*) the making of the record was not prohibited by the speaker and, where copyright already subsisted in the work, did not infringe copyright;
(*c*) the use made of the record or material taken from it is not of a kind prohibited by or on behalf of the speaker or copyright owner before the record was made; and
(*d*) the use is by or with the authority of a person who is lawfully in possession of the record.

**59 Public reading or recitation**

(1) The reading or recitation in public by one person of a reasonable extract from a published literary or dramatic work does not infringe any copyright in the work if it is accompanied by a sufficient acknowledgement.

(2) Copyright in a work is not infringed by the making of a sound recording, or the broadcasting or inclusion in a cable programme service, of a reading or recitation which by virtue of subsection (1) does not infringe copyright in the work, provided that the recording, broadcast or cable programme consists mainly of material in relation to which it is not necessary to rely on that subsection.

**60 Abstracts of scientific or technical articles**

(1) Where an article on a scientific or technical subject is published in a periodical accompanied by an abstract indicating the contents of the article, it is not an infringement of copyright in the abstract, or in the article, to copy the abstract or issue copies of it to the public.

(2) This section does not apply if or to the extent that there is a licensing scheme certified for the purposes of this section under section 143 providing for the grant of licences.

**61 Recordings of folksongs**

(1) A sound recording of a performance of a song may be made for the purpose of including it in an archive maintained by a designated body without infringing any copyright in the words as a literary work or in the accompanying musical work, provided the conditions in subsection (2) below are met.

(2) The conditions are that—

(*a*) the words are unpublished and of unknown authorship at the time the recording is made,
(*b*) the making of the recording does not infringe any other copyright, and
(*c*) its making is not prohibited by any performer.

(3) Copies of a sound recording made in reliance on subsection (1) and included in an archive maintained by a designated body may, if the prescribed conditions are met, be made and supplied by the archivist without infringing copyright in the recording or the works included in it.

(4) The prescribed conditions shall include the following—

(*a*) that copies are only supplied to persons satisfying the archivist that they require them for purposes of research or private study and will not use them for any other purpose; and
(*b*) that no person is furnished with more than one copy of the same recording.

(5) In this section—

(*a*) "designated" means designated for the purposes of this section by order of the Secretary of State, who shall not designate a body unless satisfied that it is not established or conducted for profit,
(*b*) "prescribed" means prescribed for the purposes of this section by order of the Secretary of State, and
(*c*) references to the archivist include a person acting on his behalf.

(6) An order under this section shall be made by statutory instrument which shall be subject to annulment in pursuance of a resolution of either House of Parliament.

### 62 Representation of certain artistic works on public display

(1) This section applies to—

(*a*) buildings, and
(*b*) sculptures, models for buildings and works of artistic craftsmanship, if permanently situated in a public place or in premises open to the public.

(2) The copyright in such a work is not infringed by—

(*a*) making a graphic work representing it,
(*b*) making a photograph or film of it, or
(*c*) broadcasting or including in a cable programme service a visual image of it.

(3) Nor is the copyright infringed by the issue to the public of copies, or the broadcasting or inclusion in a cable programme service, of anything whose making was, by virtue of this section, not an infringement of the copyright.

### 63 Advertisement of sale of artistic work

(1) It is not an infringement of copyright in an artistic work to copy it, or to issue copies to the public, for the purpose of advertising the sale of the work.

(2) Where a copy which would otherwise be an infringing copy is made in accordance with this section but is subsequently dealt with for any other purpose, it shall be treated as an infringing copy for the purposes of that dealing, and if that dealing infringes copyright for all subsequent purposes.

For this purpose "dealt with" means sold or let for hire, offered or exposed for sale or hire, exhibited in public or distributed.

### 64 Making of subsequent works by same artist

Where the author of an artistic work is not the copyright owner, he does not infringe the copyright by copying the work in making another artistic work, provided he does not repeat or imitate the main design of the earlier work.

### 65 Reconstruction of buildings

Anything done for the purposes of reconstructing a building does not infringe any copyright—

(*a*) in the building, or
(*b*) in any drawings or plans in accordance with which the building was, by or with the licence of the copyright owner, constructed.

*Miscellaneous: sound recordings, films and computer programs*

**66 Rental of sound recordings, films and computer programs**

(1) The Secretary of State may by order provide that in such cases as may be specified in the order the rental to the public of copies of sound recordings, films or computer programs shall be treated as licensed by the copyright owner subject only to the payment of such reasonable royalty or other payment as may be agreed or determined in default of agreement by the Copyright Tribunal.

(2) No such order shall apply if, or to the extent that, there is a licensing scheme certified for the purposes of this section under section 143 providing for the grant of licences.

(3) An order may make different provision for different cases and may specify cases by reference to any factor relating to the work, the copies rented, the renter or the circumstances of the rental.

(4) An order shall be made by statutory instrument; and no order shall be made unless a draft of it has been laid before and approved by a resolution of each House of Parliament.

(5) Copyright in a computer program is not infringed by the rental of copies to the public after the end of the period of 50 years from the end of the calendar year in which copies of it were first issued to the public in electronic form.

(6) Nothing in this section affects any liability under section 23 (secondary infringement) in respect of the rental of infringing copies.

**67 Playing of sound recordings for purposes of club, society, &c**

(1) It is not an infringement of the copyright in a sound recording to play it as part of the activities of, or for the benefit of, a club, society or other organisation if the following conditions are met.

(2) The conditions are—

(*a*) that the organisation is not established or conducted for profit and its main objects are charitable or are otherwise concerned with the advancement of religion, education or social welfare, and

(*b*) that the proceeds of any charge for admission to the place where the recording is to be heard are applied solely for the purposes of the organisation.

*Miscellaneous: broadcasts and cable programmes*

**68 Incidental recording for purposes of broadcast or cable programme**

(1) This section applies where by virtue of a licence or assignment of copyright a person is authorised to broadcast or include in a cable programme service—

(*a*) a literary, dramatic or musical work, or an adaptation of such a work,
(*b*) an artistic work, or
(*c*) a sound recording or film.

(2) He shall by virtue of this section be treated as licensed by the owner of the copyright in the work to do or authorise any of the following for the purposes of the broadcast or cable programme—

(*a*) in the case of a literary, dramatic or musical work, or an adaptation of such a work, to make a sound recording or film of the work or adaptation;

(*b*) in the case of an artistic work, to take a photograph or make a film of the work;

(*c*) in the case of a sound recording or film, to make a copy of it.

(3) That licence is subject to the condition that the recording, film, photograph or copy in question—

(*a*) shall not be used for any other purpose, and
(*b*) shall be destroyed within 28 days of being first used for broadcasting the work or, as the case may be, including it in a cable programme service.

(4) A recording, film, photograph or copy made in accordance with this section shall be treated as an infringing copy—

(*a*) for the purposes of any use in breach of the condition mentioned in subsection (3)(*a*), and
(*b*) for all purposes after that condition or the condition mentioned in subsection (3)(*b*) is broken.

**69 Recording for purposes of supervision and control of broadcasts and cable programmes**

(1) Copyright is not infringed by the making or use by the British Broadcasting Corporation, for the purpose of maintaining supervision and control over programmes broadcast by them, of recordings of those programmes.

(2) Copyright is not infringed by—

(*a*) the making or use of recordings by the Independent Broadcasting Authority for the purposes mentioned in section 4(7) of the Broadcasting Act 1981 (maintenance of supervision and control over programmes and advertisements); or
(*b*) anything done under or in pursuance of provision included in a contract between a programme contractor and the Authority in accordance with section 21 of that Act.

(3) Copyright is not infringed by—

(*a*) the making by or with the authority of the Cable Authority, or the use by that Authority, for the purpose of maintaining supervision and control over programmes included in services licensed under Part I of the Cable and Broadcasting Act 1984, of recordings of those programmes; or
(*b*) anything done under or in pursuance of—
  (i) a notice or direction given under section 16 of the Cable and Broadcasting Act 1984 (power of Cable Authority to require production of recordings); or
  (ii) a condition included in a licence by virtue of section 35 of that Act (duty of Authority to secure that recordings are available for certain purposes).

**70 Recording for purposes of time-shifting**

The making for private and domestic use of a recording of a broadcast or cable programme solely for the purpose of enabling it to be viewed or listened to at a more convenient time does not infringe any copyright in the broadcast or cable programme or in any work included in it.

**71 Photographs of television broadcasts or cable programmes**

The making for private and domestic use of a photograph of the whole or any part of an image forming part of a television broadcast or cable programme, or a copy of such a photograph, does not infringe any copyright in the broadcast or cable programme or in any film included in it.

**72 Free public showing or playing of broadcast or cable programme**

(1) The showing or playing in public of a broadcast or cable programme to an audience who have not paid for admission to the place where the broadcast or programme is to be seen or heard does not infringe any copyright in—

(*a*) the broadcast or cable programme, or
(*b*) any sound recording or film included in it.

(2) The audience shall be treated as having paid for admission to a place—

(*a*) if they have paid for admission to a place of which that place forms part; or
(*b*) if goods or services are supplied at that place (or a place of which it forms part)—
   (i) at prices which are substantially attributable to the facilities afforded for seeing or hearing the broadcast or programme, or
   (ii) at prices exceeding those usually charged there and which are partly attributable to those facilities.

(3) The following shall not be regarded as having paid for admission to a place—

(*a*) persons admitted as residents or inmates of the place;
(*b*) persons admitted as members of a club or society where the payment is only for membership of the club or society and the provision of facilities for seeing or hearing broadcasts or programmes is only incidental to the main purposes of the club or society.

(4) Where the making of the broadcast or inclusion of the programme in a cable programme service was an infringement of the copyright in a sound recording or film, the fact that it was heard or seen in public by the reception of the broadcast or programme shall be taken into account in assessing the damages for that infringement.

**73 Reception and re-transmission of broadcast in cable programme service**

(1) This section applies where a broadcast made from a place in the United Kingdom is, by reception and immediate re-transmission, included in a cable programme service.

(2) The copyright in the broadcast is not infringed—

(*a*) if the inclusion is in pursuance of a requirement imposed under section 13(1) of the Cable and Broadcasting Act 1984 (duty of Cable Authority to secure inclusion in cable service of certain programmes), or
(*b*) if and to the extent that the broadcast is made for reception in the area in which the cable programme service is provided and is not a satellite transmission or an encrypted transmission.

(3) The copyright in any work included in the broadcast is not infringed—

(*a*) if the inclusion is in pursuance of a requirement imposed under section 13(1) of the Cable and Broadcasting Act 1984 (duty of Cable Authority to secure inclusion in cable service of certain programmes), or
(*b*) if and to the extent that the broadcast is made for reception in the area in which the cable programme service is provided;

but where the making of the broadcast was an infringement of the copyright in the work, the fact that the broadcast was re-transmitted as a programme in a cable programme service shall be taken into account in assessing the damages for that infringement.

**74 Provision of sub-titled copies of broadcast or cable programme**

(1) A designated body may, for the purpose of providing people who are deaf or hard of hearing, or physically or mentally handicapped in other ways, with copies

which are sub-titled or otherwise modified for their special needs, make copies of television broadcasts or cable programmes and issue copies to the public, without infringing any copyright in the broadcasts or cable programmes or works included in them.

(2) A "designated body" means a body designated for the purposes of this section by order of the Secretary of State, who shall not designate a body unless he is satisfied that it is not established or conducted for profit.

(3) An order under this section shall be made by statutory instrument which shall be subject to annulment in pursuance of a resolution of either House of Parliament.

(4) This section does not apply if, or to the extent that, there is a licensing scheme certified for the purposes of this section under section 143 providing for the grant of licences.

### 75 Recording for archival purposes

(1) A recording of a broadcast or cable programme of a designated class, or a copy of such a recording, may be made for the purpose of being placed in an archive maintained by a designated body without thereby infringing any copyright in the broadcast or cable programme or in any work included in it.

(2) In subsection (1) "designated" means designated for the purposes of this section by order of the Secretary of State, who shall not designate a body unless he is satisfied that it is not established or conducted for profit.

(3) An order under this section shall be made by statutory instrument which shall be subject to annulment in pursuance of a resolution of either House of Parliament.

*Adaptations*

### 76 Adaptations

An act which by virtue of this Chapter may be done without infringing copyright in a literary, dramatic or musical work does not, where that work is an adaptation, infringe any copyright in the work from which the adaptation was made.

## Chapter IV

## Moral Rights

*Right to be identified as author or director*

### 77 Right to be identified as author or director

(1) The author of a copyright literary, dramatic, musical or artistic work, and the director of a copyright film, has the right to be identified as the author or director of the work in the circumstances mentioned in this section; but the right is not infringed unless it has been asserted in accordance with section 78.

(2) The author of a literary work (other than words intended to be sung or spoken with music) or a dramatic work has the right to be identified whenever—

(*a*) the work is published commercially, performed in public, broadcast or included in a cable programme service; or
(*b*) copies of a film or sound recording including the work are issued to the public;

and that right includes the right to be identified whenever any of those events occur in relation to an adaptation of the work as the author of the work from which the adaptation was made.

(3) The author of a musical work, or a literary work consisting of words intended to be sung or spoken with music, has the right to be identified whenever—

(*a*) the work is published commercially;
(*b*) copies of a sound recording of the work are issued to the public; or
(*c*) a film of which the sound-track includes the work is shown in public or copies of such a film are issued to the public;

and that right includes the right to be identified whenever any of those events occur in relation to an adaptation of the work as the author of the work from which the adaptation was made.

(4) The author of an artistic work has the right to be identified whenever—

(*a*) the work is published commercially or exhibited in public, or a visual image of it is broadcast or included in a cable programme service;
(*b*) a film including a visual image of the work is shown in public or copies of such a film are issued to the public; or
(*c*) in the case of a work of architecture in the form of a building or a model for a building, a sculpture or a work of artistic craftsmanship, copies of a graphic work representing it, or of a photograph of it, are issued to the public.

(5) The author of a work of architecture in the form of a building also has the right to be identified on the building as constructed or, where more than one building is constructed to the design, on the first to be constructed.

(6) The director of a film has the right to be identified whenever the film is shown in public, broadcast or included in a cable programme service or copies of the film are issued to the public.

(7) The right of the author or director under this section is—

(*a*) in the case of commercial publication or the issue to the public of copies of a film or sound recording, to be identified in or on each copy or, if that is not appropriate, in some other manner likely to bring his identity to the notice of a person acquiring a copy,
(*b*) in the case of identification on a building, to be identified by appropriate means visible to persons entering or approaching the building, and
(*c*) in any other case, to be identified in a manner likely to bring his identity to the attention of a person seeing or hearing the performance, exhibition, showing, broadcast or cable programme in question;

and the identification must in each case be clear and reasonably prominent.

(8) If the author or director in asserting his right to be identified specifies a pseudonym, initials or some other particular form of identification, that form shall be used; otherwise any reasonable form of identification may be used.

(9) This section has effect subject to section 79 (exceptions to right).

**78 Requirement that right be asserted**

(1) A person does not infringe the right conferred by section 77 (right to be identified as author or director) by doing any of the acts mentioned in that section unless the right has been asserted in accordance with the following provisions so as to bind him in relation to that act.

(2) The right may be asserted generally, or in relation to any specified act or description of acts—

(*a*) on an assignment of copyright in the work, by including in the instrument effecting the assignment a statement that the author or director asserts in relation to that work his right to be identified, or (*b*) by instrument in writing signed by the author or director.

(3) The right may also be asserted in relation to the public exhibition of an artistic work—

(*a*) by securing that when the author or other first owner of copyright parts with possession of the original, or of a copy made by him or under his direction or control, the author is identified on the original or copy, or on a frame, mount or other thing to which it is attached, or

(*b*) by including in a licence by which the author or other first owner of copyright authorises the making of copies of the work a statement signed by or on behalf of the person granting the licence that the author asserts his right to be identified in the event of the public exhibition of a copy made in pursuance of the licence.

(4) The persons bound by an assertion of the right under subsection (2) or (3) are—

(*a*) in the case of an assertion under subsection (2)(*a*), the assignee and anyone claiming through him, whether or not he has notice of the assertion;

(*b*) in the case of an assertion under subsection (2)(*b*), anyone to whose notice the assertion is brought;

(*c*) in the case of an assertion under subsection (3)(*a*), anyone into whose hands that original or copy comes, whether or not the identification is still present or visible;

(*d*) in the case of an assertion under subsection (3)(*b*), the licensee and anyone into whose hands a copy made in pursuance of the licence comes, whether or not he has notice of the assertion.

(5) In an action for infringement of the right the court shall, in considering remedies, take into account any delay in asserting the right.

**79 Exceptions to right**

(1) The right conferred by section 77 (right to be identified as author or director) is subject to the following exceptions.

(2) The right does not apply in relation to the following descriptions of work—

(*a*) a computer program;
(*b*) the design of a typeface;
(*c*) any computer-generated work.

(3) The right does not apply to anything done by or with the authority of the copyright owner where copyright in the work originally vested—

(*a*) in the author's employer by virtue of section 11(2) (works produced in course of employment), or

(*b*) in the director's employer by virtue of section 9(2)(*a*) (person to be treated as author of film).

(4) The right is not infringed by an act which by virtue of any of the following provisions would not infringe copyright in the work—

(*a*) section 30 (fair dealing for certain purposes), so far as it relates to the reporting of current events by means of a sound recording, film, broadcast or cable programme;
(*b*) section 31 (incidental inclusion of work in an artistic work, sound recording, film, broadcast or cable programme);
(*c*) section 32(3) (examination questions);
(*d*) section 45 (parliamentary and judicial proceedings);
(*e*) section 46(1) or (2) (Royal Commissions and statutory inquiries);
(*f*) section 51 (use of design documents and models);
(*g*) section 52 (effect of exploitation of design derived from artistic work);

(*h*) section 57 (anonymous or pseudonymous works: acts permitted on assumptions as to expiry of copyright or death of author).

(5) The right does not apply in relation to any work made for the purpose of reporting current events.

(6) The right does not apply in relation to the publication in—

(*a*) a newspaper, magazine or similar periodical, or

(*b*) an encyclopaedia, dictionary, yearbook or other collective work of reference,

of a literary, dramatic, musical or artistic work made for the purposes of such publication or made available with the consent of the author for the purposes of such publication.

(7) The right does not apply in relation to—

(*a*) a work in which Crown copyright or Parliamentary copyright subsists, or

(*b*) a work in which copyright originally vested in an international organisation by virtue of section 168,

unless the author or director has previously been identified as such in or on published copies of the work.

*Right to object to derogatory treatment of work*

**80 Right to object to derogatory treatment of work**

(1) The author of a copyright literary, dramatic, musical or artistic work, and the director of a copyright film, has the right in the circumstances mentioned in this section not to have his work subjected to derogatory treatment.

(2) For the purposes of this section—

(*a*) "treatment" of a work means any addition to, deletion from or alteration to or adaptation of the work, other than—

(i) a translation of a literary or dramatic work, or

(ii) an arrangement or transcription of a musical work involving no more than a change of key or register; and

(*b*) the treatment of a work is derogatory if it amounts to distortion or mutilation of the work or is otherwise prejudicial to the honour or reputation of the author or director;

and in the following provisions of this section references to a derogatory treatment of a work shall be construed accordingly.

(3) In the case of a literary, dramatic or musical work the right is infringed by a person who—

(*a*) publishes commercially, performs in public, broadcasts or includes in a cable programme service a derogatory treatment of the work; or

(*b*) issues to the public copies of a film or sound recording of, or including, a derogatory treatment of the work.

(4) In the case of an artistic work the right is infringed by a person who—

(*a*) publishes commercially or exhibits in public a derogatory treatment of the work, or broadcasts or includes in a cable programme service a visual image of a derogatory treatment of the work,

(*b*) shows in public a film including a visual image of a derogatory treatment of the work or issues to the public copies of such a film, or

(*c*) in the case of—

(i) a work of architecture in the form of a model for a building,

(ii) a sculpture, or

(iii) a work of artistic craftsmanship,

issues to the public copies of a graphic work representing, or of a photograph of, a derogatory treatment of the work.

(5) Subsection (4) does not apply to a work of architecture in the form of a building; but where the author of such a work is identified on the building and it is the subject of derogatory treatment he has the right to require the identification to be removed.

(6) In the case of a film, the right is infringed by a person who—

(*a*) shows in public, broadcasts or includes in a cable programme service a derogatory treatment of the film; or
(*b*) issues to the public copies of a derogatory treatment of the film,

or who, along with the film, plays in public, broadcasts or includes in a cable programme service, or issues to the public copies of, a derogatory treatment of the film sound-track.

(7) The right conferred by this section extends to the treatment of parts of a work resulting from a previous treatment by a person other than the author or director, if those parts are attributed to, or are likely to be regarded as the work of, the author or director.

(8) This section has effect subject to sections 81 and 82 (exceptions to and qualifications of right).

**81 Exceptions to right**

(1) The right conferred by section 80 (right to object to derogatory treatment of work) is subject to the following exceptions.

(2) The right does not apply to a computer program or to any computer-generated work.

(3) The right does not apply in relation to any work made for the purpose of reporting current events.

(4) The right does not apply in relation to the publication in—

(*a*) a newspaper, magazine or similar periodical, or
(*b*) an encyclopaedia, dictionary, yearbook or other collective work of reference,

of a literary, dramatic, musical or artistic work made for the purposes of such publication or made available with the consent of the author for the purposes of such publication.

Nor does the right apply in relation to any subsequent exploitation elsewhere of such a work without any modification of the published version.

(5) The right is not infringed by an act which by virtue of section 57 (anonymous or pseudonymous works: acts permitted on assumptions as to expiry of copyright or death of author) would not infringe copyright.

(6) The right is not infringed by anything done for the purpose of—

(*a*) avoiding the commission of an offence,
(*b*) complying with a duty imposed by or under an enactment, or
(*c*) in the case of the British Broadcasting Corporation, avoiding the inclusion in a programme broadcast by them of anything which offends against good taste or decency or which is likely to encourage or incite to crime or to lead to disorder or to be offensive to public feeling,

provided, where the author or director is identified at the time of the relevant act or has previously been identified in or on published copies of the work, that there is a sufficient disclaimer.

**82 Qualification of right in certain cases**

(1) This section applies to—

(*a*) works in which copyright originally vested in the author's employer by virtue of section 11(2) (works produced in course of employment) or in the director's employer by virtue of section 9(2)(*a*) (person to be treated as author of film),

(*b*) works in which Crown copyright or Parliamentary copyright subsists, and

(*c*) works in which copyright originally vested in an international organisation by virtue of section 168.

(2) The right conferred by section 80 (right to object to derogatory treatment of work) does not apply to anything done in relation to such a work by or with the authority of the copyright owner unless the author or director—

(*a*) is identified at the time of the relevant act, or

(*b*) has previously been identified in or on published copies of the work;

and where in such a case the right does apply, it is not infringed if there is a sufficient disclaimer.

**83 Infringement of right by possessing or dealing with infringing article**

(1) The right conferred by section 80 (right to object to derogatory treatment of work) is also infringed by a person who—

(*a*) possesses in the course of a business, or

(*b*) sells or lets for hire, or offers or exposes for sale or hire, or

(*c*) in the course of a business exhibits in public or distributes, or

(*d*) distributes otherwise than in the course of a business so as to affect prejudicially the honour or reputation of the author or director,

an article which is, and which he knows or has reason to believe is, an infringing article.

(2) An "infringing article" means a work or a copy of a work which—

(*a*) has been subjected to derogatory treatment within the meaning of section 80, and

(*b*) has been or is likely to be the subject of any of the acts mentioned in that section in circumstances infringing that right.

*False attribution of work*

**84 False attribution of work**

(1) A person has the right in the circumstances mentioned in this section—

(*a*) not to have a literary, dramatic, musical or artistic work falsely attributed to him as author, and

(*b*) not to have a film falsely attributed to him as director;

and in this section an "attribution", in relation to such a work, means a statement (express or implied) as to who is the author or director.

(2) The right is infringed by a person who—

(*a*) issues to the public copies of a work of any of those descriptions in or on which there is a false attribution, or

(*b*) exhibits in public an artistic work, or a copy of an artistic work, in or on which there is a false attribution.

(3) The right is also infringed by a person who—

(*a*) in the case of a literary, dramatic or musical work, performs the work in public, broadcasts it or includes it in a cable programme service as being the work of a person, or
(*b*) in the case of a film, shows it in public, broadcasts it or includes it in a cable programme service as being directed by a person,

knowing or having reason to believe that the attribution is false.

(4) The right is also infringed by the issue to the public or public display of material containing a false attribution in connection with any of the acts mentioned in subsection (2) or (3).

(5) The right is also infringed by a person who in the course of a business—

(*a*) possesses or deals with a copy of a work of any of the descriptions mentioned in subsection (1) in or on which there is a false attribution, or
(*b*) in the case of an artistic work, possesses or deals with the work itself when there is a false attribution in or on it,

knowing or having reason to believe that there is such an attribution and that it is false.

(6) In the case of an artistic work the right is also infringed by a person who in the course of a business—

(*a*) deals with a work which has been altered after the author parted with possession of it as being the unaltered work of the author, or
(*b*) deals with a copy of such a work as being a copy of the unaltered work of the author,

knowing or having reason to believe that that is not the case.

(7) References in this section to dealing are to selling or letting for hire, offering or exposing for sale or hire, exhibiting in public, or distributing.

(8) This section applies where, contrary to the fact—

(*a*) a literary, dramatic or musical work is falsely represented as being an adaptation of the work of a person, or
(*b*) a copy of an artistic work is falsely represented as being a copy made by the author of the artistic work,

as it applies where the work is falsely attributed to a person as author.

*Right to privacy of certain photographs and films*

**85 Right to privacy of certain photographs and films**

(1) A person who for private and domestic purposes commissions the taking of a photograph or the making of a film has, where copyright subsists in the resulting work, the right not to have—

(*a*) copies of the work issued to the public,
(*b*) the work exhibited or shown in public, or
(*c*) the work broadcast or included in a cable programme service;

and, except as mentioned in subsection (2), a person who does or authorises the doing of any of those acts infringes that right.

(2) The right is not infringed by an act which by virtue of any of the following provisions would not infringe copyright in the work—

(*a*) section 31 (incidental inclusion of work in an artistic work, film, broadcast or cable programme);
(*b*) section 45 (parliamentary and judicial proceedings);
(*c*) section 46 (Royal Commissions and statutory inquiries);
(*d*) section 50 (acts done under statutory authority);

(*e*) section 57 (anonymous or pseudonymous works: acts permitted on assumptions as to expiry of copyright or death of author).

*Supplementary*

**86 Duration of rights**

(1) The rights conferred by section 77 (right to be identified as author or director), section 80 (right to object to derogatory treatment of work) and section 85 (right to privacy of certain photographs and films) continue to subsist so long as copyright subsists in the work.

(2) The right conferred by section 84 (false attribution) continues to subsist until 20 years after a person's death.

**87 Consent and waiver of rights**

(1) It is not an infringement of any of the rights conferred by this Chapter to do any act to which the person entitled to the right has consented.

(2) Any of those rights may be waived by instrument in writing signed by the person giving up the right.

(3) A waiver—

(*a*) may relate to a specific work, to works of a specified description or to works generally, and may relate to existing or future works, and

(*b*) may be conditional or unconditional and may be expressed to be subject to revocation;

and if made in favour of the owner or prospective owner of the copyright in the work or works to which it relates, it shall be presumed to extend to his licensees and successors in title unless a contrary intention is expressed.

(4) Nothing in this Chapter shall be construed as excluding the operation of the general law of contract or estoppel in relation to an informal waiver or other transaction in relation to any of the rights mentioned in subsection (1).

**88 Application of provisions to joint works**

(1) The right conferred by section 77 (right to be identified as author or director) is, in the case of a work of joint authorship, a right of each joint author to be identified as a joint author and must be asserted in accordance with section 78 by each joint author in relation to himself.

(2) The right conferred by section 80 (right to object to derogatory treatment of work) is, in the case of a work of joint authorship, a right of each joint author and his right is satisfied if he consents to the treatment in question.

(3) A waiver under section 87 of those rights by one joint author does not affect the rights of the other joint authors.

(4) The right conferred by section 84 (false attribution) is infringed, in the circumstances mentioned in that section—

(*a*) by any false statement as to the authorship of a work of joint authorship, and

(*b*) by the false attribution of joint authorship in relation to a work of sole authorship;

and such a false attribution infringes the right of every person to whom authorship of any description is, whether rightly or wrongly, attributed.

(5) The above provisions also apply (with any necessary adaptations) in relation to a film which was, or is alleged to have been, jointly directed, as they apply to a work which is, or is alleged to be, a work of joint authorship.

A film is "jointly directed" if it is made by the collaboration of two or more directors and the contribution of each director is not distinct from that of the other director or directors.

(6) The right conferred by section 85 (right to privacy of certain photographs and films) is, in the case of a work made in pursuance of a joint commission, a right of each person who commissioned the making of the work, so that—

(*a*) the right of each is satisfied if he consents to the act in question, and

(*b*) a waiver under section 87 by one of them does not affect the rights of the others.

**89 Application of provisions to parts of works**

(1) The rights conferred by section 77 (right to be identified as author or director) and section 85 (right to privacy of certain photographs and films) apply in relation to the whole or any substantial part of a work.

(2) The rights conferred by section 80 (right to object to derogatory treatment of work) and section 84 (false attribution) apply in relation to the whole or any part of a work.

## CHAPTER V

## DEALINGS WITH RIGHTS IN COPYRIGHT WORKS

### *Copyright*

**90 Assignment and licences**

(1) Copyright is transmissible by assignment, by testamentary disposition or by operation of law, as personal or moveable property.

(2) An assignment or other transmission of copyright may be partial, that is, limited so as to apply—

(*a*) to one or more, but not all, of the things the copyright owner has the exclusive right to do;

(*b*) to part, but not the whole, of the period for which the copyright is to subsist.

(3) An assignment of copyright is not effective unless it is in writing signed by or on behalf of the assignor.

(4) A licence granted by a copyright owner is binding on every successor in title to his interest in the copyright, except a purchaser in good faith for valuable consideration and without notice (actual or constructive) of the licence or a person deriving title from such a purchaser; and references in this Part to doing anything with, or without, the licence of the copyright owner shall be construed accordingly.

**91 Prospective ownership of copyright**

(1) Where by an agreement made in relation to future copyright, and signed by or on behalf of the prospective owner of the copyright, the prospective owner purports to assign the future copyright (wholly or partially) to another person, then if, on the copyright coming into existence, the assignee or another person claiming under him would be entitled as against all other persons to require the copyright to be vested in him, the copyright shall vest in the assignee or his successor in title by virtue of this subsection.

(2) In this Part—

"future copyright" means copyright which will or may come into existence in respect of a future work or class of works or on the occurrence of a future event; and "prospective owner" shall be construed accordingly, and includes a person who is prospectively entitled to copyright by virtue of such an agreement as is mentioned in subsection (1).

(3) A licence granted by a prospective owner of copyright is binding on every successor in title to his interest (or prospective interest) in the right, except a purchaser in good faith for valuable consideration and without notice (actual or constructive) of the licence or a person deriving title from such a purchaser; and references in this Part to doing anything with, or without, the licence of the copyright owner shall be construed accordingly.

**92 Exclusive licences**

(1) In this Part an "exclusive licence" means a licence in writing signed by or on behalf of the copyright owner authorising the licensee to the exclusion of all other persons, including the person granting the licence, to exercise a right which would otherwise be exercisable exclusively by the copyright owner.

(2) The licensee under an exclusive licence has the same rights against a successor in title who is bound by the licence as he has against the person granting the licence.

**93 Copyright to pass under will with unpublished work**

Where under a bequest (whether specific or general) a person is entitled, beneficially or otherwise, to—

(*a*) an original document or other material thing recording or embodying a literary, dramatic, musical or artistic work which was not published before the death of the testator, or

(*b*) an original material thing containing a sound recording or film which was not published before the death of the testator,

the bequest shall, unless a contrary intention is indicated in the testator's will or a codicil to it, be construed as including the copyright in the work in so far as the testator was the owner of the copyright immediately before his death.

*Moral rights*

**94 Moral rights not assignable**

The rights conferred by Chapter IV (moral rights) are not assignable.

**95 Transmission of moral rights on death**

(1) On the death of a person entitled to the right conferred by section 77 (right to identification of author or director), section 80 (right to object to derogatory treatment of work) or section 85 (right to privacy of certain photographs and films)—

(*a*) the right passes to such person as he may by testamentary disposition specifically direct,

(*b*) if there is no such direction but the copyright in the work in question forms part of his estate, the right passes to the person to whom the copyright passes, and

(*c*) if or to the extent that the right does not pass under paragraph (*a*) or (*b*) it is exercisable by his personal representatives.

(2) Where copyright forming part of a person's estate passes in part to one person and in part to another, as for example where a bequest is limited so as to apply—

(*a*) to one or more, but not all, of the things the copyright owner has the exclusive right to do or authorise, or

(*b*) to part, but not the whole, of the period for which the copyright is to subsist,

any right which passes with the copyright by virtue of subsection (1) is correspondingly divided.

(3) Where by virtue of subsection (1)(*a*) or (*b*) a right becomes exercisable by more than one person—

(*a*) it may, in the case of the right conferred by section 77 (right to identification of author or director), be asserted by any of them;

(*b*) it is, in the case of the right conferred by section 80 (right to object to derogatory treatment of work) or section 85 (right to privacy of certain photographs and films), a right exercisable by each of them and is satisfied in relation to any of them if he consents to the treatment or act in question; and

(*c*) any waiver of the right in accordance with section 87 by one of them does not affect the rights of the others.

(4) A consent or waiver previously given or made binds any person to whom a right passes by virtue of subsection (1).

(5) Any infringement after a person's death of the right conferred by section 84 (false attribution) is actionable by his personal representatives.

(6) Any damages recovered by personal representatives by virtue of this section in respect of an infringement after a person's death shall devolve as part of his estate as if the right of action had subsisted and been vested in him immediately before his death.

## CHAPTER VI

## REMEDIES FOR INFRINGEMENT

*Rights and remedies of copyright owner*

### 96 Infringement actionable by copyright owner

(1) An infringement of copyright is actionable by the copyright owner.

(2) In an action for infringement of copyright all such relief by way of damages, injunctions, accounts or otherwise is available to the plaintiff as is available in respect of the infringement of any other property right.

(3) This section has effect subject to the following provisions of this Chapter.

### 97 Provisions as to damages in infringement action

(1) Where in an action for infringement of copyright it is shown that at the time of the infringement the defendant did not know, and had no reason to believe, that copyright subsisted in the work to which the action relates, the plaintiff is not entitled to damages against him, but without prejudice to any other remedy.

(2) The court may in an action for infringement of copyright having regard to all the circumstances, and in particular to—

(*a*) the flagrancy of the infringement, and

(*b*) any benefit accruing to the defendant by reason of the infringement,

award such additional damages as the justice of the case may require.

### 98 Undertaking to take licence of right in infringement proceedings

(1) If in proceedings for infringement of copyright in respect of which a licence is available as of right under section 144 (powers exercisable in consequence of

report of Monopolies and Mergers Commission) the defendant undertakes to take a licence on such terms as may be agreed or, in default of agreement, settled by the Copyright Tribunal under that section—

(*a*) no injunction shall be granted against him,
(*b*) no order for delivery up shall be made under section 99, and
(*c*) the amount recoverable against him by way of damages or on an account of profits shall not exceed double the amount which would have been payable by him as licensee if such a licence on those terms had been granted before the earliest infringement.

(2) An undertaking may be given at any time before final order in the proceedings, without any admission of liability.

(3) Nothing in this section affects the remedies available in respect of an infringement committed before licences of right were available.

**99 Order for delivery up**

(1) Where a person—

(*a*) has an infringing copy of a work in his possession, custody or control in the course of a business, or
(*b*) has in his possession, custody or control an article specifically designed or adapted for making copies of a particular copyright work, knowing or having reason to believe that it has been or is to be used to make infringing copies,

the owner of the copyright in the work may apply to the court for an order that the infringing copy or article be delivered up to him or to such other person as the court may direct.

(2) An application shall not be made after the end of the period specified in section 113 (period after which remedy of delivery up not available); and no order shall be made unless the court also makes, or it appears to the court that there are grounds for making, an order under section 114 (order as to disposal of infringing copy or other article).

(3) A person to whom an infringing copy or other article is delivered up in pursuance of an order under this section shall, if an order under section 114 is not made, retain it pending the making of an order, or the decision not to make an order, under that section.

(4) Nothing in this section affects any other power of the court.

**100 Right to seize infringing copies and other articles**

(1) An infringing copy of a work which is found exposed or otherwise immediately available for sale or hire, and in respect of which the copyright owner would be entitled to apply for an order under section 99, may be seized and detained by him or a person authorised by him.

The right to seize and detain is exercisable subject to the following conditions and is subject to any decision of the court under section 114.

(2) Before anything is seized under this section notice of the time and place of the proposed seizure must be given to a local police station.

(3) A person may for the purpose of exercising the right conferred by this section enter premises to which the public have access but may not seize anything in the possession, custody or control of a person at a permanent or regular place of business of his, and may not use any force.

(4) At the time when anything is seized under this section there shall be left at the place where it was seized a notice in the prescribed form containing the

prescribed particulars as to the person by whom or on whose authority the seizure is made and the grounds on which it is made.

(5) In this section—

"premises" includes land, buildings, moveable structures, vehicles, vessels, aircraft and hovercraft; and

"prescribed" means prescribed by order of the Secretary of State.

(6) An order of the Secretary of State under this section shall be made by statutory instrument which shall be subject to annulment in pursuance of a resolution of either House of Parliament.

*Rights and remedies of exclusive licensee*

**101 Rights and remedies of exclusive licensee**

(1) An exclusive licensee has, except against the copyright owner, the same rights and remedies in respect of matters occurring after the grant of the licence as if the licence had been an assignment.

(2) His rights and remedies are concurrent with those of the copyright owner; and references in the relevant provisions of this Part to the copyright owner shall be construed accordingly.

(3) In an action brought by an exclusive licensee by virtue of this section a defendant may avail himself of any defence which would have been available to him if the action had been brought by the copyright owner.

**102 Exercise of concurrent rights**

(1) Where an action for infringement of copyright brought by the copyright owner or an exclusive licensee relates (wholly or partly) to an infringement in respect of which they have concurrent rights of action, the copyright owner or, as the case may be, the exclusive licensee may not, without the leave of the court, proceed with the action unless the other is either joined as a plaintiff or added as a defendant.

(2) A copyright owner or exclusive licensee who is added as a defendant in pursuance of subsection (1) is not liable for any costs in the action unless he takes part in the proceedings.

(3) The above provisions do not affect the granting of interlocutory relief on an application by a copyright owner or exclusive licensee alone.

(4) Where an action for infringement of copyright is brought which relates (wholly or partly) to an infringement in respect of which the copyright owner and an exclusive licensee have or had concurrent rights of action—

(*a*) the court shall in assessing damages take into account—

(i) the terms of the licence, and

(ii) any pecuniary remedy already awarded or available to either of them in respect of the infringement;

(*b*) no account of profits shall be directed if an award of damages has been made, or an account of profits has been directed, in favour of the other of them in respect of the infringement; and

(*c*) the court shall if an account of profits is directed apportion the profits between them as the court considers just, subject to any agreement between them;

and these provisions apply whether or not the copyright owner and the exclusive licensee are both parties to the action.

(5) The copyright owner shall notify any exclusive licensee having concurrent rights before applying for an order under section 99 (order for delivery up) or exercising the right conferred by section 100 (right of seizure); and the court may on the application of the licensee make such order under section 99 or, as the case may be, prohibiting or permitting the exercise by the copyright owner of the right conferred by section 100, as it thinks fit having regard to the terms of the licence.

*Remedies for infringement of moral rights*

## 103 Remedies for infringement of moral rights

(1) An infringement of a right conferred by Chapter IV (moral rights) is actionable as a breach of statutory duty owed to the person entitled to the right.

(2) In proceedings for infringement of the right conferred by section 80 (right to object to derogatory treatment of work) the court may, if it thinks it is an adequate remedy in the circumstances, grant an injunction on terms prohibiting the doing of any act unless a disclaimer is made, in such terms and in such manner as may be approved by the court, dissociating the author or director from the treatment of the work.

*Presumptions*

## 104 Presumptions relevant to literary, dramatic, musical and artistic works

(1) The following presumptions apply in proceedings brought by virtue of this Chapter with respect to a literary, dramatic, musical or artistic work.

(2) Where a name purporting to be that of the author appeared on copies of the work as published or on the work when it was made, the person whose name appeared shall be presumed, until the contrary is proved—

(*a*) to be the author of the work;
(*b*) to have made it in circumstances not falling within section 11(2), 163, 165 or 168 (works produced in course of employment, Crown copyright, Parliamentary copyright or copyright of certain international organisations).

(3) In the case of a work alleged to be a work of joint authorship, subsection (2) applies in relation to each person alleged to be one of the authors.

(4) Where no name purporting to be that of the author appeared as mentioned in subsection (2) but—

(*a*) the work qualifies for copyright protection by virtue of section 155 (qualification by reference to country of first publication), and
(*b*) a name purporting to be that of the publisher appeared on copies of the work as first published,

the person whose name appeared shall be presumed, until the contrary is proved, to have been the owner of the copyright at the time of publication.

(5) If the author of the work is dead or the identity of the author cannot be ascertained by reasonable inquiry, it shall be presumed, in the absence of evidence to the contrary—

(*a*) that the work is an original work, and
(*b*) that the plaintiff's allegations as to what was the first publication of the work and as to the country of first publication are correct.

**105 Presumptions relevant to sound recordings and films**

(1) In proceedings brought by virtue of this Chapter with respect to a sound recording, where copies of the recording as issued to the public bear a label or other mark stating—

(*a*) that a named person was the owner of copyright in the recording at the date of issue of the copies, or
(*b*) that the recording was first published in a specified year or in a specified country,

the label or mark shall be admissible as evidence of the facts stated and shall be presumed to be correct until the contrary is proved.

(2) In proceedings brought by virtue of this Chapter with respect to a film, where copies of the film as issued to the public bear a statement—

(*a*) that a named person was the author or director of the film,
(*b*) that a named person was the owner of copyright in the film at the date of issue of the copies, or
(*c*) that the film was first published in a specified year or in a specified country,

the statement shall be admissible as evidence of the facts stated and shall be presumed to be correct until the contrary is proved.

(3) In proceedings brought by virtue of this Chapter with respect to a computer program, where copies of the program are issued to the public in electronic form bearing a statement—

(*a*) that a named person was the owner of copyright in the program at the date of issue of the copies, or
(*b*) that the program was first published in a specified country or that copies of it were first issued to the public in electronic form in a specified year,

the statement shall be admissible as evidence of the facts stated and shall be presumed to be correct until the contrary is proved.

(4) The above presumptions apply equally in proceedings relating to an infringement alleged to have occurred before the date on which the copies were issued to the public.

(5) In proceedings brought by virtue of this Chapter with respect to a film, where the film as shown in public, broadcast or included in a cable programme service bears a statement—

(*a*) that a named person was the author or director of the film, or
(*b*) that a named person was the owner of copyright in the film immediately after it was made,

the statement shall be admissible as evidence of the facts stated and shall be presumed to be correct until the contrary is proved.

This presumption applies equally in proceedings relating to an infringement alleged to have occurred before the date on which the film was shown in public, broadcast or included in a cable programme service.

**106 Presumptions relevant to works subject to Crown copyright**

In proceedings brought by virtue of this Chapter with respect to a literary, dramatic or musical work in which Crown copyright subsists, where there appears on printed copies of the work a statement of the year in which the work was first published commercially, that statement shall be admissible as evidence of the fact stated and shall be presumed to be correct in the absence of evidence to the contrary.

*Offences*

**107 Criminal liability for making or dealing with infringing articles, &c**

(1) A person commits an offence who, without the licence of the copyright owner—

(*a*) makes for sale or hire, or
(*b*) imports into the United Kingdom otherwise than for his private and domestic use, or
(*c*) possesses in the course of a business with a view to committing any act infringing the copyright, or
(*d*) in the course of a business—

(i) sells or lets for hire, or
(ii) offers or exposes for sale or hire, or
(iii) exhibits in public, or
(iv) distributes, or

(*e*) distributes otherwise than in the course of a business to such an extent as to affect prejudicially the owner of the copyright,

an article which is, and which he knows or has reason to believe is, an infringing copy of a copyright work.

(2) A person commits an offence who—

(*a*) makes an article specifically designed or adapted for making copies of a particular copyright work, or
(*b*) has such an article in his possession,

knowing or having reason to believe that it is to be used to make infringing copies for sale or hire or for use in the course of a business.

(3) Where copyright is infringed (otherwise than by reception of a broadcast or cable programme)—

(*a*) by the public performance of a literary, dramatic or musical work, or
(*b*) by the playing or showing in public of a sound recording or film,

any person who caused the work to be so performed, played or shown is guilty of an offence if he knew or had reason to believe that copyright would be infringed.

(4) A person guilty of an offence under subsection (1)(*a*), (*b*), (*d*)(iv) or (*e*) is liable—

(*a*) on summary conviction to imprisonment for a term not exceeding six months or a fine not exceeding the statutory maximum, or both;
(*b*) on conviction on indictment to a fine or imprisonment for a term not exceeding two years, or both.

(5) A person guilty of any other offence under this section is liable on summary conviction to imprisonment for a term not exceeding six months or a fine not exceeding level 5 on the standard scale, or both.

(6) Sections 104 to 106 (presumptions as to various matters connected with copyright) do not apply to proceedings for an offence under this section; but without prejudice to their application in proceedings for an order under section 108 below.

**108 Order for delivery up in criminal proceedings**

(1) The court before which proceedings are brought against a person for an offence under section 107 may, if satisfied that at the time of his arrest or charge—

(*a*) he had in his possession, custody or control in the course of a business an infringing copy of a copyright work, or (*b*) he had in his possession, custody or control an article specifically designed or adapted for making copies of a particular copyright work, knowing or having reason to believe that it had been or was to be used to make infringing copies,

order that the infringing copy or article be delivered up to the copyright owner or to such other person as the court may direct.

(2) For this purpose a person shall be treated as charged with an offence—

(*a*) in England, Wales and Northern Ireland, when he is orally charged or is served with a summons or indictment;
(*b*) in Scotland, when he is cautioned, charged or served with a complaint or indictment.

(3) An order may be made by the court of its own motion or on the application of the prosecutor (or, in Scotland, the Lord Advocate or procurator-fiscal), and may be made whether or not the person is convicted of the offence, but shall not be made—

(*a*) after the end of the period specified in section 113 (period after which remedy of delivery up not available), or
(*b*) if it appears to the court unlikely that any order will be made under section 114 (order as to disposal of infringing copy or other article);

(4) An appeal lies from an order made under this section by a magistrates' court—

(*a*) in England and Wales, to the Crown Court, and
(*b*) in Northern Ireland, to the county court;

and in Scotland, where an order has been made under this section, the person from whose possession, custody or control the infringing copy or article has been removed may, without prejudice to any other form of appeal under any rule of law, appeal against that order in the same manner as against sentence.

(5) A person to whom an infringing copy or other article is delivered up in pursuance of an order under this section shall retain it pending the making of an order, or the decision not to make an order, under section 114.

(6) Nothing in this section affects the powers of the court under section 43 of the Powers of Criminal Courts Act 1973, section 223 or 436 of the Criminal Procedure (Scotland) Act 1975 or Article 7 of the Criminal Justice (Northern Ireland) Order 1980 (general provisions as to forfeiture in criminal proceedings).

**109 Search warrants**

(1) Where a justice of the peace (in Scotland, a sheriff or justice of the peace) is satisfied by information on oath given by a constable (in Scotland, by evidence on oath) that there are reasonable grounds for believing—

(*a*) that an offence under section 107(1)(*a*), (*b*) (*d*)(iv) or (*e*) has been or is about to be committed in any premises, and
(*b*) that evidence that such an offence has been or is about to be committed is in those premises,

he may issue a warrant authorising a constable to enter and search the premises, using such reasonable force as is necessary.

(2) The power conferred by subsection (1) does not, in England and Wales, extend to authorising a search for material of the kinds mentioned in section 9(2) of the Police and Criminal Evidence Act 1984 (certain classes of personal or confidential material).

(3) A warrant under this section—

(*a*) may authorise persons to accompany any constable executing the warrant, and
(*b*) remains in force for 28 days from the date of its issue.

(4) In executing a warrant issued under this section a constable may seize an article if he reasonably believes that it is evidence that any offence under section 107(1) has been or is about to be committed.

(5) In this section "premises" includes land, buildings, moveable structures, vehicles, vessels, aircraft and hovercraft.

**110 Offence by body corporate: liability of officers**

(1) Where an offence under section 107 committed by a body corporate is proved to have been committed with the consent or connivance of a director, manager, secretary or other similar officer of the body, or a person purporting to act in any such capacity, he as well as the body corporate is guilty of the offence and liable to be proceeded against and punished accordingly.

(2) In relation to a body corporate whose affairs are managed by its members "director" means a member of the body corporate.

*Provision for preventing importation of infringing copies*

**111 Infringing copies may be treated as prohibited goods**

(1) The owner of the copyright in a published literary, dramatic or musical work may give notice in writing to the Commissioners of Customs and Excise—

(*a*) that he is the owner of the copyright in the work, and
(*b*) that he requests the Commissioners, for a period specified in the notice, to treat as prohibited goods printed copies of the work which are infringing copies.

(2) The period specified in a notice under subsection (1) shall not exceed five years and shall not extend beyond the period for which copyright is to subsist.

(3) The owner of the copyright in a sound recording or film may give notice in writing to the Commissioners of Customs and Excise—

(*a*) that he is the owner of the copyright in the work,
(*b*) that infringing copies of the work are expected to arrive in the United Kingdom at a time and a place specified in the notice, and
(*c*) that he requests the Commissioners to treat the copies as prohibited goods.

(4) When a notice is in force under this section the importation of goods to which the notice relates, otherwise than by a person for his private and domestic use, is prohibited; but a person is not by reason of the prohibition liable to any penalty other than forfeiture of the goods.

**112 Power of Commissioners of Customs and Excise to make regulations**

(1) The Commissioners of Customs and Excise may make regulations prescribing the form in which notice is to be given under section 111 and requiring a person giving notice—

(*a*) to furnish the Commissioners with such evidence as may be specified in the regulations, either on giving notice or when the goods are imported, or at both those times, and
(*b*) to comply with such other conditions as may be specified in the regulations.

(2) The regulations may, in particular, require a person giving such a notice—

(*a*) to pay such fees in respect of the notice as may be specified by the regulations;
(*b*) to give such security as may be so specified in respect of any liability or expense which the Commissioners may incur in consequence of the notice by reason of the detention of any article or anything done to an article detained;
(*c*) to indemnify the Commissioners against any such liability or expense, whether security has been given or not.

(3) The regulations may make different provision as respects different classes of case to which they apply and may include such incidental and supplementary provisions as the Commissioners consider expedient.

(4) Regulations under this section shall be made by statutory instrument which shall be subject to annulment in pursuance of a resolution of either House of Parliament.

(5) Section 17 of the Customs and Excise Management Act 1979 (general provisions as to Commissioners' receipts) applies to fees paid in pursuance of regulations under this section as to receipts under the enactments relating to customs and excise.

*Supplementary*

**113 Period after which remedy of delivery up not available**

(1) An application for an order under section 99 (order for delivery up in civil proceedings) may not be made after the end of the period of six years from the date on which the infringing copy or article in question was made, subject to the following provisions.

(2) If during the whole or any part of that period the copyright owner—

(*a*) is under a disability, or
(*b*) is prevented by fraud or concealment from discovering the facts entitling him to apply for an order,

an application may be made at any time before the end of the period of six years from the date on which he ceased to be under a disability or, as the case may be, could with reasonable diligence have discovered those facts.

(3) In subsection (2) "disability"—

(*a*) in England and Wales, has the same meaning as in the Limitation Act 1980;
(*b*) in Scotland, means legal disability within the meaning of the Prescription and Limitation (Scotland) Act 1973;
(*c*) in Northern Ireland, has the same meaning as in the Statute of Limitations (Northern Ireland) 1958.

(4) An order under section 108 (order for delivery up in criminal proceedings) shall not, in any case, be made after the end of the period of six years from the date on which the infringing copy or article in question was made.

**114 Order as to disposal of infringing copy or other article**

(1) An application may be made to the court for an order that an infringing copy or other article delivered up in pursuance of an order under section 99 or 108, or seized and detained in pursuance of the right conferred by section 100, shall be—

(*a*) forfeited to the copyright owner, or
(*b*) destroyed or otherwise dealt with as the court may think fit,

or for a decision that no such order should be made.

(2) In considering what order (if any) should be made, the court shall consider

whether other remedies available in an action for infringement of copyright would be adequate to compensate the copyright owner and to protect his interests.

(3) Provision shall be made by rules of court as to the service of notice on persons having an interest in the copy or other articles, and any such person is entitled—

(*a*) to appear in proceedings for an order under this section, whether or not he was served with notice, and

(*b*) to appeal against any order made, whether or not he appeared;

and an order shall not take effect until the end of the period within which notice of an appeal may be given or, if before the end of that period notice of appeal is duly given, until the final determination or abandonment of the proceedings on the appeal.

(4) Where there is more than one person interested in a copy or other article, the court shall make such order as it thinks just and may (in particular) direct that the article be sold, or otherwise dealt with, and the proceeds divided.

(5) If the court decides that no order should be made under this section, the person in whose possession, custody or control the copy or other article was before being delivered up or seized is entitled to its return.

(6) References in this section to a person having an interest in a copy or other article include any person in whose favour an order could be made in respect of it under this section or under section 204 or 231 of this Act or section 58C of the Trade Marks Act 1938 (which make similar provision in relation to infringement of rights in performances, design right and trade marks).

**115 Jurisdiction of county court and sheriff court**

(1) In England, Wales and Northern Ireland a county court may entertain proceedings under—

section 99 (order for delivery up of infringing copy or other article),
section 101(5) (order as to exercise of rights by copyright owner where exclusive licensee has concurrent rights), or
section 114 (order as to disposal of infringing copy or other article),

where the value of the infringing copies and other articles in question does not exceed the county court limit for actions in tort.

(2) In Scotland proceedings for an order under any of those provisions may be brought in the sheriff court.

(3) Nothing in this section shall be construed as affecting the jurisdiction of the High Court or, in Scotland, the Court of Session.

## Chapter VII

## Copyright Licensing

*Licensing schemes and licensing bodies*

**116 Licensing schemes and licensing bodies**

(1) In this Part a "licensing scheme" means a scheme setting out—

(*a*) the classes of case in which the operator of the scheme, or the person on whose behalf he acts, is willing to grant copyright licences, and

(*b*) the terms on which licences would be granted in those classes of case;

and for this purpose a "scheme" includes anything in the nature of a scheme, whether described as a scheme or as a tariff or by any other name.

(2) In this Chapter a "licensing body" means a society or other organisation

which has as its main object, or one of its main objects, the negotiation or granting, either as owner or prospective owner of copyright or as agent for him, of copyright licences, and whose objects include the granting of licences covering works of more than one author.

(3) In this section "copyright licences" means licences to do, or authorise the doing of, any of the acts restricted by copyright.

(4) References in this Chapter to licences or licensing schemes covering works of more than one author do not include licences or schemes covering only—

(*a*) a single collective work or collective works of which the authors are the same, or

(*b*) works made by, or by employees of or commissioned by, a single invididual, firm, company or group of companies.

For this purpose a group of companies means a holding company and its subsidiaries, within the meaning of section 736 of the Companies Act 1985.

*References and applications with respect to licensing schemes*

**117 Licensing schemes to which ss 118 to 123 apply**

Sections 118 to 123 (references and applications with respect to licensing schemes) apply to—

(*a*) licensing schemes operated by licensing bodies in relation to the copyright in literary, dramatic, musical or artistic works or films (or film sound-tracks when accompanying a film) which cover works of more than one author, so far as they relate to licences for—

(i) copying the work,

(ii) performing, playing or showing the work in public, or

(iii) broadcasting the work or including it in a cable programme service;

(*b*) all licensing schemes in relation to the copyright in sound recordings (other than film sound-tracks when accompanying a film), broadcasts or cable programmes, or the typographical arrangement of published editions; and

(*c*) all licensing schemes in relation to the copyright in sound recordings, films or computer programs so far as they relate to licences for the rental of copies to the public;

and in those sections "licensing scheme" means a licensing scheme of any of those descriptions.

**118 Reference of proposed licensing scheme to tribunal**

(1) The terms of a licensing scheme proposed to be operated by a licensing body may be referred to the Copyright Tribunal by an organisation claiming to be representative of persons claiming that they require licences in cases of a description to which the scheme would apply, either generally or in relation to any description of case.

(2) The Tribunal shall first decide whether to entertain the reference, and may decline to do so on the ground that the reference is premature.

(3) If the Tribunal decides to entertain the reference it shall consider the matter referred and make such order, either confirming or varying the proposed scheme, either generally or so far as it relates to cases of the description to which the reference relates, as the Tribunal may determine to be reasonable in the circumstances.

(4) The order may be made so as to be in force indefinitely or for such period as the Tribunal may determine.

**119 Reference of licensing scheme to tribunal**

(1) If while a licensing scheme is in operation a dispute arises between the operator of the scheme and—

(*a*) a person claiming that he requires a licence in a case of a description to which the scheme applies, or
(*b*) an organisation claiming to be representative of such persons,

that person or organisation may refer the scheme to the Copyright Tribunal in so far as it relates to cases of that description.

(2) A scheme which has been referred to the Tribunal under this section shall remain in operation until proceedings on the reference are concluded.

(3) The Tribunal shall consider the matter in dispute and make such order, either confirming or varying the scheme so far as it relates to cases of the description to which the reference relates, as the Tribunal may determine to be reasonable in the circumstances.

(4) The order may be made so as to be in force indefinitely or for such period as the Tribunal may determine.

**120 Further reference of scheme to tribunal**

(1) Where the Copyright Tribunal has on a previous reference of a licensing scheme under section 118 or 119, or under this section, made an order with respect to the scheme, then, while the order remains in force—

(*a*) the operator of the scheme,
(*b*) a person claiming that he requires a licence in a case of the description to which the order applies, or
(*c*) an organisation claiming to be representative of such persons,

may refer the scheme again to the Tribunal so far as it relates to cases of that description.

(2) A licensing scheme shall not, except with the special leave of the Tribunal, be referred again to the Tribunal in respect of the same description of cases—

(*a*) within twelve months from the date of the order on the previous reference, or
(*b*) if the order was made so as to be in force for 15 months or less, until the last three months before the expiry of the order.

(3) A scheme which has been referred to the Tribunal under this section shall remain in operation until proceedings on the reference are concluded.

(4) The Tribunal shall consider the matter in dispute and make such order, either confirming, varying or further varying the scheme so far as it relates to cases of the description to which the reference relates, as the Tribunal may determine to be reasonable in the circumstances.

(5) The order may be made so as to be in force indefinitely or for such period as the Tribunal may determine.

**121 Application for grant of licence in connection with licensing scheme**

(1) A person who claims, in a case covered by a licensing scheme, that the operator of the scheme has refused to grant him or procure the grant to him of a licence in accordance with the scheme, or has failed to do so within a reasonable time after being asked, may apply to the Copyright Tribunal.

(2) A person who claims, in a case excluded from a licensing scheme, that the operator of the scheme either—

(*a*) has refused to grant him a licence or procure the grant to him of a licence, or has failed to do so within a reasonable time of being asked, and that in the circumstances it is unreasonable that a licence should not be granted, or
(*b*) proposes terms for a licence which are unreasonable,

may apply to the Copyright Tribunal.

(3) A case shall be regarded as excluded from a licensing scheme for the purposes of subsection (2) if—

(*a*) the scheme provides for the grant of licences subject to terms excepting matters from the licence and the case falls within such an exception, or
(*b*) the case is so similar to those in which licences are granted under the scheme that it is unreasonable that it should not be dealt with in the same way.

(4) If the Tribunal is satisfied that the claim is well-founded, it shall make an order declaring that, in respect of the matters specified in the order, the applicant is entitled to a licence on such terms as the Tribunal may determine to be applicable in accordance with the scheme or, as the case may be, to be reasonable in the circumstances.

(5) The order may be made so as to be in force indefinitely or for such period as the Tribunal may determine.

### 122 Application for review of order as to entitlement to licence

(1) Where the Copyright Tribunal has made an order under section 121 that a person is entitled to a licence under a licensing scheme, the operator of the scheme or the original applicant may apply to the Tribunal to review its order.

(2) An application shall not be made, except with the special leave of the Tribunal—

(*a*) within twelve months from the date of the order, or of the decision on a previous application under this section, or
(*b*) if the order was made so as to be in force for 15 months or less, or as a result of the decision on a previous application under this section is due to expire within 15 months of that decision, until the last three months before the expiry date.

(3) The Tribunal shall on an application for review confirm or vary its order as the Tribunal may determine to be reasonable having regard to the terms applicable in accordance with the licensing scheme or, as the case may be, the circumstances of the case.

### 123 Effect of order of tribunal as to licensing scheme

(1) A licensing scheme which has been confirmed or varied by the Copyright Tribunal—

(*a*) under section 118 (reference of terms of proposed scheme), or
(*b*) under section 119 or 120 (reference of existing scheme to Tribunal),

shall be in force or, as the case may be, remain in operation, so far as it relates to the description of case in respect of which the order was made, so long as the order remains in force.

(2) While the order is in force a person who in a case of a class to which the order applies—

(*a*) pays to the operator of the scheme any charges payable under the scheme in respect of a licence covering the case in question or, if the amount cannot be ascertained, gives an undertaking to the operator to pay them when ascertained, and (*b*) complies with the other terms applicable to such a licence under the scheme,

shall be in the same position as regards infringement of copyright as if he had at all material times been the holder of a licence granted by the owner of the copyright in question in accordance with the scheme.

(3) The Tribunal may direct that the order, so far as it varies the amount of charges payable, has effect from a date before that on which it is made, but not earlier than the date on which the reference was made or, if later, on which the scheme came into operation.

If such a direction is made—

(*a*) any necessary repayments, or further payments, shall be made in respect of charges already paid, and
(*b*) the reference in subsection (2)(*a*) to the charges payable under the scheme shall be construed as a reference to the charges so payable by virtue of the order.

No such direction may be made where subsection (4) below applies.

(4) An order of the Tribunal under section 119 or 120 made with respect to a scheme which is certified for any purpose under section 143 has effect, so far as it varies the scheme by reducing the charges payable for licences, from the date on which the reference was made to the Tribunal.

(5) Where the Tribunal has made an order under section 121 (order as to entitlement to licence under licensing scheme) and the order remains in force, the person in whose favour the order is made shall if he—

(*a*) pays to the operator of the scheme any charges payable in accordance with the order or, if the amount cannot be ascertained, gives an undertaking to pay the charges when ascertained, and
(*b*) complies with the other terms specified in the order,

be in the same position as regards infringement of copyright as if he had at all material times been the holder of a licence granted by the owner of the copyright in question on the terms specified in the order.

*References and applications with respect to licensing by licensing bodies*

### 124 Licences to which ss 125 to 128 apply

Sections 125 to 128 (references and applications with respect to licensing by licensing bodies) apply to the following descriptions of licence granted by a licensing body otherwise than in pursuance of a licensing scheme—

(*a*) licences relating to the copyright in literary, dramatic, musical or artistic works or films (or film sound-tracks when accompanying a film) which cover works of more than one author, so far as they authorise—

  (i) copying the work,
  (ii) performing, playing or showing the work in public, or
  (iii) broadcasting the work or including it in a cable programme service;

(*b*) any licence relating to the copyright in a sound recording (other than a film sound-track when accompanying a film), broadcast or cable programme, or the typographical arrangement of a published edition; and
(*c*) all licences in relation to the copyright in sound recordings, films or computer programs so far as they relate to the rental of copies to the public;

and in those sections a "licence" means a licence of any of those descriptions.

**125 Reference to tribunal of proposed licence**

(1) The terms on which a licensing body proposes to grant a licence may be referred to the Copyright Tribunal by the prospective licensee.

(2) The Tribunal shall first decide whether to entertain the reference, and may decline to do so on the ground that the reference is premature.

(3) If the Tribunal decides to entertain the reference it shall consider the terms of the proposed licence and make such order, either confirming or varying the terms, as it may determine to be reasonable in the circumstances.

(4) The order may be made so as to be in force indefinitely or for such period as the Tribunal may determine.

**126 Reference to tribunal of expiring licence**

(1) A licensee under a licence which is due to expire, by effluxion of time or as a result of notice given by the licensing body, may apply to the Copyright Tribunal on the ground that it is unreasonable in the circumstances that the licence should cease to be in force.

(2) Such an application may not be made until the last three months before the licence is due to expire.

(3) A licence in respect of which a reference has been made to the Tribunal shall remain in operation until proceedings on the reference are concluded.

(4) If the Tribunal finds the application well-founded, it shall make an order declaring that the licensee shall continue to be entitled to the benefit of the licence on such terms as the Tribunal may determine to be reasonable in the circumstances.

(5) An order of the Tribunal under this section may be made so as to be in force indefinitely or for such period as the Tribunal may determine.

**127 Application for review of order as to licence**

(1) Where the Copyright Tribunal has made an order under section 125 or 126, the licensing body or the person entitled to the benefit of the order may apply to the Tribunal to review its order.

(2) An application shall not be made, except with the special leave of the Tribunal—

(*a*) within twelve months from the date of the order or of the decision on a previous application under this section, or

(*b*) if the order was made so as to be in force for 15 months or less, or as a result of the decision on a previous application under this section is due to expire within 15 months of that decision, until the last three months before the expiry date.

(3) The Tribunal shall on an application for review confirm or vary its order as the Tribunal may determine to be reasonable in the circumstances.

**128 Effect of order of Tribunal as to licence**

(1) Where the Copyright Tribunal has made an order under section 125 or 126 and the order remains in force, the person entitled to the benefit of the order shall if he—

(*a*) pays to the licensing body any charges payable in accordance with the order or, if the amount cannot be ascertained, gives an undertaking to pay the charges when ascertained, and

(*b*) complies with the other terms specified in the order,

be in the same position as regards infringement of copyright as if he had at all material times been the holder of a licence granted by the owner of the copyright in question on the terms specified in the order.

(2) The benefit of the order may be assigned—

(*a*) in the case of an order under section 125, if assignment is not prohibited under the terms of the Tribunal's order; and

(*b*) in the case of an order under section 126, if assignment was not prohibited under the terms of the original licence.

(3) The Tribunal may direct that an order under section 125 or 126, or an order under section 127 varying such an order, so far as it varies the amount of charges payable, has effect from a date before that on which it is made, but not earlier than the date on which the reference or application was made or, if later, on which the licence was granted or, as the case may be, was due to expire.

If such a direction is made—

(*a*) any necessary repayments, or further payments, shall be made in respect of charges already paid, and

(*b*) the reference in subsection (1)(*a*) to the charges payable in accordance with the order shall be construed, where the order is varied by a later order, as a reference to the charges so payable by virtue of the later order.

*Factors to be taken into account in certain classes of case*

### 129 General considerations: unreasonable discrimination

In determining what is reasonable on a reference or application under this Chapter relating to a licensing scheme or licence, the Copyright Tribunal shall have regard to—

(*a*) the availability of other schemes, or the granting of other licences, to other persons in similar circumstances, and

(*b*) the terms of those schemes or licences,

and shall exercise its powers so as to secure that there is no unreasonable discrimination between licensees, or prospective licensees, under the scheme or licence to which the reference or application relates and licensees under other schemes operated by, or other licences granted by, the same person.

### 130 Licences for reprographic copying

Where a reference or application is made to the Copyright Tribunal under this Chapter relating to the licensing of reprographic copying of published literary, dramatic, musical or artistic works, or the typographical arrangement of published editions, the Tribunal shall have regard to—

(*a*) the extent to which published editions of the works in question are otherwise available,

(*b*) the proportion of the work to be copied, and

(*c*) the nature of the use to which the copies are likely to be put.

### 131 Licences for educational establishments in respect of works included in broadcasts or cable programmes

(1) This section applies to references or applications under this Chapter relating to licences for the recording by or on behalf of educational establishments of broadcasts or cable programmes which include copyright works, or the making of copies of such recordings, for educational purposes.

(2) The Copyright Tribunal shall, in considering what charges (if any) should be paid for a licence, have regard to the extent to which the owners of copyright in

the works included in the broadcast or cable programme have already received, or are entitled to receive, payment in respect of their inclusion.

**132 Licences to reflect conditions imposed by promoters of events**

(1) This section applies to references or applications under this Chapter in respect of licences relating to sound recordings, films, broadcasts or cable programmes which include, or are to include, any entertainment or other event.

(2) The Copyright Tribunal shall have regard to any conditions imposed by the promoters of the entertainment or other event; and, in particular, the Tribunal shall not hold a refusal or failure to grant a licence to be unreasonable if it could not have been granted consistently with those conditions.

(3) Nothing in this section shall require the Tribunal to have regard to any such conditions in so far as they—

(*a*) purport to regulate the charges to be imposed in respect of the grant of licences, or

(*b*) relate to payments to be made to the promoters of any event in consideration of the grant of facilities for making the recording, film, broadcast or cable programme.

**133 Licences to reflect payments in respect of underlying rights**

(1) In considering what charges should be paid for a licence—

(*a*) on a reference or application under this Chapter relating to licences for the rental to the public of copies of sound recordings, films or computer programs, or

(*b*) on an application under section 142 (settlement of royalty or other sum payable for deemed licence),

the Copyright Tribunal shall take into account any reasonable payments which the owner of the copyright in the sound recording, film or computer program is liable to make in consequence of the granting of the licence, or of the acts authorised by the licence, to owners of copyright in works included in that work.

(2) On any reference or application under this Chapter relating to licensing in respect of the copyright in sound recordings, films, broadcasts or cable programmes, the Copyright Tribunal shall take into account, in considering what charges should be paid for a licence, any reasonable payments which the copyright owner is liable to make in consequence of the granting of the licence, or of the acts authorised by the licence, in respect of any performance included in the recording, film, broadcast or cable programme.

**134 Licences in respect of works included in re-transmissions**

(1) This section applies to references or applications under this Chapter relating to licences to include in a broadcast or cable programme service—

(*a*) literary, dramatic, musical or artistic works, or,

(*b*) sound recordings or films,

where one broadcast or cable programme ("the first transmission") is, by reception and immediate re-transmission, to be further broadcast or included in a cable programme service ("the further transmission").

(2) So far as the further transmission is to the same area as the first transmission, the Copyright Tribunal shall, in considering what charges (if any) should be paid for licences for either transmission, have regard to the extent to which the copyright owner has already received, or is entitled to receive, payment for the other transmission which adequately remunerates him in respect of transmissions to that area.

(3) So far as the further transmission is to an area outside that to which the first transmission was made, the Tribunal shall (except where subsection (4) applies) leave the further transmission out of account in considering what charges (if any) should be paid for licences for the first transmission.

(4) If the Tribunal is satisfied that requirements imposed under section 13(1) of the Cable and Broadcasting Act 1984 (duty of Cable Authority to secure inclusion of certain broadcasts in cable programme services) will result in the further transmission being to areas part of which fall outside the area to which the first transmission is made, the Tribunal shall exercise its powers so as to secure that the charges payable for licences for the first transmission adequately reflect that fact.

**135 Mention of specific matters not to exclude other relevant considerations**

The mention in sections 129 to 134 of specific matters to which the Copyright Tribunal is to have regard in certain classes of case does not affect the Tribunal's general obligation in any case to have regard to all relevant considerations.

*Implied indemnity in schemes or licences for reprographic copying*

**136 Implied indemnity in certain schemes and licences for reprographic copying**

(1) This section applies to—

(*a*) schemes for licensing reprographic copying of published literary, dramatic, musical or artistic works, or the typographical arrangement of published editions, and

(*b*) licences granted by licensing bodies for such copying,

where the scheme or licence does not specify the works to which it applies with such particularity as to enable licensees to determine whether a work falls within the scheme or licence by inspection of the scheme or licence and the work.

(2) There is implied—

(*a*) in every scheme to which this section applies an undertaking by the operator of the scheme to indemnify a person granted a licence under the scheme, and

(*b*) in every licence to which this section applies an undertaking by the licensing body to indemnify the licensee,

against any liability incurred by him by reason of his having infringed copyright by making or authorising the making of reprographic copies of a work in circumstances within the apparent scope of his licence.

(3) The circumstances of a case are within the apparent scope of a licence if—

(*a*) it is not apparent from inspection of the licence and the work that it does not fall within the description of works to which the licence applies; and

(*b*) the licence does not expressly provide that it does not extend to copyright of the description infringed.

(4) In this section "liability" includes liability to pay costs; and this section applies in relation to costs reasonably incurred by a licensee in connection with actual or contemplated proceedings against him for infringement of copyright as it applies to sums which he is liable to pay in respect of such infringement.

(5) A scheme or licence to which this section applies may contain reasonable provision—

(*a*) with respect to the manner in which, and time within which, claims under the undertaking implied by this section are to be made;

(*b*) enabling the operator of the scheme or, as the case may be, the licensing body to take over the conduct of any proceedings affecting the amount of his liability to indemnify.

*Reprographic copying by educational establishments*

**137 Power to extend coverage of scheme or licence**

(1) This section applies to—

(*a*) a licensing scheme to which sections 118 to 123 apply (see section 117) and which is operated by a licensing body, or

(*b*) a licence to which sections 125 to 128 apply (see section 124),

so far as it provides for the grant of licences, or is a licence, authorising the making by or on behalf of educational establishments for the purposes of instruction of reprographic copies of published literary, dramatic, musical or artistic works, or of the typographical arrangement of published editions.

(2) If it appears to the Secretary of State with respect to a scheme or licence to which this section applies that—

(*a*) works of a description similar to those covered by the scheme or licence are unreasonably excluded from it, and

(*b*) making them subject to the scheme or licence would not conflict with the normal exploitation of the works or unreasonably prejudice the legitimate interests of the copyright owners,

he may by order provide that the scheme or licence shall extend to those works.

(3) Where he proposes to make such an order, the Secretary of State shall give notice of the proposal to—

(*a*) the copyright owners,

(*b*) the licensing body in question, and

(*c*) such persons or organisations representative of educational establishments, and such other persons or organisations, as the Secretary of State thinks fit.

(4) The notice shall inform those persons of their right to make written or oral representations to the Secretary of State about the proposal within six months from the date of the notice; and if any of them wishes to make oral representations, the Secretary of State shall appoint a person to hear the representations and report to him.

(5) In considering whether to make an order the Secretary of State shall take into account any representations made to him in accordance with subsection (4), and such other matters as appear to him to be relevant.

**138 Variation or discharge of order extending scheme or licence**

(1) The owner of the copyright in a work in respect of which an order is in force under section 137 may apply to the Secretary of State for the variation or discharge of the order, stating his reasons for making the application.

(2) The Secretary of State shall not entertain an application made within two years of the making of the original order, or of the making of an order on a previous application under this section, unless it appears to him that the circumstances are exceptional.

(3) On considering the reasons for the application the Secretary of State may confirm the order forthwith; if he does not do so, he shall give notice of the application to—

(*a*) the licensing body in question, and

(*b*) such persons or organisations representative of educational establishments, and such other persons or organisations, as he thinks fit.

(4) The notice shall inform those persons of their right to make written or oral representations to the Secretary of State about the application within the period of two months from the date of the notice; and if any of them wishes to make oral representations, the Secretary of State shall appoint a person to hear the representations and report to him.

(5) In considering the application the Secretary of State shall take into account the reasons for the application, any representations made to him in accordance with subsection (4), and such other matters as appear to him to be relevant.

(6) The Secretary of State may make such order as he thinks fit confirming or discharging the order (or, as the case may be, the order as previously varied), or varying (or further varying) it so as to exclude works from it.

**139 Appeals against orders**

(1) The owner of the copyright in a work which is the subject of an order under section 137 (order extending coverage of scheme or licence) may appeal to the Copyright Tribunal which may confirm or discharge the order, or vary it so as to exclude works from it, as it thinks fit having regard to the considerations mentioned in subsection (2) of that section.

(2) Where the Secretary of State has made an order under section 138 (order confirming, varying or discharging order extending coverage of scheme or licence)—

(*a*) the person who applied for the order, or
(*b*) any person or organisation representative of educational establishments who was given notice of the application for the order and made representations in accordance with subsection (4) of that section,

may appeal to the Tribunal which may confirm or discharge the order or make any other order which the Secretary of State might have made.

(3) An appeal under this section shall be brought within six weeks of the making of the order or such further period as the Tribunal may allow.

(4) An order under section 137 or 138 shall not come into effect until the end of the period of six weeks from the making of the order or, if an appeal is brought before the end of that period, until the appeal proceedings are disposed of or withdrawn.

(5) If an appeal is brought after the end of that period, any decision of the Tribunal on the appeal does not affect the validity of anything done in reliance on the order appealed against before that decision takes effect.

**140 Inquiry whether new scheme or general licence required**

(1) The Secretary of State may appoint a person to inquire into the question whether new provision is required (whether by way of a licensing scheme or general licence) to authorise the making by or on behalf of educational establishments for the purposes of instruction of reprographic copies of—

(*a*) published literary, dramatic, musical or artistic works, or
(*b*) the typographical arrangement of published editions,

of a description which appears to the Secretary of State not to be covered by an existing licensing scheme or general licence and not to fall within the power conferred by section 137 (power to extend existing schemes and licences to similar works).

(2) The procedure to be followed in relation to an inquiry shall be such as may be prescribed by regulations made by the Secretary of State.

(3) The regulations shall, in particular, provide for notice to be given to—

(*a*) persons or organisations appearing to the Secretary of State to represent the owners of copyright in works of that description, and

(*b*) persons or organisations appearing to the Secretary of State to represent educational establishments,

and for the making of written or oral representations by such persons; but without prejudice to the giving of notice to, and the making of representations by, other persons and organisations.

(4) The person appointed to hold the inquiry shall not recommend the making of new provision unless he is satisfied—

(*a*) that it would be of advantage to educational establishments to be authorised to make reprographic copies of the works in question, and

(*b*) that making those works subject to a licensing scheme or general licence would not conflict with the normal exploitation of the works or unreasonably prejudice the legitimate interests of the copyright owners.

(5) If he does recommend the making of new provision he shall specify any terms, other than terms as to charges payable, on which authorisation under the new provision should be available.

(6) Regulations under this section shall be made by statutory instrument which shall be subject to annulment in pursuance of a resolution of either House of Parliament.

(7) In this section (and section 141) a "general licence" means a licence granted by a licensing body which covers all works of the description to which it applies.

**141 Statutory licence where recommendation not implemented**

(1) The Secretary of State may, within one year of the making of a recommendation under section 140 by order provide that if, or to the extent that, provision has not been made in accordance with the recommendation, the making by or on behalf of an educational establishment, for the purposes of instruction, of reprographic copies of the works to which the recommendation relates shall be treated as licensed by the owners of the copyright in the works.

(2) For that purpose provision shall be regarded as having been made in accordance with the recommendation if—

(*a*) a certified licensing scheme has been established under which a licence is available to the establishment in question, or

(*b*) a general licence has been—

(i) granted to or for the benefit of that establishment, or

(ii) referred by or on behalf of that establishment to the Copyright Tribunal under section 125 (reference of terms of proposed licence), or

(iii) offered to or for the benefit of that establishment and refused without such a reference,

and the terms of the scheme or licence accord with the recommendation.

(3) The order shall also provide that any existing licence authorising the making of such copies (not being a licence granted under a certified licensing scheme or a general licence) shall cease to have effect to the extent that it is more restricted or more onerous than the licence provided for by the order.

(4) The order shall provide for the licence to be free of royalty but, as respects other matters, subject to any terms specified in the recommendation and to such other terms as the Secretary of State may think fit.

(5) The order may provide that where a copy which would otherwise be an infringing copy is made in accordance with the licence provided by the order but is subsequently dealt with, it shall be treated as an infringing copy for the purposes of that dealing, and if that dealing infringes copyright for all subsequent purposes.

In this subsection "dealt with" means sold or let for hire, offered or exposed for sale or hire, or exhibited in public.

(6) The order shall not come into force until at least six months after it is made.

(7) An order may be varied from time to time, but not so as to include works other than those to which the recommendation relates or remove any terms specified in the recommendation, and may be revoked.

(8) An order under this section shall be made by statutory instrument which shall be subject to annulment in pursuance of a resolution of either House of Parliament.

(9) In this section a "certified licensing scheme" means a licensing scheme certified for the purposes of this section under section 143.

*Royalty or other sum payable for rental of certain works*

### 142 Royalty or other sum payable for rental of sound recording, film or computer program

(1) An application to settle the royalty or other sum payable in pursuance of section 66 (rental of sound recordings, films and computer programs) may be made to the Copyright Tribunal by the copyright owner or the person claiming to be treated as licensed by him.

(2) The Tribunal shall consider the matter and make such order as it may determine to be reasonable in the circumstances.

(3) Either party may subsequently apply to the Tribunal to vary the order, and the Tribunal shall consider the matter and make such order confirming or varying the original order as it may determine to be reasonable in the circumstances.

(4) An application under subsection (3) shall not, except with the special leave of the Tribunal, be made within twelve months from the date of the original order or of the order on a previous application under that subsection.

(5) An order under subsection (3) has effect from the date on which it is made or such later date as may be specified by the Tribunal.

*Certification of licensing schemes*

### 143 Certification of licensing schemes

(1) A person operating or proposing to operate a licensing scheme may apply to the Secretary of State to certify the scheme for the purposes of—

(*a*) section 35 (educational recording of broadcasts or cable programmes),
(*b*) section 60 (abstracts of scientific or technical articles),
(*c*) section 66 (rental of sound recordings, films and computer programs),
(*d*) section 74 (sub-titled copies of broadcasts or cable programmes for people who are deaf or hard of hearing), or
(*e*) section 141 (reprographic copying of published works by educational establishments).

(2) The Secretary of State shall by order made by statutory instrument certify the scheme if he is satisfied that it—

(*a*) enables the works to which it relates to be identified with sufficient certainty by persons likely to require licences, and
(*b*) sets out clearly the charges (if any) payable and the other terms on which licences will be granted.

(3) The scheme shall be scheduled to the order and the certification shall come into operation for the purposes of section 35, 60, 66, 74 or 141, as the case may be—

(*a*) on such date, not less than eight weeks after the order is made, as may be specified in the order, or
(*b*) if the scheme is the subject of a reference under section 118 (reference of proposed scheme), any later date on which the order of the Copyright Tribunal under that section comes into force or the reference is withdrawn.

(4) A variation of the scheme is not effective unless a corresponding amendment of the order is made; and the Secretary of State shall make such an amendment in the case of a variation ordered by the Copyright Tribunal on a reference under section 118, 119 or 120, and may do so in any other case if he thinks fit.

(5) The order shall be revoked if the scheme ceases to be operated and may be revoked if it appears to the Secretary of State that it is no longer being operated according to its terms.

*Powers exercisable in consequence of competition report*

## 144 Powers exercisable in consequence of report of Monopolies and Mergers Commission

(1) Where the matters specified in a report of the Monopolies and Mergers Commission as being those which in the Commission's opinion operate, may be expected to operate or have operated against the public interest include—

(*a*) conditions in licences granted by the owner of copyright in a work restricting the use of the work by the licensee or the right of the copyright owner to grant other licences, or
(*b*) a refusal of a copyright owner to grant licences on reasonable terms,

the powers conferred by Part I of Schedule 8 to the Fair Trading Act 1973 (powers exercisable for purpose of remedying or preventing adverse effects specified in report of Commission) include power to cancel or modify those conditions and, instead or in addition, to provide that licences in respect of the copyright shall be available as of right.

(2) The references in sections 56(2) and 73(2) of that Act, and sections 10(2)(*b*) and 12(5) of the Competition Act 1980, to the powers specified in that Part of that Schedule shall be construed accordingly.

(3) A Minister shall only exercise the powers available by virtue of this section if he is satisfied that to do so does not contravene any Convention relating to copyright to which the United Kingdom is a party.

(4) The terms of a licence available by virtue of this section shall, in default of agreement, be settled by the Copyright Tribunal on an application by the person requiring the licence; and terms so settled shall authorise the licensee to do everything in respect of which a licence is so available.

(5) Where the terms of a licence are settled by the Tribunal, the licence has effect from the date on which the application to the Tribunal was made.

## CHAPTER VIII

## THE COPYRIGHT TRIBUNAL

### *The Tribunal*

**145 The Copyright Tribunal**

(1) The Tribunal established under section 23 of the Copyright Act 1956 is renamed the Copyright Tribunal.

(2) The Tribunal shall consist of a chairman and two deputy chairmen appointed by the Lord Chancellor, after consultation with the Lord Advocate, and not less than two or more than eight ordinary members appointed by the Secretary of State.

(3) A person is not eligible for appointment as chairman or deputy chairman unless he is a barrister, advocate or solicitor of not less than seven years' standing or has held judicial office.

**146 Membership of the Tribunal**

(1) The members of the Copyright Tribunal shall hold and vacate office in accordance with their terms of appointment, subject to the following provisions.

(2) A member of the Tribunal may resign his office by notice in writing to the Secretary of State or, in the case of the chairman or a deputy chairman, to the Lord Chancellor.

(3) The Secretary of State or, in the case of the chairman or a deputy chairman, the Lord Chancellor may by notice in writing to the member concerned remove him from office if—

(*a*) he has become bankrupt or made an arrangement with his creditors or, in Scotland, his estate has been sequestrated or he has executed a trust deed for his creditors or entered into a composition contract, or

(*b*) he is incapacitated by physical or mental illness,

or if he is in the opinion of the Secretary of State or, as the case may be, the Lord Chancellor otherwise unable or unfit to perform his duties as member.

(4) If a member of the Tribunal is by reason of illness, absence or other reasonable cause for the time being unable to perform the duties of his office, either generally or in relation to particular proceedings, a person may be appointed to discharge his duties for a period not exceeding six months at one time or, as the case may be, in relation to those proceedings.

(5) The appointment shall be made—

(*a*) in the case of the chairman or deputy chairman, by the Lord Chancellor, who shall appoint a person who would be eligible for appointment to that office, and

(*b*) in the case of an ordinary member, by the Secretary of State;

and a person so appointed shall have during the period of his appointment, or in relation to the proceedings in question, the same powers as the person in whose place he is appointed.

(6) The Lord Chancellor shall consult the Lord Advocate before exercising his powers under this section.

**147 Financial provisions**

(1) There shall be paid to the members of the Copyright Tribunal such remuneration (whether by way of salaries or fees), and such allowances, as the Secretary of State with the approval of the Treasury may determine.

(2) The Secretary of State may appoint such staff for the Tribunal as, with the approval of the Treasury as to numbers and remuneration, he may determine.

(3) The remuneration and allowances of members of the Tribunal, the remuneration of any staff and such other expenses of the Tribunal as the Secretary of State with the approval of the Treasury may determine shall be paid out of money provided by Parliament.

**148 Constitution for purposes of proceedings**

(1) For the purposes of any proceedings the Copyright Tribunal shall consist of—

(*a*) a chairman, who shall be either the chairman or a deputy chairman of the Tribunal, and

(*b*) two or more ordinary members.

(2) If the members of the Tribunal dealing with any matter are not unanimous, the decision shall be taken by majority vote; and if, in such a case, the votes are equal the chairman shall have a further, casting vote.

(3) Where part of any proceedings before the Tribunal has been heard and one or more members of the Tribunal are unable to continue, the Tribunal shall remain duly constituted for the purpose of those proceedings so long as the number of members is not reduced to less than three.

(4) If the chairman is unable to continue, the chairman of the Tribunal shall—

(*a*) appoint one of the remaining members to act as chairman, and

(*b*) appoint a suitably qualified person to attend the proceedings and advise the members on any questions of law arising.

(5) A person is "suitably qualified" for the purposes of subsection (4)(*b*) if he is, or is eligible for appointment as, a deputy chairman of the Tribunal.

*Jurisdiction and procedure*

**149 Jurisdiction of the Tribunal**

The function of the Copyright Tribunal is to hear and determine proceedings under—

(*a*) section 118, 119 or 120 (reference of licensing scheme);

(*b*) section 121 or 122 (application with respect to entitlement to licence under licensing scheme);

(*c*) section 125, 126 or 127 (reference or application with respect to licensing by licensing body);

(*d*) section 139 (appeal against order as to coverage of licensing scheme or licence);

(*e*) section 142 (application to settle royalty or other sum payable for rental of sound recording, film or computer program);

(*f*) section 144(4) (application to settle terms of copyright licence available as of right);

(*g*) section 190 (application to give consent for purposes of Part II on behalf of performer);

(*h*) paragraph 5 of Schedule 6 (determination of royalty or other remuneration to be paid to trustees for the Hospital for Sick Children).

**150 General power to make rules**

(1) The Lord Chancellor may, after consultation with the Lord Advocate, make rules for regulating proceedings before the Copyright Tribunal and, subject to the approval of the Treasury, as to the fees chargeable in respect of such proceedings.

(2) The rules may apply in relation to the Tribunal—

(*a*) as respects proceedings in England and Wales, any of the provisions of the Arbitration Act 1950;
(*b*) as respects proceedings in Northern Ireland, any of the provisions of the Arbitration Act (Northern Ireland) 1937;

and any provisions so applied shall be set out in or scheduled to the rules.

(3) Provision shall be made by the rules—

(*a*) prohibiting the Tribunal from entertaining a reference under section 118, 119, or 120 by a representative organisation unless the Tribunal is satisfied that the organisation is reasonably representative of the class of persons which it claims to represent;
(*b*) specifying the parties to any proceedings and enabling the Tribunal to make a party to the proceedings any person or organisation satisfying the Tribunal that they have a substantial interest in the matter; and
(*c*) requiring the Tribunal to give the parties to proceedings an opportunity to state their case, in writing or orally as the rules may provide.

(4) The rules may make provision for regulating or prescribing any matters incidental to or consequential upon any appeal from the Tribunal under section 152 (appeal to the court on point of law).

(5) Rules under this section shall be made by statutory instrument which shall be subject to annulment in pursuance of a resolution of either House of Parliament.

**151 Costs, proof of orders, &c**

(1) The Copyright Tribunal may order that the costs of a party to proceedings before it shall be paid by such other party as the Tribunal may direct; and the Tribunal may tax or settle the amount of the costs, or direct in what manner they are to be taxed.

(2) A document purporting to be a copy of an order of the Tribunal and to be certified by the chairman to be a true copy shall, in any proceedings, be sufficient evidence of the order unless the contrary is proved.

(3) As respect proceedings in Scotland, the Tribunal has the like powers for securing the attendance of witnesses and the production of documents, and with regard to the examination of witnesses on oath, as an arbiter under a submission.

*Appeals*

**152 Appeal to the court on point of law**

(1) An appeal lies on any point of law arising from a decision of the Copyright Tribunal to the High Court or, in the case of proceedings of the Tribunal in Scotland, to the Court of Session.

(2) Provision shall be made by rules under section 150 limiting the time within which an appeal may be brought.

(3) Provision may be made by rules under that section—

(*a*) for suspending, or authorising or requiring the Tribunal to suspend, the operation of orders of the Tribunal in cases where its decision is appealed against;
(*b*) for modifying in relation to an order of the Tribunal whose operation is suspended the operation of any provision of this Act as to the effect of the order;

(*c*) for the publication of notices or the taking of other steps for securing that persons affected by the suspension of an order of the Tribunal will be informed of its suspension.

## CHAPTER IX

## QUALIFICATION FOR AND EXTENT OF COPYRIGHT PROTECTION

### *Qualification for copyright protection*

#### 153 Qualification for copyright protection

(1) Copyright does not subsist in a work unless the qualification requirements of this Chapter are satisfied as regards—

(*a*) the author (see section 154), or
(*b*) the country in which the work was first published (see section 155), or
(*c*) in the case of a broadcast or cable programme, the country from which the broadcast was made or the cable programme was sent (see section 156).

(2) Subsection (1) does not apply in relation to Crown copyright or Parliamentary copyright (see sections 163 to 166) or to copyright subsisting by virtue of section 168 (copyright of certain international organisations).

(3) If the qualification requirements of this Chapter, or section 163, 165 or 168, are once satisfied in respect of a work, copyright does not cease to subsist by reason of any subsequent event.

#### 154 Qualification by reference to author

(1) A work qualifies for copyright protection if the author was at the material time a qualifying person, that is—

(*a*) a British citizen, a British Dependent Territories citizen, a British National (Overseas), a British Overseas citizen, a British subject or a British protected person within the meaning of the British Nationality Act 1981, or
(*b*) an individual domiciled or resident in the United Kingdom or another country to which the relevant provisions of this Part extend, or
(*c*) a body incorporated under the law of a part of the United Kingdom or of another country to which the relevant provisions of this Part extend.

(2) Where, or so far as, provision is made by Order under section 159 (application of this Part to countries to which it does not extend), a work also qualifies for copyright protection if at the material time the author was a citizen or subject of, an individual domiciled or resident in, or a body incorporated under the law of, a country to which the Order relates.

(3) A work of joint authorship qualifies for copyright protection if at the material time any of the authors satisfies the requirements of subsection (1) or (2); but where a work qualifies for copyright protection only under this section, only those authors who satisfy those requirements shall be taken into account for the purposes of—

section 11(1) and (2) (first ownership of copyright; entitlement of author or author's employer),
section 12(1) and (2) (duration of copyright; dependent on life of author unless work of unknown authorship), and section 9(4) (meaning of "unknown authorship") so far as it applies for the purposes of section 12(2), and
section 57 (anonymous or pseudonymous works: acts permitted on assumptions as to expiry of copyright or death of author).

(4) The material time in relation to a literary, dramatic, musical or artistic work is—

(*a*) in the case of an unpublished work, when the work was made or, if the making of the work extended over a period, a substantial part of that period;
(*b*) in the case of a published work, when the work was first published or, if the author had died before that time, immediately before his death.

(5) The material time in relation to other descriptions of work is as follows—

(*a*) in the case of a sound recording or film, when it was made;
(*b*) in the case of a broadcast, when the broadcast was made;
(*c*) in the case of a cable programme, when the programme was included in a cable programme service;
(*d*) in the case of the typographical arrangement of a published edition, when the edition was first published.

### 155 Qualification by reference to country of first publication

(1) A literary, dramatic, musical or artistic work, a sound recording or film, or the typographical arrangement of a published edition, qualifies for copyright protection if it is first published—

(*a*) in the United Kingdom, or
(*b*) in another country to which the relevant provisions of this Part extend.

(2) Where, or so far as, provision is made by Order under section 159 (application of this Part to countries to which it does not extend), such a work also qualifies for copyright protection if it is first published in a country to which the Order relates.

(3) For the purposes of this section, publication in one country shall not be regarded as other than the first publication by reason of simultaneous publication elsewhere; and for this purpose publication elsewhere within the previous 30 days shall be treated as simultaneous.

### 156 Qualification by reference to place of transmission

(1) A broadcast qualifies for copyright protection if it is made from, and a cable programme qualifies for copyright protection if it is sent from, a place in—

(*a*) the United Kingdom, or
(*b*) another country to which the relevant provisions of this Part extend.

(2) Where, or so far as, provision is made by Order under section 159 (application of this Part to countries to which it does not extend), a broadcast or cable programme also qualifies for copyright protection if it is made from or, as the case may be, sent from a place in a country to which the Order relates.

*Extent and application of this Part*

### 157 Countries to which this Part extends

(1) This Part extends to England and Wales, Scotland and Northern Ireland.

(2) Her Majesty may by Order in Council direct that this Part shall extend, subject to such exceptions and modifications as may be specified in the Order, to—

(*a*) any of the Channel Islands,
(*b*) the Isle of Man, or
(*c*) any colony.

(3) That power includes power to extend, subject to such exceptions and modifications as may be specified in the Order, any Order in Council made under the following provisions of this Chapter.

(4) The legislature of a country to which this Part has been extended may modify or add to the provisions of this Part, in their operation as part of the law of that country, as the legislature may consider necessary to adapt the provisions to the circumstances of that country—

(*a*) as regards procedure and remedies, or

(*b*) as regards works qualifying for copyright protection by virtue of a connection with that country.

(5) Nothing in this section shall be construed as restricting the extent of paragraph 36 of Schedule 1 (transitional provisions: dependent territories where the Copyright Act 1956 or the Copyright Act 1911 remains in force) in relation to the law of a dependent territory to which this Part does not extend.

**158 Countries ceasing to be colonies**

(1) The following provisions apply where a country to which this Part has been extended ceases to be a colony of the United Kingdom.

(2) As from the date on which it ceases to be a colony it shall cease to be regarded as a country to which this Part extends for the purposes of—

(*a*) section 160(2)(*a*) (denial of copyright protection to citizens of countries not giving adequate protection to British works), and

(*b*) sections 163 and 165 (Crown and Parliamentary copyright).

(3) But it shall continue to be treated as a country to which this Part extends for the purposes of sections 154 to 156 (qualification for copyright protection) until—

(*a*) an Order in Council is made in respect of that country under section 159 (application of this Part to countries to which it does not extend), or

(*b*) an Order in Council is made declaring that it shall cease to be so treated by reason of the fact that the provisions of this Part as part of the law of that country have been repealed or amended.

(4) A statutory instrument containing an Order in Council under subsection (3)(*b*) shall be subject to annulment in pursuance of a resolution of either House of Parliament.

**159 Application of this Part to countries to which it does not extend**

(1) Her Majesty may by Order in Council make provision for applying in relation to a country to which this Part does not extend any of the provisions of this Part specified in the Order, so as to secure that those provisions—

(*a*) apply in relation to persons who are citizens or subjects of that country or are domiciled or resident there, as they apply to persons who are British citizens or are domiciled or resident in the United Kingdom, or

(*b*) apply in relation to bodies incorporated under the law of that country as they apply in relation to bodies incorporated under the law of a part of the United Kingdom, or

(*c*) apply in relation to works first published in that country as they apply in relation to works first published in the United Kingdom, or

(*d*) apply in relation to broadcasts made from or cable programmes sent from that country as they apply in relation to broadcasts made from or cable programmes sent from the United Kingdom.

(2) An Order may make provision for all or any of the matters mentioned in subsection (1) and may—

(*a*) apply any provisions of this Part subject to such exceptions and modifications as are specified in the Order; and

(*b*) direct that any provisions of this Part apply either generally or in relation to such classes of works, or other classes of case, as are specified in the Order.

(3) Except in the case of a Convention country or another member State of the European Economic Community, Her Majesty shall not make an Order in Council under this section in relation to a country unless satisfied that provision has been or will be made under the law of that country, in respect of the class of works to which the Order relates, giving adequate protection to the owners of copyright under this Part.

(4) In subsection (3) "Convention country" means a country which is a party to a Convention relating to copyright to which the United Kingdom is also a party.

(5) A statutory instrument containing an Order in Council under this section shall be subject to annulment in pursuance of a resolution of either House of Parliament.

### 160 Denial of copyright protection to citizens of countries not giving adequate protection to British works

(1) If it appears to Her Majesty that the law of a country fails to give adequate protection to British works to which this section applies, or to one or more classes of such works, Her Majesty may make provision by Order in Council in accordance with this section restricting the rights conferred by this Part in relation to works of authors connected with that country.

(2) An Order in Council under this section shall designate the country concerned and provide that, for the purposes specified in the Order, works first published after a date specified in the Order shall not be treated as qualifying for copyright protection by virtue of such publication if at that time the authors are—

(*a*) citizens or subjects of that country (not domiciled or resident in the United Kingdom or another country to which the relevant provisions of this Part extend), or

(*b*) bodies incorporated under the law of that country;

and the Order may make such provision for all the purposes of this Part or for such purposes as are specified in the Order, and either generally or in relation to such class of cases as are specified in the Order, having regard to the nature and extent of that failure referred to in subsection (1).

(3) This section applies to literary, dramatic, musical and artistic works, sound recordings and films; and "British works" means works of which the author was a qualifying person at the material time within the meaning of section 154.

(4) A statutory instrument containing an Order in Council under this section shall be subject to annulment in pursuance of a resolution of either House of Parliament.

*Supplementary*

### 161 Territorial waters and the continental shelf

(1) For the purposes of this Part the territorial waters of the United Kingdom shall be treated as part of the United Kingdom.

(2) This Part applies to things done in the United Kingdom sector of the continental shelf on a structure or vessel which is present there for purposes directly connected with the exploration of the sea bed or subsoil or the exploitation of their natural resources as it applies to things done in the United Kingdom.

(3) The United Kingdom sector of the continental shelf means the areas designated by order under section 1(7) of the Continental Shelf Act 1964.

**162 British ships, aircraft and hovercraft**

(1) This Part applies to things done on a British ship, aircraft or hovercraft as it applies to things done in the United Kingdom.

(2) In this section—

"British ship" means a ship which is a British ship for the purposes of the Merchant Shipping Acts (see section 2 of the Merchant Shipping Act 1988) otherwise than by virtue of registration in a country outside the United Kingdom; and

"British aircraft" and "British hovercraft" mean an aircraft or hovercraft registered in the United Kingdom.

## CHAPTER X

## MISCELLANEOUS AND GENERAL

### *Crown and Parliamentary copyright*

**163 Crown copyright**

(1) Where a work is made by Her Majesty or by an officer or servant of the Crown in the course of his duties—

(*a*) the work qualifies for copyright protection notwithstanding section 153(1) (ordinary requirement as to qualification for copyright protection), and

(*b*) Her Majesty is the first owner of any copyright in the work.

(2) Copyright in such a work is referred to in this Part as "Crown copyright", notwithstanding that it may be, or have been, assigned to another person.

(3) Crown copyright in a literary, dramatic, musical or artistic work continues to subsist—

(*a*) until the end of the period of 125 years from the end of the calendar year in which the work was made, or

(*b*) if the work is published commercially before the end of the period of 75 years from the end of the calendar year in which it was made, until the end of the period of 50 years from the end of the calendar year in which it was first so published.

(4) In the case of a work of joint authorship where one or more but not all of the authors are persons falling within subsection (1), this section applies only in relation to those authors and the copyright subsisting by virtue of their contribution to the work.

(5) Except as mentioned above, and subject to any express exclusion elsewhere in this Part, the provisions of this Part apply in relation to Crown copyright as to other copyright.

(6) This section does not apply to work if, or to the extent that, Parliamentary copyright subsists in the work (see sections 165 and 166).

**164 Copyright in Acts and Measures**

(1) Her Majesty is entitled to copyright in every Act of Parliament or Measure of the General Synod of the Church of England.

(2) The copyright subsists from Royal Assent until the end of the period of 50 years from the end of the calendar year in which Royal Assent was given.

(3) References in this Part to Crown copyright (except in section 163) include copyright under this section; and, except as mentioned above, the provisions of

this Part apply in relation to copyright under this section as to other Crown copyright.

(4) No other copyright, or right in the nature of copyright, subsists in an Act or Measure.

**165 Parliamentary copyright**

(1) Where a work is made by or under the direction or control of the House of Commons or the House of Lords—

(*a*) the work qualifies for copyright protection notwithstanding section 153(1) (ordinary requirement as to qualification for copyright protection), and

(*b*) the House by whom, or under whose direction or control, the work is made is the first owner of any copyright in the work, and if the work is made by or under the direction or control of both Houses, the two Houses are joint first owners of copyright.

(2) Copyright in such a work is referred to in this Part as "Parliamentary copyright", notwithstanding that it may be, or have been, assigned to another person.

(3) Parliamentary copyright in a literary, dramatic, musical or artistic work continues to subsist until the end of the period of 50 years from the end of the calendar year in which the work was made.

(4) For the purposes of this section, works made by or under the direction or control of the House of Commons or the House of Lords include—

(*a*) any work made by an officer or employee of that House in the course of his duties, and

(*b*) any sound recording, film, live broadcast or live cable programme of the proceedings of that House;

but a work shall not be regarded as made by or under the direction or control of either House by reason only of its being commissioned by or on behalf of that House.

(5) In the case of a work of joint authorship where one or more but not all of the authors are acting on behalf of, or under the direction or control of, the House of Commons or the House of Lords, this section applies only in relation to those authors and the copyright subsisting by virtue of their contribution to the work.

(6) Except as mentioned above, and subject to any express exclusion elsewhere in this Part, the provisions of this Part apply in relation to Parliamentary copyright as to other copyright.

(7) The provisions of this section also apply, subject to any exceptions or modifications specified by Order in Council, to works made by or under the direction or control of any other legislative body of a country to which this Part extends; and references in this Part to "Parliamentary copyright" shall be construed accordingly.

(8) A statutory instrument containing an Order in Council under subsection (7) shall be subject to annulment in pursuance of a resolution of either House of Parliament.

**166 Copyright in Parliamentary Bills**

(1) Copyright in every Bill introduced into Parliament belongs, in accordance with the following provisions, to one or both of the Houses of Parliament.

(2) Copyright in a public Bill belongs in the first instance to the House into which the Bill is introduced, and after the Bill has been carried to the second House

to both Houses jointly, and subsists from the time when the text of the Bill is handed in to the House in which it is introduced.

(3) Copyright in a private Bill belongs to both Houses jointly and subsists from the time when a copy of the Bill is first deposited in either House.

(4) Copyright in a personal Bill belongs in the first instance to the House of Lords, and after the Bill has been carried to the House of Commons to both Houses jointly, and subsists from the time when it is given a First Reading in the House of Lords.

(5) Copyright under this section ceases—

(*a*) on Royal Assent, or

(*b*) if the Bill does not receive Royal Assent, on the withdrawal or rejection of the Bill or the end of the Session:

Provided that, copyright in a Bill continues to subsist notwithstanding its rejection in any Session by the House of Lords if, by virtue of the Parliament Acts 1911 and 1949, it remains possible for it to be presented for Royal Assent in that Session.

(6) References in this Part to Parliamentary copyright (except in section 165) include copyright under this section; and, except as mentioned above, the provisions of this Part apply in relation to copyright under this section as to other Parliamentary copyright.

(7) No other copyright, or right in the nature of copyright, subsists in a Bill after copyright has once subsisted under this section; but without prejudice to the subsequent operation of this section in relation to a Bill which, not having passed in one Session, is reintroduced in a subsequent Session.

**167 Houses of Parliament: supplementary provisions with respect to copyright**

(1) For the purposes of holding, dealing with and enforcing copyright, and in connection with all legal proceedings relating to copyright, each House of Parliament shall be treated as having the legal capacities of a body corporate, which shall not be affected by a prorogation or dissolution.

(2) The functions of the House of Commons as owner of copyright shall be exercised by the Speaker on behalf of the House; and if so authorised by the Speaker, or in case of a vacancy in the office of Speaker, those functions may be discharged by the Chairman of Ways and Means or a Deputy Chairman.

(3) For this purpose a person who on the dissolution of Parliament was Speaker of the House of Commons, Chairman of Ways and Means or a Deputy Chairman may continue to act until the corresponding appointment is made in the next Session of Parliament.

(4) The functions of the House of Lords as owner of copyright shall be exercised by the Clerk of the Parliaments on behalf of the House; and if so authorised by him, or in case of a vacancy in the office of Clerk of the Parliaments, those functions may be discharged by the Clerk Assistant or the Reading Clerk.

(5) Legal proceedings relating to copyright—

(*a*) shall be brought by or against the House of Commons in the name of "The Speaker of the House of Commons"; and

(*b*) shall be brought by or against the House of Lords in the name of "The Clerk of the Parliaments".

*Other miscellaneous provisions*

**168 Copyright vesting in certain international organisations**

(1) Where an original literary, dramatic, musical or artistic work—

(*a*) is made by an officer or employee of, or is published by, an international organisation to which this section applies, and

(*b*) does not qualify for copyright protection under section 154 (qualification by reference to author) or section 155 (qualification by reference to country of first publication),

copyright nevertheless subsists in the work by virtue of this section and the organisation is first owner of that copyright.

(2) The international organisations to which this section applies are those as to which Her Majesty has by Order in Council declared that it is expedient that this section should apply.

(3) Copyright of which an international organisation is first owner by virtue of this section continues to subsist until the end of the period of 50 years from the end of the calendar year in which the work was made or such longer period as may be specified by Her Majesty by Order in Council for the purpose of complying with the international obligations of the United Kingdom.

(4) An international organisation to which this section applies shall be deemed to have, and to have had at all material times, the legal capacities of a body corporate for the purpose of holding, dealing with and enforcing copyright and in connection with all legal proceedings relating to copyright.

(5) A statutory instrument containing an Order in Council under this section shall be subject to annulment in pursuance of a resolution of either House of Parliament.

### 169 Folklore, &c: anonymous unpublished works

(1) Where in the case of an unpublished literary, dramatic, musical or artistic work of unknown authorship there is evidence that the author (or, in the case of a joint work, any of the authors) was a qualifying individual by connection with a country outside the United Kingdom, it shall be presumed until the contrary is proved that he was such a qualifying individual and that copyright accordingly subsists in the work, subject to the provisions of this Part.

(2) If under the law of that country a body is appointed to protect and enforce copyright in such works, Her Majesty may by Order in Council designate that body for the purposes of this section.

(3) A body so designated shall be recognised in the United Kingdom as having authority to do in place of the copyright owner anything, other than assign copyright, which it is empowered to do under the law of that country; and it may, in particular, bring proceedings in its own name.

(4) A statutory instrument containing an Order in Council under this section shall be subject to annulment in pursuance of a resolution of either House of Parliament.

(5) In subsection (1) a "qualifying individual" means an individual who at the material time (within the meaning of section 154) was a person whose works qualified under that section for copyright protection.

(6) This section does not apply if there has been an assignment of copyright in the work by the author of which notice has been given to the designated body; and nothing in this section affects the validity of an assignment of copyright made, or licence granted, by the author or a person lawfully claiming under him.

*Transitional provisions and savings*

### 170 Transitional provisions and savings

Schedule 1 contains transitional provisions and savings relating to works made, and acts or events occurring, before the commencement of this Part, and otherwise with respect to the operation of the provisions of this Part.

### 171 Rights and privileges under other enactments or the common law

(1) Nothing in this Part affects—

(*a*) any right or privilege of any person under any enactment (except where the enactment is expressly repealed, amended or modified by this Act);

(*b*) any right or privilege of the Crown subsisting otherwise than under an enactment;

(*c*) any right or privilege of either House of Parliament;

(*d*) the right of the Crown or any person deriving title from the Crown to sell, use or otherwise deal with articles forfeited under the laws relating to customs and excise;

(*e*) the operation of any rule of equity relating to breaches of trust or confidence.

(2) Subject to those savings, no copyright or right in the nature of copyright shall subsist otherwise than by virtue of this Part or some other enactment in that behalf.

(3) Nothing in this Part affects any rule of law preventing or restricting the enforcement of copyright, on grounds of public interest or otherwise.

(4) Nothing in this Part affects any right of action or other remedy, whether civil or criminal, available otherwise than under this Part in respect of acts infringing any of the rights conferred by Chapter IV (moral rights).

(5) The savings in subsection (1) have effect subject to section 164(4) and section 166(7) (copyright in Acts, Measures and Bills: exclusion of other rights in the nature of copyright).

*Interpretation*

### 172 General provisions as to construction

(1) This Part restates and amends the law of copyright, that is, the provisions of the Copyright Act 1956, as amended.

(2) A provision of this Part which corresponds to a provision of the previous law shall not be construed as departing from the previous law merely because of a change of expression.

(3) Decisions under the previous law may be referred to for the purpose of establishing whether a provision of this Part departs from the previous law, or otherwise for establishing the true construction of this Part.

### 173 Construction of references to copyright owner

(1) Where different persons are (whether in consequence of a partial assignment or otherwise) entitled to different aspects of copyright in a work, the copyright owner for any purpose of this Part is the person who is entitled to the aspect of copyright relevant for that purpose.

(2) Where copyright (or any aspect of copyright) is owned by more than one person jointly, references in this Part to the copyright owner are to all the owners, so that, in particular, any requirement of the licence of the copyright owner requires the licence of all of them.

### 174 Meaning of "educational establishment" and related expressions

(1) The expression "educational establishment" in a provision of this Part means—

(*a*) any school, and

(*b*) any other description of educational establishment specified for the purposes of this Part, or that provision, by order of the Secretary of State.

(2) The Secretary of State may by order provide that the provisions of this Part relating to educational establishments shall apply, with such modifications and adaptations as may be specified in the order, in relation to teachers who are employed by a local education authority to give instruction elsewhere to pupils who are unable to attend an educational establishment.

(3) In subsection (1)(*a*) "school"—

(*a*) in relation to England and Wales, has the same meaning as in the Education Act 1944;
(*b*) in relation to Scotland, has the same meaning as in the Education (Scotland) Act 1962, except that it includes an approved school within the meaning of the Social Work (Scotland) Act 1968; and
(*c*) in relation to Northern Ireland, has the same meaning as in the Education and Libraries (Northern Ireland) Order 1986.

(4) An order under subsection (1)(*b*) may specify a description of educational establishment by reference to the instruments from time to time in force under any enactment specified in the order.

(5) In relation to an educational establishment the expressions "teacher" and "pupil" in this Part include, respectively, any person who gives and any person who receives instruction.

(6) References in this Part to anything being done "on behalf of" an educational establishment are to its being done for the purposes of that establishment by any person.

(7) An order under this section shall be made by statutory instrument which shall be subject to annulment in pursuance of a resolution of either House of Parliament.

**175 Meaning of publication and commercial publication**

(1) In this Part "publication", in relation to a work—

(*a*) means the issue of copies to the public, and
(*b*) includes, in the case of a literary, dramatic, musical or artistic work, making it available to the public by means of an electronic retrieval system;

and related expressions shall be construed accordingly.

(2) In this Part "commercial publication", in relation to a literary, dramatic, musical or artistic work means—

(*a*) issuing copies of the work to the public at a time when copies made in advance of the receipt of orders are generally available to the public, or
(*b*) making the work available to the public by means of an electronic retrieval system;

and related expressions shall be construed accordingly.

(3) In the case of a work of architecture in the form of a building, or an artistic work incorporated in a building, construction of the building shall be treated as equivalent to publication of the work.

(4) The following do not constitute publication for the purposes of this Part and references to commercial publication shall be construed accordingly—

(*a*) in the case of a literary, dramatic or musical work—

  (i) the performance of the work, or
  (ii) the broadcasting of the work or its inclusion in a cable programme service (otherwise than for the purposes of an electronic retrieval system);

(*b*) in the case of an artistic work—

(i) the exhibition of the work;
(ii) the issue to the public of copies of a graphic work representing, or of photographs of, a work of architecture in the form of a building or a model for a building, a sculpture or a work of artistic craftsmanship,
(iii) the issue to the public of copies of a film including the work, or
(iv) the broadcasting of the work or its inclusion in a cable programme service (otherwise than for the purposes of an electronic retrieval system);

(*c*) in the case of a sound recording or film—
(i) the work being played or shown in public, or
(ii) the broadcasting of the work or its inclusion in a cable programme service.

(5) References in this Part to publication or commercial publication do not include publication which is merely colourable and not intended to satisfy the reasonable requirements of the public.

(6) No account shall be taken for the purposes of this section of any unauthorised act.

**176 Requirement of signature: application in relation to body corporate**

(1) The requirement in the following provisions that an instrument be signed by or on behalf of a person is also satisfied in the case of a body corporate by the affixing of its seal—

section 78(3)(*b*) (assertion by licensor of right to identification of author in case of public exhibition of copy made in pursuance of the licence),
section 90(3) (assignment of copyright),
section 91(1) (assignment of future copyright),
section 92(1) (grant of exclusive licence).

(2) The requirement in the following provisions that an instrument be signed by a person is satisfied in the case of a body corporate by signature on behalf of the body or by the affixing of its seal—

section 78(2)(*b*) (assertion by instrument in writing of right to have author identified),
section 87(2) (waiver of moral rights).

**177 Adaptation of expressions for Scotland**

In the application of this Part to Scotland—

"account of profits" means accounting and payment of profits;
"accounts" means count, reckoning and payment;
"assignment" means assignation;
"costs" means expenses;
"defendant" means defender;
"delivery up" means delivery;
"estoppel" means personal bar;
"injunction" means interdict;
"interlocutory relief" means interim remedy; and
"plaintiff" means pursuer.

**178 Minor definitions**

In this Part—

"article", in the context of an article in a periodical, includes an item of any description;
"business" includes a trade or profession;

"collective work" means—

(*a*) a work of joint authorship, or
(*b*) a work in which there are distinct contributions by different authors or in which works or parts of works of different authors are incorporated;

"computer-generated", in relation to a work, means that the work is generated by computer in circumstances such that there is no human author of the work;

"country" includes any territory;

"the Crown" includes the Crown in right of Her Majesty's Government in Northern Ireland or in any country outside the United Kingdom to which this Part extends;

"electronic" means actuated by electric, magnetic, electro-magnetic, electro-chemical or electro-mechanical energy, and "in electronic form" means in a form usable only by electronic means;

"employed", "employee", "employer" and "employment" refer to employment under a contract of service or of apprenticeship;

"facsimile copy" includes a copy which is reduced or enlarged in scale;

"international organisation" means an organisation the members of which include one or more states;

"judicial proceedings" includes proceedings before any court, tribunal or person having authority to decide any matter affecting a person's legal rights or liabilities;

"parliamentary proceedings" includes proceedings of the Northern Ireland Assembly or of the European Parliament;

"rental" means any arrangement under which a copy of a work is made available—

(*a*) for payment (in money or money's worth), or
(*b*) in the course of a business, as part of services or amenities for which payment is made;

on terms that it will or may be returned;

"reprographic copy" and "reprographic copying" refer to copying by means of a reprographic process;

"reprographic process" means a process—

(*a*) for making facsimile copies, or
(*b*) involving the use of an appliance for making multiple copies,

and includes, in relation to a work held in electronic form, any copying by electronic means, but does not include the making of a film or sound recording;

"sufficient acknowledgement" means an acknowledgement identifying the work in question by its title or other description, and identifying the author unless—

(*a*) in the case of a published work, it is published anonymously;
(*b*) in the case of an unpublished work, it is not possible for a person to ascertain the identity of the author by reasonable inquiry;

"sufficient disclaimer", in relation to an act capable of infringing the right conferred by section 80 (right to object to derogatory treatment of work), means a clear and reasonably prominent indication—

(*a*) given at the time of the act, and
(*b*) if the author or director is then identified, appearing along with the identification,

that the work has been subjected to treatment to which the author or director has not consented;

"telecommunications system" means a system for conveying visual images, sounds or other information by electronic means;

"typeface" includes an ornamental motif used in printing;

"unauthorised", as regards anything done in relation to a work, means done otherwise than—

(*a*) by or with the licence of the copyright owner, or

(*b*) if copyright does not subsist in the work, by or with the licence of the author or, in a case where section 11(2) would have applied, the author's employer or, in either case, persons lawfully claiming under him, or

(*c*) in pursuance of section 48 (copying, &c of certain material by the Crown);

"wireless telegraphy" means the sending of electro-magnetic energy over paths not provided by a material substance constructed or arranged for that purpose;

"writing" includes any form of notation or code, whether by hand or otherwise and regardless of the method by which, or medium in or on which, it is recorded, and "written" shall be construed accordingly.

**179 Index of defined expressions**

The following Table shows provisions defining or otherwise explaining expressions used in this Part (other than provisions defining or explaining an expression used only in the same section)—

| | |
|---|---|
| account of profits and accounts (in Scotland) | section 177 |
| acts restricted by copyright | section 16(1) |
| adaptation | section 21(3) |
| archivist (in sections 37 to 43) | section 37(6) |
| article (in a periodical) | section 178 |
| artistic work | section 4(1) |
| assignment (in Scotland) | section 177 |
| author | sections 9 and 10(3) |
| broadcast (and related expressions) | section 6 |
| building | section 4(2) |
| business | section 178 |
| cable programme, cable programme service (and related expressions) | section 7 |
| collective work | section 178 |
| commencement (in Schedule 1) | paragraph 1(2) of that Schedule |
| commercial publication | section 175 |
| computer-generated | section 178 |
| copy and copying | section 17 |
| copyright (generally) | section 1 |
| copyright (in Schedule 1) | paragraph 2(2) of that Schedule |
| copyright owner | sections 101(2) and 173 |
| Copyright Tribunal | section 145 |
| copyright work | section 1(2) |
| costs (in Scotland) | section 177 |
| country | section 178 |
| the Crown | section 178 |
| Crown copyright | sections 163(2) and 164(3) |

| | |
|---|---|
| defendant (in Scotland) | section 177 |
| delivery up (in Scotland) | section 177 |
| dramatic work | section 3(1) |
| educational establishment | sections 174(1) to (4) |
| electronic and electronic form | section 178 |
| employed, employee, employer and employment | section 178 |
| exclusive licence | section 92(1) |
| existing works (in Schedule 1) | paragraph 1(3) of that Schedule |
| facsimile copy | section 178 |
| film | section 5 |
| future copyright | section 91(2) |
| general licence (in sections 140 and 141) | section 140(7) |
| graphic work | section 4(2) |
| infringing copy | section 27 |
| injunction (in Scotland) | section 177 |
| interlocutory relief (in Scotland) | section 177 |
| international organisation | section 178 |
| issue of copies to the public | section 18(2) |
| joint authorship (work of) | sections 10(1) and (2) |
| judicial proceedings | section 178 |
| librarian (in sections 37 to 43) | section 37(6) |
| licence (in sections 125 to 128) | section 124 |
| licence of copyright owner | sections 90(4), 91(3) and 173 |
| licensing body (in Chapter VII) | section 116(2) |
| licensing scheme (generally) | section 116(1) |
| licensing scheme (in sections 118 to 121) | section 117 |
| literary work | section 3(1) |
| made (in relation to a literary, dramatic or musical work) | section 3(2) |
| musical work | section 3(1) |
| the new copyright provisions (in Schedule 1) | paragraph 1(1) of that Schedule |
| the 1911 Act (in Schedule 1) | paragraph 1(1) of that Schedule |
| the 1956 Act (in Schedule 1) | paragraph 1(1) of that Schedule |
| on behalf of (in relation to an educational establishment) | section 174(5) |
| Parliamentary copyright | sections 165(2) and (7) and 166(6) |
| parliamentary proceedings | section 178 |
| performance | section 19(2) |
| photograph | section 4(2) |
| plaintiff (in Scotland) | section 177 |
| prescribed conditions (in sections 38 to 43) | section 37(1)(*b*) |
| prescribed library or archive (in sections 38 to 43) | section 37(1)(*a*) |
| programme (in the context of broadcasting) | section 6(3) |
| prospective owner (of copyright) | section 91(2) |
| publication and related expressions | section 175 |
| published edition (in the context of copyright in the typographical arrangement) | section 8 |

| | |
|---|---|
| pupil | section 174(5) |
| rental | section 178 |
| reprographic copies and reprographic copying | section 178 |
| reprographic process | section 178 |
| sculpture | section 4(2) |
| signed | section 176 |
| sound recording | section 5 |
| sufficient acknowledgement | section 178 |
| sufficient disclaimer | section 178 |
| teacher | section 174(5) |
| telecommunications system | section 178 |
| typeface | section 178 |
| unauthorised (as regards things done in relation to a work) | section 178 |
| unknown (in relation to the author of a work) | section 9(5) |
| unknown authorship (work of) | section 9(4) |
| wireless telegraphy | section 178 |
| work (in Schedule 1) | paragraph 2(1) of that Schedule |
| work of more than one author (in Chapter VII) | section 116(4) |
| writing and written | section 178 |

## PART II

## RIGHTS IN PERFORMANCES

*Introductory*

### 180 Rights conferred on performers and persons having recording rights

(1) This Part confers rights—

(*a*) on a performer, by requiring his consent to the exploitation of his performances (see sections 181 to 184), and

(*b*) on a person having recording rights in relation to a performance, in relation to recordings made without his consent or that of the performer (see sections 185 to 188),

and creates offences in relation to dealing with or using illicit recordings and certain other related acts (see sections 198 and 201).

(2) In this Part—

"performance" means—

(*a*) a dramatic performance (which includes dance and mime),
(*b*) a musical performance,
(*c*) a reading or recitation of a literary work, or
(*d*) a performance of a variety act or any similar presentation,

which is, or so far as it is, a live performance given by one or more individuals; and

"recording", in relation to a performance, means a film or sound recording—

(*a*) made directly from the live performance,

(*b*) made from a broadcast of, or cable programme including, the performance, or

(*c*) made, directly or indirectly, from another recording of the performance.

(3) The rights conferred by this Part apply in relation to performances taking place before the commencement of this Part; but no act done before commencement, or in pursuance of arrangements made before commencement, shall be regarded as infringing those rights.

(4) The rights conferred by this Part are independent of—

(*a*) any copyright in, or moral rights relating to, any work performed or any film or sound recording of, or broadcast or cable programme including, the performance, and

(*b*) any other right or obligation arising otherwise than under this Part.

*Performers' rights*

### 181 Qualifying performances

A performance is a qualifying performance for the purposes of the provisions of this Part relating to performers' rights if it is given by a qualifying individual (as defined in section 206) or takes place in a qualifying country (as so defined).

### 182 Consent required for recording or live transmission of performance

(1) A performer's rights are infringed by a person who, without his consent—

(*a*) makes, otherwise than for his private and domestic use, a recording of the whole or any substantial part of a qualifying performance, or

(*b*) broadcasts live, or includes live in a cable programme service, the whole or any substantial part of a qualifying performance.

(2) In an action for infringement of a performer's rights brought by virtue of this section damages shall not be awarded against a defendant who shows that at the time of the infringement he believed on reasonable grounds that consent had been given.

### 183 Infringement of performer's rights by use of recording made without consent

A performer's rights are infringed by a person who, without his consent—

(*a*) shows or plays in public the whole or any substantial part of a qualifying performance, or

(*b*) broadcasts or includes in a cable programme service the whole or any substantial part of a qualifying performance,

by means of a recording which was, and which that person knows or has reason to believe was, made without the performer's consent.

### 184 Infringement of performer's rights by importing, possessing or dealing with illicit recording

(1) A performer's rights are infringed by a person who, without his consent—

(*a*) imports into the United Kingdom otherwise than for his private and domestic use, or

(*b*) in the course of a business possesses, sells or lets for hire, offers or exposes for sale or hire, or distributes,

a recording of a qualifying performance which is, and which that person knows or has reason to believe is, an illicit recording.

(2) Where in an action for infringement of a performer's rights brought by virtue of this section a defendant shows that the illicit recording was innocently acquired by him or a predecessor in title of his, the only remedy available against him in respect of the infringement is damages not exceeding a reasonable payment in respect of the act complained of.

(3) In subsection (2) "innocently acquired" means that the person acquiring the recording did not know and had no reason to believe that it was an illicit recording.

*Rights of person having recording rights*

**185 Exclusive recording contracts and persons having recording rights**

(1) In this Part an "exclusive recording contract" means a contract between a performer and another person under which that person is entitled to the exclusion of all other persons (including the performer) to make recordings of one or more of his performances with a view to their commercial exploitation.

(2) References in this Part to a "person having recording rights", in relation to a performance, are (subject to subsection (3)) to a person—

(*a*) who is party to and has the benefit of an exclusive recording contract to which the performance is subject, or

(*b*) to whom the benefit of such a contract has been assigned,

and who is a qualifying person.

(3) If a performance is subject to an exclusive recording contract but the person mentioned in subsection (2) is not a qualifying person, references in this Part to a "person having recording rights" in relation to the performance are to any person—

(*a*) who is licensed by such a person to make recordings of the performance with a view to their commercial exploitation, or

(*b*) to whom the benefit of such a licence has been assigned,

and who is a qualifying person.

(4) In this section "with a view to commercial exploitation" means with a view to the recordings being sold or let for hire, or shown or played in public.

**186 Consent required for recording of performance subject to exclusive contract**

(1) A person infringes the rights of a person having recording rights in relation to a performance who, without his consent or that of the performer, makes a recording of the whole or any substantial part of the performance, otherwise than for his private and domestic use.

(2) In an action for infringement of those rights brought by virtue of this section damages shall not be awarded against a defendant who shows that at the time of the infringement he believed on reasonable grounds that consent had been given.

**187 Infringement of recording rights by use of recording made without consent**

(1) A person infringes the rights of a person having recording rights in relation to a performance who, without his consent or, in the case of a qualifying performance, that of the performer—

(*a*) shows or plays in public the whole or any substantial part of the performance, or

(*b*) broadcasts or includes in a cable programme service the whole or any substantial part of the performance, by means of a recording which was, and which that person knows or has reason to believe was, made without the appropriate consent.

(2) The reference in subsection (1) to "the appropriate consent" is to the consent of—

(*a*) the performer, or
(*b*) the person who at the time the consent was given had recording rights in relation to the performance (or, if there was more than one such person, of all of them).

### 188 Infringement of recording rights by importing, possessing or dealing with illicit recording

(1) A person infringes the rights of a person having recording rights in relation to a performance who, without his consent or, in the case of a qualifying performance, that of the performer—

(*a*) imports into the United Kingdom otherwise than for his private and domestic use, or
(*b*) in the course of a business possesses, sells or lets for hire, offers or exposes for sale or hire, or distributes,

a recording of the performance which is, and which that person knows or has reason to believe is, an illicit recording.

(2) Where in an action for infringement of those rights brought by virtue of this section a defendant shows that the illicit recording was innocently acquired by him or a predecessor in title of his, the only remedy available against him in respect of the infringement is damages not exceeding a reasonable payment in respect of the act complained of.

(3) In subsection (2) "innocently acquired" means that the person acquiring the recording did not know and had no reason to believe that it was an illicit recording.

*Exceptions to rights conferred*

### 189 Acts permitted notwithstanding rights conferred by this Part

The provisions of Schedule 2 specify acts which may be done notwithstanding the rights conferred by this Part, being acts which correspond broadly to certain of those specified in Chapter III of Part I (acts permitted notwithstanding copyright).

### 190 Power of tribunal to give consent on behalf of performer in certain cases

(1) The Copyright Tribunal may, on the application of a person wishing to make a recording from a previous recording of a performance, give consent in a case where—

(*a*) the identity or whereabouts of a performer cannot be ascertained by reasonable inquiry, or
(*b*) a performer unreasonably withholds his consent.

(2) Consent given by the Tribunal has effect as consent of the performer for the purposes of—

(*a*) the provisions of this Part relating to performers' rights, and
(*b*) section 198(3)(*a*) (criminal liability: sufficient consent in relation to qualifying performances),

and may be given subject to any conditions specified in the Tribunal's order.

(3) The Tribunal shall not give consent under subsection (1)(*a*) except after the service or publication of such notices as may be required by rules made under section 150 (general procedural rules) or as the Tribunal may in any particular case direct.

(4) The Tribunal shall not give consent under subsection (1)(*b*) unless satisfied that the performer's reasons for withholding consent do not include the protection of any legitimate interest of his; but it shall be for the performer to show what his reasons are for withholding consent, and in default of evidence as to his reasons the Tribunal may draw such inferences as it thinks fit.

(5) In any case the Tribunal shall take into account the following factors—

(*a*) whether the original recording was made with the performer's consent and is lawfully in the possession or control of the person proposing to make the further recording;

(*b*) whether the making of the further recording is consistent with the obligations of the parties to the arrangements under which, or is otherwise consistent with the purposes for which, the original recording was made.

(6) Where the Tribunal gives consent under this section it shall, in default of agreement between the applicant and the performer, make such order as it thinks fit as to the payment to be made to the performer in consideration of consent being given.

*Duration and transmission of rights; consent*

**191 Duration of rights**

The rights conferred by this Part continue to subsist in relation to a performance until the end of the period of 50 years from the end of the calendar year in which the performance takes place.

**192 Transmission of rights**

(1) The rights conferred by this Part are not assignable or transmissible, except to the extent that performers' rights are transmissible in accordance with the following provisions.

(2) On the death of a person entitled to performer's rights—

(*a*) the rights pass to such person as he may by testamentary disposition specifically direct, and

(*b*) if or to the extent that there is no such direction, the rights are exercisable by his personal representatives;

and references in this Part to the performer, in the context of the person having performers' rights, shall be construed as references to the person for the time being entitled to exercise those rights.

(3) Where by virtue of subsection (2)(*a*) a right becomes exercisable by more than one person, it is exercisable by each of them independently of the other or others.

(4) The above provisions do not affect section 185(2)(*b*) or (3)(*b*), so far as those provisions confer rights under this Part on a person to whom the benefit of a contract or licence is assigned.

(5) Any damages recovered by personal representatives by virtue of this section in respect of an infringement after a person's death shall devolve as part of his estate as if the right of action had subsisted and been vested in him immediately before his death.

**193 Consent**

(1) Consent for the purposes of this Part may be given in relation to a specific performance, a specified description of performances or performances generally, and may relate to past or future performances.

(2) A person having recording rights in a performance is bound by any consent given by a person through whom he derives his rights under the exclusive recording contract or licence in question, in the same way as if the consent had been given by him.

(3) Where a right conferred by this Part passes to another person, any consent binding on the person previously entitled binds the person to whom the right passes in the same way as if the consent had been given by him.

*Remedies for infringement*

**194 Infringement actionable as breach of statutory duty**

An infringement of any of the rights conferred by this Part is actionable by the person entitled to the right as a breach of statutory duty.

**195 Order for delivery up**

(1) Where a person has in his possession, custody or control in the course of a business an illicit recording of a performance, a person having performer's rights or recording rights in relation to the performance under this Part may apply to the court for an order that the recording be delivered up to him or to such other person as the court may direct.

(2) An application shall not be made after the end of the period specified in section 203; and no order shall be made unless the court also makes, or it appears to the court that there are grounds for making, an order under section 204 (order as to disposal of illicit recording).

(3) A person to whom a recording is delivered up in pursuance of an order under this section shall, if an order under section 204 is not made, retain it pending the making of an order, or the decision not to make an order, under that section.

(4) Nothing in this section affects any other power of the court.

**196 Right to seize illicit recordings**

(1) An illicit recording of a performance which is found exposed or otherwise immediately available for sale or hire, and in respect of which a person would be entitled to apply for an order under section 195, may be seized and detained by him or a person authorised by him.

The right to seize and detain is exercisable subject to the following conditions and is subject to any decision of the court under section 204 (order as to disposal of illicit recording).

(2) Before anything is seized under this section notice of the time and place of the proposed seizure must be given to a local police station.

(3) A person may for the purpose of exercising the right conferred by this section enter premises to which the public have access but may not seize anything in the possession, custody or control of a person at a permanent or regular place of business of his and may not use any force.

(4) At the time when anything is seized under this section there shall be left at the place where it was seized a notice in the prescribed form containing the prescribed particulars as to the person by whom or on whose authority the seizure is made and the grounds on which it is made.

(5) In this section—

"premises" includes land, buildings, fixed or moveable structures, vehicles, vessels, aircraft and hovercraft; and

"prescribed" means prescribed by order of the Secretary of State.

(6) An order of the Secretary of State under this section shall be made by statutory instrument which shall be subject to annulment in pursuance of a resolution of either House of Parliament.

**197 Meaning of "illicit recording"**

(1) In this Part "illicit recording", in relation to a performance, shall be construed in accordance with this section.

(2) For the purposes of a performer's rights, a recording of the whole or any substantial part of a performance of his is an illicit recording if it is made, otherwise than for private purposes, without his consent.

(3) For the purposes of the rights of a person having recording rights, a recording of the whole or any substantial part of a performance subject to the exclusive recording contract is an illicit recording if it is made, otherwise than for private purposes, without his consent or that of the performer.

(4) For the purposes of sections 198 and 199 (offences and orders for delivery up in criminal proceedings), a recording is an illicit recording if it is an illicit recording for the purposes mentioned in subsection (2) or subsection (3).

(5) In this Part "illicit recording" includes a recording falling to be treated as an illicit recording by virtue of any of the following provisions of Schedule 2—

paragraph 4(3) (recordings made for purposes of instruction or examination),
paragraph 6(2) (recordings made by educational establishments for educational purposes),
paragraph 12(2) (recordings of performance in electronic form retained on transfer of principal recording), or
paragraph 16(3) (recordings made for purposes of broadcast or cable programme),

but otherwise does not include a recording made in accordance with any of the provisions of that Schedule.

(6) It is immaterial for the purposes of this section where the recording was made.

*Offences*

**198 Criminal liability for making, dealing with or using illicit recordings**

(1) A person commits an offence who without sufficient consent—

(*a*) makes for sale or hire, or
(*b*) imports into the United Kingdom otherwise than for his private and domestic use, or
(*c*) possesses in the course of a business with a view to committing any act infringing the rights conferred by this Part, or
(*d*) in the course of a business—
  (i) sells or lets for hire, or
  (ii) offers or exposes for sale or hire, or

(iii) distributes,

a recording which is, and which he knows or has reason to believe is, an illicit recording.

(2) A person commits an offence who causes a recording of a performance made without sufficient consent to be—

(*a*) shown or played in public, or
(*b*) broadcast or included in a cable programme service,

thereby infringing any of the rights conferred by this Part, if he knows or has reason to believe that those rights are thereby infringed.

(3) In subsections (1) and (2) "sufficient consent" means—

(*a*) in the case of a qualifying performance, the consent of the performer, and
(*b*) in the case of a non-qualifying performance subject to an exclusive recording contract—
    (i) for the purposes of subsection (1)(*a*) (making of recording), the consent of the performer or the person having recording rights, and
    (ii) for the purposes of subsection (1)(*b*), (*c*) and (*d*) and subsection (2) (dealing with or using recording), the consent of the person having recording rights.

The references in this subsection to the person having recording rights are to the person having those rights at the time the consent is given or, if there is more than one such person, to all of them.

(4) No offence is committed under subsection (1) or (2) by the commission of an act which by virtue of any provision of Schedule 2 may be done without infringing the rights conferred by this Part.

(5) A person guilty of an offence under subsection (1)(*a*), (*b*) or (*d*)(iii) is liable—

(*a*) on summary conviction to imprisonment for a term not exceeding six months or a fine not exceeding the statutory maximum, or both;
(*b*) on conviction on indictment to a fine or imprisonment for a term not exceeding two years, or both.

(6) A person guilty of any other offence under this section is liable on summary conviction to a fine not exceeding level 5 on the standard scale or imprisonment for a term not exceeding six months, or both.

**199 Order for delivery up in criminal proceedings**

(1) The court before which proceedings are brought against a person for an offence under section 198 may, if satisfied that at the time of his arrest or charge he had in his possession, custody or control in the course of a business an illicit recording of a performance, order that it be delivered up to a person having performers' rights or recording rights in relation to the performance or to such other person as the court may direct.

(2) For this purpose a person shall be treated as charged with an offence—

(*a*) in England, Wales and Northern Ireland, when he is orally charged or is served with a summons or indictment;
(*b*) in Scotland, when he is cautioned, charged or served with a complaint or indictment.

(3) An order may be made by the court of its own motion or on the application of the prosecutor (or, in Scotland, the Lord Advocate or procurator-fiscal), and may be made whether or not the person is convicted of the offence, but shall not be made—

(*a*) after the end of the period specified in section 203 (period after which remedy of delivery up not available), or

(*b*) if it appears to the court unlikely that any order will be made under section 204 (order as to disposal of illicit recording).

(4) An appeal lies from an order made under this section by a magistrates' court—

(*a*) in England and Wales, to the Crown Court, and

(*b*) in Northern Ireland, to the county court;

and in Scotland, where an order has been made under this section, the person from whose possession, custody or control the illicit recording has been removed may, without prejudice to any other form of appeal under any rule of law, appeal against that order in the same manner as against sentence.

(5) A person to whom an illicit recording is delivered up in pursuance of an order under this section shall retain it pending the making of an order, or the decision not to make an order, under section 204.

(6) Nothing in this section affects the powers of the court under section 43 of the Powers of Criminal Courts Act 1973, section 223 or 436 of the Criminal Procedure (Scotland) Act 1975 or Article 7 of the Criminal Justice (Northern Ireland) Order 1980 (general provisions as to forfeiture in criminal proceedings).

**200 Search warrants**

(1) Where a justice of the peace (in Scotland, a sheriff or justice of the peace) is satisfied by information on oath given by a constable (in Scotland, by evidence on oath) that there are reasonable grounds for believing—

(*a*) that an offence under section 198(1)(*a*), (*b*) or (*d*)(iii) (offences of making, importing or distributing illicit recordings) has been or is about to be committed in any premises, and

(*b*) that evidence that such an offence has been or is about to be committed is in those premises,

he may issue a warrant authorising a constable to enter and search the premises, using such reasonable force as is necessary.

(2) The power conferred by subsection (1) does not, in England and Wales, extend to authorising a search for material of the kinds mentioned in section 9(2) of the Police and Criminal Evidence Act 1984 (certain classes of personal or confidential material).

(3) A warrant under subsection (1)—

(*a*) may authorise persons to accompany any constable executing the warrant, and

(*b*) remains in force for 28 days from the date of its issue.

(4) In this section "premises" includes land, buildings, fixed or moveable structures, vehicles, vessels, aircraft and hovercraft.

**201 False representation of authority to give consent**

(1) It is an offence for a person to represent falsely that he is authorised by any person to give consent for the purposes of this Part in relation to a performance, unless he believes on reasonable grounds that he is so authorised.

(2) A person guilty of an offence under this section is liable on summary conviction to imprisonment for a term not exceeding six months or a fine not exceeding level 5 on the standard scale or both.

**202 Offence by body corporate: liability of officers**

(1) Where an offence under this Part committed by a body corporate is proved to have been committed with the consent or connivance of a director, manager,

secretary or other similar officer of the body, or a person purporting to act in any such capacity, he as well as the body corporate is guilty of the offence and liable to be proceeded against and punished accordingly.

(2) In relation to a body corporate whose affairs are managed by its members "director" means a member of the body corporate.

*Supplementary provisions with respect to delivery up and seizure*

**203 Period after which remedy of delivery up not available**

(1) An application for an order under section 195 (order for delivery up in civil proceedings) may not be made after the end of the period of six years from the date on which the illicit recording in question was made, subject to the following provisions.

(2) If during the whole or any part of that period a person entitled to apply for an order—

(*a*) is under a disability, or

(*b*) is prevented by fraud or concealment from discovering the facts entitling him to apply,

an application may be made by him at any time before the end of the period of six years from the date on which he ceased to be under a disability or, as the case may be, could with reasonable diligence have discovered those facts.

(3) In subsection (2) "disability"—

(*a*) in England and Wales, has the same meaning as in the Limitation Act 1980;

(*b*) in Scotland, means legal disability within the meaning of the Prescription and Limitations (Scotland) Act 1973;

(*c*) in Northern Ireland, has the same meaning as in the Statute of Limitation (Northern Ireland) 1958.

(4) An order under section 199 (order for delivery up in criminal proceedings) shall not, in any case, be made after the end of the period of six years from the date on which the illicit recording in question was made.

**204 Order as to disposal of illicit recording**

(1) An application may be made to the court for an order that an illicit recording of a performance delivered up in pursuance of an order under section 195 or 199, or seized and detained in pursuance of the right conferred by section 196, shall be—

(*a*) forfeited to such person having performer's rights or recording rights in relation to the performance as the court may direct, or

(*b*) destroyed or otherwise dealt with as the court may think fit,

or for a decision that no such order should be made.

(2) In considering what order (if any) should be made, the court shall consider whether other remedies available in an action for infringement of the rights conferred by this Part would be adequate to compensate the person or persons entitled to the rights and to protect their interests.

(3) Provision shall be made by rules of court as to the service of notice on persons having an interest in the recording, and any such person is entitled—

(*a*) to appear in proceedings for an order under this section, whether or not he was served with notice, and

(*b*) to appeal against any order made, whether or not he appeared;

and an order shall not take effect until the end of the period within which notice of an appeal may be given or, if before the end of that period notice of appeal is duly given, until the final determination or abandonment of the proceedings on the appeal.

(4) Where there is more than one person interested in a recording, the court shall make such order as it thinks just and may (in particular) direct that the recording be sold, or otherwise dealt with, and the proceeds divided.

(5) If the court decides that no order should be made under this section, the person in whose possession, custody or control the recording was before being delivered up or seized is entitled to its return.

(6) References in this section to a person having an interest in a recording include any person in whose favour an order could be made in respect of the recording under this section or under section 114 or 231 of this Act or section 58C of the Trade Marks Act 1938 (which make similar provision in relation to infringement of copyright, design right and trade marks).

**205 Jurisdiction of county court and sheriff court**

(1) In England, Wales and Northern Ireland a county court may entertain proceedings under—

section 195 (order for delivery up of illicit recording), or
section 204 (order as to disposal of illicit recording),

where the value of the illicit recordings in question does not exceed the county court limit for actions in tort.

(2) In Scotland proceedings for an order under either of those provisions may be brought in the sheriff court.

(3) Nothing in this section shall be construed as affecting the jurisdiction of the High Court or, in Scotland, the Court of Session.

*Qualification for protection and extent*

**206 Qualifying countries, individuals and persons**

(1) In this Part—

"qualifying country" means—

(*a*) the United Kingdom,
(*b*) another member State of the European Economic Community, or
(*c*) to the extent that an Order under section 208 so provides, a country designated under that section as enjoying reciprocal protection;

"qualifying individual" means a citizen or subject of, or an individual resident in, a qualifying country; and

"qualifying person" means a qualifying individual or a body corporate or other body having legal personality which—

(*a*) is formed under the law of a part of the United Kingdom or another qualifying country, and
(*b*) has in any qualifying country a place of business at which substantial business activity is carried on.

(2) The reference in the definition of "qualifying individual" to a person's being a citizen or subject of a qualifying country shall be construed—

(*a*) in relation to the United Kingdom, as a reference to his being a British citizen, and
(*b*) in relation to a colony of the United Kingdom, as a reference to his being a British Dependent Territories' citizen by connection with that colony.

(3) In determining for the purpose of the definition of "qualifying person"

whether substantial business activity is carried on at a place of business in any country, no account shall be taken of dealings in goods which are at all material times outside that country.

**207 Countries to which this Part extends**

This Part extends to England and Wales, Scotland and Northern Ireland.

**208 Countries enjoying reciprocal protection**

(1) Her Majesty may by Order in Council designate as enjoying reciprocal protection under this Part—

(*a*) a Convention country, or

(*b*) a country as to which Her Majesty is satisfied that provision has been or will be made under its law giving adequate protection for British performances.

(2) A "Convention country" means a country which is a party to a Convention relating to performers' rights to which the United Kingdom is also a party.

(3) A "British performance" means a performance—

(*a*) given by an individual who is a British citizen or resident in the United Kingdom, or

(*b*) taking place in the United Kingdom.

(4) If the law of that country provides adequate protection only for certain descriptions of performance, an Order under subsection (1)(*b*) designating that country shall contain provision limiting to a corresponding extent the protection afforded by this Part in relation to performances connected with that country.

(5) The power conferred by subsection (1)(*b*) is exercisable in relation to any of the Channel Islands, the Isle of Man or any colony of the United Kingdom, as in relation to a foreign country.

(6) A statutory instrument containing an Order in Council under this section shall be subject to annulment in pursuance of a resolution of either House of Parliament.

**209 Territorial waters and the continental shelf**

(1) For the purposes of this Part the territorial waters of the United Kingdom shall be treated as part of the United Kingdom.

(2) This Part applies to things done in the United Kingdom sector of the continental shelf on a structure or vessel which is present there for purposes directly connected with the exploration of the sea bed or subsoil or the exploitation of their natural resources as it applies to things done in the United Kingdom.

(3) The United Kingdom sector of the continental shelf means the areas designated by order under section 1(7) of the Continental Shelf Act 1964.

**210 British ships, aircraft and hovercraft**

(1) This Part applies to things done on a British ship, aircraft or hovercraft as it applies to things done in the United Kingdom.

(2) In this section—

"British ship" means a ship which is a British ship for the purposes of the Merchant Shipping Acts (see section 2 of the Merchant Shipping Act 1988) otherwise than by virtue of registration in a country outside the United Kingdom; and

"British aircraft" and "British hovercraft" mean an aircraft or hovercraft registered in the United Kingdom.

*Interpretation*

### 211 Expressions having same meaning as in copyright provisions

(1) The following expressions have the same meaning in this Part as in Part I (copyright)—

broadcast,
business,
cable programme,
cable programme service,
country,
defendant (in Scotland),
delivery up (in Scotland),
film,
literary work,
published, and
sound recording.

(2) The provisions of section 6(3) to (5), section 7(5) and 19(4) (supplementary provisions relating to broadcasting and cable programme services) apply for the purposes of this Part, and in relation to an infringement of the rights conferred by this Part, as they apply for the purposes of Part I and in relation to an infringement of copyright.

### 212 Index of defined expressions

The following Table shows provisions defining or otherwise explaining expressions used in this Part (other than provisions defining or explaining an expression used only in the same section)—

| | |
|---|---|
| broadcast (and related expressions) | section 211 (and section 6) |
| business | section 211(1) (and section 178) |
| cable programme, cable programme service (and related expressions) | section 211 (and section 7) |
| country | section 211(1) (and section 178) |
| defendant (in Scotland) | section 211(1) (and section 177) |
| delivery up (in Scotland) | section 211(1) (and section 177) |
| exclusive recording contract | section 185(1) |
| film | section 211(1) (and section 5) |
| illicit recording | section 197 |
| literary work | section 211(1) (and section 3(1)) |
| performance | section 180(2) |
| published | section 211(1) (and section 175) |
| qualifying country | section 206(1) |
| qualifying individual | section 206(1) and (2) |
| qualifying performance | section 181 |
| qualifying person | section 206(1) and (3) |
| recording (of a performance) | section 180(2) |
| recording rights (person having) | section 185(2) and (3) |
| sound recording | section 211(1) (and section 5). |

## PART III

## DESIGN RIGHT

## CHAPTER I

## DESIGN RIGHT IN ORIGINAL DESIGNS

*Introductory*

### 213 Design right

(1) Design right is a property right which subsists in accordance with this Part in an original design.

(2) In this Part "design" means the design of any aspect of the shape or configuration (whether internal or external) of the whole or part of an article.

(3) Design right does not subsist in—

(*a*) a method or principle of construction,
(*b*) features of shape or configuration of an article which—
  (i) enable the article to be connected to, or placed in, around or against, another article so that either article may perform its function, or
  (ii) are dependent upon the appearance of another article of which the article is intended by the designer to form an integral part, or
(*c*) surface decoration.

(4) A design is not "original" for the purposes of this Part if it is commonplace in the design field in question at the time of its creation.

(5) Design right subsists in a design only if the design qualifies for design right protection by reference to—

(*a*) the designer or the person by whom the design was commissioned or the designer employed (see sections 218 and 219), or
(*b*) the person by whom and country in which articles made to the design were first marketed (see section 220),

or in accordance with any Order under section 221 (power to make further provision with respect to qualification).

(6) Design right does not subsist unless and until the design has been recorded in a design document or an article has been made to the design.

(7) Design right does not subsist in a design which was so recorded, or to which an article was made, before the commencement of this Part.

### 214 The designer

(1) In this Part the "designer", in relation to a design, means the person who creates it.

(2) In the case of a computer-generated design the person by whom the arrangements necessary for the creation of the design are undertaken shall be taken to be the designer.

### 215 Ownership of design right

(1) The designer is the first owner of any design right in a design which is not created in pursuance of a commission or in the course of employment.

(2) Where a design is created in pursuance of a commission, the person commissioning the design is the first owner of any design right in it.

(3) Where, in a case not falling within subsection (2) a design is created by an

employee in the course of his employment, his employer is the first owner of any design right in the design.

(4) If a design qualifies for design right protection by virtue of section 220 (qualification by reference to first marketing of articles made to the design), the above rules do not apply and the person by whom the articles in question are marketed is the first owner of the design right.

**216 Duration of design right**

(1) Design right expires—

(*a*) fifteen years from the end of the calendar year in which the design was first recorded in a design document or an article was first made to the design, whichever first occurred, or

(*b*) if articles made to the design are made available for sale or hire within five years from the end of that calendar year, ten years from the end of the calendar year in which that first occurred.

(2) The reference in subsection (1) to articles being made available for sale or hire is to their being made so available anywhere in the world by or with the licence of the design right owner.

*Qualification for design right protection*

**217 Qualifying individuals and qualifying persons**

(1) In this Part—

"qualifying individual" means a citizen or subject of, or an individual habitually resident in, a qualifying country; and

"qualifying person" means a qualifying individual or a body corporate or other body having legal personality which—

(*a*) is formed under the law of a part of the United Kingdom or another qualifying country, and

(*b*) has in any qualifying country a place of business at which substantial business activity is carried on.

(2) References in this Part to a qualifying person include the Crown and the government of any other qualifying country.

(3) In this section "qualifying country" means—

(*a*) the United Kingdom,

(*b*) a country to which this Part extends by virtue of an Order under section 255,

(*c*) another member State of the European Economic Community, or

(*d*) to the extent that an Order under section 256 so provides, a country designated under that section as enjoying reciprocal protection.

(4) The reference in the definition of "qualifying individual" to a person's being a citizen or subject of a qualifying country shall be construed—

(*a*) in relation to the United Kingdom, as a reference to his being a British citizen, and

(*b*) in relation to a colony of the United Kingdom, as a reference to his being a British Dependent Territories' citizen by connection with that colony.

(5) In determining for the purpose of the definition of "qualifying person" whether substantial business activity is carried on at a place of business in any country, no account shall be taken of dealings in goods which are at all material times outside that country.

**218 Qualification by reference to designer**

(1) This section applies to a design which is not created in pursuance of a commission or in the course of employment.

(2) A design to which this section applies qualifies for design right protection if the designer is a qualifying individual or, in the case of a computer-generated design, a qualifying person.

(3) A joint design to which this section applies qualifies for design right protection if any of the designers is a qualifying individual or, as the case may be, a qualifying person.

(4) Where a joint design qualifies for design right protection under this section, only those designers who are qualifying individuals or qualifying persons are entitled to design right under section 215(1) (first ownership of design right: entitlement of designer).

**219 Qualification by reference to commissioner or employer**

(1) A design qualifies for design right protection if it is created in pursuance of a commission from, or in the course of employment with, a qualifying person.

(2) In the case of a joint commission or joint employment a design qualifies for design right protection if any of the commissioners or employers is a qualifying person.

(3) Where a design which is jointly commissioned or created in the course of joint employment qualifies for design right protection under this section, only those commissioners or employers who are qualifying persons are entitled to design right under section 215(2) or (3) (first ownership of design right: entitlement of commissioner or employer).

**220 Qualification by reference to first marketing**

(1) A design which does not qualify for design right protection under section 218 or 219 (qualification by reference to designer, commissioner or employer) qualifies for design right protection if the first marketing of articles made to the design—

(*a*) is by a qualifying person who is exclusively authorised to put such articles on the market in the United Kingdom, and
(*b*) takes place in the United Kingdom, another country to which this Part extends by virtue of an Order under section 255, or another member State of the European Economic Community.

(2) If the first marketing of articles made to the design is done jointly by two or more persons, the design qualifies for design right protection if any of those persons meets the requirements specified in subsection (1)(*a*).

(3) In such a case only the persons who meet those requirements are entitled to design right under section 215(4) (first ownership of design right: entitlement of first marketer of articles made to the design).

(4) In subsection (1)(*a*) "exclusively authorised" refers—

(*a*) to authorisation by the person who would have been first owner of design right as designer, commissioner of the design or employer of the designer if he had been a qualifying person, or by a person lawfully claiming under such a person, and
(*b*) to exclusivity capable of being enforced by legal proceedings in the United Kingdom.

**221 Power to make further provision as to qualification**

(1) Her Majesty may, with a view to fulfilling an international obligation of the United Kingdom, by Order in Council provide that a design qualifies for design right protection if such requirements as are specified in the Order are met.

(2) An Order may make different provision for different descriptions of design or article; and may make such consequential modifications of the operation of sections 215 (ownership of design right) and sections 218 to 220 (other means of qualification) as appear to Her Majesty to be appropriate.

(3) A statutory instrument containing an Order in Council under this section shall be subject to annulment in pursuance of a resolution of either House of Parliament.

*Dealings with design right*

**222 Assignment and licences**

(1) Design right is transmissible by assignment, by testamentary disposition or by operation of law, as personal or moveable property.

(2) An assignment or other transmission of design right may be partial, that is, limited so as to apply—

(*a*) to one or more, but not all, of the things the design right owner has the exclusive right to do;

(*b*) to part, but not the whole, of the period for which the right is to subsist.

(3) An assignment of design right is not effective unless it is in writing signed by or on behalf of the assignor.

(4) A licence granted by the owner of design right is binding on every successor in title to his interest in the right, except a purchaser in good faith for valuable consideration and without notice (actual or constructive) of the licence or a person deriving title from such a purchaser; and references in this Part to doing anything with, or without, the licence of the design right owner shall be construed accordingly.

**223 Prospective ownership of design right**

(1) Where by an agreement made in relation to future design right, and signed by or on behalf of the prospective owner of the design right, the prospective owner purports to assign the future design right (wholly or partially) to another person, then if, on the right coming into existence, the assignee or another person claiming under him would be entitled as against all other persons to require the right to be vested in him, the right shall vest in him by virtue of this section.

(2) In this section—

"future design right" means design right which will or may come into existence in respect of a future design or class of designs or on the occurrence of a future event; and

"prospective owner" shall be construed accordingly, and includes a person who is prospectively entitled to design right by virtue of such an agreement as is mentioned in subsection (1).

(3) A licence granted by a prospective owner of design right is binding on every successor in title to his interest (or prospective interest) in the right, except a purchaser in good faith for valuable consideration and without notice (actual or constructive) of the licence or a person deriving title from such a purchaser; and references in this Part to doing anything with, or without, the licence of the design right owner shall be construed accordingly.

### 224 Assignment of right in registered design presumed to carry with it design right

Where a design consisting of a design in which design right subsists is registered under the Registered Designs Act 1949 and the proprietor of the registered design is also the design right owner, an assignment of the right in the registered design shall be taken to be also an assignment of the design right, unless a contrary intention appears.

### 225 Exclusive licences

(1) In this Part an "exclusive licence" means a licence in writing signed by or on behalf of the design right owner authorising the licensee to the exclusion of all other persons, including the person granting the licence, to exercise a right which would otherwise be exercisable exclusively by the design right owner.

(2) The licensee under an exclusive licence has the same rights against any successor in title who is bound by the licence as he has against the person granting the licence.

## CHAPTER II

## RIGHTS OF DESIGN RIGHT OWNER AND REMEDIES

*Infringement of design right*

### 226 Primary infringement of design right

(1) The owner of design right in a design has the exclusive right to reproduce the design for commercial purposes—

(*a*) by making articles to that design, or
(*b*) by making a design document recording the design for the purpose of enabling such articles to be made.

(2) Reproduction of a design by making articles to the design means copying the design so as to produce articles exactly or substantially to that design, and references in this Part to making articles to a design shall be construed accordingly.

(3) Design right is infringed by a person who without the licence of the design right owner does, or authorises another to do, anything which by virtue of this section is the exclusive right of the design right owner.

(4) For the purposes of this section reproduction may be direct or indirect, and it is immaterial whether any intervening acts themselves infringe the design right.

(5) This section has effect subject to the provisions of Chapter III (exceptions to rights of design right owner).

### 227 Secondary infringement: importing or dealing with infringing article

(1) Design right is infringed by a person who, without the licence of the design right owner—

(*a*) imports into the United Kingdom for commercial purposes, or
(*b*) has in his possession for commercial purposes, or
(*c*) sells, lets for hire, or offers or exposes for sale or hire, in the course of a business,

an article which is, and which he knows or has reason to believe is, an infringing article.

(2) This section has effect subject to the provisions of Chapter III (exceptions to rights of design right owner).

**228 Meaning of "infringing article"**

(1) In this Part "infringing article", in relation to a design, shall be construed in accordance with this section.

(2) An article is an infringing article if its making to that design was an infringement of design right in the design.

(3) An article is also an infringing article if—

(*a*) it has been or is proposed to be imported into the United Kingdom, and

(*b*) its making to that design in the United Kingdom would have been an infringement of design right in the design or a breach of an exclusive licence agreement relating to the design.

(4) Where it is shown that an article is made to a design in which design right subsists or has subsisted at any time, it shall be presumed until the contrary is proved that the article was made at a time when design right subsisted.

(5) Nothing in subsection (3) shall be construed as applying to an article which may lawfully be imported into the United Kingdom by virtue of any enforceable Community right within the meaning of section 2(1) of the European Communities Act 1972.

(6) The expression "infringing article" does not include a design document, notwithstanding that its making was or would have been an infringement of design right.

*Remedies for infringement*

**229 Rights and remedies of design right owner**

(1) An infringement of design right is actionable by the design right owner.

(2) In an action for infringement of design right all such relief by way of damages, injunctions, accounts or otherwise is available to the plaintiff as is available in respect of the infringement of any other property right.

(3) The court may in an action for infringement of design right, having regard to all the circumstances and in particular to—

(*a*) the flagrancy of the infringement, and

(*b*) any benefit accruing to the defendant by reason of the infringement,

award such additional damages as the justice of the case may require.

(4) This section has effect subject to section 233 (innocent infringement).

**230 Order for delivery up**

(1) Where a person—

(*a*) has in his possession, custody or control for commercial purposes an infringing article, or

(*b*) has in his possession, custody or control anything specifically designed or adapted for making articles to a particular design, knowing or having reason to believe that it has been or is to be used to make an infringing article,

the owner of the design right in the design in question may apply to the court for an order that the infringing article or other thing be delivered up to him or to such other person as the court may direct.

(2) An application shall not be made after the end of the period specified in the following provisions of this section; and no order shall be made unless the court

also makes, or it appears to the court that there are grounds for making, an order under section 231 (order as to disposal of infringing article, &c).

(3) An application for an order under this section may not be made after the end of the period of six years from the date on which the article or thing in question was made, subject to subsection (4).

(4) If during the whole or any part of that period the design right owner—

(*a*) is under a disability, or

(*b*) is prevented by fraud or concealment from discovering the facts entitling him to apply for an order,

an application may be made at any time before the end of the period of six years from the date on which he ceased to be under a disability or, as the case may be, could with reasonable diligence have discovered those facts.

(5) In subsection (4) "disability"—

(*a*) in England and Wales, has the same meaning as in the Limitation Act 1980;

(*b*) in Scotland, means legal disability within the meaning of the Prescription and Limitation (Scotland) Act 1973;

(*c*) in Northern Ireland, has the same meaning as in the Statute of Limitations (Northern Ireland) 1958.

(6) A person to whom an infringing article or other thing is delivered up in pursuance of an order under this section shall, if an order under section 231 is not made, retain it pending the making of an order, or the decision not to make an order, under that section.

(7) Nothing in this section affects any other power of the court.

**231 Order as to disposal of infringing articles, &c**

(1) An application may be made to the court for an order that an infringing article or other thing delivered up in pursuance of an order under section 230 shall be—

(*a*) forfeited to the design right owner, or

(*b*) destroyed or otherwise dealt with as the court may think fit,

or for a decision that no such order should be made.

(2) In considering what order (if any) should be made, the court shall consider whether other remedies available in an action for infringement of design right would be adequate to compensate the design right owner and to protect his interests.

(3) Provision shall be made by rules of court as to the service of notice on persons having an interest in the article or other thing, and any such person is entitled—

(*a*) to appear in proceedings for an order under this section, whether or not he was served with notice, and

(*b*) to appeal against any order made, whether or not he appeared;

and an order shall not take effect until the end of the period within which notice of an appeal may be given or, if before the end of that period notice of appeal is duly given, until the final determination or abandonment of the proceedings on the appeal.

(4) Where there is more than one person interested in an article or other thing, the court shall make such order as it thinks just and may (in particular) direct that the thing be sold, or otherwise dealt with, and the proceeds divided.

(5) If the court decides that no order should be made under this section, the person in whose possession, custody or control the article or other thing was before being delivered up or seized is entitled to its return.

(6) References in this section to a person having an interest in an article or other

thing include any person in whose favour an order could be made in respect of it under this section or under section 114 or 204 of this Act or section 58C of the Trade Marks Act 1938 (whch make similar provision in relation to infringement of copyright, rights in performances and trade marks).

**232 Jurisdiction of county court and sheriff court**

(1) In England, Wales and Northern Ireland a county court may entertain proceedings under—

section 230 (order for delivery up of infringing article, &c),
section 231 (order as to disposal of infringing article, &c), or
section 235(5) (application by exclusive licensee having concurrent rights),

where the value of the infringing articles and other things in question does not exceed the county court limit for actions in tort.

(2) In Scotland proceedings for an order under any of those provisions may be brought in the sheriff court.

(3) Nothing in this section shall be construed as affecting the jurisdiction of the High Court or, in Scotland, the Court of Session.

**233 Innocent infringement**

(1) Where in an action for infringement of design right brought by virtue of section 226 (primary infringement) it is shown that at the time of the infringement the defendant did not know, and had no reason to believe, that design right subsisted in the design to which the action relates, the plaintiff is not entitled to damages against him, but without prejudice to any other remedy.

(2) Where in an action for infringement of design right brought by virtue of section 227 (secondary infringement) a defendant shows that the infringing article was innocently acquired by him or a predecessor in title of his, the only remedy available against him in respect of the infringement is damages not exceeding a reasonable royalty in respect of the act complained of.

(3) In subsection (2) "innocently acquired" means that the person acquiring the article did not know and had no reason to believe that it was an infringing article.

**234 Rights and remedies of exclusive licensee**

(1) An exclusive licensee has, except against the design right owner, the same rights and remedies in respect of matters occurring after the grant of the licence as if the licence had been an assignment.

(2) His rights and remedies are concurrent with those of the design right owner; and references in the relevant provisions of this Part to the design right owner shall be construed accordingly.

(3) In an action brought by an exclusive licensee by virtue of this section a defendant may avail himself of any defence which would have been available to him if the action had been brought by the design right owner.

**235 Exercise of concurrent rights**

(1) Where an action for infringement of design right brought by the design right owner or an exclusive licensee relates (wholly or partly) to an infringement in respect of which they have concurrent rights of action, the design right owner or, as the case may be, the exclusive licensee may not, without the leave of the court, proceed with the action unless the other is either joined as a plaintiff or added as a defendant.

(2) A design right owner or exclusive licensee who is added as a defendant in

pursuance of subsection (1) is not liable for any costs in the action unless he takes part in the proceedings.

(3) The above provisions do not affect the granting of interlocutory relief on the application of the design right owner or an exclusive licensee.

(4) Where an action for infringement of design right is brought which relates (wholly or partly) to an infringement in respect of which the design right owner and an exclusive licensee have concurrent rights of action—

(*a*) the court shall, in assessing damages, take into account—

(i) the terms of the licence, and

(ii) any pecuniary remedy already awarded or available to either of them in respect of the infringement;

(*b*) no account of profits shall be directed if an award of damages has been made, or an account of profits has been directed, in favour of the other of them in respect of the infringement; and

(*c*) the court shall if an account of profits is directed apportion the profits between them as the court considers just, subject to any agreement between them;

and these provisions apply whether or not the design right owner and the exclusive licensee are both parties to the action.

(5) The design right owner shall notify any exclusive licensee having concurrent rights before applying for an order under section 230 (order for delivery up of infringing article, &c); and the court may on the application of the licensee make such order under that section as it thinks fit having regard to the terms of the licence.

## CHAPTER III

## EXCEPTIONS TO RIGHTS OF DESIGN RIGHT OWNERS

*Infringement of copyright*

### 236 Infringement of copyright

Where copyright subsists in a work which consists of or includes a design in which design right subsists, it is not an infringement of design right in the design to do anything which is an infringement of the copyright in that work.

*Availability of licences of right*

### 237 Licences available in last five years of design right

(1) Any person is entitled as of right to a licence to do in the last five years of the design right term anything which would otherwise infringe the design right.

(2) The terms of the licence shall, in default of agreement, be settled by the comptroller.

(3) The Secretary of State may if it appears to him necessary in order to—

(*a*) comply with an international obligation of the United Kingdom, or

(*b*) secure or maintain reciprocal protection for British designs in other countries,

by order exclude from the operation of subsection (1) designs of a description specified in the order or designs applied to articles of a description so specified.

(4) An order shall be made by statutory instrument; and no order shall be made

unless a draft of it has been laid before and approved by a resolution of each House of Parliament.

**238 Powers exercisable for protection of the public interest**

(1) Where the matters specified in a report of the Monopolies and Mergers Commission as being those which in the Commission's opinion operate, may be expected to operate or have operated against the public interest include—

(*a*) conditions in licences granted by a design right owner restricting the use of the design by the licensee or the right of the design right owner to grant other licences, or

(*b*) a refusal of a design right owner to grant licences on reasonable terms,

the powers conferred by Part I of Schedule 8 to the Fair Trading Act 1973 (powers exercisable for purpose of remedying or preventing adverse effects specified in report of Commission) include power to cancel or modify those conditions and, instead or in addition, to provide that licences in respect of the design right shall be available as of right.

(2) The references in sections 56(2) and 73(2) of that Act, and sections 10(2)(*b*) and 12(5) of the Competition Act 1980, to the powers specified in that Part of that Schedule shall be construed accordingly.

(3) The terms of a licence available by virtue of this section shall, in default of agreement, be settled by the comptroller.

**239 Undertaking to take licence of right in infringement proceedings**

(1) If in proceedings for infringement of design right in a design in respect of which a licence is available as of right under section 237 or 238 the defendant undertakes to take a licence on such terms as may be agreed or, in default of agreement, settled by the comptroller under that section—

(*a*) no injunction shall be granted against him,

(*b*) no order for delivery up shall be made under section 230, and

(*c*) the amount recoverable against him by way of damages or on an account of profits shall not exceed double the amount which would have been payable by him as licensee if such a licence on those terms had been granted before the earliest infringement.

(2) An undertaking may be given at any time before final order in the proceedings, without any admission of liability.

(3) Nothing in this section affects the remedies available in respect of an infringement committed before licences of right were available.

*Crown use of designs*

**240 Crown use of designs**

(1) A government department, or a person authorised in writing by a government department, may without the licence of the design right owner—

(*a*) do anything for the purpose of supplying articles for the services of the Crown, or

(*b*) dispose of articles no longer required for the services of the Crown;

and nothing done by virtue of this section infringes the design right.

(2) References in this Part to "the services of the Crown" are to—

(*a*) the defence of the realm,

(*b*) foreign defence purposes, and

(*c*) health service purposes.

(3) The reference to the supply of articles for "foreign defence purposes" is to their supply—

(*a*) for the defence of a country outside the realm in pursuance of an agreement or arrangement to which the government of that country and Her Majesty's Government in the United Kingdom are parties; or

(*b*) for use by armed forces operating in pursuance of a resolution of the United Nations or one of its organs.

(4) The reference to the supply of articles for "health service purposes" are to their supply for the purpose of providing—

(*a*) pharmaceutical services,
(*b*) general medical services, or
(*c*) general dental services,

that is, services of those kinds under Part II of the National Health Service Act 1977, Part II of the National Health Service (Scotland) Act 1978 or the corresponding provisions of the law in force in Northern Ireland.

(5) In this Part—

"Crown use", in relation to a design, means the doing of anything by virtue of this section which would otherwise be an infringement of design right in the design; and

"the government department concerned", in relation to such use, means the government department by whom or on whose authority the act was done.

(6) The authority of a government department in respect of Crown use of a design may be given to a person either before or after the use and whether or not he is authorised, directly or indirectly, by the design right owner to do anything in relation to the design.

(7) A person acquiring anything sold in the exercise of powers conferred by this section, and any person claiming under him, may deal with it in the same manner as if the design right were held on behalf of the Crown.

**241 Settlement of terms for Crown use**

(1) Where Crown use is made of a design, the government department concerned shall—

(*a*) notify the design right owner as soon as practicable, and

(*b*) give him such information as to the extent of the use as he may from time to time require,

unless it appears to the department that it would be contrary to the public interest to do so or the identity of the design right owner cannot be ascertained on reasonable inquiry.

(2) Crown use of a design shall be on such terms as, either before or after the use, are agreed between the government department concerned and the design right owner with the approval of the Treasury or, in default of agreement, are determined by the court.

In the application of this subsection to Northern Ireland the reference to the Treasury shall, where the government department referred to in that subsection is a Northern Ireland department, be construed as a reference to the Department of Finance and Personnel.

(3) Where the identity of the design right owner cannot be ascertained on reasonable inquiry, the government department concerned may apply to the court who may order that no royalty or other sum shall be payable in respect of Crown

use of the design until the owner agrees terms with the department or refers the matter to the court for determination.

**242 Rights of third parties in case of Crown use**

(1) The provisions of any licence, assignment or agreement made between the design right owner (or anyone deriving title from him or from whom he derives title) and any person other than a government department are of no effect in relation to Crown use of a design, or any act incidental to Crown use, so far as they—

(*a*) restrict or regulate anything done in relation to the design, or the use of any model, document or other information relating to it, or

(*b*) provide for the making of payments in respect of, or calculated by reference to such use;

and the copying or issuing to the public of copies of any such model or document in connection with the thing done, or any such use, shall be deemed not to be an infringement of any copyright in the model or document.

(2) Subsection (1) shall not be construed as authorising the disclosure of any such model, document or information in contravention of the licence, assignment or agreement.

(3) Where an exclusive licence is in force in respect of the design—

(*a*) if the licence was granted for royalties—

(i) any agreement between the design right owner and a government department under section 241 (settlement of terms for Crown use) requires the consent of the licensee, and

(ii) the licensee is entitled to recover from the design right owner such part of the payment for Crown use as may be agreed between them or, in default of agreement, determined by the court;

(*b*) if the licence was granted otherwise than for royalties—

(i) section 241 applies in relation to anything done which but for section 240 (Crown use) and subsection (1) above would be an infringement of the rights of the licensee with the substitution for references to the design right owner of references to the licensee, and

(ii) section 241 does not apply in relation to anything done by the licensee by virtue of an authority given under section 240.

(4) Where the design right has been assigned to the design right owner in consideration of royalties—

(*a*) section 241 applies in relation to Crown use of the design as if the references to the design right owner included the assignor, and any payment for Crown use shall be divided between them in such proportion as may be agreed or, in default of agreement, determined by the court; and

(*b*) section 241 applies in relation to any act incidental to Crown use as it applies in relation to Crown use of the design.

(5) Where any model, document or other information relating to a design is used in connection with Crown use of the design, or any act incidental to Crown use, section 241 applies to the use of the model, document or other information with the substitution for the references to the design right owner of references to the person entitled to the benefit of any provision of an agreement rendered inoperative by subsection (1) above.

(6) In this section—

"act incidental to Crown use" means anything done for the services of the Crown to the order of a government department by the design right owner in respect of a design;

"payment for Crown use" means such amount as is payable by the government department concerned by virtue of section 241; and

"royalties" includes any benefit determined by reference to the use of the design.

**243 Crown use: compensation for loss of profit**

(1) Where Crown use is made of a design, the government department concerned shall pay—

(*a*) to the design right owner, or

(*b*) if there is an exclusive licence in force in respect of the design, to the exclusive licensee,

compensation for any loss resulting from his not being awarded a contract to supply the articles made to the design.

(2) Compensation is payable only to the extent that such a contract could have been fulfilled from his existing manufacturing capacity; but is payable notwithstanding the existence of circumstances rendering him ineligible for the award of such a contract.

(3) In determining the loss, regard shall be had to the profit which would have been made on such a contract and to the extent to which any manufacturing capacity was under-used.

(4) No compensation is payable in respect of any failure to secure contracts for the supply of articles made to the design otherwise than for the services of the Crown.

(5) The amount payable shall, if not agreed between the design right owner or licensee and the government department concerned with the approval of the Treasury, be determined by the court on a reference under section 252; and it is in addition to any amount payable under section 241 or 242.

(6) In the application of this section to Northern Ireland, the reference in subsection (5) to the Treasury shall, where the government department concerned is a Northern Ireland department, be construed as a reference to the Department of Finance and Personnel.

**244 Special provision for Crown use during emergency**

(1) During a period of emergency the powers exercisable in relation to a design by virtue of section 240 (Crown use) include power to do any act which would otherwise be an infringement of design right for any purpose which appears to the government department concerned necessary or expedient—

(*a*) for the efficient prosecution of any war in which Her Majesty may be engaged;

(*b*) for the maintenance of supplies and services essential to the life of the community;

(*c*) for securing a sufficiency of supplies and services essential to the well-being of the community;

(*d*) for promoting the productivity of industry, commerce and agriculture;

(*e*) for fostering and directing exports and reducing imports, or imports of any classes, from all or any countries and for redressing the balance of trade;

(*f*) generally for ensuring that the whole resources of the community are available for use, and are used, in a manner best calculated to serve the interests of the community; or

(*g*) for assisting the relief of suffering and the restoration and distribution of essential supplies and services in any country outside the United Kingdom which is in grave distress as the result of war.

(2) References in this Part to the services of the Crown include, as respects a

period of emergency, those purposes; and references to "Crown use" include any act which would apart from this section be an infringement of design right.

(3) In this section "period of emergency" means a period beginning with such date as may be declared by Order in Council to be the beginning, and ending with such date as may be so declared to be the end, of a period of emergency for the purposes of this section.

(4) No Order in Council under this section shall be submitted to Her Majesty unless a draft of it has been laid before and approved by a resolution of each House of Parliament.

*General*

**245 Power to provide for further exceptions**

(1) The Secretary of State may if it appears to him necessary in order to—

(*a*) comply with an international obligation of the United Kingdom, or

(*b*) secure or maintain reciprocal protection for British designs in other countries,

by order provide that acts of a description specified in the order do not infringe design right.

(2) An order may make different provision for different descriptions of design or article.

(3) An order shall be made by statutory instrument and no order shall be made unless a draft of it has been laid before and approved by a resolution of each House of Parliament.

## CHAPTER IV

## JURISDICTION OF THE COMPTROLLER AND THE COURT

*Jurisdiction of the comptroller*

**246 Jurisdiction to decide matters relating to design right**

(1) A party to a dispute as to any of the following matters may refer the dispute to the comptroller for his decision—

(*a*) the subsistence of design right,

(*b*) the term of design right, or

(*c*) the identity of the person in whom design right first vested;

and the comptroller's decision on the reference is binding on the parties to the dispute.

(2) No other court or tribunal shall decide any such matter except—

(*a*) on a reference or appeal from the comptroller,

(*b*) in infringement or other proceedings in which the issue arises incidentally, or

(*c*) in proceedings brought with the agreement of the parties or the leave of the comptroller.

(3) The comptroller has jurisdiction to decide any incidental question of fact or law arising in the course of a reference under this section.

**247 Application to settle terms of licence of right**

(1) A person requiring a licence which is available as of right by virtue of—

(*a*) section 237 (licences available in last five years of design right), or
(*b*) an order under section 238 (licences made available in the public interest),

may apply to the comptroller to settle the terms of the licence.

(2) No application for the settlement of the terms of a licence available by virtue of section 237 may be made earlier than one year before the earliest date on which the licence may take effect under that section.

(3) The terms of a licence settled by the comptroller shall authorise the licensee to do—

(*a*) in the case of licence available by virtue of section 237, everything which would be an infringement of the design right in the absence of a licence;
(*b*) in the case of a licence available by virtue of section 238, everything in respect of which a licence is so available.

(4) In settling the terms of a licence the comptroller shall have regard to such factors as may be prescribed by the Secretary of State by order made by statutory instrument.

(5) No such order shall be made unless a draft of it has been laid before and approved by a resolution of each House of Parliament.

(6) Where the terms of a licence are settled by the comptroller, the licence has effect—

(*a*) in the case of an application in respect of a licence available by virtue of section 237 made before the earliest date on which the licence may take effect under that section, from that date;
(*b*) in any other case, from the date on which the application to the comptroller was made.

**248 Settlement of terms where design right owner unknown**

(1) This section applies where a person making an application under section 247 (settlement of terms of licence of right) is unable on reasonable inquiry to discover the identity of the design right owner.

(2) The comptroller may in settling the terms of the licence order that the licence shall be free of any obligation as to royalties or other payments.

(3) If such an order is made the design right owner may apply to the comptroller to vary the terms of the licence with effect from the date on which his application is made.

(4) If the terms of a licence are settled by the comptroller and it is subsequently established that a licence was not available as of right, the licensee shall not be liable in damages for, or for an account of profits in respect of, anything done before he was aware of any claim by the design right owner that a licence was not available.

**249 Appeals as to terms of licence of right**

(1) An appeal lies from any decision of the comptroller under section 247 or 248 (settlement of terms of licence of right) to the Appeal Tribunal constituted under section 28 of the Registered Designs Act 1949.

(2) Section 28 of that Act applies to appeals from the comptroller under this section as it applies to appeals from the registrar under that Act; but rules made under that section may make different provision for appeals under this section.

**250 Rules**

(1) The Secretary of State may make rules for regulating the procedure to be followed in connection with any proceeding before the comptroller under this Part.

(2) Rules may, in particular, make provision—

(*a*) prescribing forms;
(*b*) requiring fees to be paid;
(*c*) authorising the rectification of irregularities of procedure;
(*d*) regulating the mode of giving evidence and empowering the comptroller to compel the attendance of witnesses and the discovery of and production of documents;
(*e*) providing for the appointment of advisers to assist the comptroller in proceedings before him;
(*f*) prescribing time limits for doing anything required to be done (and providing for the alteration of any such limit); and
(*g*) empowering the comptroller to award costs and to direct how, to what party and from what parties, costs are to be paid.

(3) Rules prescribing fees require the consent of the Treasury.

(4) The remuneration of an adviser appointed to assist the comptroller shall be determined by the Secretary of State with the consent of the Treasury and shall be defrayed out of money provided by Parliament.

(5) Rules shall be made by statutory instrument which shall be subject to annulment in pursuance of a resolution of either House of Parliament.

*Jurisdiction of the court*

**251 References and appeals on design right matters**

(1) In any proceedings before him under section 246 (reference of matter relating to design right), the comptroller may at any time order the whole proceedings or any question or issue (whether of fact or law) to be referred, on such terms as he may direct, to the High Court or, in Scotland, the Court of Session.

(2) The comptroller shall make such an order if the parties to the proceedings agree that he should do so.

(3) On a reference under this section the court may exercise any power available to the comptroller by virtue of this Part as respects the matter referred to it and, following its determination, may refer any matter back to the comptroller.

(4) An appeal lies from any decision of the comptroller in proceedings before him under section 246 (decisions on matters relating to design right) to the High Court or, in Scotland, the Court of Session.

**252 Reference of disputes relating to Crown use**

(1) A dispute as to any matter which falls to be determined by the court in default of agreement under—

(*a*) section 241 (settlement of terms for Crown use),
(*b*) section 242 (rights of third parties in case of Crown use), or
(*c*) section 243 (Crown use: compensation for loss of profit),

may be referred to the court by any party to the dispute.

(2) In determining a dispute between a government department and any person as to the terms for Crown use of a design the court shall have regard to—

(*a*) any sums which that person or a person from whom he derives title has received or is entitled to receive, directly or indirectly, from any government department in respect of the design; and
(*b*) whether that person or a person from whom he derives title has in the court's opinion without reasonable cause failed to comply with a request of the department for the use of the design on reasonable terms.

(3) One of two or more joint owners of design right may, without the concurrence of the others, refer a dispute to the court under this section, but shall not do so unless the others are made parties; and none of those others is liable for any costs unless he takes part in the proceedings.

(4) Where the consent of an exclusive licensee is required by section 242(3)(*a*)(i) to the settlement by agreement of the terms for Crown use of a design, a determination by the court of the amount of any payment to be made for such use is of no effect unless the licensee has been notified of the reference and given an opportunity to be heard.

(5) On the reference of a dispute as to the amount recoverable as mentioned in section 242(3)(*a*)(ii) (right of exclusive licensee to recover part of amount payable to design right owner) the court shall determine what is just having regard to any expenditure incurred by the licensee—

(*a*) in developing the design, or
(*b*) in making payments to the design right owner in consideration of the licence (other than royalties or other payments determined by reference to the use of the design).

(6) In this section "the court" means—

(*a*) in England and Wales, the High Court or any patents county court having jurisdiction by virtue of an order under section 287 of this Act,
(*b*) in Scotland, the Court of Session, and
(*c*) in Northern Ireland, the High Court.

## CHAPTER V

## MISCELLANEOUS AND GENERAL

### *Miscellaneous*

### 253 Remedy for groundless threats of infringement proceedings

(1) Where a person threatens another person with proceedings for infringement of design right, a person aggrieved by the threats may bring an action against him claiming—

(*a*) a declaration to the effect that the threats are unjustifiable;
(*b*) an injunction against the continuance of the threats;
(*c*) damages in respect of any loss which he has sustained by the threats.

(2) If the plaintiff proves that the threats were made and that he is a person aggrieved by them, he is entitled to the relief claimed unless the defendant shows that the acts in respect of which proceedings were threatened did constitute, or if done would have constituted, an infringement of the design right concerned.

(3) Proceedings may not be brought under this section in respect of a threat to bring proceedings for an infringement alleged to consist of making or importing anything.

(4) Mere notification that a design is protected by design right does not constitute a threat of proceedings for the purposes of this section.

### 254 Licensee under licence of right not to claim connection with design right owner

(1) A person who has a licence in respect of a design by virtue of section 237 or 238 (licences of right) shall not, without the consent of the design right owner—

(*a*) apply to goods which he is marketing, or proposes to market, in reliance on that licence a trade description indicating that he is the licensee of the design right owner, or
(*b*) use any such trade description in an advertisement in relation to such goods.

(2) A contravention of subsection (1) is actionable by the design right owner.

(3) In this section "trade description", the reference to applying a trade description to goods and "advertisement" have the same meaning as in the Trade Descriptions Act 1968.

*Extent of operation of this Part*

**255 Countries to which this Part extends**

(1) This Part extends to England and Wales, Scotland and Northern Ireland.

(2) Her Majesty may by Order in Council direct that this Part shall extend, subject to such exceptions and modifications as may be specified in the Order, to—

(*a*) any of the Channel Islands,
(*b*) the Isle of Man, or
(*c*) any colony.

(3) That power includes power to extend, subject to such exceptions and modifications as may be specified in the Order, any Order in Council made under section 221 (further provision as to qualification for design right protection) or section 256 (countries enjoying reciprocal protection).

(4) The legislature of a country to which this Part has been extended may modify or add to the provisions of this Part, in their operation as part of the law of that country, as the legislature may consider necessary to adapt the provisions to the circumstances of that country; but not so as to deny design right protection in a case where it would otherwise exist.

(5) Where a country to which this Part extends ceases to be a colony of the United Kingdom, it shall continue to be treated as such a country for the purposes of this Part until—

(*a*) an Order in Council is made under section 256 designating it as a country enjoying reciprocal protection, or
(*b*) an Order in Council is made declaring that it shall cease to be so treated by reason of the fact that the provisions of this Part as part of the law of that country have been amended or repealed.

(6) A statutory instrument containing an Order in Council under subsection (5)(*b*) shall be subject to annulment in pursuance of a resolution of either House of Parliament.

**256 Countries enjoying reciprocal protection**

(1) Her Majesty may, if it appears to Her that the law of a country provides adequate protection for British designs, by Order in Council designate that country as one enjoying reciprocal protection under this Part.

(2) If the law of a country provides adequate protection only for certain classes of British design, or only for designs applied to certain classes of article, any Order designating that country shall contain provision limiting, to a corresponding extent, the protection afforded by this Part in relation to designs connected with that country.

(3) An Order under this section shall be subject to annulment in pursuance of a resolution of either House of Parliament.

**257 Territorial waters and the continental shelf**

(1) For the purposes of this Part the territorial waters of the United Kingdom shall be treated as part of the United Kingdom.

(2) This Part applies to things done in the United Kingdom sector of the continental shelf on a structure or vessel which is present there for purposes directly connected with the exploration of the sea bed or subsoil or the exploitation of their natural resources as it applies to things done in the United Kingdom.

(3) The United Kingdom sector of the continental shelf means the areas designated by order under section 1(7) of the Continental Shelf Act 1964.

*Interpretation*

**258 Construction of references to design right owner**

(1) Where different persons are (whether in consequence of a partial assignment or otherwise) entitled to different aspects of design right in a work, the design right owner for any purpose of this Part is the person who is entitled to the right in the respect relevant for that purpose.

(2) Where design right (or any aspect of design right) is owned by more than one person jointly, references in this Part to the design right owner are to all the owners, so that, in particular, any requirement of the licence of the design right owner requires the licence of all of them.

**259 Joint designs**

(1) In this Part a "joint design" means a design produced by the collaboration of two or more designers in which the contribution of each is not distinct from that of the other or others.

(2) References in this Part to the designer of a design shall, except as otherwise provided, be construed in relation to a joint design as references to all the designers of the design.

**260 Application of provisions to articles in kit form**

(1) The provisions of this Part apply in relation to a kit, that is, a complete or substantially complete set of components intended to be assembled into an article, as they apply in relation to the assembled article.

(2) Subsection (1) does not affect the question whether design right subsists in any aspect of the design of the components of a kit as opposed to the design of the assembled article.

**261 Requirement of signature: application in relation to body corporate**

The requirement in the following provisions that an instrument be signed by or on behalf of a person is also satisfied in the case of a body corporate by the affixing of its seal—

section 222(3) (assignment of design right),
section 223(1) (assignment of future design right),
section 225(1) (grant of exclusive licence).

**262 Adaptation of expressions in relation to Scotland**

In the application of this Part to Scotland—

"account of profits" means accounting and payment of profits;
"accounts" means count, reckoning and payment;
"assignment" means assignation;

"costs" means expenses;
"defendant" means defender;
"delivery up" means delivery;
"injunction" means interdict;
"interlocutory relief" means interim remedy; and
"plaintiff" means pursuer.

**263 Minor definitions**

(1) In this Part—

"British design" means a design which qualifies for design right protection by reason of a connection with the United Kingdom of the designer or the person by whom the design is commissioned or the designer is employed;
"business" includes a trade or profession;
"commission" means a commission for money or money's worth;
"the comptroller" means the Comptroller-General of Patents, Designs and Trade Marks;
"computer-generated", in relation to a design, means that the design is generated by computer in circumstances such that there is no human designer,
"country" includes any territory;
"the Crown" includes the Crown in right of Her Majesty's Government in Northern Ireland;
"design document" means any record of a design, whether in the form of a drawing, a written description, a photograph, data stored in a computer or otherwise;
"employee", "employment" and "employer" refer to employment under a contract of service or of apprenticeship;
"government department" includes a Northern Ireland department.

(2) References in this Part to "marketing", in relation to an article, are to its being sold or let for hire, or offered or exposed for sale or hire, in the course of a business, and related expressions shall be construed accordingly; but no account shall be taken for the purposes of this Part of marketing which is merely colourable and not intended to satisfy the reasonable requirements of the public.

(3) References in this Part to an act being done in relation to an article for "commercial purposes" are to its being done with a view to the article in question being sold or hired in the course of a business.

**264 Index of defined expressions**

The following Table shows provisions defining or otherwise explaining expressions used in this Part (other than provisions defining or explaining an expression used only in the same section)—

| | |
|---|---|
| account of profits and accounts (in Scotland) | section 262 |
| assignment (in Scotland) | section 262 |
| British designs | section 263(1) |
| business | section 263(1) |
| commercial purposes | section 263(3) |
| commission | section 263(1) |
| the comptroller | section 263(1) |
| computer-generated | section 263(1) |
| costs (in Scotland) | section 262 |
| country | section 263(1) |
| the Crown | section 263(1) |
| Crown use | sections 240(5) and 244(2) |

| | |
|---|---|
| defendant (in Scotland) | section 262 |
| delivery up (in Scotland) | section 262 |
| design | section 213(2) |
| design document | section 263(1) |
| designer | sections 214 and 259(2) |
| design right | section 213(1) |
| design right owner | sections 234(2) and 258 |
| employee, employment and employer | section 263(1) |
| exclusive licence | section 225(1) |
| government department | section 263(1) |
| government department concerned (in relation to Crown use) | section 240(5) |
| infringing article | section 228 |
| injunction (in Scotland) | section 262 |
| interlocutory relief (in Scotland) | section 262 |
| joint design | section 259(1) |
| licence (of the design right owner) | sections 222(4), 223(3) and 258 |
| making articles to a design | section 226(2) |
| marketing (and related expressions) | section 263(2) |
| original | section 213(4) |
| plaintiff (in Scotland) | section 262 |
| qualifying individual | section 217(1) |
| qualifying person | sections 217(1) and (2) |
| signed | section 261 |

## PART IV

## REGISTERED DESIGNS

*Amendments of the Registered Designs Act 1949*

### 265 Registrable designs

(1) For section 1 of the Registered Designs Act 1949 (designs registrable under that Act) substitute—

"**1 Designs registrable under Act**

(1) In this Act "design" means features of shape, configuration, pattern or ornament applied to an article by any industrial process, being features which in the finished article appeal to and are judged by the eye, but does not include—

(*a*) a method or principle of construction, or

(*b*) features of shape or configuration of an article which—

(i) are dictated solely by the function which the article has to perform, or

(ii) are dependent upon the appearance of another article of which the article is intended by the author of the design to form an integral part.

(2) A design which is new may, upon application by the person claiming to be the proprietor, be registered under this Act in respect of any article, or set of articles, specified in the application.

(3) A design shall not be registered in respect of an article if the appearance of the article is not material, that is, if aesthetic considerations are not normally taken into account to a material extent by persons acquiring or using articles of

that description, and would not be so taken into account if the design were to be applied to the article.

(4) A design shall not be regarded as new for the purposes of this Act if it is the same as a design—

(*a*) registered in respect of the same or any other article in pursuance of a prior application, or

(*b*) published in the United Kingdom in respect of the same or any other article before the date of the application,

or if it differs from such a design only in immaterial details or in features which are variants commonly used in the trade.

This subsection has effect subject to the provisions of sections 4, 6 and 16 of this Act.

(5) The Secretary of State may by rules provide for excluding from registration under this Act designs for such articles of a primarily literary or artistic character as the Secretary of State thinks fit.".

(2) The above amendment does not apply in relation to applications for registration made before the commencement of this Part; but the provisions of section 266 apply with respect to the right in certain designs registered in pursuance of such an application.

### 266 Provisions with respect to certain designs registered in pursuance of application made before commencement

(1) Where a design is registered under the Registered Designs Act 1949 in pursuance of an application made after 12th January 1988 and before the commencement of this Part which could not have been registered under section 1 of that Act as substituted by section 265 above—

(*a*) the right in the registered design expires ten years after the commencement of this Part, if it does not expire earlier in accordance with the 1949 Act, and

(*b*) any person is, after the commencement of this Part, entitled as of right to a licence to do anything which would otherwise infringe the right in the registered design.

(2) The terms of a licence available by virtue of this section shall, in default of agreement, be settled by the registrar on an application by the person requiring the licence; and the terms so settled shall authorise the licensee to do everything which would be an infringement of the right in the registered design in the absence of a licence.

(3) In settling the terms of a licence the registrar shall have regard to such factors as may be prescribed by the Secretary of State by order made by statutory instrument.

No such order shall be made unless a draft of it has been laid before and approved by a resolution of each House of Parliament.

(4) Where the terms of a licence are settled by the registrar, the licence has effect from the date on which the application to the registrar was made.

(5) Section 11B of the 1949 Act (undertaking to take licence of right in infringement proceedings), as inserted by section 270 below, applies where a licence is available as of right under this section, as it applies where a licence is available as of right under section 11A of that Act.

(6) Where a licence is available as of right under this section, a person to whom a licence was granted before the commencement of this Part may apply to the registrar for an order adjusting the terms of that licence.

(7) An appeal lies from any decision of the registrar under this section.

(8) This section shall be construed as one with the Registered Designs Act 1949.

**267 Authorship and first ownership of designs**

(1) Section 2 of the Registered Designs Act 1949 (proprietorship of designs) is amended as follows.

(2) For subsection (1) substitute—

"(1) The author of a design shall be treated for the purposes of this Act as the original proprietor of the design, subject to the following provisions.

(1A) Where a design is created in pursuance of a commission for money or money's worth, the person commissioning the design shall be treated as the original proprietor of the design.

(1B) Where, in a case not falling within subsection (1A), a design is created by an employee in the course of his employment, his employer shall be treated as the original proprietor of the design.".

(3) After subsection (2) insert—

"(3) In this Act the "author" of a design means the person who creates it.

(4) In the case of a design generated by computer in circumstances such that there is no human author, the person by whom the arrangements necessary for the creation of the design are made shall be taken to be the author.".

(4) The amendments made by this section do not apply in relation to an application for registration made before the commencement of this Part.

**268 Right given by registration of design**

(1) For section 7 of the Registered Designs Act 1949 (right given by registration) substitute—

"**7 Right given by registration**

(1) The registration of a design under this Act gives the registered proprietor the exclusive right—

(*a*) to make or import—

(i) for sale or hire, or

(ii) for use for the purposes of a trade or business, or

(*b*) to sell, hire or offer or expose for sale or hire,

an article in respect of which the design is registered and to which that design or a design not substantially different from it has been applied.

(2) The right in the registered design is infringed by a person who without the licence of the registered proprietor does anything which by virtue of subsection (1) is the exclusive right of the proprietor.

(3) The right in the registered design is also infringed by a person who without the licence of the registered proprietor makes anything for enabling any such article to be made, in the United Kingdom or elsewhere, as mentioned in subsection (1).

(4) The right in the registered design is also infringed by a person who without the licence of the registered proprietor—

(*a*) does anything in relation to a kit that would be an infringement if done in relation to the assembled article (see subsection (1)), or (*b*) makes anything for enabling a kit to be made or assembled, in the United Kingdom or elsewhere, if the assembled article would be such an article as is mentioned in subsection (1);

and for this purpose a "kit" means a complete or substantially complete set of components intended to be assembled into an article.

(5) No proceedings shall be taken in respect of an infringement committed before the date on which the certificate of registration of the design under this Act is granted.

(6) The right in a registered design is not infringed by the reproduction of a feature of the design which, by virtue of section 1(1)(*b*), is left out of account in determining whether the design is registrable.".

(2) The above amendment does not apply in relation to a design registered in pursuance of an application made before the commencement of this Part.

**269 Duration of right in registered design**

(1) For section 8 of the Registered Designs Act 1949 (period of right) substitute—

"**8 Duration of right in registered design**

(1) The right in a registered design subsists in the first instance for a period of five years from the date of the registration of the design.

(2) The period for which the right subsists may be extended for a second, third, fourth and fifth period of five years, by applying to the registrar for an extension and paying the prescribed renewal fee.

(3) If the first, second, third or fourth period expires without such application and payment being made, the right shall cease to have effect; and the registrar shall, in accordance with rules made by the Secretary of State, notify the proprietor of that fact.

(4) If during the period of six months immediately following the end of that period an application for extension is made and the prescribed renewal fee and any prescribed additional fee is paid, the right shall be treated as if it had never expired, with the result that—

(*a*) anything done under or in relation to the right during that further period shall be treated as valid,
(*b*) an act which would have constituted an infringement of the right if it had not expired shall be treated as an infringement, and
(*c*) an act which would have constituted use of the design for the services of the Crown if the right had not expired shall be treated as such use.

(5) Where it is shown that a registered design—

(*a*) was at the time it was registered a corresponding design in relation to an artistic work in which copyright subsists, and
(*b*) by reason of a previous use of that work would not have been registrable but for section 6(4) of this Act (registration despite certain prior applications of design),

the right in the registered design expires when the copyright in that work expires, if that is earlier than the time at which it would otherwise expire, and it may not thereafter be renewed.

(6) The above provisions have effect subject to the proviso to section 4(1) (registration of same design in respect of other articles, &c).

**8A Restoration of lapsed right in design**

(1) Where the right in a registered design has expired by reason of a failure to extend, in accordance with section 8(2) or (4), the period for which the right

subsists, an application for the restoration of the right in the design may be made to the registrar within the prescribed period.

(2) The application may be made by the person who was the registered proprietor of the design or by any other person who would have been entitled to the right in the design if it had not expired; and where the design was held by two or more persons jointly, the application may, with the leave of the registrar, be made by one or more of them without joining the others.

(3) Notice of the application shall be published by the registrar in the prescribed manner.

(4) If the registrar is satisfied that the proprietor took reasonable care to see that the period for which the right subsisted was extended in accordance with section 8(2) or (4), he shall, on payment of any unpaid renewal fee and any prescribed additional fee, order the restoration of the right in the design.

(5) The order may be made subject to such conditions as the registrar thinks fit, and if the proprietor of the design does not comply with any condition the registrar may revoke the order and give such consequential directions as he thinks fit.

(6) Rules altering the period prescribed for the purposes of subsection (1) may contain such transitional provisions and savings as appear to the Secretary of State to be necessary or expedient.

**8B Effect of order for restoration of right**

(1) The effect of an order under section 8A for the restoration of the right in a registered design is as follows.

(2) Anything done under or in relation to the right during the period between expiry and restoration shall be treated as valid.

(3) Anything done during that period which would have constituted an infringement if the right had not expired shall be treated as an infringement—

(*a*) if done at a time when it was possible for an application for extension to be made under section 8(4); or

(*b*) if it was a continuation or repetition of an earlier infringing act.

(4) If, after it was no longer possible for such an application for extension to be made and before publication of notice of the application for restoration, a person—

(*a*) began in good faith to do an act which would have constituted an infringement of the right in the design if it had not expired, or

(*b*) made in good faith effective and serious preparations to do such an act,

he has the right to continue to do the act or, as the case may be, to do the act, notwithstanding the restoration of the right in the design; but this does not extend to granting a licence to another person to do the act.

(5) If the act was done, or the preparations were made, in the course of a business, the person entitled to the right conferred by subsection (4) may—

(*a*) authorise the doing of that act by any partners of his for the time being in that business, and

(*b*) assign that right, or transmit it on death (or in the case of a body corporate on its dissolution), to any person who acquires that part of the business in the course of which the act was done or the preparations were made.

(6) Where an article is disposed of to another in exercise of the rights conferred by subsection (4) or subsection (5), that other and any person claiming through him may deal with the article in the same way as if it had been disposed of by the registered proprietor of the design.

(7) The above provisions apply in relation to the use of a registered design for

the services of the Crown as they apply in relation to infringement of the right in the design.".

(2) The above amendment does not apply in relation to the right in a design registered in pursuance of an application made before the commencement of this Part.

**270 Powers exercisable for protection of the public interest**

In the Registered Designs Act 1949 after section 11 insert—

"**11A Powers exercisable for protection of the public interest**

(1) Where a report of the Monopolies and Mergers Commission has been laid before Parliament containing conclusions to the effect—

(*a*) on a monopoly reference, that a monopoly situation exists and facts found by the Commission operate or may be expected to operate against the public interest,

(*b*) on a merger reference, that a merger situation qualifying for investigation has been created and the creation of the situation, or particular elements in or consequences of it specified in the report, operate or may be expected to operate against the public interest,

(*c*) on a competition reference, that a person was engaged in an anti-competitive practice which operated or may be expected to operate against the public interest, or

(*d*) on a reference under section 11 of the Competition Act 1980 (reference of public bodies and certain other persons), that a person is pursuing a course of conduct which operates against the public interest,

the appropriate Minister or Ministers may apply to the registrar to take action under this section.

(2) Before making an application the appropriate Minister or Ministers shall publish, in such a manner as he or they think appropriate, a notice describing the nature of the proposed application and shall consider any representations which may be made within 30 days of such publication by persons whose interests appear to him or them to be affected.

(3) If on an application under this section it appears to the registrar that the matters specified in the Commission's report as being those which in the Commission's opinion operate or operated or may be expected to operate against the public interest include—

(*a*) conditions in licences granted in respect of a registered design by its proprietor restricting the use of the design by the licensee or the right of the proprietor to grant other licences, or

(*b*) a refusal by the proprietor of a registered design to grant licences on reasonable terms,

he may by order cancel or modify any such condition or may, instead or in addition, make an entry in the register to the effect that licences in respect of the design are to be available as of right.

(4) The terms of a licence available by virtue of this section shall, in default of agreement, be settled by the registrar on an application by the person requiring the licence; and terms so settled shall authorise the licensee to do everything which would be an infringement of the right in the registered design in the absence of a licence.

(5) Where the terms of a licence are settled by the registrar the licence has effect from the date on which the application to him was made.

(6) An appeal lies from any order of the registrar under this section.

(7) In this section "the appropriate Minister or Ministers" means the Minister or Ministers to whom the report of the Monopolies and Mergers Commission was made.

**11B Undertaking to take licence of right in infringement proceedings**

(1) If in proceedings for infringement of the right in a registered design in respect of which a licence is available as of right under section 11A of this Act the defendant undertakes to take a licence on such terms as may be agreed or, in default of agreement, settled by the registrar under that section—

(*a*) no injunction shall be granted against him, and

(*b*) the amount recoverable against him by way of damages or on an account of profits shall not exceed double the amount which would have been payable by him as licensee if such a licence on those terms had been granted before the earliest infringement.

(2) An undertaking may be given at any time before final order in the proceedings, without any admission of liability.

(3) Nothing in this section affects the remedies available in respect of an infringement committed before licences of right were available.".

## 271 Crown use: compensation for loss of profit

(1) In Schedule 1 to the Registered Designs Act 1949 (Crown use), after paragraph 2 insert—

"**2A Compensation for loss of profit**

(1) Where Crown use is made of a registered design, the government department concerned shall pay—

(*a*) to the registered proprietor, or

(*b*) if there is an exclusive licence in force in respect of the design, to the exclusive licensee,

compensation for any loss resulting from his not being awarded a contract to supply the articles to which the design is applied.

(2) Compensation is payable only to the extent that such a contract could have been fulfilled from his existing manufacturing capacity; but is payable notwithstanding the existence of circumstances rendering him ineligible for the award of such a contract.

(3) In determining the loss, regard shall be had to the profit which would have been made on such a contract and to the extent to which any manufacturing capacity was underused.

(4) No compensation is payable in respect of any failure to secure contracts for the supply of articles to which the design is applied otherwise than for the services of the Crown.

(5) The amount payable under this paragraph shall, if not agreed between the registered proprietor or licensee and the government department concerned with the approval of the Treasury, be determined by the court on a reference under paragraph 3; and it is in addition to any amount payable under paragraph 1 or 2 of this Schedule.

(6) In this paragraph—

"Crown use", in relation to a design, means the doing of anything by virtue of paragraph 1 which would otherwise be an infringement of the right in the design; and

"the government department concerned", in relation to such use, means the government department by whom or on whose authority the act was done.".

(2) In paragraph 3 of that Schedule (reference of disputes as to Crown use), for sub-paragraph (1) substitute—

"(1) Any dispute as to—

(*a*) the exercise by a Government department, or a person authorised by a Government department, of the powers conferred by paragraph 1 of this Schedule,

(*b*) terms for the use of a design for the services of the Crown under that paragraph,

(*c*) the right of any person to receive any part of a payment made under paragraph 1(3), or

(*d*) the right of any person to receive a payment under paragraph 2A,

may be referred to the court by either party to the dispute.".

(3) The above amendments apply in relation to any Crown use of a registered design after the commencement of this section, even if the terms for such use were settled before commencement.

**272 Minor and consequential amendments**

The Registered Designs Act 1949 is further amended in accordance with Schedule 3 which contains minor amendments and amendments consequential upon the provisions of this Act.

*Supplementary*

**273 Text of Registered Designs Act 1949 as amended**

Schedule 4 contains the text of the Registered Designs Act 1949 as amended.

## PART V

## PATENT AGENTS AND TRADE MARK AGENTS

*Patent agents*

**274 Persons permitted to carry on business of a patent agent**

(1) Any individual, partnership or body corporate may, subject to the following provisions of this Part, carry on the business of acting as agent for others for the purpose of—

(*a*) applying for or obtaining patents, in the United Kingdom or elsewhere, or

(*b*) conducting proceedings before the comptroller relating to applications for, or otherwise in connection with, patents.

(2) This does not affect any restriction under the European Patent Convention as to who may act on behalf of another for any purpose relating to European patents.

**275 The register of patent agents**

(1) The Secretary of State may make rules requiring the keeping of a register of persons who act as agent for others for the purposes of applying for or obtaining patents; and in this Part a "registered patent agent" means a person whose name is entered in the register kept under this section.

(2) The rules may contain such provision as the Secretary of State thinks fit regulating the registration of persons, and may in particular—

(*a*) require the payment of such fees as may be prescribed, and (*b*) authorise in prescribed cases the erasure from the register of the name of any person registered in it, or the suspension of a person's registration.

(3) The rules may delegate the keeping of the register to another person, and may confer on that person—

(*a*) power to make regulations—

(i) with respect to the payment of fees, in the cases and subject to the limits prescribed by rules, and

(ii) with respect to any other matter which could be regulated by rules, and

(*b*) such other functions, including disciplinary functions, as may be prescribed by rules.

(4) Rules under this section shall be made by statutory instrument which shall be subject to annulment in pursuance of a resolution of either House of Parliament.

**276 Persons entitled to describe themselves as patent agents**

(1) An individual who is not a registered patent agent shall not—

(*a*) carry on a business (otherwise than in partnership) under any name or other description which contains the words "patent agent" or "patent attorney"; or

(*b*) in the course of a business otherwise describe himself, or permit himself to be described, as a "patent agent" or "patent attorney".

(2) A partnership shall not—

(*a*) carry on a business under any name or other description which contains the words "patent agent" or "patent attorney"; or

(*b*) in the course of a business otherwise describe itself, or permit itself to be described as, a firm of "patent agents" or "patent attorneys",

unless all the partners are registered patent agents or the partnership satisfies such conditions as may be prescribed for the purposes of this section.

(3) A body corporate shall not—

(*a*) carry on a business (otherwise than in partnership) under any name or other description which contains the words "patent agent" or "patent attorney"; or

(*b*) in the course of a business otherwise describe itself, or permit itself to be described as, a "patent agent" or "patent attorney",

unless all the directors of the body corporate are registered patent agents or the body satisfies such conditions as may be prescribed for the purposes of this section.

(4) Subsection (3) does not apply to a company which began to carry on business as a patent agent before 17th November 1917 if the name of a director or the manager of the company who is a registered patent agent is mentioned as being so registered in all professional advertisements, circulars or letters issued by or with the company's consent on which its name appears.

(5) Where this section would be contravened by the use of the words "patent agent" or "patent attorney" in reference to an individual, partnership or body corporate, it is equally contravened by the use of other expressions in reference to that person, or his business or place of business, which are likely to be understood as indicating that he is entitled to be described as a "patent agent" or "patent attorney".

(6) A person who contravenes this section commits an offence and is liable on summary conviction to a fine not exceeding level 5 on the standard scale; and proceedings for such an offence may be begun at any time within a year from the date of the offence.

(7) This section has effect subject to—

(*a*) section 277 (persons entitled to describe themselves as European patent attorneys, &c), and

(*b*) section 278(1) (use of term "patent attorney" in reference to solicitors).

**277 Persons entitled to describe themselves as European patent attorneys, &c**

(1) The term "European patent attorney" or "European patent agent" may be used in the following cases without any contravention of section 276.

(2) An individual who is on the European list may—

(*a*) carry on business under a name or other description which contains the words "European patent attorney" or "European patent agent", or

(*b*) otherwise describe himself, or permit himself to be described, as a "European patent attorney" or "European patent agent".

(3) A partnership of which not less than the prescribed number or proportion of partners is on the European list may—

(*a*) carry on a business under a name or other description which contains the words "European patent attorneys" or "European patent agents", or

(*b*) otherwise describe itself, or permit itself to be described, as a firm which carries on the business of a "European patent attorney" or "European patent agent".

(4) A body corporate of which not less than the prescribed number or proportion of directors is on the European list may—

(*a*) carry on a business under a name or other description which contains the words "European patent attorney" or "European patent agent", or

(*b*) otherwise describe itself, or permit itself to be described as, a company which carries on the business of a "European patent attorney" or "European patent agent".

(5) Where the term "European patent attorney" or "European patent agent" may, in accordance with this section, be used in reference to an individual, partnership or body corporate, it is equally permissible to use other expressions in reference to that person, or to his business or place of business, which are likely to be understood as indicating that he is entitled to be described as a "European patent attorney" or "European patent agent."

**278 Use of the term "patent attorney": supplementary provisions**

(1) The term "patent attorney" may be used in reference to a solicitor, and a firm of solicitors may be described as a firm of "patent attorneys", without any contravention of section 276.

(2) No offence is committed under the enactments restricting the use of certain expressions in reference to persons not qualified to act as solicitors—

(*a*) by the use of the term "patent attorney" in reference to a registered patent agent, or

(*b*) by the use of the term "European patent attorney" in reference to a person on the European list.

(3) The enactments referred to in subsection (2) are section 21 of the Solicitors Act 1974, section 31 of the Solicitors (Scotland) Act 1980 and Article 22 of the Solicitors (Northern Ireland) Order 1976.

**279 Power to prescribe conditions, &c for mixed partnerships and bodies corporate**

(1) The Secretary of State may make rules—

(*a*) prescribing the conditions to be satisfied for the purposes of section 276 (persons entitled to describe themselves as patent agents) in relation to a partnership where not all the partners are qualified persons or a body corporate where not all the directors are qualified persons, and
(*b*) imposing requirements to be complied with by such partnerships and bodies corporate.

(2) The rules may, in particular—

(*a*) prescribe conditions as to the number or proportion of partners or directors who must be qualified persons;
(*b*) impose requirements as to—
   (i) the identification of qualified and unqualified persons in professional advertisements, circulars or letters issued by or with the consent of the partnership or body corporate and which relate to it or to its business; and
   (ii) the manner in which a partnership or body corporate is to organise its affairs so as to secure that qualified persons exercise a sufficient degree of control over the activities of unqualified persons.

(3) Contravention of a requirement imposed by the rules is an offence for which a person is liable on summary conviction to a fine not exceeding level 5 on the standard scale.

(4) The Secretary of State may make rules prescribing for the purposes of section 277 the number or proportion of partners of a partnership or directors of a body corporate who must be qualified persons in order for the partnership or body to take advantage of that section.

(5) In this section "qualified person"—

(*a*) in subsections (1) and (2), means a person who is a registered patent agent, and
(*b*) in subsection (4), means a person who is on the European list.

(6) Rules under this section shall be made by statutory instrument which shall be subject to annulment in pursuance of a resolution of either House of Parliament.

**280 Privilege for communications with patent agents**

(1) This section applies to communications as to any matter relating to the protection of any invention, design, technical information, trade mark or service mark, or as to any matter involving passing off.

(2) Any such communication—

(*a*) between a person and his patent agent, or
(*b*) for the purpose of obtaining, or in response to a request for, information which a person is seeking for the purpose of instructing his patent agent,

is privileged from disclosure in legal proceedings in England, Wales or Northern Ireland in the same way as a communication between a person and his solicitor or, as the case may be, a communication for the purpose of obtaining, or in response to a request for, information which a person seeks for the purpose of instructing his solicitor.

(3) In subsection (2) "patent agent" means—

(*a*) a registered patent agent or a person who is on the European list,
(*b*) a partnership entitled to describe itself as a firm of patent agents or as a firm carrying on the business of a European patent attorney, or
(*c*) a body corporate entitled to describe itself as a patent agent or as a company carrying on the business of a European patent attorney.

(4) It is hereby declared that in Scotland the rules of law which confer privilege

from disclosure in legal proceedings in respect of communications extend to such communications as are mentioned in this section.

**281 Power of comptroller to refuse to deal with certain agents**

(1) This section applies to business under the Patents Act 1949, the Registered Designs Act 1949 or the Patents Act 1977.

(2) The Secretary of State may make rules authorising the comptroller to refuse to recognise as agent in respect of any business to which this section applies—

(*a*) a person who has been convicted of an offence under section 88 of the Patents Act 1949, section 114 of the Patents Act 1977 or section 276 of this Act;
(*b*) an individual whose name has been erased from and not restored to, or who is suspended from, the register of patent agents on the ground of misconduct;
(*c*) a person who is found by the Secretary of State to have been guilty of such conduct as would, in the case of an individual registered in the register of patent agents, render him liable to have his name erased from the register on the ground of misconduct;
(*d*) a partnership or body corporate of which one of the partners or directors is a person whom the comptroller could refuse to recognise under paragraph (*a*), (*b*) or (*c*) above.

(3) The rules may contain such incidental and supplementary provisions as appear to the Secretary of State to be appropriate and may, in particular, prescribe circumstances in which a person is or is not to be taken to have been guilty of misconduct.

(4) Rules made under this section shall be made by statutory instrument which shall be subject to annulment in pursuance of a resolution of either House of Parliament.

(5) The comptroller shall refuse to recognise as agent in respect of any business to which this section applies a person who neither resides nor has a place of business in the United Kingdom, the Isle of Man or another member State of the European Economic Community.

*Trade mark agents*

**282 The register of trade mark agents**

(1) The Secretary of State may make rules requiring the keeping of a register of persons who act as agent for others for the purpose of applying for or obtaining the registration of trade marks; and in this Part a "registered trade mark agent" means a person whose name is entered in the register kept under this section.

(2) The rules may contain such provision as the Secretary of State thinks fit regulating the registration of persons, and may in particular—

(*a*) require the payment of such fees as may be prescribed, and
(*b*) authorise in prescribed cases the erasure from the register of the name of any person registered in it, or the suspension of a person's registration.

(3) The rules may delegate the keeping of the register to another person, and may confer on that person—

(*a*) power to make regulations—
  (i) with respect to the payment of fees, in the cases and subject to the limits prescribed by rules, and
  (ii) with respect to any other matter which could be regulated by rules, and

(*b*) such other functions, including disciplinary functions, as may be prescribed by rules.

(4) Rules under this section shall be made by statutory instrument which shall be subject to annulment in pursuance of a resolution of either House of Parliament.

**283 Unregistered persons not to be described as registered trade mark agents**

(1) An individual who is not a registered trade mark agent shall not—

(*a*) carry on a business (otherwise than in partnership) under any name or other description which contains the words "registered trade mark agent"; or
(*b*) in the course of a business otherwise describe or hold himself out, or permit himself to be described or held out, as a registered trade mark agent.

(2) A partnership shall not—

(*a*) carry on a business under any name or other description which contains the words "registered trade mark agent"; or
(*b*) in the course of a business otherwise describe or hold itself out, or permit itself to be described or held out, as a firm of registered trade mark agents,

unless all the partners are registered trade mark agents or the partnership satisfies such conditions as may be prescribed for the purposes of this section.

(3) A body corporate shall not—

(*a*) carry on a business (otherwise than in partnership) under any name or other description which contains the words "registered trade mark agent"; or
(*b*) in the course of a business otherwise describe or hold itself out, or permit itself to be described or held out, as a registered trade mark agent,

unless all the directors of the body corporate are registered trade mark agents or the body satisfies such conditions as may be prescribed for the purposes of this section.

(4) The Secretary of State may make rules prescribing the conditions to be satisfied for the purposes of this section in relation to a partnership where not all the partners are registered trade mark agents or a body corporate where not all the directors are registered trade mark agents; and the rules may, in particular, prescribe conditions as to the number or proportion of partners or directors who must be registered trade mark agents.

(5) Rules under this section shall be made by statutory instrument which shall be subject to annulment in pursuance of a resolution of either House of Parliament.

(6) A person who contravenes this section commits an offence and is liable on summary conviction to a fine not exceeding level 5 on the standard scale; and proceedings for such an offence may be begun at any time within a year from the date of the offence.

**284 Privilege for communications with registered trade mark agents**

(1) This section applies to communications as to any matter relating to the protection of any design, trade mark or service mark, or as to any matter involving passing off.

(2) Any such communication—

(*a*) between a person and his trade mark agent, or
(*b*) for the purpose of obtaining, or in response to a request for, information which a person is seeking for the purpose of instructing his trade mark agent,

is privileged from disclosure in legal proceedings in England, Wales or Northern Ireland in the same way as a communication between a person and his solicitor or, as the case may be, a communication for the purpose of obtaining, or in response to a request for, information which a person seeks for the purpose of instructing his solicitor.

(3) In subsection (1) "trade mark agent" means—

(*a*) a registered trade mark agent, or
(*b*) a partnership entitled to describe itself as a firm of registered trade mark agents, or
(*c*) a body corporate entitled to describe itself as a registered trade mark agent.

(4) It is hereby declared that in Scotland the rules of law which confer privilege from disclosure in legal proceedings in respect of communications extend to such communications as are mentioned in subsection (1).

*Supplementary*

**285 Offences committed by partnerships and bodies corporate**

(1) Proceedings for an offence under this Part alleged to have been committed by a partnership shall be brought in the name of the partnership and not in that of the partners; but without prejudice to any liability of theirs under subsection (4) below.

(2) The following provisions apply for the purposes of such proceedings as in relation to a body corporate—

(*a*) any rules of court relating to the service of documents;
(*b*) in England, Wales or Northern Ireland, Schedule 3 to the Magistrates' Courts Act 1980 or Schedule 4 to the Magistrates' Courts (Northern Ireland) Order 1981 (procedure on charge of offence).

(3) A fine imposed on a partnership on its conviction in such proceedings shall be paid out of the partnership assets.

(4) Where a partnership is guilty of an offence under this Part, every partner, other than a partner who is proved to have been ignorant of or to have attempted to prevent the commission of the offence, is also guilty of the offence and liable to be proceeded against and punished accordingly.

(5) Where an offence under this Part committed by a body corporate is proved to have been committed with the consent or connivance of a director, manager, secretary or other similar officer of the body, or a person purporting to act in any such capacity, he as well as the body corporate is guilty of the offence and liable to be proceeded against and punished accordingly.

**286 Interpretation**

In this Part—

"the comptroller" means the Comptroller-General of Patents, Designs and Trade Marks;
"director", in relation to a body corporate whose affairs are managed by its members, means any member of the body corporate;
"the European list" means the list of professional representatives maintained by the European Patent Office in pursuance of the European Patent Convention;
"registered patent agent" has the meaning given by section 275(1);
"registered trade mark agent" has the meaning given by section 282(1).

# PART VI

# PATENTS

## *Patents county courts*

### 287 Patents county courts: special jurisdiction

(1) The Lord Chancellor may by order made by statutory instrument designate any county court as a patents county court and confer on it jurisdiction (its "special jurisdiction") to hear and determine such descriptions of proceedings—

(*a*) relating to patents or designs, or

(*b*) ancillary to, or arising out of the same subject matter as, proceedings relating to patents or designs,

as may be specified in the order.

(2) The special jurisdiction of a patents county court is exercisable throughout England and Wales, but rules of court may provide for a matter pending in one such court to be heard and determined in another or partly in that and partly in another.

(3) A patents county court may entertain proceedings within its special jurisdiction notwithstanding that no pecuniary remedy is sought.

(4) An order under this section providing for the discontinuance of any of the special jurisdiction of a patents county court may make provision as to proceedings pending in the court when the order comes into operation.

(5) Nothing in this section shall be construed as affecting the ordinary jurisdiction of a county court.

### 288 Financial limits in relation to proceedings within special jurisdiction of patents county court

(1) Her Majesty may by Order in Council provide for limits of amount or value in relation to any description of proceedings within the special jurisdiction of a patents county court.

(2) If a limit is imposed on the amount of a claim of any description and the plaintiff has a cause of action for more than that amount, he may abandon the excess; in which case a patents county court shall have jurisdiction to hear and determine the action, but the plaintiff may not recover more than that amount.

(3) Where the court has jurisdiction to hear and determine an action by virtue of subsection (2), the judgment of the court in the action is in full discharge of all demands in respect of the cause of action, and entry of the judgment shall be made accordingly.

(4) If the parties agree, by a memorandum signed by them or by their respective solicitors or other agents, that a patents county court shall have jurisdiction in any proceedings, that court shall have jurisdiction to hear and determine the proceedings notwithstanding any limit imposed under this section.

(5) No recommendation shall be made to Her Majesty to make an Order under this section unless a draft of the Order has been laid before and approved by a resolution of each House of Parliament.

### 289 Transfer of proceedings between High Court and patents county court

(1) No order shall be made under section 41 of the County Courts Act 1984 (power of High Court to order proceedings to be transferred from the county court) in respect of proceedings within the special jurisdiction of a patents county court.

(2) In considering in relation to proceedings within the special jurisdiction of a patents county court whether an order should be made under section 40 or 42 of the County Courts Act 1984 (transfer of proceedings from or to the High Court), the court shall have regard to the financial position of the parties and may order the transfer of the proceedings to a patents county court or, as the case may be, refrain from ordering their transfer to the High Court notwithstanding that the proceedings are likely to raise an important question of fact or law.

**290 Limitation of costs where pecuniary claim could have been brought in patents county court**

(1) Where an action is commenced in the High Court which could have been commenced in a patents county court and in which a claim for a pecuniary remedy is made, then, subject to the provisions of this section, if the plaintiff recovers less than the prescribed amount, he is not entitled to recover any more costs than those to which he would have been entitled if the action had been brought in the county court.

(2) For this purpose a plaintiff shall be treated as recovering the full amount recoverable in respect of his claim without regard to any deduction made in respect of matters not falling to be taken into account in determining whether the action could have been commenced in a patents county court.

(3) This section does not affect any question as to costs if it appears to the High Court that there was reasonable ground for supposing the amount recoverable in respect of the plaintiff's claim to be in excess of the prescribed amount.

(4) The High Court, if satisfied that there was sufficient reason for bringing the action in the High Court, may make an order allowing the costs or any part of the costs on the High Court scale or on such one of the county court scales as it may direct.

(5) This section does not apply to proceedings brought by the Crown.

(6) In this section "the prescribed amount" means such amount as may be prescribed by Her Majesty for the purposes of this section by Order in Council.

(7) No recommendation shall be made to Her Majesty to make an Order under this section unless a draft of the Order has been laid before and approved by a resolution of each House of Parliament.

**291 Proceedings in patents county court**

(1) Where a county court is designated a patents county court, the Lord Chancellor shall nominate a person entitled to sit as a judge of that court as the patents judge.

(2) County court rules shall make provision for securing that, so far as is practicable and appropriate—

- (*a*) proceedings within the special jurisdiction of a patents county court are dealt with by the patents judge, and
- (*b*) the judge, rather than a registrar or other officer of the court, deals with interlocutory matters in the proceedings.

(3) County court rules shall make provision empowering a patents county court in proceedings within its special jurisdiction, on or without the application of any party—

- (*a*) to appoint scientific advisers or assessors to assist the court, or
- (*b*) to order the Patent Office to inquire into and report on any question of fact or opinion.

(4) Where the court exercises either of those powers on the application of a party, the remuneration or fees payable to the Patent Office shall be at such rate as may be determined in accordance with county court rules and shall be costs of the proceedings unless otherwise ordered by the judge.

(5) Where the court exercises either of those powers of its own motion, the remuneration or fees payable to the Patent Office shall be at such rate as may be determined by the Lord Chancellor with the approval of the Treasury and shall be paid out of money provided by Parliament.

**292 Rights and duties of registered patent agents in relation to proceedings in patents county court**

(1) A registered patent agent may do, in or in connection with proceedings in a patents county court which are within the special jurisdiction of that court, anything which a solicitor of the Supreme Court might do, other than prepare a deed.

(2) The Lord Chancellor may by regulations provide that the right conferred by subsection (1) shall be subject to such conditions and restrictions as appear to the Lord Chancellor to be necessary or expedient; and different provision may be made for different descriptions of proceedings.

(3) A patents county court has the same power to enforce an undertaking given by a registered patent agent acting in pursuance of this section as it has, by virtue of section 142 of the County Courts Act 1984, in relation to a solicitor.

(4) Nothing in section 143 of the County Courts Act 1984 (prohibition on persons other than solicitors receiving remuneration) applies to a registered patent agent acting in pursuance of this section.

(5) The provisions of county court rules prescribing scales of costs to be paid to solicitors apply in relation to registered patent agents acting in pursuance of this section.

(6) Regulations under this section shall be made by statutory instrument which shall be subject to annulment in pursuance of a resolution of either House of Parliament.

*Licences of right in respect of certain patents*

**293 Restriction of acts authorised by certain licences**

In paragraph 4(2)(*c*) of Schedule 1 to the Patents Act 1977 (licences to be available as of right where term of existing patent extended), at the end insert ", but subject to paragraph 4A below", and after that paragraph insert—

"4A.—(1) If the proprietor of a patent for an invention which is a product files a declaration with the Patent Office in accordance with this paragraph, the licences to which persons are entitled by virtue of paragraph 4(2)(*c*) above shall not extend to a use of the product which is excepted by or under this paragraph.

(2) Pharmaceutical use is excepted, that is—

(*a*) use as a medicinal product within the meaning of the Medicines Act 1968, and

(*b*) the doing of any other act mentioned in section 60(1)(*a*) above with a view to such use.

(3) The Secretary of State may by order except such other uses as he thinks fit; and an order may—

(*a*) specify as an excepted use any act mentioned in section 60(1)(*a*) above, and (*b*) make different provision with respect to acts done in different circumstances or for different purposes.

(4) For the purposes of this paragraph the question what uses are excepted, so far as that depends on—

(*a*) orders under section 130 of the Medicines Act 1968 (meaning of "medicinal product"), or
(*b*) orders under sub-paragraph (3) above,

shall be determined in relation to a patent at the beginning of the sixteenth year of the patent.

(5) A declaration under this paragraph shall be in the prescribed form and shall be filed in the prescribed manner and within the prescribed time limits.

(6) A declaration may not be filed—

(*a*) in respect of a patent which has at the commencement of section 293 of the Copyright, Designs and Patents Act 1988 passed the end of its fifteenth year; or
(*b*) if at the date of filing there is—
   (i) an existing licence for any description of excepted use of the product, or
   (ii) an outstanding application under section 46(3)(*a*) or (*b*) above for the settlement by the comptroller of the terms of a licence for any description of excepted use of the product,

and, in either case, the licence took or is to take effect at or after the end of the sixteenth year of the patent.

(7) Where a declaration has been filed under this paragraph in respect of a patent—

(*a*) section 46(3)(*c*) above (restriction of remedies for infringement where licences available as of right) does not apply to an infringement of the patent in so far as it consists of the excepted use of the product after the filing of the declaration; and
(*b*) section 46(3)(*d*) above (abatement of renewal fee if licences available as of right) does not apply to the patent.".

### 294 When application may be made for settlement of terms of licence

In Schedule 1 to the Patents Act 1977, after the paragraph inserted by section 293 above, insert—

"4B.—(1) An application under section 46(3)(*a*) or (*b*) above for the settlement by the comptroller of the terms on which a person is entitled to a licence by virtue of paragraph 4(2)(*c*) above is ineffective if made before the beginning of the sixteenth year of the patent.

(2) This paragraph applies to applications made after the commencement of section 294 of the Copyright, Designs and Patents Act 1988 and to any application made before the commencement of that section in respect of a patent which has not at the commencement of that section passed the end of its fifteenth year.".

*Patents: miscellaneous amendments*

### 295 Patents: miscellaneous amendments

The Patents Act 1949 and the Patents Act 1977 are amended in accordance with Schedule 5.

## PART VII

## MISCELLANEOUS AND GENERAL

*Devices designed to circumvent copy-protection*

### 296 Devices designed to circumvent copy-protection

(1) This section applies where copies of a copyright work are issued to the public, by or with the licence of the copyright owner, in an electronic form which is copy-protected.

(2) The person issuing the copies to the public has the same rights against a person who, knowing or having reason to believe that it will be used to make infringing copies—

(*a*) makes, imports, sells or lets for hire, offers or exposes for sale or hire, or advertises for sale or hire, any device or means specifically designed or adapted to circumvent the form of copy-protection employed, or

(*b*) publishes information intended to enable or assist persons to circumvent that form of copy-protection,

as a copyright owner has in respect of an infringement of copyright.

(3) Further, he has the same rights under section 99 or 100 (delivery up or seizure of certain articles) in relation to any such device or means which a person has in his possession, custody or control with the intention that it should be used to make infringing copies of copyright works, as a copyright owner has in relation to an infringing copy.

(4) References in this section to copy-protection include any device or means intended to prevent or restrict copying of a work or to impair the quality of copies made.

(5) Expressions used in this section which are defined for the purposes of Part I of this Act (copyright) have the same meaning as in that Part.

(6) The following provisions apply in relation to proceedings under this section as in relation to proceedings under Part I (copyright)—

(*a*) sections 104 to 106 of this Act (presumptions as to certain matters relating to copyright), and

(*b*) section 72 of the Supreme Court Act 1981, section 15 of the Law Reform (Miscellaneous Provisions) (Scotland) Act 1985 and section 94A of the Judicature (Northern Ireland) Act 1978 (withdrawal of privilege against self-incrimination in certain proceedings relating to intellectual property);

and section 114 of this Act applies, with the necessary modifications, in relation to the disposal of anything delivered up or seized by virtue of subsection (3) above.

*Fraudulent reception of transmissions*

### 297 Offence of fraudulently receiving programmes

(1) A person who dishonestly receives a programme included in a broadcasting or cable programme service provided from a place in the United Kingdom with intent to avoid payment of any charge applicable to the reception of the programme commits an offence and is liable on summary conviction to a fine not exceeding level 5 on the standard scale.

(2) Where an offence under this section committed by a body corporate is proved to have been committed with the consent or connivance of a director, manager, secretary or other similar officer of the body, or a person purporting to act in any

such capacity, he as well as the body corporate is guilty of the offence and liable to be proceeded against and punished accordingly.

In relation to a body corporate whose affairs are managed by its members "director" means a member of the body corporate.

**298 Rights and remedies in respect of apparatus, &c for unauthorised reception of transmissions**

(1) A person who—

(*a*) makes charges for the reception of programmes included in a broadcasting or cable programme service provided from a place in the United Kingdom, or

(*b*) sends encrypted transmissions of any other description from a place in the United Kingdom,

is entitled to the following rights and remedies.

(2) He has the same rights and remedies against a person who—

(*a*) makes, imports or sells or lets for hire any apparatus or device designed or adapted to enable or assist persons to receive the programmes or other transmissions when they are not entitled to do so, or

(*b*) publishes any information which is calculated to enable or assist persons to receive the programmes or other transmissions when they are not entitled to do so,

as a copyright owner has in respect of an infringement of copyright.

(3) Further, he has the same rights under section 99 or 100 (delivery up or seizure of certain articles) in relation to any such apparatus or device as a copyright owner has in relation to an infringing copy.

(4) Section 72 of the Supreme Court Act 1981, section 15 of the Law Reform (Miscellaneous Provisions) (Scotland) Act 1985 and section 94A of the Judicature (Northern Ireland) Act 1978 (withdrawal of privilege against self-incrimination in certain proceedings relating to intellectual property) apply to proceedings under this section as to proceedings under Part I of this Act (copyright).

(5) In section 97(1) (innocent infringement of copyright) as it applies to proceedings for infringement of the rights conferred by this section, the reference to the defendant not knowing or having reason to believe that copyright subsisted in the work shall be construed as a reference to his not knowing or having reason to believe that his acts infringed the rights conferred by this section.

(6) Section 114 of this Act applies, with the necessary modifications, in relation to the disposal of anything delivered up or seized by virtue of subsection (3) above.

**299 Supplementary provisions as to fraudulent reception**

(1) Her Majesty may by Order in Council—

(*a*) provide that section 297 applies in relation to programmes included in services provided from a country or territory outside the United Kingdom, and

(*b*) provide that section 298 applies in relation to such programmes and to encrypted transmissions sent from such a country or territory.

(2) No such Order shall be made unless it appears to Her Majesty that provision has been or will be made under the laws of that country or territory giving adequate protection to persons making charges for programmes included in broadcasting or cable programme services provided from the United Kingdom or, as the case may be, for encrypted transmissions sent from the United Kingdom.

(3) A statutory instrument containing an Order in Council under subsection (1)

shall be subject to annulment in pursuance of a resolution of either House of Parliament.

(4) Where sections 297 and 298 apply in relation to a broadcasting service or cable programme service, they also apply to any service run for the person providing that service, or a person providing programmes for that service, which consists wholly or mainly in the sending by means of a telecommunications system of sounds or visual images, or both.

(5) In sections 297 and 298, and this section, "programme", "broadcasting" and "cable programme service", and related expressions, have the same meaning as in Part I (copyright).

*Fraudulent application or use of trade mark*

**300 Fraudulent application or use of trade mark an offence**

In the Trade Marks Act 1938 the following sections are inserted before section 59, after the heading "*Offences and restraint of use of Royal Arms*"—

"**58A Fraudulent application or use of trade mark an offence**

(1) It is an offence, subject to subsection (3) below, for a person—

(*a*) to apply a mark identical to or nearly resembling a registered trade mark to goods, or to material used or intended to be used for labelling, packaging or advertising goods, or

(*b*) to sell, let for hire, or offer or expose for sale or hire, or distribute—

(i) goods bearing such a mark, or

(ii) material bearing such a mark which is used or intended to be used for labelling, packaging or advertising goods, or

(*c*) to use material bearing such a mark in the course of a business for labelling, packaging or advertising goods, or

(*d*) to possess in the course of a business goods or material bearing such a mark with a view to doing any of the things mentioned in paragraphs (*a*) to (*c*),

when he is not entitled to use the mark in relation to the goods in question and the goods are not connected in the course of trade with a person who is so entitled.

(2) It is also an offence, subject to subsection (3) below, for a person to possess in the course of a business goods or material bearing a mark identical to or nearly resembling a registered trade mark with a view to enabling or assisting another person to do any of the things mentioned in subsection (1)(*a*) to (*c*), knowing or having reason to believe that the other person is not entitled to use the mark in relation to the goods in question and that the goods are not connected in the course of trade with a person who is so entitled.

(3) A person commits an offence under subsection (1) or (2) only if—

(*a*) he acts with a view to gain for himself or another, or with intent to cause loss to another, and

(*b*) he intends that the goods in question should be accepted as connected in the course of trade with a person entitled to use the mark in question;

and it is a defence for a person charged with an offence under subsection (1) to show that he believed on reasonable grounds that he was entitled to use the mark in relation to the goods in question.

(4) A person guilty of an offence under this section is liable—

(*a*) on summary conviction to imprisonment for a term not exceeding six months or a fine not exceeding the statutory maximum, or both;

(*b*) on conviction on indictment to a fine or imprisonment for a term not exceeding ten years, or both.

(5) Where an offence under this section committed by a body corporate is proved to have been committed with the consent or connivance of a director, manager, secretary or other similar officer of the body, or a person purporting to act in any such capacity, he as well as the body corporate is guilty of the offence and liable to be proceeded against and punished accordingly.

In relation to a body corporate whose affairs are managed by its members "director" means a member of the body corporate.

(6) In this section "business" includes a trade or profession."

**58B Delivery up of offending goods and material**

(1) The court by which a person is convicted of an offence under section 58A may, if satisfied that at the time of his arrest or charge he had in his possession, custody or control—

(*a*) goods or material in respect of which the offence was committed, or
(*b*) goods of the same description as those in respect of which the offence was committed, or material similar to that in respect of which the offence was committed, bearing a mark identical to or nearly resembling that in relation to which the offence was committed,

order that the goods or material be delivered up to such person as the court may direct.

(2) For this purpose a person shall be treated as charged with an offence—

(*a*) in England, Wales and Northern Ireland, when he is orally charged or is served with a summons or indictment;
(*b*) in Scotland, when he is cautioned, charged or served with a complaint or indictment.

(3) An order may be made by the court of its own motion or on the application of the prosecutor (or, in Scotland, the Lord Advocate or procurator-fiscal), but shall not be made if it appears to the court unlikely that any order will be made under section 58C (order as to disposal of offending goods or material).

(4) An appeal lies from an order made under this section by a magistrates' court—

(*a*) in England and Wales, to the Crown Court, and
(*b*) in Northern Ireland, to the county court;

and in Scotland, where an order has been made under this section, the person from whose possession, custody or control the goods or material have been removed may, without prejudice to any other form of appeal under any rule of law, appeal against that order in the same manner as against sentence.

(5) A person to whom goods or material are delivered up in pursuance of an order under this section shall retain it pending the making of an order under section 58C.

(6) Nothing in this section affects the powers of the court under section 43 of the Powers of Criminal Courts Act 1973, section 223 or 436 of the Criminal Procedure (Scotland) Act 1975 or Article 7 of the Criminal Justice (Northern Ireland) Order 1980 (general provisions as to forfeiture in criminal proceedings).

**58C Order as to disposal of offending goods or material**

(1) Where goods or material have been delivered up in pursuance of an order under section 58B, an application may be made to the court for an order that they be destroyed or forfeited to such person as the court may think fit.

(2) Provision shall be made by rules of court as to the service of notice on

persons having an interest in the goods or material, and any such person is entitled—

(*a*) to appear in proceedings for an order under this section, whether or not he was served with notice, and

(*b*) to appeal against any order made, whether or not he appeared;

and an order shall not take effect until the end of the period within which notice of an appeal may be given or, if before the end of that period notice of appeal is duly given, until the final determination or abandonment of the proceedings on the appeal.

(3) Where there is more than one person interested in goods or material, the court shall make such order as it thinks just.

(4) References in this section to a person having an interest in goods or material include any person in whose favour an order could be made under this section or under sections 114, 204 or 231 of the Copyright, Designs and Patents Act 1988 (which make similar provision in relation to infringement of copyright, rights in performances and design right).

(5) Proceedings for an order under this section may be brought—

(*a*) in a county court in England, Wales and Northern Ireland, provided the value of the goods or material in question does not exceed the county court limit for actions in tort, and

(*b*) in a sheriff court in Scotland;

but this shall not be construed as affecting the jurisdiction of the High Court or, in Scotland, the Court of Session.

**58D Enforcement of section 58A**

(1) The functions of a local weights and measures authority include the enforcement in their area of section 58A.

(2) The following provisions of the Trade Descriptions Act 1968 apply in relation to the enforcement of that section as in relation to the enforcement of that Act—

section 27 (power to make test purchases),

section 28 (power to enter premises and inspect and seize goods and documents),

section 29 (obstruction of authorised officers), and

section 33 (compensation for loss, &c of goods seized under s 28).

(3) Subsection (1) above does not apply in relation to the enforcement of section 58A in Northern Ireland, but the functions of the Department of Economic Development include the enforcement of that section in Northern Ireland.

For that purpose the provisions of the Trade Descriptions Act 1968 specified in subsection (2) apply as if for the references to a local weights and measures authority and any officer of such an authority there were substituted references to that Department and any of its officers.

(4) Any enactment which authorises the disclosure of information for the purpose of facilitating the enforcement of the Trade Descriptions Act 1968 shall apply as if section 58A above were contained in that Act and as if the functions of any person in relation to the enforcement of that section were functions under that Act.".

*Provisions for the benefit of the Hospital for Sick Children*

**301 Provisions for the benefit of the Hospital for Sick Children**

The provisions of Schedule 6 have effect for conferring on trustees for the benefit of the Hospital for Sick Children, Great Ormond Street, London, a right to a royalty in respect of the public performance, commercial publication, broadcasting or inclusion in a cable programme service of the play "Peter Pan" by Sir James Matthew Barrie, or of any adaptation of that work, notwithstanding that copyright in the work expired on 31st December 1987.

*Financial assistance for certain international bodies*

**302 Financial assistance for certain international bodies**

(1) The Secretary of State may give financial assistance, in the form of grants, loans or guarantees to—

(*a*) any international organisation having functions relating to trade marks or other intellectual property, or

(*b*) any Community institution or other body established under any of the Community Treaties having any such functions,

with a view to the establishment or maintenance by that organisation, institution or body of premises in the United Kingdom.

(2) Any expenditure of the Secretary of State under this section shall be defrayed out of money provided by Parliament; and any sums received by the Secretary of State in consequence of this section shall be paid into the Consolidated Fund.

*General*

**303 Consequential amendments and repeals**

(1) The enactments specified in Schedule 7 are amended in accordance with that Schedule, the amendments being consequential on the provisions of this Act.

(2) The enactments specified in Schedule 8 are repealed to the extent specified.

**304 Extent**

(1) Provision as to the extent of Part I (copyright), Part II (rights in performances) and Part III (design right) is to be found in sections 157, 207 and 255 respectively; the extent of the other provisions of this Act is as follows.

(2) Parts IV to VII extend to England and Wales, Scotland and Northern Ireland, except that—

(*a*) sections 287 to 292 (patents county courts) extend to England and Wales only,

(*b*) the proper law of the trust created by Schedule 6 (provisions for the benefit of the Hospital for Sick Children) is the law of England and Wales, and

(*c*) the amendments and repeals in Schedules 7 and 8 have the same extent as the enactments amended or repealed.

(3) The following provisions extend to the Isle of Man subject to any modifications contained in an Order made by Her Majesty in Council—

(*a*) sections 293 and 294 (patents: licences of right), and

(*b*) paragraphs 24 and 29 of Schedule 5 (patents: effect of filing international application for patent and power to extend time limits).

(4) Her Majesty may by Order in Council direct that the following provisions extend to the Isle of Man, with such exceptions and modifications as may be specified in the Order—

(*a*) Part IV (registered designs),

(*b*) Part V (patent agents),

(*c*) the provisions of Schedule 5 (patents: miscellaneous amendments) not mentioned in subsection (3) above,
(*d*) sections 297 to 299 (fraudulent reception of transmissions), and
(*e*) section 300 (fraudulent application or use of trade mark).

(5) Her Majesty may by Order in Council direct that sections 297 to 299 (fraudulent reception of transmissions) extend to any of the Channel Islands, with such exceptions and modifications as may be specified in the Order.

(6) Any power conferred by this Act to make provision by Order in Council for or in connection with the extent of provisions of this Act to a country outside the United Kingdom includes power to extend to that country, subject to any modifications specified in the Order, any provision of this Act which amends or repeals an enactment extending to that country.

### 305 Commencement

(1) The following provisions of this Act come into force on Royal Assent—

paragraphs 24 and 29 of Schedule 5 (patents: effect of filing international application for patent and power to extend time limits);
section 301 and Schedule 6 (provisions for the benefit of the Hospital for Sick Children).

(2) Sections 293 and 294 (licences of right) come into force at the end of the period of two months beginning with the passing of this Act.

(3) The other provisions of this Act come into force on such day as the Secretary of State may appoint by order made by statutory instrument, and different days may be appointed for different provisions and different purposes.

### 306 Short title

This Act may be cited as the Copyright, Designs and Patents Act 1988.

## SCHEDULES

### SCHEDULE 1

Section 170

COPYRIGHT: TRANSITIONAL PROVISIONS AND SAVINGS

*Introductory*

1.—(1) In this Schedule—

"the 1911 Act" means the Copyright Act 1911,
"the 1956 Act" means the Copyright Act 1956, and
"the new copyright provisions" means the provisions of this Act relating to copyright, that is, Part I (including this Schedule) and Schedules 3, 7 and 8 so far as they make amendments or repeals consequential on the provisions of Part I.

(2) References in this Schedule to "commencement", without more, are to the date on which the new copyright provisions come into force.

(3) References in this Schedule to "existing works" are to works made before commencement; and for this purpose a work of which the making extended over a period shall be taken to have been made when its making was completed.

2.—(1) In relation to the 1956 Act, references in this Schedule to a work include any work or other subject-matter within the meaning of that Act.

(2) In relation to the 1911 Act—

(*a*) references in this Schedule to copyright include the right conferred by section 24 of that Act in substitution for a right subsisting immediately before the commencement of that Act;
(*b*) references in this Schedule to copyright in a sound recording are to the copyright under that Act in records embodying the recording; and

(*c*) references in this Schedule to copyright in a film are to any copyright under that Act in the film (so far as it constituted a dramatic work for the purposes of that Act) or in photographs forming part of the film.

*General principles: continuity of the law*

3. The new copyright provisions apply in relation to things existing at commencement as they apply in relation to things coming into existence after commencement, subject to any express provision to the contrary.

4.—(1) The provisions of this paragraph have effect for securing the continuity of the law so far as the new copyright provisions re-enact (with or without modification) earlier provisions.

(2) A reference in an enactment, instrument or other document to copyright, or to a work or other subject-matter in which copyright subsists, which apart from this Act would be construed as referring to copyright under the 1956 Act shall be construed, so far as may be required for continuing its effect, as being, or as the case may require, including, a reference to copyright under this Act or to works in which copyright subsists under this Act.

(3) Anything done (including subordinate legislation made), or having effect as done, under or for the purposes of a provision repealed by this Act has effect as if done under or for the purposes of the corresponding provision of the new copyright provisions.

(4) References (expressed or implied) in this Act or any other enactment, instrument or document to any of the new copyright provisions shall, so far as the context permits, be construed as including, in relation to times, circumstances and purposes before commencement, a reference to corresponding earlier provisions.

(5) A reference (express or implied) in an enactment, instrument or other document to a provision repealed by this Act shall be construed, so far as may be required for continuing its effect, as a reference to the corresponding provision of this Act.

(6) The provisions of this paragraph have effect subject to any specific transitional provision or saving and to any express amendment made by this Act.

*Subsistence of copyright*

5.—(1) Copyright subsists in an existing work after commencement only if copyright subsisted in it immediately before commencement.

(2) Sub-paragraph (1) does not prevent an existing work qualifying for copyright protection after commencement—

(*a*) under section 155 (qualification by virtue of first publication), or
(*b*) by virtue of an Order under section 159 (application of Part I to countries to which it does not extend).

6.—(1) Copyright shall not subsist by virtue of this Act in an artistic work made before 1st June 1957 which at the time when the work was made constituted a design capable of registration under the Registered Designs Act 1949 or under the enactments repealed by that Act, and was used, or intended to be used, as a model or pattern to be multiplied by an industrial process.

(2) For this purpose a design shall be deemed to be used as a model or pattern to be multiplied by any industrial process—

(*a*) when the design is reproduced or is intended to be reproduced on more than 50 single articles, unless all the articles in which the design is reproduced or is intended to be reproduced together form only a single set of articles as defined in section 44(1) of the Registered Designs Act 1949, or
(*b*) when the design is to be applied to—
  (i) printed paper hangings,
  (ii) carpets, floor cloths or oil cloths, manufactured or sold in lengths or pieces,
  (iii) textile piece goods, or textile goods manufactured or sold in lengths or pieces, or
  (iv) lace, not made by hand.

7.—(1) No copyright subsists in a film, as such, made before 1st June 1957.

(2) Where a film made before that date was an original dramatic work within the meaning of the 1911 Act, the new copyright provisions have effect in relation to the film as if it was an original dramatic work within the meaning of Part I.

(3) The new copyright provisions have effect in relation to photographs forming part of a film made before 1st June 1957 as they have effect in relation to photographs not forming part of a film.

8.—(1) A film sound-track to which section 13(9) of the 1956 Act applied before commencement (film to be taken to include sounds in associated sound-track) shall be treated for the purposes of the new copyright provisions not as part of the film, but as a sound recording.

(2) However—

(*a*) copyright subsists in the sound recording only if copyright subsisted in the film immediately before commencement, and it continues to subsist until copyright in the film expires;

(*b*) the author and first owner of copyright in the film shall be treated as having been author and first owner of the copyright in the sound recording; and

(*c*) anything done before commencement under or in relation to the copyright in the film continues to have effect in relation to the sound recording as in relation to the film.

9. No copyright subsists in—

(*a*) a broadcast made before 1st June 1957, or

(*b*) a cable programme included in a cable programme service before 1st January 1985;

and any such broadcast or cable programme shall be disregarded for the purposes of section 14(2) (duration of copyright in repeats).

*Authorship of work*

10. The question who was the author of an existing work shall be determined in accordance with the new copyright provisions for the purposes of the rights conferred by Chapter IV of Part I (moral rights), and for all other purposes shall be determined in accordance with the law in force at the time the work was made.

*First ownership of copyright*

11.—(1) The question who was first owner of copyright in an existing work shall be determined in accordance with the law in force at the time the work was made.

(2) Where before commencement a person commissioned the making of a work in circumstances falling within—

(*a*) section 4(3) of the 1956 Act or paragraph (*a*) of the proviso to section 5(1) of the 1911 Act (photographs, portraits and engravings), or

(*b*) the proviso to section 12(4) of the 1956 Act (sound recordings),

those provisions apply to determine first ownership of copyright in any work made in pursuance of the commission after commencement.

*Duration of copyright in existing works*

12.—(1) The following provisions have effect with respect to the duration of copyright in existing works.

The question which provision applies to a work shall be determined by reference to the facts immediately before commencement; and expressions used in this paragraph which were defined for the purposes of the 1956 Act have the same meaning as in that Act.

(2) Copyright in the following descriptions of work continues to subsist until the date on which it would have expired under the 1956 Act—

(*a*) literary, dramatic or musical works in relation to which the period of 50 years mentioned in the proviso to section 2(3) of the 1956 Act (duration of copyright in works made available to the public after the death of the author) has begun to run;

(*b*) engravings in relation to which the period of 50 years mentioned in the proviso to section 3(4) of the 1956 Act (duration of copyright in works published after the death of the author) has begun to run;

(*c*) published photographs and photographs taken before 1st June 1957;

(*d*) published sound recordings and sound recordings made before 1st June 1957;

(*e*) published films and films falling within section 13(3)(*a*) of the 1956 Act (films registered under former enactments relating to registration of films).

(3) Copyright in anonymous or pseudonymous literary, dramatic, musical or artistic works (other than photographs) continues to subsist—

(*a*) if the work is published, until the date on which it would have expired in accordance with the 1956 Act, and
(*b*) if the work is unpublished, until the end of the period of 50 years from the end of the calendar year in which the new copyright provisions come into force or, if during that period the work is first made available to the public within the meaning of section 12(2) (duration of copyright in works of unknown authorship), the date on which copyright expires in accordance with that provision;

unless, in any case, the identity of the author becomes known before that date, in which case section 12(1) applies (general rule: life of the author plus 50 years).

(4) Copyright in the following descriptions of work continues to subsist until the end of the period of 50 years from the end of the calendar year in which the new copyright provisions come into force—

(*a*) literary, dramatic and musical works of which the author has died and in relation to which none of the acts mentioned in paragraphs (*a*) to (*e*) of the proviso to section 2(3) of the 1956 Act has been done;
(*b*) unpublished engravings of which the author has died;
(*c*) unpublished photographs taken on or after 1st June 1957.

(5) Copyright in the following descriptions of work continues to subsist until the end of the period of 50 years from the end of the calendar year in which the new copyright provisions come into force—

(*a*) unpublished sound recordings made on or after 1st June 1957;
(*b*) films not falling within sub-paragraph (2)(*e*) above,

unless the recording or film is published before the end of that period in which case copyright in it shall continue until the end of the period of 50 years from the end of the calendar year in which the recording or film is published.

(6) Copyright in any other description of existing work continues to subsist until the date on which copyright in that description of work expires in accordance with sections 12 to 15 of this Act.

(7) The above provisions do not apply to works subject to Crown or Parliamentary copyright (see paragraphs 41 to 43 below).

*Perpetual copyright under the Copyright Act 1775*

13.—(1) The rights conferred on universities and colleges by the Copyright Act 1775 shall continue to subsist until the end of the period of 50 years from the end of the calendar year in which the new copyright provisions come into force and shall then expire.

(2) The provisions of the following Chapters of Part I—

Chapter III (acts permitted in relation to copyright works),
Chapter VI (remedies for infringement),
Chapter VII (provisions with respect to copyright licensing), and
Chapter VIII (the Copyright Tribunal),

apply in relation to those rights as they apply in relation to copyright under this Act.

*Acts infringing copyright*

14.—(1) The provisions of Chapters II and III of Part I as to the acts constituting an infringement of copyright apply only in relation to acts done after commencement; the provisions of the 1956 Act continue to apply in relation to acts done before commencement.

(2) So much of section 18(2) as extends the restricted act of issuing copies to the public to include the rental to the public of copies of sound recordings, films or computer programs does not apply in relation to a copy of a sound recording, film or computer program acquired by any person before commencement for the purpose of renting it to the public.

(3) For the purposes of section 27 (meaning of "infringing copy") the question whether the making of an article constituted an infringement of copyright, or would have done if the article had been made in the United Kingdom, shall be determined—

(*a*) in relation to an article made on or after 1st June 1957 and before commencement, by reference to the 1956 Act, and

(*b*) in relation to an article made before 1st June 1957, by reference to the 1911 Act.

(4) For the purposes of the application of sections 31(2), 51(2) and 62(3) (subsequent exploitation of things whose making was, by virtue of an earlier provision of the section, not an infringement of copyright) to things made before commencement, it shall be assumed that the new copyright provisions were in force at all material times.

(5) Section 55 (articles for producing material in a particular typeface) applies where articles have been marketed as mentioned in subsection (1) before commencement with the substitution for the period mentioned in subsection (3) of the period of 25 years from the end of the calendar year in which the new copyright provisions come into force.

(6) Section 56 (transfer of copies, adaptations, &c of work in electronic form) does not apply in relation to a copy purchased before commencement.

(7) In section 65 (reconstruction of buildings) the reference to the owner of the copyright in the drawings or plans is, in relation to buildings constructed before commencement, to the person who at the time of the construction was the owner of the copyright in the drawings or plans under the 1956 Act, the 1911 Act or any enactment repealed by the 1911 Act.

15.—(1) Section 57 (anonymous or pseudonymous works: acts permitted on assumptions as to expiry of copyright or death of author) has effect in relation to existing works subject to the following provisions.

(2) Subsection (1)(*b*)(i) (assumption as to expiry of copyright) does not apply in relation to—

(*a*) photographs, or

(*b*) the rights mentioned in paragraph 13 above (rights conferred by the Copyright Act 1775).

(3) Subsection (1)(*b*)(ii) (assumption as to death of author) applies only—

(*a*) where paragraph 12(3)(*b*) above applies (unpublished anonymous or pseudonymous works), after the end of the period of 50 years from the end of the calendar year in which the new copyright provisions come into force, or

(*b*) where paragraph 12(6) above applies (cases in which the duration of copyright is the same under the new copyright provisions as under the previous law).

16. The following provisions of section 7 of the 1956 Act continue to apply in relation to existing works—

(*a*) subsection (6) (copying of unpublished works from manuscript or copy in library, museum or other institution);

(*b*) subsection (7) (publication of work containing material to which subsection (6) applies), except paragraph (*a*) (duty to give notice of intended publication);

(*c*) subsection (8) (subsequent broadcasting, performance, &c of material published in accordance with subsection (7));

and subsection (9)(*d*) (illustrations) continues to apply for the purposes of those provisions.

17. Where in the case of a dramatic or musical work made before 1st July 1912, the right conferred by the 1911 Act did not include the sole right to perform the work in public, the acts restricted by the copyright shall be treated as not including—

(*a*) performing the work in public,

(*b*) broadcasting the work or including it in a cable programme service, or

(*c*) doing any of the above in relation to an adaptation of the work;

and where the right conferred by the 1911 Act consisted only of the sole right to perform the work in public, the acts restricted by the copyright shall be treated as consisting only of those acts.

18. Where a work made before 1st July 1912 consists of an essay, article or portion forming part of and first published in a review, magazine or other periodical or work of a like nature, the copyright is subject to any right of publishing the essay, article, or portion in a separate form to which the author was entitled at the commencement of the 1911 Act, or would if that Act had not been passed, have become entitled under section 18 of the Copyright Act 1842.

*Designs*

19.—(1) Section 51 (exclusion of copyright protection in relation to works recorded or embodied in design document or models) does not apply for ten years after commencement in relation to a design recorded or embodied in a design document or model before commencement.

(2) During those ten years the following provisions of Part III (design right) apply to any relevant copyright as in relation to design right—

(*a*) sections 237 to 239 (availability of licences of right), and
(*b*) sections 247 and 248 (application to comptroller to settle terms of licence of right).

(3) In section 237 as it applies by virtue of this paragraph, for the reference in subsection (1) to the last five years of the design right term there shall be substituted a reference to the last five years of the period of ten years referred to in sub-paragraph (1) above, or to so much of those last five years during which copyright subsists.

(4) In section 239 as it applies by virtue of this paragraph, for the reference in subsection (1)(*b*) to section 230 there shall be substituted a reference to section 99.

(5) Where a licence of right is available by virtue of this paragraph, a person to whom a licence was granted before commencement may apply to the comptroller for an order adjusting the terms of that licence.

(6) The provisions of sections 249 and 250 (appeals and rules) apply in relation to proceedings brought under or by virtue of this paragraph as to proceedings under Part III.

(7) A licence granted by virtue of this paragraph shall relate only to acts which would be permitted by section 51 if the design document or model had been made after commencement.

(8) Section 100 (right to seize infringing copies, &c) does not apply during the period of ten years referred to in sub-paragraph (1) in relation to anything to which it would not apply if the design in question had been first recorded or embodied in a design document or model after commencement.

(9) Nothing in this paragraph affects the operation of any rule of law preventing or restricting the enforcement of copyright in relation to a design.

20.—(1) Where section 10 of the 1956 Act (effect of industrial application of design corresponding to artistic work) applied in relation to an artistic work at any time before commencement, section 52(2) of this Act applies with the substitution for the period of 25 years mentioned there of the relevant period of 15 years as defined in section 10(3) of the 1956 Act.

(2) Except as provided in sub-paragraph (1), section 52 applies only where articles are marketed as mentioned in subsection (1)(*b*) after commencement.

*Abolition of statutory recording licence*

21. Section 8 of the 1956 Act (statutory licence to copy records sold by retail) continues to apply where notice under subsection (1)(*b*) of that section was given before the repeal of that section by this Act, but only in respect of the making of records—

(*a*) within one year of the repeal coming into force, and
(*b*) up to the number stated in the notice as intended to be sold.

*Moral rights*

22.—(1) No act done before commencement is actionable by virtue of any provision of Chapter IV of Part I (moral rights).

(2) Section 43 of the 1956 Act (false attribution of authorship) continues to apply in relation to acts done before commencement.

23.—(1) The following provisions have effect with respect to the rights conferred by—

(*a*) section 77 (right to be identified as author or director), and
(*b*) section 80 (right to object to derogatory treatment of work).

(2) The rights do not apply—

(*a*) in relation to a literary, dramatic, musical and artistic work of which the author died before commencement; or
(*b*) in relation to a film made before commencement.

(3) The rights in relation to an existing literary, dramatic, musical or artistic work do not apply—

(*a*) where copyright first vested in the author, to anything which by virtue of an assignment of copyright made or licence granted before commencement may be done without infringing copyright;
(*b*) where copyright first vested in a person other than the author, to anything done by or with the licence of the copyright owner.

(4) The rights do not apply to anything done in relation to a record made in pursuance of section 8 of the 1956 Act (statutory recording licence).

24. The right conferred by section 85 (right to privacy of certain photographs and films) does not apply to photographs taken or films made before commencement.

*Assignments and licences*

25.—(1) Any document made or event occurring before commencement which had any operation—

(*a*) affecting the ownership of the copyright in an existing work, or
(*b*) creating, transferring or terminating an interest, right or licence in respect of the copyright in an existing work,

has the corresponding operation in relation to copyright in the work under this Act.

(2) Expressions used in such a document shall be construed in accordance with their effect immediately before commencement.

26.—(1) Section 91(1) of this Act (assignment of future copyright: statutory vesting of legal interest on copyright coming into existence) does not apply in relation to an agreement made before 1st June 1957.

(2) The repeal by this Act of section 37(2) of the 1956 Act (assignment of future copyright: devolution of right where assignee dies before copyright comes into existence) does not affect the operation of that provision in relation to an agreement made before commencement.

27.—(1) Where the author of a literary, dramatic, musical or artistic work was the first owner of the copyright in it, no assignment of the copyright and no grant of any interest in it, made by him (otherwise than by will) after the passing of the 1911 Act and before 1st June 1957, shall be operative to vest in the assignee or grantee any rights with respect to the copyright in the work beyond the expiration of 25 years from the death of the author.

(2) The reversionary interest in the copyright expectant on the termination of that period may after commencement be assigned by the author during his life but in the absence of any assignment shall, on his death, devolve on his legal personal representatives as part of his estate.

(3) Nothing in this paragraph affects—

(*a*) an assignment of the reversionary interest by a person to whom it has been assigned,
(*b*) an assignment of the reversionary interest after the death of the author by his personal representatives or any person becoming entitled to it, or
(*c*) any assignment of the copyright after the reversionary interest has fallen in.

(4) Nothing in this paragraph applies to the assignment of the copyright in a collective work or a licence to publish a work or part of a work as part of a collective work.

(5) In sub-paragraph (4) "collective work" means—

(*a*) any encyclopaedia, dictionary, yearbook, or similar work;
(*b*) a newspaper, review, magazine, or similar periodical; and
(*c*) any work written in distinct parts by different authors, or in which works or parts of works of different authors are incorporated.

28.—(1) This paragraph applies where copyright subsists in a literary, dramatic, musical or artistic work made before 1st July 1912 in relation to which the author, before the commencement of the 1911 Act, made such an assignment or grant as was mentioned in paragraph (*a*) of the proviso to section 24(1) of that Act (assignment or grant of copyright or performing right for full term of the right under the previous law).

(2) If before commencement any event has occurred or notice has been given which by virtue of paragraph 38 of Schedule 7 to the 1956 Act had any operation in relation to copyright in the work under that Act, the event or notice has the corresponding operation in relation to copyright under this Act.

(3) Any right which immediately before commencement would by virtue of paragraph

38(3) of that Schedule have been exercisable in relation to the work, or copyright in it, is exercisable in relation to the work or copyright in it under this Act.

(4) If in accordance with paragraph 38(4) of that Schedule copyright would, on a date after the commencement of the 1956 Act, have reverted to the author or his personal representatives and that date falls after the commencement of the new copyright provisions—

(*a*) the copyright in the work shall revert to the author or his personal representatives, as the case may be, and

(*b*) any interest of any other person in the copyright which subsists on that date by virtue of any document made before the commencement of the 1911 Act shall thereupon determine.

29. Section 92(2) of this Act (rights of exclusive licensee against successors in title of person granting licence) does not apply in relation to an exclusive licence granted before commencement.

*Bequests*

30.—(1) Section 93 of this Act (copyright to pass under will with original document or other material thing embodying unpublished work)—

(*a*) does not apply where the testator died before 1st June 1957, and

(*b*) where the testator died on or after that date and before commencement, applies only in relation to an original document embodying a work.

(2) In the case of an author who died before 1st June 1957, the ownership after his death of a manuscript of his, where such ownership has been acquired under a testamentary disposition made by him and the manuscript is of a work which has not been published or performed in public, is prima facie proof of the copyright being with the owner of the manuscript.

*Remedies for infringement*

31.—(1) Sections 96 and 97 of this Act (remedies for infringement) apply only in relation to an infringement of copyright committed after commencement; section 17 of the 1956 Act continues to apply in relation to infringements committed before commencement.

(2) Sections 99 and 100 of this Act (delivery up or seizure of infringing copies, &c) apply to infringing copies and other articles made before or after commencement; section 18 of the 1956 Act, and section 7 of the 1911 Act, (conversion damages, &c), do not apply after commencement except for the purposes of proceedings begun before commencement.

(3) Sections 101 to 102 of this Act (rights and remedies of exclusive licensee) apply where sections 96 to 100 of this Act apply; section 19 of the 1956 Act continues to apply where section 17 or 18 of that Act applies.

(4) Sections 104 to 106 of this Act (presumptions) apply only in proceedings brought by virtue of this Act; section 20 of the 1956 Act continues to apply in proceedings brought by virtue of that Act.

32. Sections 101 and 102 of this Act (rights and remedies of exclusive licensee) do not apply to a licence granted before 1st June 1957.

33.—(1) The provisions of section 107 of this Act (criminal liability for making or dealing with infringing articles, &c) apply only in relation to acts done after commencement; section 21 of the 1956 Act (penalties and summary proceedings in respect of dealings which infringe copyright) continues to apply in relation to acts done before commencement.

(2) Section 109 of this Act (search warrants) applies in relation to offences committed before commencement in relation to which section 21A or 21B of the 1956 Act applied; sections 21A and 21B continue to apply in relation to warrants issued before commencement.

*Copyright Tribunal: proceedings pending on commencement*

34.—(1) The Lord Chancellor may, after consultation with the Lord Advocate, by rules make such provision as he considers necessary or expedient with respect to proceedings pending under Part IV of the 1956 Act immediately before commencement.

(2) Rules under this paragraph shall be made by statutory instrument which shall be subject to annulment in pursuance of a resolution of either House of Parliament.

*Qualification for copyright protection*

35. Every work in which copyright subsisted under the 1956 Act immediately before commencement shall be deemed to satisfy the requirements of Part I of this Act as to qualification for copyright protection.

*Dependent territories*

36.—(1) The 1911 Act shall remain in force as part of the law of any dependent territory in which it was in force immediately before commencement until—

(*a*) the new copyright provisions come into force in that territory by virtue of an Order under section 157 of this Act (power to extend new copyright provisions), or

(*b*) in the case of any of the Channel Islands, the Act is repealed by Order under sub-paragraph (3) below.

(2) An Order in Council in force immediately before commencement which extends to any dependent territory any provisions of the 1956 Act shall remain in force as part of the law of that territory until—

(*a*) the new copyright provisions come into force in that territory by virtue of an Order under section 157 of this Act (power to extend new copyright provisions), or

(*b*) in the case of the Isle of Man, the Order is revoked by Order under sub-paragraph (3) below;

and while it remains in force such an Order may be varied under the provisions of the 1956 Act under which it was made.

(3) If it appears to Her Majesty that provision with respect to copyright has been made in the law of any of the Channel Islands or the Isle of Man otherwise than by extending the provisions of Part I of this Act, Her Majesty may by Order in Council repeal the 1911 Act as it has effect as part of the law of that territory or, as the case may be, revoke the Order extending the 1956 Act there.

(4) A dependent territory in which the 1911 or 1956 Act remains in force shall be treated, in the law of the countries to which Part I extends, as a country to which that Part extends; and those countries shall be treated in the law of such a territory as countries to which the 1911 Act or, as the case may be, the 1956 Act extends.

(5) If a country in which the 1911 or 1956 Act is in force ceases to be a colony of the United Kingdom, section 158 of this Act (consequences of country ceasing to be colony) applies with the substitution for the reference in subsection (3)(*b*) to the provisions of Part I of this Act of a reference to the provisions of the 1911 or 1956 Act, as the case may be.

(6) In this paragraph "dependent territory" means any of the Channel Islands, the Isle of Man or any colony.

37.—(1) This paragraph applies to a country which immediately before commencement was not a dependent territory within the meaning of paragraph 36 above but—

(*a*) was a country to which the 1956 Act extended, or

(*b*) was treated as such a country by virtue of paragraph 39(2) of Schedule 7 to that Act (countries to which the 1911 Act extended or was treated as extending);

and Her Majesty may by Order in Council conclusively declare for the purposes of this paragraph whether a country was such a country or was so treated.

(2) A country to which this paragraph applies shall be treated as a country to which Part I extends for the purposes of sections 154 to 156 (qualification for copyright protection) until—

(*a*) an Order in Council is made in respect of that country under section 159 (application of Part I to countries to which it does not extend), or

(*b*) an Order in Council is made declaring that it shall cease to be so treated by reason of the fact that the provisions of the 1956 Act or, as the case may be, the 1911 Act, which extended there as part of the law of that country have been repealed or amended.

(3) A statutory instrument containing an Order in Council under this paragraph shall be subject to annulment in pursuance of a resolution of either House of Parliament.

*Territorial waters and the continental shelf*

38. Section 161 of this Act (application of Part I to things done in territorial waters or the United Kingdom sector of the continental shelf) does not apply in relation to anything done before commencement.

*British ships, aircraft and hovercraft*

39. Section 162 (British ships, aircraft and hovercraft) does not apply in relation to anything done before commencement.

*Crown copyright*

40.—(1) Section 163 of this Act (general provisions as to Crown copyright) applies to an existing work if—

(*a*) section 39 of the 1956 Act applies to the work immediately before commencement, and

(*b*) the work is not one to which section 164, 165 or 166 applies (copyright in Acts, Measures and Bills and Parliamentary copyright: see paragraphs 42 and 43 below).

(2) Section 163(1)(*b*) (first ownership of copyright) has effect subject to any agreement entered into before commencement under section 39(6) of the 1956 Act.

41.—(1) The following provisions have effect with respect to the duration of copyright in existing works to which section 163 (Crown copyright) applies.

The question which provision applies to a work shall be determined by reference to the facts immediately before commencement; and expressions used in this paragraph which were defined for the purposes of the 1956 Act have the same meaning as in that Act.

(2) Copyright in the following descriptions of work continues to subsist until the date on which it would have expired in accordance with the 1956 Act—

(*a*) published literary, dramatic or musical works;
(*b*) artistic works other than engravings or photographs;
(*c*) published engravings;
(*d*) published photographs and photographs taken before 1st June 1957;
(*e*) published sound recordings and sound recordings made before 1st June 1957;
(*f*) published films and films falling within section 13(3)(*a*) of the 1956 Act (films registered under former enactments relating to registration of films).

(3) Copyright in unpublished literary, dramatic or musical works continues to subsist until—

(*a*) the date on which copyright expires in accordance with section 163(3), or
(*b*) the end of the period of 50 years from the end of the calendar year in which the new copyright provisions come into force,

whichever is the later.

(4) Copyright in the following descriptions of work continues to subsist until the end of the period of 50 years from the end of the calendar year in which the new copyright provisions come into force—

(*a*) unpublished engravings;
(*b*) unpublished photographs taken on or after 1st June 1957.

(5) Copyright in a film or sound recording not falling within sub-paragraph (2) above continues to subsist until the end of the period of 50 years from the end of the calendar year in which the new copyright provisions come into force, unless the film or recording is published before the end of that period, in which case copyright expires 50 years from the end of the calendar year in which it is published.

42.—(1) Section 164 (copyright in Acts and Measures) applies to existing Acts of Parliament and Measures of the General Synod of the Church of England.

(2) References in that section to Measures of the General Synod of the Church of England include Church Assembly Measures.

*Parliamentary copyright*

43.—(1) Section 165 of this Act (general provisions as to Parliamentary copyright) applies to existing unpublished literary, dramatic, musical or artistic works, but does not otherwise apply to existing works.

(2) Section 166 (copyright in Parliamentary Bills) does not apply—

(*a*) to a public Bill which was introduced into Parliament and published before commencement, (*b*) to a private Bill of which a copy was deposited in either House before commencement, or

(*c*) to a personal Bill which was given a First Reading in the House of Lords before commencement.

*Copyright vesting in certain international organisations*

44.—(1) Any work in which immediately before commencement copyright subsisted by virtue of section 33 of the 1956 Act shall be deemed to satisfy the requirements of section 168(1); but otherwise section 168 does not apply to works made or, as the case may be, published before commencement.

(2) Copyright in any such work which is unpublished continues to subsist until the date on which it would have expired in accordance with the 1956 Act, or the end of the period of 50 years from the end of the calendar year in which the new copyright provisions come into force, whichever is the earlier.

*Meaning of "publication"*

45. Section 175(3) (construction of building treated as equivalent to publication) applies only where the construction of the building began after commencement.

*Meaning of "unauthorised"*

46. For the purposes of the application of the definition in section 178 (minor definitions) of the expression "unauthorised" in relation to things done before commencement—

(*a*) paragraph (*a*) applies in relation to things done before 1st June 1957 as if the reference to the licence of the copyright owner were a reference to his consent or acquiescence;

(*b*) paragraph (*b*) applies with the substitution for the words from "or, in a case" to the end of the words "or any person lawfully claiming under him"; and

(*c*) paragraph (*c*) shall be disregarded.

## SCHEDULE 2

Section 189

### Rights in performances: permitted acts

*Introductory*

1.—(1) The provisions of this Schedule specify acts which may be done in relation to a performance or recording notwithstanding the rights conferred by Part II; they relate only to the question of infringement of those rights and do not affect any other right or obligation restricting the doing of any of the specified acts.

(2) No inference shall be drawn from the description of any act which may by virtue of this Schedule be done without infringing the rights conferred by Part II as to the scope of those rights.

(3) The provisions of this Schedule are to be construed independently of each other, so that the fact that an act does not fall within one provision does not mean that it is not covered by another provision.

*Criticism, reviews and news reporting*

2.—(1) Fair dealing with a performance or recording—

(*a*) for the purpose of criticism or review, of that or another performance or recording, or of a work, or

(*b*) for the purpose of reporting current events,

does not infringe any of the rights conferred by Part II.

(2) Expressions used in this paragraph have the same meaning as in section 30.

*Incidental inclusion of performance or recording*

3.—(1) The rights conferred by Part II are not infringed by the incidental inclusion of a performance or recording in a sound recording, film, broadcast or cable programme.

(2) Nor are those rights infringed by anything done in relation to copies of, or the playing,

showing, broadcasting or inclusion in a cable programme service of, anything whose making was, by virtue of sub-paragraph (1), not an infringement of those rights.

(3) A performance or recording so far as it consists of music, or words spoken or sung with music, shall not be regarded as incidentally included in a sound recording, broadcast or cable programme if it is deliberately included.

(4) Expressions used in this paragraph have the same meaning as in section 31.

*Things done for purposes of instruction or examination*

4.—(1) The rights conferred by Part II are not infringed by the copying of a recording of a performance in the course of instruction, or of preparation for instruction, in the making of films or film sound-tracks, provided the copying is done by a person giving or receiving instruction.

(2) The rights conferred by Part II are not infringed—

(*a*) by the copying of a recording of a performance for the purposes of setting or answering the questions in an examination, or

(*b*) by anything done for the purposes of an examination by way of communicating the questions to the candidates.

(3) Where a recording which would otherwise be an illicit recording is made in accordance with this paragraph but is subsequently dealt with, it shall be treated as an illicit recording for the purposes of that dealing, and if that dealing infringes any right conferred by Part II for all subsequent purposes.

For this purpose "dealt with" means sold or let for hire, or offered or exposed for sale or hire.

(4) Expressions used in this paragraph have the same meaning as in section 32.

*Playing or showing sound recording, film, broadcast or cable programme at educational establishment*

5.—(1) The playing or showing of a sound recording, film, broadcast or cable programme at an educational establishment for the purposes of instruction before an audience consisting of teachers and pupils at the establishment and other persons directly connected with the activities of the establishment is not a playing or showing of a performance in public for the purposes of infringement of the rights conferred by Part II.

(2) A person is not for this purpose directly connected with the activities of the educational establishment simply because he is the parent of a pupil at the establishment.

(3) Expressions used in this paragraph have the same meaning as in section 34 and any provision made under section 174(2) with respect to the application of that section also applies for the purposes of this paragraph.

*Recording of broadcasts and cable programmes by educational establishments*

6.—(1) A recording of a broadcast or cable programme, or a copy of such a recording, may be made by or on behalf of an educational establishment for the educational purposes of that establishment without thereby infringing any of the rights conferred by Part II in relation to any performance or recording included in it.

(2) Where a recording which would otherwise be an illicit recording is made in accordance with this paragraph but is subsequently dealt with, it shall be treated as an illicit recording for the purposes of that dealing, and if that dealing infringes any right conferred by Part II for all subsequent purposes.

For this purpose "dealt with" means sold or let for hire, or offered or exposed for sale or hire.

(3) Expressions used in this paragraph have the same meaning as in section 35 and any provision made under section 174(2) with respect to the application of that section also applies for the purposes of this paragraph.

*Copy of work required to be made as condition of export*

7.—(1) If an article of cultural or historical importance or interest cannot lawfully be exported from the United Kingdom unless a copy of it is made and deposited in an appropriate library or archive, it is not an infringement of any right conferred by Part II to make that copy.

(2) Expressions used in this paragraph have the same meaning as in section 44.

*Parliamentary and judicial proceedings*

8.—(1) The rights conferred by Part II are not infringed by anything done for the purposes of parliamentary or judicial proceedings or for the purpose of reporting such proceedings.

(2) Expressions used in this paragraph have the same meaning as in section 45.

*Royal Commissions and statutory inquiries*

9.—(1) The rights conferred by Part II are not infringed by anything done for the purposes of the proceedings of a Royal Commission or statutory inquiry or for the purpose of reporting any such proceedings held in public.

(2) Expressions used in this paragraph have the same meaning as in section 46.

*Public records*

10.—(1) Material which is comprised in public records within the meaning of the Public Records Act 1958, the Public Records (Scotland) Act 1937 or the Public Records Act (Northern Ireland) 1923 which are open to public inspection in pursuance of that Act, may be copied, and a copy may be supplied to any person, by or with the authority of any officer appointed under that Act, without infringing any right conferred by Part II.

(2) Expressions used in this paragraph have the same meaning as in section 49.

*Acts done under statutory authority*

11.—(1) Where the doing of a particular act is specifically authorised by an Act of Parliament, whenever passed, then, unless the Act provides otherwise, the doing of that act does not infringe the rights conferred by Part II.

(2) Sub-paragraph (1) applies in relation to an enactment contained in Northern Ireland legislation as it applies to an Act of Parliament.

(3) Nothing in this paragraph shall be construed as excluding any defence of statutory authority otherwise available under or by virtue of any enactment.

(4) Expressions used in this paragraph have the same meaning as in section 50.

*Transfer of copies of works in electronic form*

12.—(1) This paragraph applies where a recording of a performance in electronic form has been purchased on terms which, expressly or impliedly or by virtue of any rule of law, allow the purchaser to make further recordings in connection with his use of the recording.

(2) If there are no express terms—

(*a*) prohibiting the transfer of the recording by the purchaser, imposing obligations which continue after a transfer, prohibiting the assignment of any consent or terminating any consent on a transfer, or

(*b*) providing for the terms on which a transferee may do the things which the purchaser was permitted to do,

anything which the purchaser was allowed to do may also be done by a transferee without infringement of the rights conferred by this Part, but any recording made by the purchaser which is not also transferred shall be treated as an illicit recording for all purposes after the transfer.

(3) The same applies where the original purchased recording is no longer usable and what is transferred is a further copy used in its place.

(4) The above provisions also apply on a subsequent transfer, with the substitution for references in sub-paragraph (2) to the purchaser of references to the subsequent transferor.

(5) This paragraph does not apply in relation to a recording purchased before the commencement of Part II.

(6) Expressions used in this paragraph have the same meaning as in section 56.

*Use of recordings of spoken works in certain cases*

13.—(1) Where a recording of the reading or recitation of a literary work is made for the purpose—

(*a*) of reporting current events, or
(*b*) of broadcasting or including in a cable programme service the whole or part of the reading or recitation,

it is not an infringement of the rights conferred by Part II to use the recording (or to copy the recording and use the copy) for that purpose, provided the following conditions are met.

(2) The conditions are that—

(*a*) the recording is a direct recording of the reading or recitation and is not taken from a previous recording or from a broadcast or cable programme;
(*b*) the making of the recording was not prohibited by or on behalf of the person giving the reading or recitation;
(*c*) the use made of the recording is not of a kind prohibited by or on behalf of that person before the recording was made; and
(*d*) the use is by or with the authority of a person who is lawfully in possession of the recording.

(3) Expressions used in this paragraph have the same meaning as in section 58.

*Recordings of folksongs*

14.—(1) A recording of a performance of a song may be made for the purpose of including it in an archive maintained by a designated body without infringing any of the rights conferred by Part II, provided the conditions in sub-paragraph (2) below are met.

(2) The conditions are that—

(*a*) the words are unpublished and of unknown authorship at the time the recording is made,
(*b*) the making of the recording does not infringe any copyright, and
(*c*) its making is not prohibited by any performer.

(3) Copies of a recording made in reliance on sub-paragraph (1) and included in an archive maintained by a designated body may, if the prescribed conditions are met, be made and supplied by the archivist without infringing any of the rights conferred by Part II.

(4) In this paragraph—

"designated body" means a body designated for the purposes of section 61, and
"the prescribed conditions" means the conditions prescribed for the purposes of subsection (3) of that section;

and other expressions used in this paragraph have the same meaning as in that section.

*Playing of sound recordings for purposes of club, society, &c*

15.—(1) It is not an infringement of any right conferred by Part II to play a sound recording as part of the activities of, or for the benefit of, a club, society or other organisation if the following conditions are met.

(2) The conditions are—

(*a*) that the organisation is not established or conducted for profit and its main objects are charitable or are otherwise concerned with the advancement of religion, education or social welfare, and
(*b*) that the proceeds of any charge for admission to the place where the recording is to be heard are applied solely for the purposes of the organisation.

(3) Expressions used in this paragraph have the same meaning as in section 67.

*Incidental recording for purposes of broadcast or cable programme*

16.—(1) A person who proposes to broadcast a recording of a performance, or include a recording of a performance in a cable programme service, in circumstances not infringing the rights conferred by Part II shall be treated as having consent for the purposes of that Part for the making of a further recording for the purposes of the broadcast or cable programme.

(2) That consent is subject to the condition that the further recording—

(*a*) shall not be used for any other purpose, and
(*b*) shall be destroyed within 28 days of being first used for broadcasting the performance or including it in a cable programme service.

(3) A recording made in accordance with this paragraph shall be treated as an illicit recording—

(*a*) for the purposes of any use in breach of the condition mentioned in sub-paragraph (2)(*a*), and
(*b*) for all purposes after that condition or the condition mentioned in sub-paragraph (2)(*b*) is broken.

(4) Expressions used in this paragraph have the same meaning as in section 68.

*Recordings for purposes of supervision and control of broadcasts and cable programmes*

17.—(1) The rights conferred by Part II are not infringed by the making or use by the British Broadcasting Corporation, for the purpose of maintaining supervision and control over programmes broadcast by them, of recordings of those programmes.

(2) The rights conferred by Part II are not infringed by—

(*a*) the making or use of recordings by the Independent Broadcasting Authority for the purposes mentioned in section 4(7) of the Broadcasting Act 1981 (maintenance of supervision and control over programmes and advertisements); or
(*b*) anything done under or in pursuance of provision included in a contract between a programme contractor and the Authority in accordance with section 21 of that Act.

(3) The rights conferred by Part II are not infringed by—

(*a*) the making by or with the authority of the Cable Authority, or the use by that Authority, for the purpose of maintaining supervision and control over programmes included in services licensed under Part I of the Cable and Broadcasting Act 1984, of recordings of those programmes; or
(*b*) anything done under or in pursuance of—
    (i) a notice or direction given under section 16 of the Cable and Broadcasting Act 1984 (power of Cable Authority to require production of recordings); or
    (ii) a condition included in a licence by virtue of section 35 of that Act (duty of Authority to secure that recordings are available for certain purposes).

(4) Expressions used in this paragraph have the same meaning as in section 69.

*Free public showing or playing of broadcast or cable programme*

18.—(1) The showing or playing in public of a broadcast or cable programme to an audience who have not paid for admission to the place where the broadcast or programme is to be seen or heard does not infringe any right conferred by Part II in relation to a performance or recording included in—

(*a*) the broadcast or cable programme, or
(*b*) any sound recording or film which is played or shown in public by reception of the broadcast or cable programme.

(2) The audience shall be treated as having paid for admission to a place—

(*a*) if they have paid for admission to a place of which that place forms part; or
(*b*) if goods or services are supplied at that place (or a place of which it forms part)—
    (i) at prices which are substantially attributable to the facilities afforded for seeing or hearing the broadcast or programme, or
    (ii) at prices exceeeding those usually charged there and which are partly attributable to those facilities.

(3) The following shall not be regarded as having paid for admission to a place—

(*a*) persons admitted as residents or inmates of the place;
(*b*) persons admitted as members of a club or society where the payment is only for membership of the club or society and the provision of facilities for seeing or hearing broadcasts or programmes is only incidental to the main purposes of the club or society.

(4) Where the making of the broadcast or inclusion of the programme in a cable programme service was an infringement of the rights conferred by Part II in relation to a performance or

recording, the fact that it was heard or seen in public by the reception of the broadcast or programme shall be taken into account in assessing the damages for that infringement.

(5) Expressions used in this paragraph have the same meaning as in section 72.

*Reception and re-transmission of broadcast in cable programme service*

19.—(1) This paragraph applies where a broadcast made from a place in the United Kingdom is, by reception and immediate re-transmission, included in a cable programme service.

(2) The rights conferred by Part II in relation to a performance or recording included in the broadcast are not infringed—

(*a*) if the inclusion of the broadcast in the cable programme service is in pursuance of a requirement imposed under section 13(1) of the Cable and Broadcasting Act 1984 (duty of Cable Authority to secure inclusion in cable service of certain programmes), or

(*b*) if and to the extent that the broadcast is made for reception in the area in which the cable programme service is provided;

but where the making of the broadcast was an infringement of those rights, the fact that the broadcast was re-transmitted as a programme in a cable programme service shall be taken into account in assessing the damages for that infringement.

(3) Expressions used in this paragraph have the same meaning as in section 73.

*Provision of sub-titled copies of broadcast or cable programme*

20.—(1) A designated body may, for the purpose of providing people who are deaf or hard of hearing, or physically or mentally handicapped in other ways, with copies which are sub-titled or otherwise modified for their special needs, make recordings of television broadcasts or cable programmes without infringing any right conferred by Part II in relation to a performance or recording included in the broadcast or cable programme.

(2) In this paragraph "designated body" means a body designated for the purposes of section 74 and other expressions used in this paragraph have the same meaning as in that section.

*Recording of broadcast or cable programme for archival purposes*

21.—(1) A recording of a broadcast or cable programme of a designated class, or a copy of such a recording, may be made for the purpose of being placed in an archive maintained by a designated body without thereby infringing any right conferred by Part II in relation to a performance or recording included in the broadcast or cable programme.

(2) In this paragraph "designated class" and "designated body" means a class or body designated for the purposes of section 75 and other expressions used in this paragraph have the same meaning as in that section.

## SCHEDULE 3

Section 272

### Registered Designs: Minor and Consequential Amendments of 1949 Act

*Section 3: proceedings for registration*

1. In section 3 of the Registered Designs Act 1949 (proceedings for registration) for subsections (2) to (6) substitute—

"(2) An application for the registration of a design in which design right subsists shall not be entertained unless made by the person claiming to be the design right owner.

(3) For the purpose of deciding whether a design is new, the registrar may make such searches, if any, as he thinks fit.

(4) The registrar may, in such cases as may be prescribed, direct that for the purpose of deciding whether a design is new an application shall be treated as made on a date earlier or later than that on which it was in fact made.

(5) The registrar may refuse an application for the registration of a design or may register the design in pursuance of the application subject to such modifications, if any, as

he thinks fit; and a design when registered shall be registered as of the date on which the application was made or is treated as having been made.

(6) An application which, owing to any default or neglect on the part of the applicant, has not been completed so as to enable registration to be effected within such time as may be prescribed shall be deemed to be abandoned.

(7) An appeal lies from any decision of the registrar under this section.".

*Section 4: registration of same design in respect of other articles, etc*

2. In section 4 of the Registered Designs Act 1949 (registration of same design in respect of other articles, &c), in subsection (1), for the proviso substitute—

"Provided that the right in a design registered by virtue of this section shall not extend beyond the end of the period, and any extended period, for which the right subsists in the original registered design.".

*Section 5: provisions for secrecy of certain designs*

3.—(1) Section 5 of the Registered Designs Act 1949 is amended as follows.

(2) For "a competent authority" or "the competent authority", wherever occurring, substitute "the Secretary of State"; and in subsection (3)(*c*) for "that authority" substitute "he".

(3) For subsection (2) substitute—

"(2) The Secretary of State shall by rules make provision for securing that where such directions are given—

(*a*) the representation or specimen of the design, and
(*b*) any evidence filed in support of the applicant's contention that the appearance of an article is material (for the purposes of section 1(3) of this Act),

shall not be open to public inspection at the Patent Office during the continuance in force of the directions."

(4) In subsection (3)(*b*) after "representation or specimen of the design" insert ", or any such evidence as is mentioned in subsection (2)(*b*) above,".

(5) Omit subsection (5).

*Section 6: provisions as to confidential disclosure, etc*

4.—(1) Section 6 of the Registered Designs Act 1949 (provisions as to confidential disclosure, &c) is amended as follows.

(2) In subsection (2) (display of design at certified exhibition), in paragraph (*a*) for "certified by the Board of Trade" substitute "certified by the Secretary of State".

(3) For subsections (4) and (5) (registration of designs corresponding to copyright artistic works) substitute—

"(4) Where an application is made by or with the consent of the owner of copyright in an artistic work for the registration of a corresponding design, the design shall not be treated for the purposes of this Act as being other than new by reason only of any use previously made of the artistic work, subject to subsection (5).

(5) Subsection (4) does not apply if the previous use consisted of or included the sale, letting for hire or offer or exposure for sale or hire of articles to which had been applied industrially—

(*a*) the design in question, or
(*b*) a design differing from it only in immaterial details or in features which are variants commonly used in the trade,

and that previous use was made by or with the consent of the copyright owner.

(6) The Secretary of State may make provision by rules as to the circumstances in which a design is to be regarded for the purposes of this section as "applied industrially" to articles, or any description of articles.".

*Section 9: exemption of innocent infringer from liability for damages*

5. In section 9 of the Registered Designs Act 1949 (exemption of innocent infringer from liability for damages), in subsections (1) and (2) for "copyright in a registered design" substitute "the right in a registered design".

*Section 11: cancellation of registration*

6.—(1) Section 11 of the Registered Designs Act 1949 (cancellation of registration) is amended as follows.

(2) In subsection (2) omit "or original".

(3) For subsections (2A) and (3) substitute—

"(3) At any time after a design has been registered, any person interested may apply to the registrar for the cancellation of the registration on the ground that—

(*a*) the design was at the time it was registered a corresponding design in relation to an artistic work in which copyright subsisted, and

(*b*) the right in the registered design has expired in accordance with section 8(4) of this Act (expiry of right in registered design on expiry of copyright in artistic work);

and the registrar may make such order on the application as he thinks fit.

(4) A cancellation under this section takes effect—

(*a*) in the case of cancellation under subsection (1), from the date of the registrar's decision,

(*b*) in the case of cancellation under subsection (2), from the date of registration,

(*c*) in the case of cancellation under subsection (3), from the date on which the right in the registered design expired,

or, in any case, from such other date as the registrar may direct.

(5) An appeal lies from any order of the registrar under this section.".

*Section 14: registration where application has been made in convention country*

7. In section 14 of the Registered Designs Act 1949 (registration where application has been made in convention country), for subsection (2) and (3) substitute—

"(2) Where an application for registration of a design is made by virtue of this section, the application shall be treated, for the purpose of determining whether that or any other design is new, as made on the date of the application for protection in the convention country or, if more than one such application was made, on the date of the first such application.

(3) Subsection (2) shall not be construed as excluding the power to give directions under section 3(4) of this Act in relation to an application made by virtue of this section.".

*Section 15: extension of time for application under s. 14 in certain cases*

8. In section 15(1) of the Registered Designs Act 1949 (power to make rules empowering registrar to extend time for applications under s. 14) for "the Board of Trade are satisfied" substitute "the Secretary of State is satisfied" and for "they" substitute "he".

*Section 16: protection of designs communicated under international agreements*

9. In section 16 of the Registered Designs Act 1949 (protection of designs communicated under international agreements)—

(*a*) in subsection (1) for "the Board of Trade" substitute "the Secretary of State", and

(*b*) in subsection (3) for "the Board of Trade" substitute "the Secretary of State" and for "the Board are satisfied" substitute "the Secretary of State is satisfied".

*Section 19: registration of assignments, &c*

10. In section 19 of the Registered Designs Act 1949 (registration of assignments, &c.), after subsection (3) insert—

"(3A) Where design right subsists in a registered design, the registrar shall not register an interest under subsection (3) unless he is satisfied that the person entitled to that interest is also entitled to a corresponding interest in the design right.

(3B) Where design right subsists in a registered design and the proprietor of the registered design is also the design right owner, an assignment of the design right shall be taken to be also an assignment of the right in the registered design, unless a contrary intention appears.".

*Section 20: rectification of the register*

11. In section 20 of the Registered Designs Act 1949 (rectification of the register), after subsection (4) add—

"(5) A rectification of the register under this section has effect as follows—

(*a*) an entry made has effect from the date on which it should have been made,
(*b*) an entry varied has effect as if it had originally been made in its varied form, and
(*c*) an entry deleted shall be deemed never to have had effect,

unless, in any case, the court directs otherwise.".

*Section 22: inspection of registered designs*

12.—(1) Section 22 of the Registered Designs Act 1949 (inspection of registered designs) is amended as follows.

(2) For subsection (1) substitute—

"(1) Where a design has been registered under this Act, there shall be open to inspection at the Patent Office on and after the day on which the certificate of registration is issued—

(*a*) the representation or specimen of the design, and
(*b*) any evidence filed in support of the applicant's contention that the appearance of an article is material (for the purposes of section 1(3) of this Act).

This subsection has effect subject to the following provisions of this section and to any rules made under section 5(2) of this Act.".

(3) In subsection (2), subsection (3) (twice) and subsection (4) for "representation or specimen of the design" substitute "representation, specimen or evidence".

*Section 23: information as to existence of right in registered design*

13. For section 23 of the Registered Designs Act 1949 (information as to existence of right in registered design) substitute—

**"23 Information as to existence of right in registered design**

On the request of a person furnishing such information as may enable the registrar to identify the design, and on payment of the prescribed fee, the registrar shall inform him—

(*a*) whether the design is registered and, if so, in respect of what articles, and
(*b*) whether any extension of the period of the right in the registered design has been granted,

and shall state the date of registration and the name and address of the registered proprietor.".

*Section 25: certificate of contested validity of registration*

14. In section 25 of the Registered Designs Act 1949 (certificate of contested validity of registration), in subsection (2) for "the copyright in the registered design" substitute "the right in the registered design".

*Section 26: remedy for groundless threats of infringement proceedings*

15.—(1) Section 26 of the Registered Designs Act 1949 (remedy for groundless threats of infringement proceedings) is amended as follows.

(2) In subsections (1) and (2) for "the copyright in a registered design" substitute "the right in a registered design".

(3) After subsection (2) insert—

"(2A) Proceedings may not be brought under this section in respect of a threat to bring proceedings for an infringement alleged to consist of the making or importing of anything.".

*Section 27: the court*

16. For section 27 of the Registered Designs Act 1949 (the court) substitute—

"**27 The court**

(1) In this Act "the court" means—

(*a*) in England and Wales the High Court or any patents county court having jurisdiction by virtue of an order under section 287 of the Copyright, Designs and Patents Act 1988,

(*b*) in Scotland, the Court of Session, and

(*c*) in Northern Ireland, the High Court.

(2) Provision may be made by rules of court with respect to proceedings in the High Court in England and Wales for references and applications under this Act to be dealt with by such judge of that court as the Lord Chancellor may select for the purpose.".

*Section 28: the Appeal Tribunal*

17.—(1) Section 28 of the Registered Designs Act 1949 (the Appeal Tribunal) is amended as follows.

(2) For subsection (2) (members of Tribunal) substitute—

"(2) The Appeal Tribunal shall consist of—

(*a*) one or more judges of the High Court nominated by the Lord Chancellor, and

(*b*) one judge of the Court of Session nominated by the Lord President of that Court.".

(3) In subsection (5) (costs), after "costs" (twice) insert "or expenses", and for the words from "and any such order" to the end substitute—

"and any such order may be enforced—

(*a*) in England and Wales or Northern Ireland, in the same way as an order of the High Court;

(*b*) in Scotland, in the same way as a decree for expenses granted by the Court of Session.".

(4) For subsection (10) (seniority of judges) substitute—

"(10) In this section "the High Court" means the High Court in England and Wales; and for the purposes of this section the seniority of judges shall be reckoned by reference to the dates on which they were appointed judges of that court or the Court of Session.".

(5) The amendments to section 28 made by section 10(5) of the Administration of Justice Act 1970 (power to make rules as to right of audience) shall be deemed always to have extended to Northern Ireland.

*Section 29: exercise of discretionary powers of registrar*

18. In section 29 of the Registered Designs Act 1949 (exercise of discretionary powers of registrar) for "the registrar shall give" substitute "rules made by the Secretary of State under this Act shall require the registrar to give".

*Section 30: costs and security for costs*

19. For section 30 of the Registered Designs Act 1949 (costs and security for costs) substitute—

"**30 Costs and security for costs**

(1) Rules made by the Secretary of State under this Act may make provision empowering the registrar, in any proceedings before him under this Act—

(*a*) to award any party such costs as he may consider reasonable, and

(*b*) to direct how and by what parties they are to be paid.

(2) Any such order of the registrar may be enforced—

(*a*) in England and Wales or Northern Ireland, in the same way as an order of the High Court;

(*b*) in Scotland, in the same way as a decree for expenses granted by the Court of Session.

(3) Rules made by the Secretary of State under this Act may make provision empowering

the registrar to require a person, in such cases as may be prescribed, to give security for the costs of—

(*a*) an application for cancellation of the registration of a design,
(*b*) an application for the grant of a licence in respect of a registered design, or
(*c*) an appeal from any decision of the registrar under this Act,

and enabling the application or appeal to be treated as abandoned in default of such security being given.".

*Section 31: evidence before registrar*

20. For section 31 of the Registered Designs Act 1949 (evidence before registrar) substitute—

"**31 Evidence before registrar**

Rules made by the Secretary of State under this Act may make provision—

(*a*) as to the giving of evidence in proceedings before the registrar under this Act by affidavit or statutory declaration;
(*b*) conferring on the registrar the powers of an official referee of the Supreme Court as regards the examination of witnesses on oath and the discovery and production of documents; and
(*c*) applying in relation to the attendance of witnesses in proceedings before the registrar the rules applicable to the attendance of witnesses in proceedings before such a referee.".

*Section 32: power of registrar to refuse to deal with certain agents*

21. Section 32 of the Registered Designs Act 1949 (power of registrar to refuse to deal with certain agents) is repealed.

*Section 33: offence under s 5 (secrecy of certain designs)*

22.—(1) Section 33 of the Registered Designs Act 1949 (offences under s 5 (secrecy of certain designs)) is amended as follows.

(2) In subsection (1), for paragraphs (*a*) and (*b*) substitute—

"(*a*) on conviction on indictment to imprisonment for a term not exceeding two years or a fine, or both;
(*b*) on summary conviction to imprisonment for a term not exceeding six months or a fine not exceeding the statutory maximum, or both.".

(3) Omit subsection (2).

(4) The above amendments do not apply in relation to offences committed before the commencement of Part IV.

*Section 34: falsification of register, &c*

23.—(1) In section 34 of the Registered Designs Act 1949 (falsification of register, &c.) for "shall be guilty of a misdemeanour" substitute—

"shall be guilty of an offence and liable—

(*a*) on conviction on indictment to imprisonment for a term not exceeding two years or a fine, or both;
(*b*) on summary conviction to imprisonment for a term not exceeding six months or a fine not exceeding the statutory maximum, or both.".

(2) The above amendment does not apply in relation to offences committed before the commencement of Part IV.

*Section 35: fine for falsely representing a design as registered*

24.—(1) Section 35 of the Registered Designs Act 1949 (fine for falsely representing a design as registered) is amended as follows.

(2) In subsection (1) for the words from "a fine not exceeding £50" substitute "a fine not exceeding level 3 on the standard scale".

(3) In subsection (2)—

(*a*) for "the copyright in a registered design" substitute "the right in a registered design";
(*b*) for "subsisting copyright in the design" substitute "subsisting right in the design under this Act"; and
(*c*) for the words from "a fine" to the end substitute "a fine not exceeding level 1 on the standard scale".

(4) The amendment in sub-paragraph (2) does not apply in relation to offences committed before the commencement of Part IV.

*Section 35A: offence by body corporate - liability of officers*

25.—(1) In the Registered Designs Act 1949 after section 35 insert—

"**35A Offence by body corporate: liability of officers**

(1) Where an offence under this Act committed by a body corporate is proved to have been committed with the consent or connivance of a director, manager, secretary or other similar officer of the body, or a person purporting to act in any such capacity, he as well as the body corporate is guilty of the offence and liable to be proceeded against and punished accordingly.

(2) In relation to a body corporate whose affairs are managed by its members "director" means a member of the body corporate.".

(2) The above amendment does not apply in relation to offences committed before the commencement of Part IV.

*Section 36: general power to make rules, &c*

26.—(1) Section 36 of the Registered Designs Act 1949 (general power to make rules, &c.) is amended as follows.

(2) In subsection (1) for "the Board of Trade" and "the Board" substitute "the Secretary of State", and for "as they think expedient" substitute "as he thinks expedient".

(3) For the words in subsection (1) from "and in particular" to the end substitute the following subsections—

"(1A) Rules may, in particular, make provision—

(*a*) prescribing the form of applications for registration of designs and of any representations or specimens of designs or other documents which may be filed at the Patent Office, and requiring copies to be furnished of any such representations, specimens or documents;
(*b*) regulating the procedure to be followed in connection with any application or request to the registrar or in connection with any proceeding before him, and authorising the rectification of irregularities of procedure;
(*c*) providing for the appointment of advisers to assist the registrar in proceedings before him;
(*d*) regulating the keeping of the register of designs;
(*e*) authorising the publication and sale of copies of representations of designs and other documents in the Patent Office;
(*f*) prescribing anything authorised or required by this Act to be prescribed by rules.

(1B) The remuneration of an adviser appointed to assist the registrar shall be determined by the Secretary of State with the consent of the Treasury and shall be defrayed out of money provided by Parliament.".

*Section 37: provisions as to rules and Orders*

27.—(1) Section 37 of the Registered Designs Act 1949 (provisions as to rules and orders) is amended as follows.

(2) Omit subsection (1) (duty to advertise making of rules).

(3) In subsections (2), (3) and (4) for "the Board of Trade" substitute "the Secretary of State".

*Section 38: proceedings of the Board of Trade*

28. Section 38 of the Registered Designs Act 1949 (proceedings of the Board of Trade) is repealed.

*Section 39: hours of business and excluded days*

29. In section 39 of the Registered Designs Act 1949 (hours of business and excluded days), in subsection (1) for "the Board of Trade" substitute "the Secretary of State".

*Section 40: fees*

30. In section 40 of the Registered Designs Act 1949 (fees) for "the Board of Trade" substitute "the Secretary of State".

*Section 44: interpretation*

31.—(1) In section 44 of the Registered Designs Act 1949 (interpretation), subsection (1) is amended as follows.

(2) In the definition of "artistic work" for "the Copyright Act 1956" substitute "Part I of the Copyright, Designs and Patents Act 1988".

(3) At the appropriate place insert—

"author" in relation to a design, has the meaning given by section 2(3) and (4);".

(4) Omit the definition of "copyright".

(5) In the definition of "corresponding design", for the words from "has the same meaning" to the end substitute ", in relation to an artistic work, means a design which if applied to an article would produce something which would be treated for the purposes of Part I of the Copyright, Designs and Patents Act 1988 as a copy of that work;".

(6) For the definition of "court" substitute—

"'the court' shall be construed in accordance with section 27 of this Act;".

(7) In the definition of "design" for "subsection (3) of section one of this Act" substitute "section 1(1) of this Act".

(8) At the appropriate place insert—

"'employee', 'employment' and 'employer' refer to employment under a contract of service or of apprenticeship,".

(9) Omit the definition of "Journal".

(10) In the definition of "prescribed" for "the Board of Trade" substitute "the Secretary of State".

*Section 45: application to Scotland*

32. In section 45 of the Registered Designs Act 1949 (application to Scotland), omit paragraphs (1) and (2).

*Section 46: application to Northern Ireland*

33.—(1) Section 46 of the Registered Designs Act 1949 (application to Northern Ireland) is amended as follows.

(2) Omit paragraphs (1) and (2).

(3) For paragraph (3) substitute—

"(3) References to enactments include enactments comprised in Northern Ireland legislation:".

(4) After paragraph (3) insert—

"(3A) References to the Crown include the Crown in right of Her Majesty's Government in Northern Ireland:".

(5) In paragraph (4) for "a department of the Government of Northern Ireland" substitute "a Northern Ireland department", and at the end add "and in relation to a Northern Ireland department references to the Treasury shall be construed as references to the Department of Finance and Personnel".

*Section 47: application to Isle of Man*

34. For section 47 of the Registered Designs Act 1949 (application to Isle of Man) substitute—

"**47 Application to Isle of Man**

This Act extends to the Isle of Man, subject to any modifications contained in an Order made by Her Majesty in Council, and accordingly, subject to any such Order, references in this Act to the United Kingdom shall be construed as including the Isle of Man.".

*Section 47A: territorial waters and the continental shelf*

35. In the Registered Designs Act 1949, after section 47 insert—

**"47A Territorial waters and the continental shelf**

(1) For the purposes of this Act the territorial waters of the United Kingdom shall be treated as part of the United Kingdom.

(2) This Act applies to things done in the United Kingdom sector of the continental shelf on a structure or vessel which is present there for purposes directly connected with the exploration of the sea bed or subsoil or the exploitation of their natural resources as it applies to things done in the United Kingdom.

(3) The United Kingdom sector of the continental shelf means the areas designated by order under section 1(7) of the Continental Shelf Act 1964.".

*Section 48: repeals, savings and transitional provisions*

36. In section 48 of the Registered Designs Act 1949 (repeals, savings and transitional provisions), omit subsection (1) (repeals).

*Schedule 1: provisions as to Crown use of registered designs*

37.—(1) The First Schedule to the Registered Designs Act 1949 (provisions as to Crown use of registered designs) is amended as follows.

(2) In paragraph 2(1) after "copyright" insert "or design right".

(3) In paragraph 3(1) omit "in such manner as may be prescribed by rules of court".

(4) In paragraph 4(2) (definition of "period of emergency") for the words from "the period ending" to "any other period" substitute "a period".

(5) For paragraph 4(3) substitute—

"(3) No Order in Council under this paragraph shall be submitted to Her Majesty unless a draft of it has been laid before and approved by a resolution of each House of Parliament.".

*Schedule 2: enactments repealed*

38. Schedule 2 to the Registered Designs Act 1949 (enactments repealed) is repealed.

## SCHEDULE 4

Section 273

### THE REGISTERED DESIGNS ACT 1949 AS AMENDED

ARRANGEMENT OF SECTIONS

*Registrable designs and proceedings for registration*



*Effect of registration, &c*

*An Act to consolidate certain enactments relating to registered designs* [16 December 1949]

*Registrable designs and proceedings for registration*

### 1 Designs registrable under Act

(1) In this Act "design" means features of shape, configuration, pattern or ornament

applied to an article by any industrial process, being features which in the finished article appeal to and are judged by the eye, but does not include—

(*a*) a method or principle of construction, or

(*b*) features of shape or configuration of an article which—

(i) are dictated solely by the function which the article has to perform, or

(ii) are dependent upon the appearance of another article of which the article is intended by the author of the design to form an integral part.

(2) A design which is new may, upon application by the person claiming to be the proprietor, be registered under this Act in respect of any article, or set of articles, specified in the application.

(3) A design shall not be registered in respect of an article if the appearance of the article is not material, that is, if aesthetic considerations are not normally taken into account to a material extent by persons acquiring or using articles of that description, and would not be so taken into account if the design were to be applied to the article.

(4) A design shall not be regarded as new for the purposes of this Act if it is the same as a design—

(*a*) registered in respect of the same or any other article in pursuance of a prior application, or

(*b*) published in the United Kingdom in respect of the same or any other article before the date of the application,

or if it differs from such a design only in immaterial details or in features which are variants commonly used in the trade.

This subsection has effect subject to the provisions of sections 4, 6 and 16 of this Act.

(5) The Secretary of State may by rules provide for excluding from registration under this Act designs for such articles of a primarily literary or artistic character as the Secretary of State thinks fit.

### 2 Proprietorship of designs

(1) The author of a design shall be treated for the purposes of this Act as the original proprietor of the design, subject to the following provisions.

(1A) Where a design is created in pursuance of a commission for money or money's worth, the person commissioning the design shall be treated as the original proprietor of the design.

(1B) Where, in a case not falling within subsection (1A), a design is created by an employee in the course of his employment, his employer shall be treated as the original proprietor of the design.

(2) Where a design, or the right to apply a design to any article, becomes vested, whether by assignment, transmission or operation of law, in any person other than the original proprietor, either alone or jointly with the original proprietor, that other person, or as the case may be the original proprietor and that other person, shall be treated for the purposes of this Act as the proprietor of the design or as the proprietor of the design in relation to that article.

(3) In this Act the "author" of a design means the person who creates it.

(4) In the case of a design generated by computer in circumstances such that there is no human author, the person by whom the arrangements necessary for the creation of the design are made shall be taken to be the author.

### 3 Proceedings for registration

(1) An application for the registration of a design shall be made in the prescribed form and shall be filed at the Patent Office in the prescribed manner.

(2) An application for the registration of a design in which design right subsists shall not be entertained unless made by the person claiming to be the design right owner.

(3) For the purpose of deciding whether a design is new, the registrar may make such searches, if any, as he thinks fit.

(4) The registrar may, in such cases as may be prescribed, direct that for the purpose of deciding whether a design is new an application shall be treated as made on a date earlier or later than that on which it was in fact made.

(5) The registrar may refuse an application for the registration of a design or may register the design in pursuance of the application subject to such modifications, if any, as he thinks fit; and a design when registered shall be registered as of the date on which the application was made or is treated as having been made.

(6) An application which, owing to any default or neglect on the part of the applicant, has not been completed so as to enable registration to be effected within such time as may be prescribed shall be deemed to be abandoned.

(7) An appeal lies from any decision of the registrar under this section.

**4 Registration of same design in respect of other articles, etc.**

(1) Where the registered proprietor of a design registered in respect of any article makes an application—

(*a*) for registration in respect of one or more other articles, of the registered design, or

(*b*) for registration in respect of the same or one or more other articles, of a design consisting of the registered design with modifications or variations not sufficient to alter the character or substantially to affect the identity thereof,

the application shall not be refused and the registration made on that application shall not be invalidated by reason only of the previous registration or publication of the registered design:

Provided that the right in a design registered by virtue of this section shall not extend beyond the end of the period, and any extended period, for which the right subsists in the original registered design.

(2) Where any person makes an application for the registration of a design in respect of any article and either—

(*a*) that design has been previously registered by another person in respect of some other article; or

(*b*) the design to which the application relates consists of a design previously registered by another person in respect of the same or some other article with modifications or variations not sufficient to alter the character or substantially to affect the identity thereof,

then, if at any time while the application is pending the applicant becomes the registered proprietor of the design previously registered, the foregoing provisions of this section shall apply as if at the time of making the application the applicant had been the registered proprietor of that design.

**5 Provisions for secrecy of certain designs**

(1) Where, either before or after the commencement of this Act, an application for the registration of a design has been made, and it appears to the registrar that the design is one of a class notified to him by the Secretary of State as relevant for defence purposes, he may give directions for prohibiting or restricting the publication of information with respect to the design, or the communication of such information to any person or class of persons specified in the directions.

(2) The Secretary of State shall by rules make provision for securing that where such directions are given—

(*a*) the representation or specimen of the design, and

(*b*) any evidence filed in support of the applicant's contention that the appearance of an article is material (for the purposes of section 1(3) of this Act),

shall not be open to public inspection at the Patent Office during the continuance in force of the directions.

(3) Where the registrar gives any such directions as aforesaid, he shall give notice of the application and of the directions to the Secretary of State, and thereupon the following provisions shall have effect, that is to say:—

(*a*) the Secretary of State shall, upon receipt of such notice, consider whether the publication of the design would be prejudicial to the defence of the realm and unless a notice under paragraph (*c*) of this subsection has previously been given by that authority to the registrar, shall reconsider that question before the expiration of nine months from the date of filing of the application for registration of the design and at least once in every subsequent year;

(*b*) for the purpose aforesaid, the Secretary of State may, at any time after the design has been registered or, with the consent of the applicant, at any time before the design has been registered, inspect the representation or specimen of the design, or any such evidence as is mentioned in subsection (2)(*b*) above, filed in pursuance of the application;

(*c*) if upon consideration of the design at any time it appears to the Secretary of State that the publication of the design would not, or would no longer, be prejudicial to the defence of the realm, he shall give notice to the registrar to that effect;

(*d*) on the receipt of any such notice the registrar shall revoke the directions and may, subject to such conditions, if any, as he thinks fit, extend the time for doing anything required or authorised to be done by or under this Act in connection with the application or registration, whether or not that time has previously expired.

(4) No person resident in the United Kingdom shall, except under the authority of a written permit granted by or on behalf of the registrar, make or cause to be made any application outside the United Kingdom for the registration of a design of any class prescribed for the purposes of this subsection unless—

(*a*) an application for registration of the same design has been made in the United Kingdom not less than six weeks before the application outside the United Kingdom; and

(*b*) either no directions have been given under subsection (1) of this section in relation to the application in the United Kingdom or all such directions have been revoked:

Provided that this subsection shall not apply in relation to a design for which an application for protection has first been filed in a country outside the United Kingdom by a person resident outside the United Kingdom.

(5) ...

**6 Provisions as to confidential disclosure, etc**

(1) An application for the registration of a design shall not be refused, and the registration of a design shall not be invalidated, by reason only of—

(*a*) the disclosure of the design by the proprietor to any other person in such circumstances as would make it contrary to good faith for that other person to use or publish the design;

(*b*) the disclosure of the design in breach of good faith by any person other than the proprietor of the design; or

(*c*) in the case of a new or original textile design intended for registration, the acceptance of a first and confidential order for goods bearing the design.

(2) An application for the registration of a design shall not be refused and the registration of a design shall not be invalidated by reason only—

(*a*) that a representation of the design, or any article to which the design has been applied, has been displayed, with the consent of the proprietor of the design, at an exhibition certified by the Secretary of State for the purposes of this subsection;

(*b*) that after any such display as aforesaid, and during the period of the exhibition, a representation of the design or any such article as aforesaid has been displayed by any person without the consent of the proprietor; or

(*c*) that a representation of the design has been published in consequence of any such display as is mentioned in paragraph (*a*) of this subsection,

if the application for registration of the design is made not later than six months after the opening of the exhibition.

(3) An application for the registration of a design shall not be refused, and the registration of a design shall not be invalidated, by reason only of the communication of the design by the proprietor thereof to a government department or to any person authorised by a government department to consider the merits of the design, or of anything done in consequence of such a communication.

(4) Where an application is made by or with the consent of the owner of copyright in an artistic work for the registration of a corresponding design, the design shall not be treated for the purposes of this Act as being other than new by reason only of any use previously made of the artistic work, subject to subsection (5).

(5) Subsection (4) does not apply if the previous use consisted of or included the sale, letting for hire or offer or exposure for sale or hire of articles to which had been applied industrially—

(*a*) the design in question, or

(*b*) a design differing from it only in immaterial details or in features which are variants commonly used in the trade,

and that previous use was made by or with the consent of the copyright owner.

(6) The Secretary of State may make provision by rules as to the circumstances in which a design is to be regarded for the purposes of this section as "applied industrially" to articles, or any description of articles.

*Effect of registration, &c*

**7 Right given by registration**

(1) The registration of a design under this Act gives the registered proprietor the exclusive right—

(*a*) to make or import—

(i) for sale or hire, or

(ii) for use for the purposes of a trade or business, or

(*b*) to sell, hire or offer or expose for sale or hire,

an article in respect of which the design is registered and to which that design or a design not substantially different from it has been applied.

(2) The right in the registered design is infringed by a person who without the licence of the registered proprietor does anything which by virtue of subsection (1) is the exclusive right of the proprietor.

(3) The right in the registered design is also infringed by a person who, without the licence of the registered proprietor makes anything for enabling any such article to be made, in the United Kingdom or elsewhere, as mentioned in subsection (1).

(4) The right in the registered design is also infringed by a person who without the licence of the registered proprietor—

(*a*) does anything in relation to a kit would be an infringement if done in relation to the assembled article (see subsection (1)), or

(*b*) makes anything for enabling a kit to be made or assembled, in the United Kingdom or elsewhere, if the assembled article would be such an article as is mentioned in subsection (1);

and for this purpose a "kit" means a complete or substantially complete set of components intended to be assembled into an article.

(5) No proceedings shall be taken in respect of an infringement committed before the date on which the certificate of registration of the design under this Act is granted.

(6) The right in a registered design is not infringed by the reproduction of a feature of the design which, by virtue of section 1(1)(*b*), is left out of account in determining whether the design is registrable.

**8 Duration of right in registered design**

(1) The right in a registered design subsists in the first instance for a period of five years from the date of the registration of the design.

(2) The period for which the right subsists may be extended for a second, third, fourth and fifth period of five years, by applying to the registrar for an extension and paying the prescribed renewal fee.

(3) If the first, second, third or fourth period expires without such application and payment being made, the right shall cease to have effect; and the registrar shall, in accordance with rules made by the Secretary of State, notify the proprietor of that fact.

(4) If during the period of six months immediately following the end of that period an application for extension is made and the prescribed renewal fee and any prescribed additional fee is paid, the right shall be treated as if it had never expired, with the result that—

(*a*) anything done under or in relation to the right during that further period shall be treated as valid, (*b*) an act which would have constituted an infringement of the right if it had not expired shall be treated as an infringement, and

(*c*) an act which would have constituted use of the design for the services of the Crown if the right had not expired shall be treated as such use.

(5) Where it is shown that a registered design—

(*a*) was at the time it was registered a corresponding design in relation to an artistic work in which copyright subsists, and

(*b*) by reason of a previous use of that work would not have been registrable but for section 6(4) of this Act (registration despite certain prior applications of design),

the right in the registered design expires when the copyright in that work expires, if that is earlier than the time at which it would otherwise expire, and it may not thereafter be renewed.

(6) The above provisions have effect subject to the proviso to section 4(1) (registration of same design in respect of other articles, &c).

### 8A Restoration of lapsed right in design

(1) Where the right in a registered design has expired by reason of a failure to extend, in accordance with section 8(2) or (4), the period for which the right subsists, an application for the restoration of the right in the design may be made to the registrar within the prescribed period.

(2) The application may be made by the person who was the registered proprietor of the design or by any other person who would have been entitled to the right in the design if it had not expired; and where the design was held by two or more persons jointly, the application may, with the leave of the registrar, be made by one or more of them without joining the others.

(3) Notice of the application shall be published by the registrar in the prescribed manner.

(4) If the registrar is satisfied that the proprietor took reasonable care to see that the period for which the right subsisted was extended in accordance with section 8(2) or (4), he shall, on payment of any unpaid renewal fee and any prescribed additional fee, order the restoration of the right in the design.

(5) The order may be made subject to such conditions as the registrar thinks fit, and if the proprietor of the design does not comply with any condition the registrar may revoke the order and give such consequential directions as he thinks fit.

(6) Rules altering the period prescribed for the purposes of subsection (1) may contain such transitional provisions and savings as appear to the Secretary of State to be necessary or expedient.

### 8B Effect of order for restoration of right

(1) The effect of an order under section 8A for the restoration of the right in a registered design is as follows.

(2) Anything done under or in relation to the right during the period between expiry and restoration shall be treated as valid.

(3) Anything done during that period which would have constituted an infringement if the right had not expired shall be treated as an infringement—

(*a*) if done at a time when it was possible for an application for extension to be made under section 8(4); or

(*b*) if it was a continuation or repetition of an earlier infringing act.

(4) If after it was no longer possible for such an application for extension to be made, and before publication of notice of the application for restoration, a person—

(*a*) began in good faith to do an act which would have constituted an infringement of the right in the design if it had not expired, or

(*b*) made in good faith effective and serious preparations to do such an act,

he has the right to continue to do the act or, as the case may be, to do the act, notwithstanding the restoration of the right in the design; but this does not extend to granting a licence to another person to do the act.

(5) If the act was done, or the preparations were made, in the course of a business, the person entitled to the right conferred by subsection (4) may—

(*a*) authorise the doing of that act by any partners of his for the time being in that business, and
(*b*) assign that right, or transmit it on death (or in the case of a body corporate on its dissolution), to any person who acquires that part of the business in the course of which the act was done or the prepations were made.

(6) Where an article is disposed of to another in exercise of the rights conferred by subsection (4) or subsection (5), that other and any person claiming through him may deal with the article in the same way as if it had been disposed of by the registered proprietor of the design.

(7) The above provisions apply in relation to the use of a registered design for the services of the Crown as they apply in relation to infringement of the right in the design.

**9 Exemption of innocent infringer from liability for damages**

(1) In proceedings for the infringement of the right in a registered design damages shall not be awarded against a defendant who proves that at the date of the infringement he was not aware, and had no reasonable ground for supposing, that the design was registered; and a person shall not be deemed to have been aware or to have had reasonable grounds for supposing as aforesaid by reason only of the marking of an article with the word "registered" or any abbreviation thereof, or any word or words expressing or implying that the design applied to the article has been registered, unless the number of the design accompanied the word or words or the abbreviation in question.

(2) Nothing in this section shall affect the power of the court to grant an injunction in any proceedings for infringement of the right in a registered design.

**10 Compulsory licence in respect of registered design**

(1) At any time after a design has been registered any person interested may apply to the registrar for the grant of a compulsory licence in respect of the design on the ground that the design is not applied in the United Kingdom by any industrial process or means to the article in respect of which it is registered to such an extent as is reasonable in the circumstances of the case; and the registrar may make such order on the application as he thinks fit.

(2) An order for the grant of a licence shall, without prejudice to any other method of enforcement, have effect as if it were a deed executed by the registered proprietor and all other necessary parties, granting a licence in accordance with the order.

(3) No order shall be made under this section which would be at variance with any treaty, convention, arrangement or engagement applying to the United Kingdom and any convention country.

(4) An appeal shall lie from any order of the registrar under this section.

**11 Cancellation of registration**

(1) The registrar may, upon a request made in the prescribed manner by the registered proprietor, cancel the registration of a design.

(2) At any time after a design has been registered any person interested may apply to the registrar for the cancellation of the registration of the design on the ground that the design was not, at the date of the registration thereof, new . . . , or on any other ground on which the registrar could have refused to register the design; and the registrar may make such order on the application as he thinks fit.

(3) At any time after a design has been registered, any person interested may apply to the registrar for the cancellation of the registration on the ground that—

(*a*) the design was at the time it was registered a corresponding design in relation to an artistic work in which copyright subsisted, and
(*b*) the right in the registered design has expired in accordance with section 8(4) of this Act (expiry of right in registered design on expiry of copyright in artistic work);

and the registrar may make such order on the application as he thinks fit.

(4) A cancellation under this section takes effect—

(*a*) in the case of cancellation under subsection (1), from the date of the registrar's decision,
(*b*) in the case of cancellation under subsection (2), from the date of registration,
(*c*) in the case of cancellation under subsection (3), from the date on which the right in the registered design expired,

or, in any case, from such other date as the registrar may direct.

(5) An appeal lies from any order of the registrar under this section.

### 11A Powers exercisable for protection of the public interest

(1) Where a report of the Monopolies and Mergers Commission has been laid before Parliament containing conclusions to the effect—

(*a*) on a monopoly reference, that a monopoly situtation exists and facts found by the Commission operate or may be expected to operate against the public interest,
(*b*) on a merger reference, that a merger situation qualifying for investigation has been created and the creation of the situation, or particular elements in or consequences of it specified in the report, operate or may be expected to operate against the public interest,
(*c*) on a competition reference, that a person was engaged in an anti-competitive practice which operated or may be expected to operate against the public interest, or
(*d*) on a reference under section 11 of the Competition Act 1980 (reference of public bodies and certain other persons), that a person is pursuing a course of conduct which operates against the public interest,

the appropriate Minister or Ministers may apply to the registrar to take action under this section.

(2) Before making an application the appropriate Minister or Ministers shall publish, in such manner as he or they think appropriate, a notice describing the nature of the proposed application and shall consider any representations which may be made within 30 days of such publication by persons whose interests appear to him or them to be affected.

(3) If on an application under this section it appears to the registrar that the matters specified in the Commission's report as being those which in the Commission's opinion operate, or operated or may be expected to operate, against the public interest include—

(*a*) conditions in licences granted in respect of a registered design by its proprietor restricting the use of the design by the licensee or the right of the proprietor to grant other licences, or
(*b*) a refusal by the proprietor of a registered design to grant licences on reasonable terms,

he may by order cancel or modify any such condition or may, instead or in addition, make an entry in the register to the effect that licences in respect of the design are to be available as of right.

(4) The terms of a licence available by virtue of this section shall, in default of agreement, be settled by the registrar on an application by the person requiring the licence; and terms so settled shall authorise the licensee to do everything which would be an infringement of the right in the registered design in the absence of a licence.

(5) Where the terms of a licence are settled by the registrar, the licence has effect from the date on which the application to him was made.

(6) An appeal lies from any order of the registrar under this section.

(7) In this section "the appropriate Minister or Ministers" means the Minister or Ministers to whom the report of the Monopolies and Mergers Commission was made.

### 11B Undertaking to take licence of right in infringement proceedings

(1) If in proceedings for infringement of the right in a registered design in respect of which a licence is available as of right under section 11A of this Act the defendant undertakes to take a licence on such terms as may be agreed or, in default of agreement, settled by the registrar under that section—

(*a*) no injunction shall be granted against him, and
(*b*) the amount recoverable against him by way of damages or on an account of profits shall not exceed double the amount which would have been payable by him as licensee if such a licence on those terms had been granted before the earliest infringement.

(2) An undertaking may be given at any time before final order in the proceedings, without any admission of liability.

(3) Nothing in this section affects the remedies available in respect of an infringement committed before licences of right were available.

**12 Use for services of the Crown**

The provisions of the First Schedule to this Act shall have effect with respect to the use of registered designs for the services of the Crown and the rights of third parties in respect of such use.

*International Arrangements*

**13 Orders in Council as to convention countries**

(1) His Majesty may, with a view to the fulfilment of a treaty, convention, arrangement or engagement, by Order in Council declare that any country specified in the Order is a convention country for the purposes of this Act:

Provided that a declaration may be made as aforesaid for the purposes either of all or of some only of the provisions of this Act, and a country in the case of which a declaration made for the purposes of some only of the provisions of this Act is in force shall be deemed to be a convention country for the purposes of those provisions only.

(2) His Majesty may by Order in Council direct that any of the Channel Islands, any colony, . . . shall be deemed to be a convention country for the purposes of all or any of the provisions of this Act; and an Order made under this subsection may direct that any such provisions shall have effect, in relation to the territory in question, subject to such conditions or limitations, if any, as may be specified in the Order.

(3) For the purposes of subsection (1) of this section, every colony, protectorate, territory subject to the authority or under the suzerainty of another country, and territory administered by another country . . . under the trusteeship system of the United Nations, shall be deemed to be a country in the case of which a declaration may be made under that subsection.

**14 Registration of design where application for protection in convention country has been made**

(1) An application for registration of a design in respect of which protection has been applied for in a convention country may be made in accordance with the provisions of this Act by the person by whom the application for protection was made or his personal representative or assignee:

Provided that no application shall be made by virtue of this section after the expiration of six months from the date of the application for protection in a convention country or, where more than one such application for protection has been made, from the date of the first application.

(2) Where an application for registration of a design is made by virtue of this section, the application shall be treated, for the purpose of determining whether that or any other design is new, as made on the date of the application for protection in the convention country or, if more than one such application was made, on the date of the first such application.

(3) Subsection (2) shall not be construed as excluding the power to give directions under section 3(4) of this Act in relation to an application made by virtue of this section.

(4) Where a person has applied for protection for a design by an application which—

(*a*) in accordance with the terms of a treaty subsisting between two or more convention countries, is equivalent to an application duly made in any one of those convention countries; or

(*b*) in accordance with the law of any convention country, is equivalent to an application duly made in that convention country,

he shall be deemed for the purposes of this section to have applied in that convention country.

**15 Extension of time for applications under s 14 in certain cases**

(1) If the Secretary of State is satisfied that provision substantially equivalent to the provision to be made by or under this section has been or will be made under the law of any convention country, he may make rules empowering the registrar to extend the time for

making application under subsection (1) of section 14 of this Act for registration of a design in respect of which protection has been applied for in that country in any case where the period specified in the proviso to that subsection expires during a period prescribed by the rules.

(2) Rules made under this section—

- (*a*) may, where any agreement or arrangement has been made between His Majesty's Government in the United Kingdom and the government of the convention country for the supply or mutual exchange of information or articles, provide, either generally or in any class of case specified in the rules, that an extension of time shall not be granted under this section unless the design has been communicated in accordance with the agreement or arrangement;
- (*b*) may, either generally or in any class of case specified in the rules, fix the maximum extension which may be granted under this section;
- (*c*) may prescribe or allow any special procedure in connection with applications made by virtue of this section;
- (*d*) may empower the registrar to extend, in relation to an application made by virtue of this section, the time limited by or under the foregoing provisions of this Act for doing any act, subject to such conditions, if any, as may be imposed by or under the rules;
- (*e*) may provide for securing that the rights conferred by registration on an application made by virtue of this section shall be subject to such restrictions or conditions as may be specified by or under the rules and in particular to restrictions and conditions for the protection of persons (including persons acting on behalf of His Majesty) who, otherwise than as the result of a communication made in accordance with such an agreement or arrangement as is mentioned in paragraph (*a*) of this subsection, and before the date of the application in question or such later date as may be allowed by the rules, may have imported or made articles to which the design is applied or may have made any application for registration of the design.

**16 Protection of designs communicated under international agreements**

(1) Subject to the provisions of this section, the Secretary of State may make rules for securing that, where a design has been communicated in accordance with an agreement or arrangement made between His Majesty's Government in the United Kingdom and the government of any other country for the supply or mutual exchange of information or articles,—

- (*a*) an application for the registration of the design made by the person from whom the design was communicated or his personal representative or assignee shall not be prejudiced, and the registration of the design in pursuance of such an application shall not be invalidated, by reason only that the design has been communicated as aforesaid or that in consequence thereof—
  - (i) the design has been published or applied, or
  - (ii) an application for registration of the design has been made by any other person, or the design has been registered on such an application;
- (*b*) any application for the registration of a design made in consequence of such a communication as aforesaid may be refused and any registration of a design made on such an application may be cancelled.

(2) Rules made under subsection (1) of this section may provide that the publication or application of a design, or the making of any application for registration thereof shall, in such circumstances and subject to such conditions or exceptions as may be prescribed by the rules, be presumed to have been in consequence of such a communication as is mentioned in that subsection.

(3) The powers of the Secretary of State under this section, so far as they are exercisable for the benefit of persons from whom designs have been communicated to His Majesty's Government in the United Kingdom by the government of any other country, shall only be exercised if and to the extent that the Secretary of State is satisfied that substantially equivalent provision has been or will be made under the law of that country for the benefit of persons from whom designs have been communicated by His Majesty's Government in the United Kingdom to the government of that country.

(4) References in the last foregoing subsection to the communication of a design to or by

His Majesty's Government or the government of any other country shall be construed as including references to the communication of the design by or to any person authorised in that behalf by the government in question.

*Register of designs, etc*

**17 Register of designs**

(1) The registrar shall maintain the register of designs, in which shall be entered—

(*a*) the names and addresses of proprietors of registered designs;
(*b*) notices of assignments and of transmissions of registered designs; and
(*c*) such other matters as may be prescribed or as the registrar may think fit.

(2) No notice of any trust, whether express, implied or constructive, shall be entered in the register of designs, and the registrar shall not be affected by any such notice.

(3) The register need not be kept in documentary form.

(4) Subject to the provisions of this Act and to rules made by the Secretary of State under it, the public shall have a right to inspect the register at the Patent Office at all convenient times.

(5) Any person who applies for a certified copy of an entry in the register or a certified extract from the register shall be entitled to obtain such a copy or extract on payment of a fee prescribed in relation to certified copies and extracts; and rules made by the Secretary of State under this Act may provide that any person who applies for an uncertified copy or extract shall be entitled to such a copy or extract on payment of a fee prescribed in relation to uncertified copies and extracts.

(6) Applications under subsection (5) above or rules made by virtue of that subsection shall be made in such manner as may be prescribed.

(7) In relation to any portion of the register kept otherwise than in documentary form—

(*a*) the right of inspection conferred by subsection (4) above is a right to inspect the material on the register; and
(*b*) the right to a copy or extract conferred by subsection (5) above or rules is a right to a copy or extract in a form in which it can be taken away and in which it is visible and legible.

(8) Subject to subsection (11) below, the register shall be prima facie evidence of anything required or authorised to be entered in it and in Scotland shall be sufficient evidence of any such thing.

(9) A certificate purporting to be signed by the registrar and certifying that any entry which he is authorised by or under this Act to make has or has not been made, or that any other thing which he is so authorised to do has or has not been done, shall be prima facie evidence, and in Scotland shall be sufficient evidence, of the matters so certified.

(10) Each of the following—

(*a*) a copy of an entry in the register or an extract from the register which is supplied under subsection (5) above;
(*b*) a copy or any representation, specimen or document kept in the Patent Office or an extract from any such document,

which purports to be a certified copy or certified extract shall, subject to subsection (11) below, be admitted in evidence without further proof and without production of any original; and in Scotland such evidence shall be sufficient evidence.

(11) In the application of this section to England and Wales nothing in it shall be taken as detracting from section 69 or 70 of the Police and Criminal Evidence Act 1984 or any provision made by virtue of either of them.

(12) In this section "certified copy" and "certified extract" means a copy and extract certified by the registrar and sealed with the seal of the Patent Office.

**18 Certificate of registration**

(1) The registrar shall grant a certificate of registration in the prescribed form to the registered proprietor of a design when the design is registered.

(2) The registrar may, in a case where he is satisfied that the certificate of registration has been lost or destroyed, or in any other case in which he thinks it expedient, furnish one or more copies of the certificate.

## 19 Registration of assignments, etc

(1) Where any person becomes entitled by assignment, transmission or operation of law to a registered design or to a share in a registered design, or becomes entitled as mortgagee, licensee or otherwise to any other interest in a registered design, he shall apply to the registrar in the prescribed manner for the registration of his title as proprietor or co-proprietor or, as the case may be, of notice of his interest, in the register of designs.

(2) Without prejudice to the provisions of the foregoing subsection, an application for the registration of the title of any person becoming entitled by assignment to a registered design or a share in a registered design, or becoming entitled by virtue of a mortgage, licence or other instrument to any other interest in a registered design, may be made in the prescribed manner by the assignor, mortgagor, licensor or other party to that instrument, as the case may be.

(3) Where application is made under this section for the registration of the title of any person, the registrar shall, upon proof of title to his satisfaction—

- (*a*) where that person is entitled to a registered design or a share in a registered design, register him in the register of designs as proprietor or co-proprietor of the design, and enter in that register particulars of the instrument or event by which he derives title; or
- (*b*) where that person is entitled to any other interest in the registered design, enter in that register notice of his interest, with particulars of the instrument (if any) creating it.

(3A) Where design right subsists in a registered design, the registrar shall not register an interest under subsection (3) unless he is satisfied that the person entitled to that interest is also entitled to a corresponding interest in the design right.

(3B) Where design right subsists in a registered design and the proprietor of the registered design is also the design right owner, an assignment of the design right shall be taken to be also an assignment of the right in the registered design, unless a contrary intention appears.

(4) Subject to any rights vested in any other person of which notice is entered in the register of designs, the person or persons registered as proprietor of a registered design shall have power to assign, grant licences under, or otherwise deal with the design, and to give effectual receipts for any consideration for any such assignment, licence or dealing.

Provided that any equities in respect of the design may be enforced in like manner as in respect of any other personal property.

(5) Except for the purposes of an application to rectify the register under the following provisions of this Act, a document in respect of which no entry has been made in the register of designs under subsection (3) of this section shall not be admitted in any court as evidence of the title of any person to a registered design or share of or interest in a registered design unless the court otherwise directs.

## 20 Rectification of register

(1) The court may, on the application of any person aggrieved, order the register of designs to be rectified by the making of any entry therein or the variation or deletion of any entry therein.

(2) In proceedings under this section the court may determine any question which it may be necessary or expedient to decide in connection with the rectification of the register.

(3) Notice of any application to the court under this section shall be given in the prescribed manner to the registrar, who shall be entitled to appear and be heard on the application, and shall appear if so directed by the court.

(4) Any order made by the court under this section shall direct that notice of the order shall be served on the registrar in the prescribed manner; and the registrar shall, on receipt of the notice, rectify the register accordingly.

(5) A rectification of the register under this section has effect as follows—

- (*a*) an entry made has effect from the date on which it should have been made,
- (*b*) an entry varied has effect as if it had originally been made in its varied form, and
- (*c*) an entry deleted shall be deemed never to have had effect,

unless, in any case, the court directs otherwise.

**21 Power to correct clerical errors**

(1) The registrar may, in accordance with the provisions of this section, correct any error in an application for the registration or in the representation of a design, or any error in the register of designs.

(2) A correction may be made in pursuance of this section either upon a request in writing made by any person interested and accompanied by the prescribed fee, or without such a request.

(3) Where the registrar proposes to make any such correction as aforesaid otherwise than in pursuance of a request made under this section, he shall give notice of the proposal to the registered proprietor or to the applicant for registration of the design, as the case may be, and to any other person who appears to him to be concerned, and shall give them an opportunity to be heard before making the correction.

**22 Inspection of registered designs**

(1) Where a design has been registered under this Act, there shall be open to inspection at the Patent Office on and after the day on which the certificate of registration is issued—

(*a*) the representation or specimen of the design, and
(*b*) any evidence filed in support of the applicant's contention that the appearance of an article is material (for the purposes of section 1(3) of this Act).

This subsection has effect subject to the following provisions of this section and to any rules made under section 5(2) of this Act.

(2) In the case of a design registered in respect of an article of any class prescribed for the purposes of this subsection, no representation, specimen or evidence filed in pursuance of the application shall, until the expiration of such period after the day on which the certificate of registration is issued as may be prescribed in relation to articles of that class, be open to inspection at the Patent Office except by the registered proprietor, a person authorised in writing by the registered proprietor, or a person authorised by the registrar or by the court:

Provided that where the registrar proposes to refuse an application for the registration of any other design on the ground that it is the same as the first-mentioned design or differs from that design only in immaterial details or in features which are variants commonly used in the trade, the applicant shall be entitled to inspect the representation or specimen of the first-mentioned design filed in pursuance of the application for registration of that design.

(3) In the case of a design registered in respect of an article of any class prescribed for the purposes of the last foregoing subsection, the representation, specimen or evidence shall not, during the period prescribed as aforesaid, be inspected by any person by virtue of this section except in the presence of the registrar or of an officer acting under him; and except in the case of an inspection authorised by the proviso to that subsection, the person making the inspection shall not be entitled to take a copy of the representation, specimen or evidence or any part thereof.

(4) Where an application for the registration of a design has been abandoned or refused, neither the application for registration nor any representation, specimen or evidence filed in pursuance thereof shall at any time be open to inspection at the Patent Office or be published by the registrar.

**23 Information as to existence of right in registered design**

On the request of a person furnishing such information as may enable the registrar to identify the design, and on payment of the prescribed fee, the registrar shall inform him—

(*a*) whether the design is registered and, if so, in respect of what articles, and
(*b*) whether any extension of the period of the right in the registered design has been granted,

and shall state the date of registration and the name and address of the registered proprietor.

**24** (*Repealed by the Patents, Designs and Marks Act 1986, s 3, Sch 3, Pt I.*)

*Legal proceedings and appeals*

**25 Certificate of contested validity of registration**

(1) If in any proceedings before the court the validity of the registration of a design is

contested, and it is found by the court that the design is validly registered, the court may certify that the validity of the registration of the design was contested in those proceedings.

(2) Where any such certificate has been granted, then if in any subsequent proceedings before the court for infringement of the right in the registered design or for cancellation of the registration of the design, a final order or judgment is made or given in favour of the registered proprietor, he shall, unless the court otherwise directs, be entitled to his costs as between solicitor and client:

Provided that this subsection shall not apply to the costs of any appeal in any such proceedings as aforesaid.

**26 Remedy for groundless threats of infringement proceedings**

(1) Where any person (whether entitled to or interested in a registered design or an application for registration of a design or not) by circulars, advertisements or otherwise threatens any other person with proceedings for infringement of the right in a registered design, any person aggrieved thereby may bring an action against him for any such relief as is mentioned in the next following subsection.

(2) Unless in any action brought by virtue of this section the defendant proves that the acts in respect of which proceedings were threatened constitute or, if done, would constitute, an infringement of the right in a registered design the registration of which is not shown by the plaintiff to be invalid, the plaintiff shall be entitled to the following relief, that is to say:—

(*a*) a declaration to the effect that the threats are unjustifiable;
(*b*) an injunction against the continuance of the threats; and
(*c*) such damages, if any, as he has sustained thereby.

(2A) Proceedings may not be brought under this section in respect of a threat to bring proceedings for an infringement alleged to consist of the making or importing of anything.

(3) For the avoidance of doubt it is hereby declared that a mere notification that a design is registered does not constitute a threat of proceedings within the meaning of this section.

**27 The court**

(1) In this Act "the court" means—

(*a*) in England and Wales, the High Court or any patents county court having jurisdiction by virtue of an order under section 287 of the Copyright, Designs and Patents Act 1988,
(*b*) in Scotland, the Court of Session, and
(*c*) in Northern Ireland, the High Court.

(2) Provision may be made by rules of court with respect to proceedings in the High Court in England and Wales for references and applications under this Act to be dealt with by such judge of that court as the Lord Chancellor may select for the purpose.

**28 The Appeal Tribunal**

(1) Any appeal from the registrar under this Act shall lie to the Appeal Tribunal.

(2) The Appeal Tribunal shall consists of—

(*a*) one or more judges of the High Court nominated by the Lord Chancellor, and
(*b*) one judge of the Court of Session nominated by the Lord President of that Court.

(2A) At any time when it consists of two or more judges, the jurisdiction of the Appeal Tribunal—

(*a*) where in the case of any particular appeal the senior of those judges so directs, shall be exercised in relation to that appeal by both of the judges, or (if there are more than two) by two of them, sitting together, and
(*b*) in relation to any appeal in respect of which no such direction is given, may be exercised by any one of the judges;

and, in the exercise of that jurisdiction, different appeals may be heard at the same time by different judges.

(3) The expenses of the Appeal Tribunal shall be defrayed and the fees to be taken therein may be fixed as if the Tribunal were a court of the High Court.

(4) The Appeal Tribunal may examine witnesses on oath and administer oaths for that purpose.

(5) Upon any appeal under this Act the Appeal Tribunal may by order award to any party such costs or expenses as the Tribunal may consider reasonable and direct how and by what parties the costs or expenses are to be paid; and any such order may be enforced—

(*a*) in England and Wales or Northern Ireland, in the same way as an order of the High Court;

(*b*) in Scotland, in the same way as a decree for expenses granted by the Court of Session.

(6) . . .

(7) Upon any appeal under this Act the Appeal Tribunal may exercise any power which could have been exercised by the registrar in the proceeding from which the appeal is brought.

(8) Subject to the foregoing provisions of this section the Appeal Tribunal may make rules for regulating all matters relating to proceedings before it under this Act, including right of audience.

(8A) At any time when the Appeal Tribunal consists of two or more judges, the power to make rules under subsection (8) of this section shall be exercisable by the senior of those judges:

Provided that another of those judges may exercise that power if it appears to him that it is necessary for rules to be made and that the judge (or, if more than one, each of the judges) senior to him is for the time being prevented by illness, absence or otherwise from making them.

(9) An appeal to the Appeal Tribunal under this Act shall not be deemed to be a proceeding in the High Court.

(10) In this section "the High Court" means the High Court in England and Wales; and for the purposes of this section the seniority of judges shall be reckoned by reference to the dates on which they were appointed judges of that court or the Court of Session.

*Powers and duties of Registrar*

### 29 Exercise of discretionary powers of registrar

Without prejudice to any provisions of this Act requiring the registrar to hear any party to proceedings thereunder, or to give to any such party an opportunity to be heard, rules made by the Secretary of State under this Act shall require the registrar to give to any applicant for registration of a design an opportunity to be heard before exercising adversely to the applicant any discretion vested in the registrar by or under this Act.

### 30 Costs and security for costs

(1) Rules made by the Secretary of State under this Act may make provision empowering the registrar, in any proceedings before him under this Act—

(*a*) to award any party such costs as he may consider reasonable, and
(*b*) to direct how and by what parties they are to be paid.

(2) Any such order of the registrar may be enforced—

(*a*) in England and Wales or Northern Ireland, in the same way as an order of the High Court;

(*b*) in Scotland, in the same way as a decree for expenses granted by the Court of Session.

(3) Rules made by the Secretary of State under this Act may make provision empowering the registrar to require a person, in such cases as may be prescribed, to give security for the costs of—

(*a*) an application for cancellation of the registration of a design,
(*b*) an application for the grant of a licence in respect of a registered design, or
(*c*) an appeal from any decision of the registrar under this Act,

and enabling the application or appeal to be treated as abandoned in default of such security being given.

### 31 Evidence before registrar

Rules made by the Secretary of State under this Act may make provision—

(*a*) as to the giving of evidence in proceedings before the registrar under this Act by affidavit or statutory declaration;

(*b*) conferring on the registrar the powers of an official referee of the Supreme Court as regards the examination of witnesses on oath and the discovery and production of documents; and

(*c*) applying in relation to the attendance of witnesses in proceedings before the registrar the rules applicable to the attendance of witnesses in proceedings before such a referee.

**32** (*Repaled by the Copyright, Designs and Patents Act 1988, s 303(2), Sch 8.*)

*Offences*

### 33 Offences under s 5

(1) If any person fails to comply with any direction given under section five of this Act or makes or causes to be made an application for the registration of a design in contravention of that section, he shall be guilty of an offence and liable—

(*a*) on conviction on indictment to imprisonment for a term not exceeding two years or a fine, or both;

(*b*) on summary conviction to imprisonment for a term not exceeding six months or a fine not exceeding the statutory maximum, or both.

(2) . . .

### 34 Falsification of register, etc

If any person makes or causes to be made a false entry in the register of designs, or a writing falsely purporting to be a copy of an entry in that register, or produces or tenders or causes to be produced or tendered in evidence any such writing, knowing the entry or writing to be false, he shall be guilty of an offence and liable—

(*a*) on conviction on indictment to imprisonment for a term not exceeding two years or a fine, or both;

(*b*) on summary conviction to imprisonment for a term not exceeding six months or a fine not exceeding the statutory maximum, or both.

### 35 Fine for falsely representing a design as registered

(1) If any person falsely represents that a design applied to any article sold by him is registered in respect of that article, he shall be liable on summary conviction to a fine not exceeding level 3 on the standard scale; and for the purposes of this provision a person who sells an article having stamped, engraved or impressed thereon or otherwise applied thereto the word "registered", or any other word expressing or implying that the design applied to the article is registered, shall be deemed to represent that the design applied to the article is registered in respect of that article.

(2) If any person, after the right in a registered design has expired, marks any article to which the design has been applied with the word "registered", or any word or words implying that there is a subsisting right in the design under this Act, or causes any such article to be so marked, he shall be liable on summary conviction to a fine not exceeding level 1 on the standard scale.

### 35A Offence by body corporate: liability of officers

(1) Where an offence under this Act committed by a body corporate is proved to have been committed with the consent or connivance of a director, manager, secretary or other similar officer of the body, or a person purporting to act in any such capacity, he as well as the body corporate is guilty of the offence and liable to be proceeded against and punished accordingly.

(2) In relation to a body corporate whose affairs are managed by its members "director" means a member of the body corporate.

*Rules, etc*

### 36 General power of Secretary of State to make rules, etc

(1) Subject to the provisions of this Act, the Secretary of State may make such rules as he thinks expedient for regulating the business of the Patent Office in relation to designs and for

regulating all matters by this Act placed under the direction or control of the registrar or the Secretary of State.

(1A) Rules may, in particular, make provision—

(*a*) prescribing the form of applications for registration of designs and of any representations or specimens of designs or other documents which may be filed at the Patent Office, and requiring copies to be furnished of any such representations, specimens or documents;

(*b*) regulating the procedure to be followed in connection with any application or request to the registrar or in connection with any proceeding before him, and authorising the rectification of irregularities of procedure;

(*c*) providing for the appointment of advisers to assist the registrar in proceedings before him;

(*d*) regulating the keeping of the register of designs;

(*e*) authorising the publication and sale of copies of representations of designs and other documents in the Patent Office;

(*f*) prescribing anything authorised or required by this Act to be prescribed by rules.

(1B) The remuneration of an adviser appointed to assist the registrar shall be determined by the Secretary of State with the consent of the Treasury and shall be defrayed out of money provided by Parliament.

(2) Rules made under this section may provide for the establishment of branch offices for designs and may authorise any document or thing required by or under this Act to be filed or done at the Patent Office to be filed or done at the branch office at Manchester or any other branch office established in pursuance of the rules.

**37 Provisions as to rules and Orders**

(1) . . .

(2) Any rules made by the Secretary of State in pursuance of section 15 or section 16 of this Act, and any order made, direction given, or other action taken under the rules by the registrar, may be made, given or taken so as to have effect as respects things done or omitted to be done on or after such date, whether before or after the coming into operation of the rules or of this Act, as may be specified in the rules.

(3) Any power to make rules conferred by this Act on the Secretary of State or on the Appeal Tribunal shall be exercisable by statutory instrument; and the Statutory Instruments Act 1946 shall apply to a statutory instrument containing rules made by the Appeal Tribunal in like manner as if the rules had been made by a Minister of the Crown.

(4) Any statutory instrument containing rules made by the Secretary of State under this Act shall be subject to annulment in pursuance of a resolution of either House of Parliament.

(5) Any Order in Council made under this Act may be revoked or varied by a subsequent Order in Council.

**38** (*Repealed by the Copyright, Designs and Patents Act 1988, s 303(2), Sch 8.*)

*Supplemental*

**39 Hours of business and excluded days**

(1) Rules made by the Secretary of State under this Act may specify the hour at which the Patent Office shall be deemed to be closed on any day for purposes of the transaction by the public of business under this Act or of any class of such business, and may specify days as excluded days for any such purposes.

(2) Any business done under this Act on any day after the hour specified as aforesaid in relation to business of that class, or on a day which is an excluded day in relation to business of that class, shall be deemed to have been done on the next following day not being an excluded day; and where the time for doing anything under this Act expires on an excluded day, that time shall be extended to the next following day not being an excluded day.

**40 Fees**

There shall be paid in respect of the registration of designs and applications therefor, and in respect of other matters relating to designs arising under this Act, such fees as may be prescribed by rules made by the Secretary of State with the consent of the Treasury.

**41 Service of notices, &c, by post**

Any notice required or authorised to be given by or under this Act, and any application or other document so authorised or required to be made or filed, may be given, made or filed by post.

**42 Annual report of registrar**

The Comptroller-General of Patents, Designs and Trade Marks shall, in his annual report with respect to the execution of the Patents Act 1977, include a report with respect to the execution of this Act as if it formed a part of or was included in that Act.

**43 Savings**

(1) Nothing in this Act shall be construed as authorising or requiring the registrar to register a design the use of which would, in his opinion, be contrary to law or morality.

(2) Nothing in this Act shall affect the right of the Crown or of any person deriving title directly or indirectly from the Crown to sell or use articles forfeited under the laws relating to customs or excise.

**44 Interpretation**

(1) In this Act, except where the context otherwise requires, the following expressions have the meanings hereby respectively assigned by them, that is to say—

"Appeal Tribunal" means the Appeal Tribunal constituted and acting in accordance with section 28 of this Act as amended by the Administration of Justice Act 1969;

"article" means any article of manufacture and includes any part of an article if that part is made and sold separately;

"artistic work" has the same meaning as in Part I of the Copyright, Designs and Patents Act 1988;

"assignee" includes the personal representative of a deceased assignee, and references to the assignee of any person include references to the assignee of the personal representative or assignee of that person;

"author", in relation to a design, has the meaning given by section 2(3) and (4);

. . . . . .

"corresponding design", in relation to an artistic work, means a design which if applied to an article would produce something which would be treated for the purposes of Part I of the Copyright, Designs and Patents Act 1988 as a copy of that work;

"the court" shall be construed in accordance with section 27 of this Act;

"design" has the meaning assigned to it by section 1(1) of this Act;

"employee", "employment" and "employer" refer to employment under a contract of service or of apprenticeship;

. . . . . .

"prescribed" means prescribed by rules made by the Secretary of State under this Act;

"proprietor" has the meaning assigned to it by section two of this Act;

"registered proprietor" means the person or persons for the time being entered in the register of designs as proprietor of the design;

"registrar" means the Comptroller-General of Patents Designs and Trade Marks;

"set of articles" means a number of articles of the same general character ordinarily on sale or intended to be used together, to each of which the same design, or the same design with modifications or variations not sufficient to alter the character or substantially to affect the identity thereof, is applied.

(2) Any reference in this Act to an article in respect of which a design is registered shall, in the case of a design registered in respect of a set of articles, be construed as a reference to any article of that set.

(3) Any question arising under this Act whether a number of articles constitute a set of articles shall be determined by the registrar; and notwithstanding anything in this Act any determination of the registrar under this subsection shall be final.

(4) For the purposes of subsection (1) of section 14 and of section 16 of this Act, the expression "personal representative", in relation to a deceased person, includes the legal representative of the deceased appointed in any country outside the United Kingdom.

**45 Application to Scotland.**

In the application of this Act to Scotland—

(1), (2) ...

(3) The expression "injunction" means "interdict"; the expression "arbitrator" means "arbiter"; the expression "plaintiff" means "pursuer"; the expression "defendant means "defender".

**46 Application to Northern Ireland**

In the application of this Act to Northern Ireland—

(1), (2) ...

(3) References to enactments include enactments comprised in Northern Ireland legislation:

(3A) References to the Crown include the Crown in right of Her Majesty's Government in Northern Ireland:

(4) References to a government department shall be construed as including references to a Northern Ireland department, and in relation to a Northern Ireland department references to the Treasury shall be construed as references to the Department of Finance and Personnel.

(5) ...

**47 Application to Isle of Man**

This Act extends to the Isle of Man, subject to any modifications contained in an Order made by Her Majesty in Council, and accordingly, subject to any such Order, references in this Act to the United Kingdom shall be construed as including the Isle of Man.

**47A Territorial waters and the continental shelf**

(1) For the purposes of this Act the territorial waters of the United Kingdom shall be treated as part of the United Kingdom.

(2) This Act applies to things done in the United Kingdom sector of the continental shelf on a structure or vessel which is present there for purposes directly connected with the exploration of the sea bed or subsoil or the exploitation of their natural resources as it applies to things done in the United Kingdom.

(3) The United Kingdom sector of the continental shelf means the areas designated by order under section 1(7) of the Continental Shelf Act 1964.

**48 Repeals, savings, and transitional provisions**

(1) ...

(2) Subject to the provisions of this section, any Order in Council, rule, order, requirement, certificate, notice, decision, direction, authorisation, consent, application, request or thing made, issued, given or done under any enactment repealed by this Act shall, if in force at the commencement of this Act, and so far as it could have been made, issued, given or done under this Act, continue in force and have effect as if made, issued, given or done under the corresponding enactment of this Act.

(3) Any register kept under the Patents and Designs Act 1907 shall be deemed to form part of the corresponding register under this Act.

(4) Any design registered before the commencement of this Act shall be deemed to be registered under this Act in respect of articles of the class in which it is registered.

(5) Where, in relation to any design, the time for giving notice to the registrar under section 59 of the Patents and Designs Act 1907 expired before the commencement of this Act and the notice was not given, subsection (2) of section 6 of this Act shall not apply in relation to that design or any registration of that design.

(6) Any document referring to any enactment repealed by this Act shall be construed as referring to the corresponding enactment of this Act.

(7) Nothing in the foregoing provisions of this section shall be taken as prejudicing the operation of section 38 of the Interpretation Act 1889 (which relates to the effect of repeals).

**49 Short title and commencement**

(1) This Act may be cited as the Registered Designs Act 1949.

(2) This Act shall come into operation on the first day of January, nineteen hundred and fifty, immediately after the coming into operation of the Patents and Designs Act 1949.

## FIRST SCHEDULE

PROVISIONS AS TO THE USE OF REGISTERED DESIGNS FOR THE SERVICES OF THE CROWN AND AS TO THE RIGHTS OF THIRD PARTIES IN RESPECT OF SUCH USE

### 1 Use of registered designs for services of the Crown

(1) Notwithstanding anything in this Act, any Government department, and any person authorised in writing by a Government department, may use any registered design for the services of the Crown in accordance with the following provisions of this paragraph.

(2) If and so far as the design has before the date or registration thereof been duly recorded by or applied by or on behalf of a Government department otherwise than in consequence of the communication of the design directly or indirectly by the registered proprietor or any person from whom he derives title, any use of the design by virtue of this paragraph may be made free of any royalty or other payment to the registered proprietor.

(3) If and so far as the design has not been so recorded or applied as aforesaid, any use of the design made by virtue of this paragraph at any time after the date of registration thereof, or in consequence of any such communication as aforesaid, shall be made upon such terms as may be agreed upon, either before or after the use, between the Government department and the registered proprietor with the approval of the Treasury, or as may in default of agreement be determined by the court on a reference under paragraph 3 of this Schedule.

(4) The authority of a Government department in respect of a design may be given under this paragraph either before or after the design is registered and either before or after the acts in respect of which the authority is given are done, and may be given to any person whether or not he is authorised directly or indirectly by the registered proprietor to use the design.

(5) Where any use of a design is made by or with the authority of a Government department under this paragraph, then, unless it appears to the department that it would be contrary to the public interest so to do, the department shall notify the registered proprietor as soon as practicable after the use is begun, and furnish him with such information as to the extent of the use as he may from time to time require.

(6) For the purposes of this and the next following paragraph "the services of the Crown" shall be deemed to include—

(*a*) the supply to the government of any country outside the United Kingdom, in pursuance of an agreement or arrangement between Her Majesty's Government in the United Kingdom and the government of that country, of articles required—

(i) for the defence of that country; or
(ii) for the defence of any other country whose government is party to an agreement or arrangement with Her Majesty's said Government in respect of defence matters;

(*b*) the supply to the United Nations, or the government of any country belonging to that organisation, in pursuance of an agreement or arrangement between Her Majesty's Government and that organisation or government, of articles required for any armed forces operating in pursuance of a resolution of that organisation or any organ of that organisation;

and the power of a Government department or a person authorised by a Government department under this paragraph to use a design shall include power to sell to any such government or to the said organisation any articles the supply of which is authorised by this sub-paragraph, and to sell to any person any articles made in the exercise of the powers conferred by this paragraph which are no longer required for the purpose for which they were made.

(7) The purchaser of any articles sold in the exercise of powers conferred by this paragraph, and any person claiming through him, shall have power to deal with them in the same manner as if the rights in the registered design were held on behalf of His Majesty.

**2 Rights of third parties in respect of Crown use**

(1) In relation to any use of a registered design, or a design in respect of which an application for registration is pending, made for the services of the Crown—

(*a*) by a Government department or a person authorised by a Government department under the last foregoing paragraph; or

(*b*) by the registered proprietor or applicant for registration to the order of a Government department,

the provisions of any licence, assignment or agreement made, whether before or after the commencement of this Act, between the registered proprietor or applicant for registration or any person who derives title from him or from whom he derives title and any person other than a Government department shall be of no effect so far as those provisions restrict or regulate the use of the design, or any model, document or information relating thereto, or provide for the making of payments in respect of any such use, or calculated by reference thereto; and the reproduction or publication of any model or document in connection with the said use shall not be deemed to be an infringement of any copyright or design right subsisting in the model or document.

(2) Where an exclusive licence granted otherwise than for royalties or other benefits determined by reference to the use of the design is in force under the registered design then—

(*a*) in relation to any use of the design which, but for the provisions of this and the last foregoing paragraph, would constitute an infringement of the rights of the licensee, sub-paragraph (3) of the last foregoing paragraph shall have effect as if for the reference to the registered proprietor there were substituted a reference to the licensee; and

(*b*) in relation to any use of the design by the licensee by virtue of an authority given under the last foregoing paragraph, that paragraph shall have effect as if the said sub-paragraph (3) were omitted.

(3) Subject to the provisions of the last foregoing sub-paragraph, where the registered design or the right to apply for or obtain registration of the design has been assigned to the registered proprietor in consideration of royalties or other benefits determined by reference to the use of the design, then—

(*a*) in relation to any use of the design by virtue of paragraph 1 of this Schedule, sub-paragraph (3) of that paragraph shall have effect as if the reference to the registered proprietor included a reference to the assignor, and any sum payable by virtue of that sub-paragraph shall be divided between the registered proprietor and the assignor in such proportion as may be agreed upon between them or as may in default of agreement be determined by the court on a reference under the next following paragraph; and

(*b*) in relation to any use of the design made for the services of the Crown by the registered proprietor to the order of a Government department, sub-paragraph (3) of paragraph 1 of this Schedule shall have effect as if that use were made by virtue of an authority given under that paragraph.

(4) Where, under sub-paragraph (3) of paragraph 1 of this Schedule, payments are required to be made by a Government department to a registered proprietor in respect of any use of a design, any person being the holder of an exclusive licence under the registered design (not being such a licence as is mentioned in sub-paragraph (2) of this paragraph) authorising him to make that use of the design shall be entitled to recover from the registered proprietor such part (if any) of those payments as may be agreed upon between that person and the registered proprietor, or as may in default of agreement be determined by the court under the next following paragraph to be just having regard to any expenditure incurred by that person—

(*a*) in developing the said design; or

(*b*) in making payments to the registered proprietor, other than royalties or other payments determined by reference to the use of the design, in consideration of the licence;

and if, at any time before the amount of any such payment has been agreed upon between the Government department and the registered proprietor, that person gives notice in writing of his interest to the department, any agreement as to the amount of that payment shall be of no effect unless it is made with his consent.

(5) In this paragraph "exclusive licence" means a licence from a registered proprietor which confers on the licensee, or on the licensee and persons authorised by him, to the exclusion of

all other persons (including the registered proprietor), any right in respect of the registered design.

### 2A Compensation for loss of profit

(1) Where Crown use is made of a registered design, the government department concerned shall pay—

(*a*) to the registered proprietor, or

(*b*) if there is an exclusive licence in force in respect of the design, to the exclusive licensee,

compensation for any loss resulting from his not being awarded a contract to supply the articles to which the design is applied.

(2) Compensation is payable only to the extent that such a contract could have been fulfilled from his existing manufacturing capacity; but is payable notwithstanding the existence of circumstances rendering him ineligible for the award of such a contract.

(3) In determining the loss, regard shall be had to the profit which would have been made on such a contract and to the extent to which any manufacturing capacity was under-used.

(4) No compensation is payable in respect of any failure to secure contracts for the supply of articles to which the design is applied otherwise than for the services of the Crown.

(5) The amount payable under this paragraph shall, if not agreed between the registered proprietor or licensee and the government department concerned with the approval of the Treasury, be determined by the court on a reference under paragraph 3; and it is in addition to any amount payable under paragraph 1 or 2 of this schedule.

(6) In this paragraph—

"Crown use", in relation to a design, means the doing of anything by virtue of paragraph 1 which would otherwise be an infringement of the right in the design; and

"the government department concerned", in relation to such use, means the government department by whom or on whose authority the act was done.

### 3 Reference of disputes as to Crown use

(1) Any dispute as to—

(*a*) the exercise by a Government department, or a person authorised by a Government department, of the powers conferred by paragraph 1 of this Schedule,

(*b*) terms for the use of a design for the services of the Crown under that paragraph,

(*c*) the right of any person to receive any part of a payment made under paragraph 1(3), or

(*d*) the right of any person to receive a payment under paragraph 2A,

may be referred to the court by either party to the dispute.

(2) In any proceedings under this paragraph to which a Government department are a party, the department may—

(*a*) if the registered proprietor is a party to the proceedings, apply for cancellation of the registration of the design upon any ground upon which the registration of a design may be cancelled on an application to the court under section twenty of this Act;

(*b*) in any case, put in issue the validity of the registration of the design without applying for its cancellation.

(3) If in such proceedings as aforesaid any question arises whether a design has been recorded or applied as mentioned in paragraph 1 of this Schedule, and the disclosure of any document recording the design, or of any evidence of the application thereof, would in the opinion of the department be prejudicial to the public interest, the disclosure may be made confidentially to counsel for the other party or to an independent expert mutually agreed upon.

(4) In determining under this paragraph any dispute between a Government department and any person as to terms for the use of a design for the services of the Crown, the court shall have regard to any benefit or compensation which that person or any person from whom he derives title may have received, or may be entitled to receive, directly or indirectly from any Government department in respect of the design in question.

(5) In any proceedings under this paragraph the court may at any time order the whole proceedings or any question or issue of fact arising therein to be referred to a special or official

referee or an arbitrator on such terms as the court may direct; and references to the court in the foregoing provisions of this paragraph shall be construed accordingly.

**4 Special provisions as to Crown use during emergency**

(1) During any period of emergency within the meaning of this paragraph, the powers exercisable in relation to a design by a Government department, or a person authorised by a Government department under paragraph 1 of this Schedule shall include power to use the design for any purpose which appears to the department necessary or expedient—

(*a*) for the efficient prosecution of any war in which His Majesty may be engaged;
(*b*) for the maintenance of supplies and services essential to the life of the community;
(*c*) for securing a sufficiency of supplies and services essential to the well-being of the community;
(*d*) for promoting the productivity of industry, commerce and agriculture;
(*e*) for fostering and directing exports and reducing imports, or imports of any classes, from all or any countries and for redressing the balance of trade;
(*f*) generally for ensuring that the whole resources of the community are available for use, and are used, in a manner best calculated to serve the interests of the community; or
(*g*) for assisting the relief of suffering and the restoration and distribution of essential supplies and services in any part of His Majesty's dominions or any foreign countries that are in grave distress as the result of war;

and any reference in this Schedule to the services of the Crown shall be construed as including a reference to the purposes aforesaid.

(2) In this paragraph the expression "period of emergency" means a period beginning on such date as may be declared by Order in Council to be the commencement, and ending on such date as may be so declared to be the termination, of a period of emergency for the purposes of this paragraph.

(3) No Order in Council under this paragraph shall be submitted to Her Majesty unless a draft of it has been laid before and approved by a resolution of each House of Parliament.

(*Sch 2 repealed by the Copyright, Designs and Patents Act 1988, s 303(2), Sch 8.*)

## SCHEDULE 5

Section 295

### PATENTS: MISCELLANEOUS AMENDMENTS

*Withdrawal of application before publication of specification*

1. In section 13(2) of the Patents Act 1949 (duty of comptroller to advertise acceptance of and publish complete specification) after the word "and", in the first place where it occurs, insert ", unless the application is withdrawn,".

*Correction of clerical errors*

2.—(1) In section 15 of the Patents Act 1977 (filing of application), after subsection (3) insert—

"(3A) Nothing in subsection (2) or (3) above shall be construed as affecting the power of the comptroller under section 117(1) below to correct errors or mistakes with respect to the filing of drawings.".

(2) The above amendment applies only in relation to applications filed after the commencement of this paragraph.

*Supplementary searches*

3.—(1) Section 17 of the Patents Act 1977 (preliminary examination and search) is amended as follows.

(2) In subsection (7) (supplementary searches) for "subsection (4) above)" substitute "subsections (4) and (5) above" and for "it applies" substitute "they apply".

(3) After that subsection add—

"(8) A reference for a supplementary search in consequence of—

(*a*) an amendment of the application made by the applicant under section 18(3) or 19(1) below, or

(*b*) a correction of the application, or of a document filed in connection with the application, under section 117 below,

shall be made only on payment of the prescribed fee, unless the comptroller directs otherwise.".

4. In section 18 of the Patents Act 1977 (substantive examination and grant or refusal of patent), after subsection (1) insert—

"(1A) If the examiner forms the view that a supplementary search under section 17 above is required for which a fee is payable, he shall inform the comptroller, who may decide that the substantive examination should not proceed until the fee is paid; and if he so decides, then unless within such period as he may allow—

(*a*) the fee is paid, or

(*b*) the application is amended so as to render the supplementary search unnecessary,

he may refuse the application.".

5. In section 130(1) of the Patents Act 1977 (interpretation), in the definition of "search fee", for "section 17 above" substitute "section 17(1) above".

*Application for restoration of lapsed patent*

6.—(1) Section 28 of the Patents Act 1977 (restoration of lapsed patents) is amended as follows.

(2) For subsection (1) (application for restoration within period of one year) substitute—

"(1) Where a patent has ceased to have effect by reason of a failure to pay any renewal fee, an application for the restoration of the patent may be made to the comptroller within the prescribed period.

(1A) Rules prescribing that period may contain such transitional provisions and savings as appear to the Secretary of State to be necessary or expedient.".

(3) After subsection (2) insert—

"(2A) Notice of the application shall be published by the comptroller in the prescribed manner.".

(4) In subsection (3), omit paragraph (*b*) (requirement that failure to renew is due to circumstances beyond proprietor's control) and the word "and" preceding it.

This amendment does not apply to a patent which has ceased to have effect in accordance with section 25(3) of the Patents Act 1977 (failure to renew within prescribed period) and in respect of which the period referred to in subsection (4) of that section (six months' period of grace for renewal) has expired before commencement.

(5) Omit subsections (5) to (9) (effect of order for restoration).

7. After that section insert—

"**28A Effect of order for restoration of patent**

(1) The effect of an order for the restoration of a patent is as follows.

(2) Anything done under or in relation to the patent during the period between expiry and restoration shall be treated as valid.

(3) Anything done during that period which would have constituted an infringement if the patent had not expired shall be treated as an infringement—

(*a*) if done at a time when it was possible for the patent to be renewed under section 25(4), or

(*b*) if it was a continuation or repetition of an earlier infringing act.

(4) If after it was no longer possible for the patent to be so renewed, and before publication of notice of the application for restoration, a person—

(*a*) began in good faith to do an act which would have constituted an infringement of the patent if it had not expired, or

(*b*) made in good faith effective and serious preparations to do such an act,

he has the right to continue to do the act or, as the case may be, to do the act, notwithstanding the restoration of the patent; but this right does not extend to granting a licence to another person to do the act.

(5) If the act was done, or the preparations were made, in the course of a business, the person entitled to the right conferred by subsection (4) may—

(*a*) authorise the doing of that act by any partners of his for the time being in that business, and

(*b*) assign that right, or transmit it on death (or in the case of a body corporate on its dissolution), to any person who acquires that part of the business in the course of which the act was done or the preparations were made.

(6) Where a product is disposed of to another in exercise of the rights conferred by subsection (4) or (5), that other and any person claiming through him may deal with the product in the same way as if it had been disposed of by the registered proprietor of the patent.

(7) The above provisions apply in relation to the use of a patent for the services of the Crown as they apply in relation to infringement of the patent.".

8. In consequence of the above amendments—

(*a*) In section 60(6)(*b*) of the Patents Act 1977, for "section 28(6)" substitute "section 28A(4) or (5)"; and

(*b*) in sections 77(5), 78(6) and 80(4) of that Act, for the words from "section 28(6)" to the end substitute "section 28A(4) and (5) above, and subsections (6) and (7) of that section shall apply accordingly.".

*Determination of right to patent after grant*

9.—(1) Section 37 of the Patents Act 1977 (determination of right to patent after grant) is amended as follows.

(2) For subsection (1) substitute—

"(1) After a patent has been granted for an invention any person having or claiming a proprietary interest in or under the patent may refer to the comptroller the question—

(*a*) who is or are the true proprietor or proprietors of the patent,

(*b*) whether the patent should have been granted to the person or persons to whom it was granted, or

(*c*) whether any right in or under the patent should be transferred or granted to any other person or persons;

and the comptroller shall determine the question and make such order as he thinks fit to give effect to the determination.".

(3) Substitute "this section"—

(*a*) in subsections (4) and (7) for "subsection (1)(*a*) above", and

(*b*) in subsection (8) for "subsection (1) above".

10. In section 74(6) (meaning of "entitlement proceedings"), for "section 37(1)(*a*) above" substitute "section 37(1) above".

*Employees' inventions*

11.—(1) In section 39 of the Patents Act 1977 (right to employees' inventions), after subsection (2) add—

"(3) Where by virtue of this section an invention belongs, as between him and his employer, to an employee, nothing done—

(*a*) by or on behalf of the employee or any person claiming under him for the purposes of pursuing an application for a patent, or

(*b*) by any person for the purpose of performing or working the invention,

shall be taken to infringe any copyright or design right to which, as between him and his employer, his employer is entitled in any model or document relating to the invention.".

(2) In section 43 of the Patents Act 1977 (supplementary provisons with respect to employees' inventions), in subsection (4) (references to patents to include other forms of protection, whether in UK or elsewhere) for "in sections 40 to 42" substitute "in sections 39 to 42.".

*Undertaking to take licence in infringement proceedings*

12.—(1) Section 46 of the Patents Act 1977 (licences of right) is amended as follows.

(2) In subsection (3)(*c*) (undertaking to take licence in infringement proceedings) after the words "(otherwise than by the importation of any article" insert "from a country which is not a member State of the European Economic Community".

(3) After subsection (3) insert—

"(3A) An undertaking under subsection (3)(*c*) above may be given at any time before final order in the proceedings, without any admission of liability.".

*Power of comptroller on grant of compulsory licence*

13. In section 49 of the Patents Act 1977 (supplementary provisions with respect to compulsory licences), omit subsection (3) (power to order that licence has effect to revoke existing licences and deprive proprietor of power to work invention or grant licences).

*Powers exercisable in consequence of report of Monopolies and Mergers Commission*

14. For section 51 of the Patents Act 1977 (licences of right: application by Crown in consequence of report of Monopolies and Mergers Commission) substitute—

**"51 Powers exercisable in consequence of report of Monopolies and Mergers Commission**

(1) Where a report of the Monopolies and Mergers Commission has been laid before Parliament containing conclusions to the effect—

(*a*) on a monopoly reference, that a monopoly situation exists and facts found by the Commission operate or may be expected to operate against the public interest,

(*b*) on a merger reference, that a merger situation qualifying for investigation has been created and the creation of the situation, or particular elements in or consequences of it specified in the report, operate or may be expected to operate against the public interest,

(*c*) on a competition reference, that a person was engaged in an anti-competitive practice which operated or may be expected to operate against the public interest, or

(*d*) on a reference under section 11 of the Competition Act 1980 (reference of public bodies and certain other persons), that a person is pursuing a course of conduct which operates against the public interest,

the appropriate Minister or Ministers may apply to the comptroller to take action under this section.

(2) Before making an application the appropriate Minister or Ministers shall publish, in such manner as he or they think appropriate, a notice describing the nature of the proposed application and shall consider any representations which may be made within 30 days of such publication by persons whose interests appear to him or them to be affected.

(3) If on an application under this section it appears to the comptroller that the matters specified in the Commission's report as being those which in the Commission's opinion operate, or operated or may be expected to operate, against the public interest include—

(*a*) conditions in licences granted under a patent by its proprietor restricting the use of the invention by the licensee or the right of the proprietor to grant other licences, or

(*b*) a refusal by the proprietor of a patent to grant licences on reasonable terms

he may by order cancel or modify any such condition or may, instead or in addition, make an entry in the register to the effect that licences under the patent are to be available as of right.

(4) In this section "the appropriate Minister or Ministers" means the Minister or Ministers to whom the report of the Commission was made.".

*Compulsory licensing: reliance on statements in competition report*

15. In section 53(2) of the Patents Act 1977 (compulsory licensing: reliance on statements in reports of Monopolies and Mergers Commission)—

(*a*) for "application made in relation to a patent under sections 48 to 51 above" substitute "application made under section 48 above in respect of patent"; and
(*b*) after "Part VIII of the Fair Trading Act 1973" insert "or section 17 of the Competition Act 1980".

*Crown use: compensation for loss of profit*

6.—(1) In the Patents Act 1977, after section 57 insert—

"**57A Compensation for loss of profit**

(1) Where use is made of an invention for the services of the Crown, the government department concerned shall pay—

(*a*) to the proprietor of the patent, or
(*b*) if there is an exclusive licence in force in respect of the patent, to the exclusive licensee,

compensation for any loss resulting from his not being awarded a contract to supply the patented product or, as the case may be, to perform the patented process or supply a thing made by means of the patented process.

(2) Compensation is payable only to the extent that such a contract could have been fulfilled from his existing manufacturing or other capacity; but is payable notwithstanding the existence of circumstances rendering him ineligible for the award of such a contract.

(3) In determining the loss, regard shall be had to the profit which would have been made on such a contract and to the extent to which any manufacturing or other capacity was under-used.

(4) No compensation is payable in respect of any failure to secure contracts to supply the patented product or, as the case may be, to perform the patented process or supply a thing made by means of the patented process, otherwise than for the services of the Crown.

(5) The amount payable shall, if not agreed between the proprietor or licensee and the government department concerned with the approval of the Treasury, be determined by the court on a reference under section 58, and is in addition to any amount payable under section 55 or 57.

(6) In this section 'the government department concerned', in relation to any use of an invention for the services of the Crown, means the government department by whom or on whose authority the use was made.

(7) In the application of this section to Northern Ireland, the reference in subsection (5) above to the Treasury shall, where the government department concerned is a department of the Government of Northern Ireland, be construed as a reference to the Department of Finance and Personnel.".

(2) In section 58 of the Patents Act 1977 (reference of disputes as to Crown use), for subsection (1) substitute—

"(1) Any dispute as to—

(*a*) the exercise by a government department, or a person authorised by a government department, of the powers conferred by section 55 above,
(*b*) terms for the use of an invention for the services of the Crown under that section,
(*c*) the right of any person to receive any part of a payment made in pursuance of subsection (4) of that section, or
(*d*) the right of any person to receive a payment under section 57A,

may be referred to the court by either party to the dispute after a patent has been granted for the invention.";

and in subsection (4) for "under this section" substitute "under subsection (1)(*a*), (*b*) or (*c*) above".

(3) In section 58(11) of the Patents Act 1977 (exclusion of right to compensation for Crown use if relevant transaction, instrument or event not registered), after "section 57(3) above)" insert ", or to any compensation under section 57A above,".

(4) The above amendments apply in relation to any use of an invention for the services of the Crown after the commencement of this section, even if the terms for such use were settled before commencement.

*Right to continue use begun before priority date*

17. For section 64 of the Patents Act 1977 (right to continue use begun before priority date) substitute—

"**64 Right to continue use begun before priority date**

(1) Where a patent is granted for an invention, a person who in the United Kingdom before the priority date of the invention—

(*a*) does in good faith an act which would constitute an infringement of the patent if it were in force, or

(*b*) makes in good faith effective and serious preparations to do such an act,

has the right to continue to do the act or, as the case may be, to do the act, notwithstanding the grant of the patent; but this right does not extend to granting a licence to another person to do the act.

(2) If the act was done, or the preparations were made, in the course of a business, the person entitled to the right conferred by subsection (1) may—

(*a*) authorise the doing of that act by any partners of his for the time being in that business, and

(*b*) assign that right, or transmit it on death (or in the case of a body corporate on its dissolution), to any person who acquires that part of the business in the course of which the act was done or the preparations were made.

(3) Where a product is disposed of to another in exercise of the rights conferred by subsection (1) or (2), that other and any person claiming through him may deal with the product in the same way as if it had been disposed of by the registered proprietor of the patent.".

*Revocation on grounds of grant to wrong person*

18. In section 72(1) of the Patents Act 1977 (grounds for revocation of patent), for paragraph (*b*) substitute—

"(*b*) that the patent was granted to a person who was not entitled to be granted that patent;".

*Revocation where two patents granted for same invention*

19. In section 73 of the Patents Act 1977 (revocation on initiative of comptroller), for subsections (2) and (3) (revocation of patent where European patent (UK) granted in respect of same invention) substitute—

"(2) If it appears to the comptroller that a patent under this Act and a European patent (UK) have been granted for the same invention having the same priority date, and that the applications for the patents were filed by the same applicant or his successor in title, he shall give the proprietor of the patent under this Act an opportunity of making observations and of amending the specification of the patent, and if the proprietor fails to satisfy the comptroller that there are not two patents in respect of the same invention, or to amend the specification so as to prevent there being two patents in respect of the same invention, the comptroller shall revoke the patent.

(3) The comptroller shall not take action under subsection (2) above before—

(*a*) the end of the period for filing an opposition to the European patent (UK) under the European Patent Convention, or

(*b*) if later, the date on which opposition proceedings are finally disposed of;

and he shall not then take any action if the decision is not to maintain the European patent or if it is amended so that there are not two patents in respect of the same invention.

(4) The comptroller shall not take action under subsection (2) above if the European patent (UK) has been surrendered under section 29(1) above before the date on which by virtue of section 25(1) above the patent under this Act is to be treated as having been granted or, if proceedings for the surrender of the European patent (UK) have been begun before that date, until those proceedings are finally disposed of; and he shall not then take any action if the decision is to accept the surrender of the European patent.".

*Applications and amendments not to include additional matter*

20. For section 76 of the Patents Act 1977 (amendments of applications and patents not to include added matter) substitute—

"**76 Amendments of applications and patents not to include added matter**

(1) An application for a patent which—

(*a*) is made in respect of matter disclosed in an earlier application, or in the specification of a patent which has been granted, and

(*b*) discloses additional matter, that is, matter extending beyond that disclosed in the earlier application, as filed, or the application for the patent, as filed,

may be filed under section 8(3), 12 or 37(4) above, or as mentioned in section 15(4) above, but shall not be allowed to proceed unless it is amended so as to exclude the additional matter.

(2) No amendment of an application for a patent shall be allowed under section 17(3), 18(3) or 19(1) if it results in the application disclosing matter extending beyond that disclosed in the application as filed.

(3) No amendment of the specification of a patent shall be allowed under section 27(1), 73 or 75 if it—

(*a*) results in the specification disclosing additional matter, or

(*b*) extends the protection conferred by the patent.".

*Effect of European patent (UK)*

21.—(1) Section 77 of the Patents Act 1977 (effect of European patent (UK)) is amended as follows.

(2) For subsection (3) (effect of finding of partial validity on pending proceedings) substitute—

"(3) Where in the case of a European patent (UK)—

(*a*) proceedings for infringement, or proceedings under section 58 above, have been commenced before the court or the comptroller and have not been finally disposed of, and

(*b*) it is established in proceedings before the European Patent Office that the patent is only partially valid,

the provisions of section 63 or, as the case may be, of subsections (7) to (9) of section 58 apply as they apply to proceedings in which the validity of a patent is put in issue and in which it is found that the patent is only partially valid.".

(3) For subsection (4) (effect of amendment or revocation under European Patent Convention) substitute—

"(4) Where a European patent (UK) is amended in accordance with the European Patent Convention, the amendment shall have effect for the purposes of Parts I and III of this Act as if the specification of the patent had been amended under this Act; but subject to subsection (6)(*b*) below.

(4A) Where a European patent (UK) is revoked in accordance with the European Patent Convention, the patent shall be treated for the purposes of Parts I and III of this Act as having been revoked under this Act.".

(4) In subsection (6) (filing of English translation), in paragraph (*b*) (amendments) for "a translation of the amendment into English" substitute "a translation into English of the specification as amended".

(5) In subsection (7) (effect of failure to file translation) for the words from "a translation" to "above" substitute "such a translation is not filed".

*The state of the art: material contained in patent applications*

22. In section 78 of the Patents Act 1977 (effect of filing an application for a European patent (UK)), for subsection (5) (effect of withdrawal of application, &c.) substitute—

"(5) Subsections (1) to (3) above shall cease to apply to an application for a European patent (UK), except as mentioned in subsection (5A) below, if—

(*a*) the application is refused or withdrawn or deemed to be withdrawn, or (*b*) the designation of the United Kingdom in the application is withdrawn or deemed to be withdrawn,

but shall apply again if the rights of the applicant are re-established under the European Patent Convention, as from their re-establishment.

(5A) The occurrence of any of the events mentioned in subsection (5)(*a*) or (*b*) shall not affect the continued operation of section 2(3) above in relation to matter contained in an application for a European patent (UK) which by virtue of that provision has become part of the state of the art as regards other inventions.".

*Jurisdiction in certain proceedings*

23. Section 88 of the Patents Act 1977 (jurisdiction in legal proceedings in connection with Community Patent Convention) is repealed.

*Effect of filing international application for patent*

24.—(1) Section 89 of the Patents Act 1977 (effect of filing international application for patent) is amended as follows.

(2) After subsection (3) insert—

"(3A) If the relevant conditions are satisfied with respect to an application which is amended in accordance with the Treaty and the relevant conditions are not satisfied with respect to any amendment, that amendment shall be disregarded.".

(3) After subsection (4) insert—

"(4A) In subsection (4)(*a*) 'a copy of the application' includes a copy of the application published in accordance with the Treaty in a language other than that in which it was filed.".

(4) For subsection (10) (exclusion of certain applications subject to European Patent Convention) substitute—

"(10) The foregoing provisions of this section do not apply to an application which falls to be treated as an international application for a patent (UK) by reason only of its containing an indication that the applicant wishes to obtain a European patent (UK); but without prejudice to the application of those provisions to an application which also separately designates the United Kingdom.".

(5) The amendments in this paragraph shall be deemed always to have had effect.

(6) This paragraph shall be repealed by the order bringing the following paragraph into force.

25. In section 89 of the Patents Act 1977 (effect of filing international application for patent) substitute—

**"89 Effect of international application for patent**

(1) An international application for a patent (UK) for which a date of filing has been accorded under the Patent Co-operation Treaty shall, subject to—

section 89A (international and national phases of application), and
section 89B (adaptation of provisions in relation to international application),

be treated for the purposes of Parts I and III of this Act as an application for a patent under this Act.

(2) If the application, or the designation of the United Kingdom in it, is withdrawn or (except as mentioned in subsection (3)) deemed to be withdrawn under the Treaty, it shall be treated as withdrawn under this Act.

(3) An application shall not be treated as withdrawn under this Act if it, or the designation of the United Kingdom in it, is deemed to be withdrawn under the Treaty—

(*a*) because of an error or omission in an institution having functions under the Treaty, or

(*b*) because, owing to circumstances outside the applicant's control, a copy of the application was not received by the International Bureau before the end of the time limited for that purpose under the Treaty,

or in such other circumstances as may be prescribed.

(4) For the purposes of the above provisions an application shall not be treated as an international application for a patent (UK) by reason only of its containing an indication that the applicant wishes to obtain a European patent (UK), but an application shall be so treated if it also separately designates the United Kingdom.

(5) If an international application for a patent which designates the United Kingdom is refused a filing date under the Treaty and the comptroller determines that the refusal was caused by an error or omission in an institution having functions under the Treaty, he may direct that the application shall be treated as an application under this Act, having such date of filing as he may direct.

**89A International and national phases of application**

(1) The provisions of the Patent Co-operation Treaty relating to publication, search, examination and amendment, and not those of this Act, apply to an international application for a patent (UK) during the international phase of the application.

(2) The international phase of the application means the period from the filing of the application in accordance with the Treaty until the national phase of the application begins.

(3) The national phase of the application begins—

(*a*) when the prescribed period expires, provided any necessary translation of the application into English has been filed at the Patent Office and the prescribed fee has been paid by the applicant; or

(*b*) on the applicant expressly requesting the comptroller to proceed earlier with the national phase of the application, filing at the Patent Office—

(i) a copy of the application, if none has yet been sent to the Patent Office in accordance with the Treaty, and

(ii) any necessary translation of the application into English,

and paying the prescribed fee.

For this purpose a "copy of the application" includes a copy published in accordance with the Treaty in a language other than that in which it was originally filed.

(4) If the prescribed period expires without the conditions mentioned in subsection (3)(*a*) being satisfied, the application shall be taken to be withdrawn.

(5) Where during the international phase the application is amended in accordance with the Treaty, the amendment shall be treated as made under this Act if—

(*a*) when the prescribed period expires, any necessary translation of the amendment into English has been filed at the Patent Office, or

(*b*) where the applicant expressly requests the comptroller to proceed earlier with the national phase of the application, there is then filed at the Patent Office—

(i) a copy of the amendment, if none has yet been sent to the Patent Office in accordance with the Treaty, and

(ii) any necessary translation of the amendment into English;

otherwise the amendment shall be disregarded.

(6) The comptroller shall on payment of the prescribed fee publish any translation filed at the Patent Office under subsection (3) or (5) above.

**89B Adaptation of provisions in relation to international application**

(1) Where an international application for a patent (UK) is accorded a filing date under the Patent Co-operation Treaty—

(*a*) that date, or if the application is re-dated under the Treaty to a later date that later date, shall be treated as the date of filing the application under this Act,

(*b*) any declaration of priority made under the Treaty shall be treated as made under section 5(2) above, and where in accordance with the Treaty any extra days are allowed, the period of 12 months specified in section 5(2) shall be treated as altered accordingly, and

(*c*) any statement of the name of the inventor under the Treaty shall be treated as a statement filed under section 13(2) above.

(2) If the application, not having been published under this Act, is published in accordance with the Treaty it shall be treated, for purposes other than those mentioned in

subsection (3), as published under section 16 above when the conditions mentioned in section 89A(3)(*a*) are complied with.

(3) For the purposes of section 55 (use of invention for service of the Crown) and section 69 (infringement of rights conferred by publication) the application, not having been published under this Act, shall be treated as published under section 16 above—

(*a*) if it is published in accordance with the Treaty in English, on its being so published; and

(*b*) if it is so published in a language other than English—

(i) on the publication of a translation of the application in accordance with section 89A(6) above, or

(ii) on the service by the applicant of a translation into English of the specification of the application on the government department concerned or, as the case may be, on the person committing the infringing act.

The reference in paragraph (*b*)(ii) to the service of a translation on a government department or other person is to its being sent by post or delivered to that department or person.

(4) During the international phase of the application, section 8 above does not apply (determination of questions of entitlement in relation to application under this Act) and section 12 above (determination of entitlement in relation to foreign and convention patents) applies notwithstanding the application; but after the end of the international phase, section 8 applies and section 12 does not.

(5) When the national phase begins the comptroller shall refer the application for so much of the examination and search under section 17 and 18 above as he considers appropriate in view of any examination or search carried out under the Treaty.".

*Proceedings before the court or the comptroller*

26. In the Patents Act 1977, after section 99 (general powers of the court) insert—

**"99A Power of Patents Court to order report**

(1) Rules of court shall make provision empowering the Patents Court in any proceedings before it under this Act, on or without the application of any party, to order the Patent Office to inquire into and report on any question of fact or opinion.

(2) Where the court makes such an order on the application of a party, the fee payable to the Patent Office shall be at such rate as may be determined in accordance with rules of court and shall be costs of the proceedings unless otherwise ordered by the court.

(3) Where the court makes such an order of its own motion, the fee payable to the Patent Office shall be at such rate as may be determined by the Lord Chancellor with the approval of the Treasury and shall be paid out of money provided by Parliament.

**99B Power of Court of Session to order report**

(1) In any proceedings before the Court of Session under this Act the court may, either of its own volition or on the application of any party, order the Patent Office to inquire into and report on any question of fact or opinion.

(2) Where the court makes an order under subsection (1) above of its own volition the fee payable to the Patent Office shall be at such rate as may be determined by the Lord President of the Court of Session with the consent of the Treasury and shall be defrayed out of moneys provided by Parliament.

(3) Where the court makes an order under subsection (1) above on the application of a party, the fee payable to the Patent Office shall be at such rate as may be provided for in rules of court and shall be treated as expenses in the cause.".

27. For section 102 of the Patents Act 1977 (right of audience in patent proceedings) substitute—

**"102 Right of audience, &c in proceedings before comptroller**

(1) A party to proceedings before the comptroller under this Act, or under any treaty or international convention to which the United Kingdom is a party, may appear before the comptroller in person or be represented by any person whom he desires to represent him.

(2) No offence is committed under the enactments relating to the preparation of

documents by persons not legally qualified by reason only of the preparation by any person of a document, other than a deed, for use in such proceedings.

(3) Subsection (1) has effect subject to rules made under section 281 of the Copyright, Designs and Patents Act 1988 (power of comptroller to refuse to recognise certain agents).

(4) In its application to proceedings in relation to applications for, or otherwise in connection with, European patents, this section has effect subject to any restrictions imposed by or under the European Patent Convention.

**102A Right of audience, &c in proceedings on appeal from the comptroller**

(1) A solicitor of the Supreme Court may appear and be heard on behalf of any party to an appeal under this Act from the comptroller to the Patents Court.

(2) A registered patent agent or a member of the Bar not in actual practice may do, in or in connection with proceedings on an appeal under this Act from the comptroller to the Patents Court, anything which a solicitor of the Supreme Court might do, other than prepare a deed.

(3) The Lord Chancellor may by regulations—

(*a*) provide that the right conferred by subsection (2) shall be subject to such conditions and restrictions as appear to the Lord Chancellor to be necessary or expedient, and

(*b*) apply to persons exercising that right such statutory provisions, rules of court and other rules of law and practice applying to solicitors as may be specified in the regulations;

and different provision may be made for different descriptions of proceedings.

(4) Regulations under this section shall be made by statutory instrument which shall be subject to annulment in pursuance of a resolution of either House of Parliament.

(5) This section is without prejudice to the right of counsel to appear before the High Court.".

*Provision of information*

28. In section 118 of the Patents Act 1977 (information about patent applications, &c.), in subsection (3) (restriction on disclosure before the publication of application: exceptions) for "section 22(6)(*a*) above" substitute "section 22(6) above".

*Power to extend time limits*

29. In section 123 of the Patents Act 1977 (rules), after subsection (3) insert—

"(3A) It is hereby declared that rules—

(*a*) authorising the rectification of irregularities of procedure, or

(*b*) providing for the alteration of any period of time,

may authorise the comptroller to extend or further extend any period notwithstanding that the period has already expired.".

*Availability of samples of micro-organisms*

30. In the Patents Act 1977 after section 125 insert—

"**125A Disclosure of invention by specification: availability of samples of micro-organisms**

(1) Provision may be made by rules prescribing the circumstances in which the specification of an application for a patent, or of a patent, for an invention which requires for its performance the use of a micro-organism is to be treated as disclosing the invention in a manner which is clear enough and complete enough for the invention to be performed by a person skilled in the art.

(2) The rules may in particular require the applicant or patentee—

(*a*) to take such steps as may be prescribed for the purposes of making available to the public samples of the micro-organism, and

(*b*) not to impose or maintain restrictions on the uses to which such samples may be put, except as may be prescribed.

(3) The rules may provide that, in such cases as may be prescribed, samples need only be made available to such persons or descriptions of persons as may be prescribed; and the

rules may identify a description of persons by reference to whether the comptroller has given his certificate as to any matter.

(4) An application for revocation of the patent under section 72(1)(*c*) above may be made if any of the requirements of the rules cease to be complied with.".

## SCHEDULE 6:

Section 301

### PROVISIONS FOR THE BENEFIT OF THE HOSPITAL FOR SICK CHILDREN

*Interpretation*

1.—(1) In this Schedule—

"the Hospital" means The Hospital for Sick Children, Great Ormond Street, London,

"the trustees" means the special trustees appointed for the Hospital under the National Health Service Act 1977; and

"the work" means the play "Peter Pan" by Sir James Matthew Barrie.

(2) Expressions used in this Schedule which are defined for the purposes of Part I of this Act (copyright) have the same meaning as in that Part.

*Entitlement to royalty*

2.—(1) The trustees are entitled, subject to the following provisions of this Schedule, to a royalty in respect of any public performance, commercial publication, broadcasting or inclusion in a cable programme service of the whole or any substantial part of the work or an adaptation of it.

(2) Where the trustees are or would be entitled to a royalty, another form of remuneration may be agreed.

*Exceptions*

3. No royalty is payable in respect of—

(*a*) anything which immediately before copyright in the work expired on 31st December 1987 could lawfully have been done without the licence, or further licence, of the trustees as copyright owners; or

(*b*) anything which if copyright still subsisted in the work could, by virtue of any provision of Chapter III of Part I of this Act (acts permitted notwithstanding copyright), be done without infringing copyright.

*Saving*

4. No royalty is payable in respect of anything done in pursuance of arrangements made before the passing of this Act.

*Procedure for determining amount payable*

5.—(1) In default of agreement application may be made to the Copyright Tribunal which shall consider the matter and make such order regarding the royalty or other remuneration to be paid as it may determine to be reasonable in the circumstances.

(2) Application may subsequently be made to the Tribunal to vary its order, and the Tribunal shall consider the matter and make such order confirming or varying the original order as it may determine to be reasonable in the circumstances.

(3) An application for variation shall not, except with the special leave of the Tribunal, be made within twelve months from the date of the original order or of the order on a previous application for variation.

(4) A variation order has effect from the date on which it is made or such later date as may be specified by the Tribunal.

*Sums received to be held on trust*

6. The sums received by the trustees by virtue of this Schedule, after deduction of any relevant expenses, shall be held by them on trust for the purposes of the Hospital.

*Right only for the benefit of the Hospital*

7.—(1) The right of the trustees under this Schedule may not be assigned and shall cease if the trustees purport to assign or charge it.

(2) The right may not be the subject of an order under section 92 of the National Health Service Act 1977 (transfers of trust property by order of the Secretary of State) and shall cease if the Hospital ceases to have a separate identity or ceases to have purposes which include the care of sick children.

(3) Any power of Her Majesty, the court (within the meaning of the Charities Act 1960) or any other person to alter the trusts of a charity is not exercisable in relation to the trust created by this Schedule.

## SCHEDULE 7

Section 303(1)

### CONSEQUENTIAL AMENDMENTS: GENERAL

*British Mercantile Marine Uniform Act 1919 (c 62)*

1. For section 2 of the British Mercantile Marine Uniform Act 1919 (copyright in distinctive marks of uniform) substitute—

> **"2 Right in registered design of distinctive marks of uniform**
>
> The right of the Secretary of State in any design forming part of the British mercantile marine uniform which is registered under the Registered Designs Act 1949 is not limited to the period prescribed by section 8 of that Act but shall continue to subsist so long as the design remains on the register.".

*Chartered Associations (Protection of Names and Uniforms) Act 1926 (c 26)*

2. In section 1(5) of the Chartered Associations (Protection of Names and Uniforms) Act 1926 for "the copyright in respect thereof" substitute "the right in the registered design".

*Patents, Designs, Copyright and Trade Marks (Emergency) Act 1939 (c 107)*

3.—(1) The Patents, Designs, Copyright and Trade Marks (Emergency) Act 1939 is amended as follows.

(2) In section 1 (effect of licence where owner is enemy or enemy subject)—

- (*a*) in subsection (1) after "a copyright" and "the copyright" insert "or design right";
- (*b*) in subsection (2) after "the copyright" insert "or design right" and for "or copyright" substitute ", copyright or design right".

(3) In section 2 (power of comptroller to grant licences)—

- (*a*) in subsection (1) after "a copyright", "the copyright" (twice) and "the said copyright" insert "or design right" and for "or copyright" (twice) substitute ", copyright or design right";
- (*b*) in subsections (2), and (3) for ", or copyright" substitute ", copyright or design right";
- (*c*) in subsection (4) and in subsection (5) (twice), after "the copyright" insert "or design right";
- (*d*) in subsection (8)(*c*) for "or work in which copyright subsists" substitute "work in which copyright subsists or design in which design right subsists".

(4) In section 5 (effect of war on international arrangements)—

- (*a*) in subsection (1) for "section twenty-nine of the Copyright Act 1911" substitute "section 159 or 256 of the Copyright, Designs and Patents Act 1988 (countries enjoying reciprocal copyright or design right protection)";
- (*b*) in subsection (2) after "copyright" (four times) insert "or design right" and for "the Copyright Act 1911" (twice) substitute "Part I or III of the Copyright, Designs and Patents Act 1988".

(5) In section 10(1) (interpretation) omit the definition of "copyright", and for the definitions of "design", "invention", "patent" and "patentee" substitute—

"'design' has in reference to a registered design the same meaning as in the Registered Designs Act 1949, and in reference to design right the same meaning as in Part III of the Copyright, Designs and Patents Act 1988;

'invention' and 'patent' have the same meaning as in the Patents Act 1977.".

*Crown Proceedings Act 1947 (c 44)*

4.—(1) In the Crown Proceedings Act 1947 for section 3 (provisions as to industrial property) substitute—

"**3 Infringement of intellectual property rights**

(1) Civil proceedings lie against the Crown for an infringement committed by a servant or agent of the Crown, with the authority of the Crown, of—

(*a*) a patent,
(*b*) a registered trade mark or registered service mark,
(*c*) the right in a registered design,
(*d*) design right, or
(*e*) copyright;

but save as provided by this subsection no proceedings lie against the Crown by virtue of this Act in respect of an infringement of any of those rights.

(2) Nothing in this section, or any other provision of this Act, shall be construed as affecting—

(*a*) the rights of a government department under section 55 of the Patents Act 1977, Schedule 1 to the Registered Designs Act 1949 or section 240 of the Copyright, Designs and Patents Act 1988 (Crown use of patents and designs), or
(*b*) the rights of the Secretary of State under section 22 of the Patents Act 1977 or section 5 of the Registered Designs Act 1949 (security of information prejudicial to defence or public safety).".

(2) In the application of sub-paragraph (1) to Northern Ireland—

(*a*) the reference to the Crown Proceedings Act 1947 is to that Act as it applies to the Crown in right of Her Majesty's Government in Northern Ireland, as well as to the Crown in right of Her Majesty's Government in the United Kingdom, and
(*b*) in the substituted section 3 as it applies in relation to the Crown in right of Her Majesty's Government in Northern Ireland, subsection (2)(*b*) shall be omitted.

*Patents Act 1949 (c 87)*

5. In section 47 of the Patents Act 1949 (rights of third parties in respect of Crown use of patent), in the closing words of subsection (1) (which relate to the use of models or documents), after "copyright" insert "or design right".

*Public Libraries (Scotland) Act 1955 (c 27)*

6. In section 4 of the Public Libraries (Scotland) Act 1955 (extension of lending power of public libraries), make the existing provision subsection (1) and after it add—

"(2) The provisions of Part I of the Copyright, Designs and Patents Act 1988 (copyright) relating to the rental of copies of sound recordings, films and computer programs apply to any lending by a statutory library authority of copies of such works, whether or not a charge is made for that facility.".

*London County Council (General Powers) Act 1958 (c xxi)*

7. In section 36 of the London County Council (General Powers) Act 1958 (power as to libraries: provision and repair of things other than books) for subsection (5) substitute—

"(5) Nothing in this section shall be construed as authorising an infringement of copyright.".

*Public Libraries and Museums Act 1964 (c 75)*

8. In section 8 of the Public Libraries and Museums Act 1964 (restrictions on charges for library facilities), after subsection (5) add—

"(6) The provisions of Part I of the Copyright, Designs and Patents Act 1988 (copyright) relating to the rental of copies of sound recordings, films and computer programs apply to any lending by a library authority of copies of such works, whether or not a charge is made for that facility.".

*Marine, &c, Broadcasting (Offences) Act 1967 (c 41)*

9. In section 5 of the Marine, &c, Broadcasting (Offences) Act 1967 (provision of material for broadcasting by pirate radio stations)—

(*a*) in subsection (3)(*a*) for the words from "cinematograph film" to "in the record" substitute "film or sound recording with intent that a broadcast of it"; and
(*b*) in subsection (6) for the words from "and references" to the end substitute "and "film", "sound recording", "literary, dramatic or musical work" and "artistic work" have the same meaning as in Part I of the Copyright, Designs and Patents Act 1988 (copyright)".

*Medicines Act 1968 (c 67)*

10.—(1) Section 92 of the Medicines Act 1968 (scope of provisions restricting promotion of sales of medicinal products) is amended as follows.

(2) In subsection (1) (meaning of "advertisement") for the words from "or by the exhibition" to "service" substitute "or by means of a photograph, film, sound recording, broadcast or cable programme,".

(3) In subsection (2) (exception for the spoken word)—

(*a*) in paragraph (*a*) omit the words from "or embodied" to "film"; and
(*b*) in paragraph (*b*) for the words from "by way of" to the end substitute "or included in a cable programme service".

(4) For subsection (6) substitute—

"(6) In this section 'film', 'sound recording', 'broadcast', 'cable programme', 'cable programme service', and related expressions, have the same meaning as in Part I of the Copyright, Designs and Patents Act 1988 (copyright).".

*Post Office Act 1969 (c 48)*

11. In Schedule 10 to the Post Office Act 1969 (special transitional provisions relating to use of patents and registered designs), in the closing words of paragraphs 8(1) and 18(1) (which relate to the use of models and documents), after "copyright" insert "or design right".

*Merchant Shipping Act 1970 (c 36)*

12. In section 87 of the Merchant Shipping Act 1970 (merchant navy uniform), for subsection (4) substitute—

"(4) Where any design forming part of the merchant navy uniform has been registered under the Registered Designs Act 1949 and the Secretary of State is the proprietor of the design, his right in the design is not limited to the period prescribed by section 8 of that Act but shall continue to subsist so long as the design remains registered.".

*Taxes Management Act 1970 (c 9)*

13. In section 16 of the Taxes Management Act 1970 (returns to be made in respect of certain payments)—

(*a*) in subsection (1)(*c*), and
(*b*) in subsection (2)(*b*),

for "or public lending right" substitute ", public lending right, right in a registered design or design right".

*Tribunals and Inquiries Act 1971 (c 62)*

14. In Part I of Schedule 1 to the Tribunals and Inquiries Act 1971 (tribunals under direct supervision of Council on Tribunals) renumber the entry inserted by the Data Protection Act 1984 as "5B" and before it insert—

"Copyright. 5A. The Copyright Tribunal."

*Fair Trading Act 1973 (c 41)*

15. In Schedule 4 to the Fair Trading Act 1973 (excluded services), for paragraph 10 (services of patent agents) substitute—

"10. The services of registered patent agents (within the meaning of Part V of the Copyright, Designs and Patents Act 1988) in their capacity as such.";

and in paragraph 10A (services of European patent attorneys) for "section 84(7) of the Patents Act 1977" substitute "Part V of the Copyright, Designs and Patents Act 1988".

*House of Commons Disqualification Act 1975 (c 24)*

16. In Part II of Schedule 1 to the House of Commons Disqualification Act 1975 (bodies of which all members are disqualified), at the appropriate place insert "The Copyright Tribunal".

*Northern Ireland Assembly Disqualification Act 1975 (c 25)*

17. In Part II of Schedule 1 to the Northern Ireland Assembly Disqualification Act 1975 (bodies of which all members are disqualified), at the appropriate place insert "The Copyright Tribunal".

*Restrictive Trade Practices Act 1976 (c 34)*

18.—(1) The Restrictive Trade Practices Act 1976 is amended as follows.

(2) In Schedule 1 (excluded services) for paragraph 10 (services of patent agents) substitute—

"10. The services of registered patent agents (within the meaning of Part V of the Copyright, Designs and Patents Act 1988) in their capacity as such.";

and in paragraph 10A (services of European patent attorneys) for "section 84(7) of the Patents Act 1977" substitute "Part V of the Copyright, Designs and Patents Act 1988".

(3) In Schedule 3 (excepted agreements), after paragraph 5A insert—

*"Design right*

5B.—(1) This Act does not apply to—

(*a*) a licence granted by the owner or a licensee of any design right,
(*b*) an assignment of design right, or
(*c*) an agreement for such a licence or assignment,

if the licence, assignment or agreement is one under which no such restrictions as are described in section 6(1) above are accepted, or no such information provisions as are described in section 7(1) above are made, except in respect of articles made to the design; but subject to the following provisions.

(2) Sub-paragraph (1) does not exclude a licence, assignment or agreement which is a design pooling agreement or is granted or made (directly or indirectly) in pursuance of a design pooling agreement.

(3) In this paragraph a "design pooling agreement" means an agreement—

(*a*) to which the parties are or include at least three persons (the "principal parties") each of whom has an interest in one or more design rights, and
(*b*) by which each principal party agrees, in respect of design right in which he has, or may during the currency of the agreement acquire, an interest to grant an interest (directly or indirectly) to one or more of the other principal parties, or to one or more of those parties and to other persons.

(4) In this paragraph—

"assignment", in Scotland, means assignation; and
"interest" means an interest as owner or licensee of design right.

(5) This paragraph applies to an interest held by or granted to more than one person jointly as if they were one person.

(6) References in this paragraph to the granting of an interest to a person indirectly are to its being granted to a third person for the purpose of enabling him to make a grant to the person in question.".

*Resale Prices Act 1976 (c 53)*

19. In section 10(4) of the Resale Prices Act 1976 (patented articles: articles to be treated in same way), in paragraph (*a*) after "protected" insert "by design right or".

*Patents Act 1977 (c 37)*

20. In section 57 of the Patents Act 1977 (rights of third parties in respect of Crown use of patent), in the closing words of subsection (1) (which relate to the use of models or documents), after "copyright" insert "or design right".

21. In section 105 of the Patents Act 1977 (privilege in Scotland for communications relating to patent proceedings), omit "within the meaning of section 104 above", make the existing text subsection (1) and after it insert—

"(2) In this section—

"patent proceedings" means proceedings under this Act or any of the relevant conventions, before the court, the comptroller or the relevant convention court, whether contested or uncontested and including an application for a patent; and

"the relevant conventions" means the European Patent Convention, the Community Patent Convention and the Patent Co-operation Treaty.".

22. In section 123(7) of the Patents Act 1977 (publication of case reports by the comptroller)—

(*a*) for "and registered designs" substitute "registered designs or design right",
(*b*) for "and copyright" substitute ", copyright and design right".

23. In section 130(1) of the Patents Act 1977 (interpretation), in the definition of "court", for paragraph (*a*) substitute—

"(*a*) as respects England and Wales, the High Court or any patents county court having jurisdiction by virtue of an order under section 287 of the Copyright, Designs and Patents Act 1988;".

*Unfair Contract Terms Act 1977 (c 50)*

24. In paragraph 1 of Schedule 1 to the Unfair Contract Terms Act 1977 (scope of main provisions: excluded contracts), in paragraph (*c*) (contracts relating to grant or transfer of interest in intellectual property) after "copyright" insert "or design right".

*Judicature (Northern Ireland) Act 1978 (c 23)*

25. In section 94A of the Judicature (Northern Ireland) Act 1978 (withdrawal of privilege against self-incrimination in certain proceedings relating to intellectual property), in subsection (5) (meaning of "intellectual property") after "copyright" insert "or design right".

*Capital Gains Tax Act 1979 (c 14)*

26. In section 18(4) of the Capital Gains Tax Act 1979 (situation of certain assets for purposes of Act), for paragraph (*h*) (intellectual property) substitute—

"(*ha*) patents, trade marks, service marks and registered designs are situated where they are registered, and if registered in more than one register, where each register is situated, and rights or licences to use a patent, trade mark, service mark or registered design are situated in the United Kingdom if they or any right derived from them are exercisable in the United Kingdom,

(*hb*) copyright, design right and franchises, and rights or licences to use any copyright work or design in which design right subsists, are situated in the United Kingdom if they or any right derived from them are exercisable in the United Kingdom,".

*British Telecommunications Act 1981 (c 38)*

27. In Schedule 5 to the British Telecommunications Act 1981 (special transitional provisions relating to use of patents and registered designs), in the closing words of paragraphs 9(1) and 19(1) (which relate to the use of models and documents), after "copyright" insert "or design right".

*Supreme Court Act 1981 (c 54)*

28.—(1) The Supreme Court Act 1981 is amended as follows.

(2) In section 72 (withdrawal of privilege against self-incrimination in certain proceedings relating to intellectual property), in subsection (5) (meaning of "intellectual property") after "copyright" insert ", design right".

(3) In Schedule 1 (distribution of business in the High Court), in paragraph 1(*i*) (business assigned to the Chancery Division: causes and matters relating to certain intellectual property) for "or copyright" substitute ", copyright or design right".

*Broadcasting Act 1981 (c 68)*

29.—(1) The Broadcasting Act 1981 is amended as follows.

(2) In section 4 (general duties of IBA as regards programmes) for subsection (7) substitute—

"(7) For the purpose of maintaining supervision and control over the programmes (including advertisements) broadcast by them the Authority may make and use recordings of those programmes or any part of them.".

(3) In section 20(9), omit paragraph (*a*).

*Cable and Broadcasting Act 1984 (c 46)*

30.—(1) The Cable and Broadcasting Act 1984 is amended as follows.

(2) In section 8, omit subsection (8).

(3) In section 49 (power of Secretary of State to give directions in the public interest), for subsection (7) substitute—

"(7) For the purposes of this section the place from which a broadcast is made is, in the case of a satellite transmission, the place from which the signals carrying the broadcast are transmitted to the satellite.".

(4) In section 56(2) (interpretation) omit the definition of "the 1956 Act".

*Companies Act 1985 (c 6)*

31.—(1) Part XII of the Companies Act 1985 (registration of charges) is amended as follows.

(2) In section 396 (registration of charges in England and Wales: charges which must be registered), in subsection (1)(*j*) for the words from "on a patent" to the end substitute "or on any intellectual property", and after subsection (3) insert—

"(3A) The following are 'intellectual property' for the purposes of this section—

(a) any patent, trade mark, service mark, registered design, copyright or design right;
(b) any licence under or in respect of any such right.".

(3) In section 410 (registration of charges in Scotland: charges which must be registered), in subsection (3)(*c*) (incorporeal moveable property) after sub-paragraph (vi) insert—

"(vii) a registered design or a licence in respect of such a design,
(viii) a design right or a licence under a design right,".

*Law Reform (Miscellaneous Provisions) (Scotland) Act 1985 (c 73)*

32. In section 15 of the Law Reform (Miscellaneous Provisions) (Scotland) Act 1985 (withdrawal of privilege against self-incrimination in certain proceedings relating to intellectual property), in subsection (5) (meaning of "intellectual property") after "copyright" insert "or design right".

*Atomic Energy Authority Act 1986 (c 3)*

33. In section 8(2) of the Atomic Energy Authority Act 1986 (powers of Authority as to exploitation of research: meaning of "intellectual property"), after "copyrights" insert ", design rights".

*Education and Libraries (Northern Ireland) Order 1986 (SI 1986/594 (NI 3))*

34. In Article 77 of the Education and Libraries (Northern Ireland) Order 1986 (charges for library services), after paragraph (2) add—

"(3) The provisions of Part I of the Copyright, Designs and Patents Act 1988 (copyright) relating to the rental of copies of sound recordings, films and computer programs apply to any lending by a board of copies of such works, whether or not a charge is made for that facility.".

*Companies (Northern Ireland) Order 1986 (SI 1986/1032 (NI 6))*

35. In Article 403 of the Companies (Northern Ireland) Order 1986 (registration of charges: charges which must be registered), in paragraph (1)(*j*) for the words from "on a patent" to the end substitute "or on any intellectual property", and after paragraph (3) insert—

"(3A) The following are "intellectual property" for the purposes of this Article—

(*a*) any patent, trade mark, service mark, registered design, copyright or design right;
(*b*) any licence under or in respect of any such right.".

*Income and Corporation Taxes Act 1988 (c 1)*

36.—(1) The Income and Corporation Taxes Act 1988 is amended as follows.

(2) In section 83 (fees and expenses deductible in computing profits and gains of trade) for "the extension of the period of copyright in a design" substitute "an extension of the period for which the right in a registered design subsists".

(3) In section 103 (charge on receipts after discontinuance of trade, profession or vocation), in subsection (3) (sums to which the section does not apply), after paragraph (*b*) insert—

"(*bb*) a lump sum paid to the personal representatives of the designer of a design in which design right subsists as consideration for the assignment by them, wholly or partially, of that right,".

(4) In section 387 (carry forward as losses of certain payments made under deduction of tax), in subsection (3) (payments to which the section does not apply), in paragraph (*e*) (copyright royalties) after "applies" insert "or royalties in respect of a right in a design to which section 537B applies".

(5) In section 536 (taxation of copyright royalties where owner abroad), for the definition of "copyright" in subsection (2) substitute—

"'copyright' does not include copyright in—

(i) a cinematograph film or video recording, or
(ii) the sound-track of such a film or recording, so far as it is not separately exploited; and".

(6) In Chapter I of Part XIII (miscellaneous special provisions: intellectual property), after section 537 insert—

*"Designs*

**537A Relief for payments in respect of designs**

(1) Where the designer of a design in which design right subsists assigns that right, or the author of a registered design assigns the right in the design, wholly or partially, or grants an interest in it by licence, and—

(*a*) the consideration for the assignment or grant consists, in whole or in part, of a payment to which this section applies, the whole amount of which would otherwise be included in computing the amount of his profits or gains for a single year of assessment, and
(*b*) he was engaged in the creation of the design for a period of more than 12 months,

he may, on making a claim, require that effect shall be given to the following provisions in connection with that payment.

(2) If the period for which he was engaged in the creation of the design does not exceed 24 months, then, for all income tax purposes, one-half only of the amount of the payment shall be treated as having become receivable on the date on which it actually became receivable and the remaining half shall be treated as having become receivable 12 months before that date.

(3) If the period for which he was engaged in the creation of the design exceeds 24 months, then, for all income tax purposes, one-third only of the amount of the payment shall be treated as having become receivable on the date on which it actually became

receivable, and one-third shall be treated as having become receivable 12 months, and one-third 24 months, before that date.

(4) This section applies to—

(*a*) a lump sum payment, including an advance on account of royalties which is not returnable, and

(*b*) any other payment of or on account of royalties or sums payable periodically which does not only become receivable more than two years after articles made to the design or, as the case may be, articles to which the design is applied are first made available for sale or hire.

(5) A claim under this section with respect to any payment to which it applies by virtue only of subsection (4)(*b*) above shall have effect as a claim with respect to all such payments in respect of rights in the design in question which are receivable by the claimant, whether before or after the claim; and such a claim may be made at any time not later than 5th April next following the expiration of eight years after articles made to the design or, as the case may be, articles to which the design is applied were first made available for sale or hire.

(6) In this section—

(*a*) "designer" includes a joint designer, and

(*b*) any reference to articles being made available for sale or hire is to their being so made available anywhere in the world by or with the licence of the design right owner or, as the case may be, the proprietor of the registered design.

**537B Taxation of design royalties where owner abroad**

(1) Where the usual place of abode of the owner of a right in a design is not within the United Kingdom, section 349(1) shall apply to any payment of or on account of any royalties or sums paid periodically for or in respect of that right as it applies to annual payments not payable out of profits or gains brought into charge to income tax.

(2) In subsection (1) above—

(*a*) "right in a design" means design right or the right in a registered design,

(*b*) the reference to the owner of a right includes a person who, notwithstanding that he has assigned the right to some other person, is entitled to receive periodical payments in respect of the right, and

(*c*) the reference to royalties or other sums paid periodically for or in respect of a right does not include royalties or sums paid in respect of articles which are shown on a claim to have been exported from the United Kingdom for distribution outside the United Kingdom.

(3) Where a payment to which subsection (1) above applies is made through an agent resident in the United Kingdom and that agent is entitled as against the owner of the right to deduct any sum by way of commission in respect of services rendered, the amount of the payment shall for the purposes of section 349(1) be taken to be diminished by the sum which the agent is entitled to deduct.

(4) Where the person by or through whom the payment is made does not know that any such commission is payable or does not know the amount of any such commission, any income tax deducted by or assessed and charged on him shall be computed in the first instance on, and the account to be delivered of the payment shall be an account of, the total amount of the payment without regard being had to any diminution thereof, and in that case, on proof of the facts on a claim, there shall be made to the agent on behalf of the owner of the right such repayment of income tax as is proper in respect of the sum deducted by way of commission.

(5) The time of the making of a payment to which subsection (1) above applies shall, for all tax purposes, be taken to be the time when it is made by the person by whom it is first made and not the time when it is made by or through any other person.

(6) Any agreement for the making of any payment to which subsection (1) above applies in full and without deduction of income tax shall be void.".

(7) In section 821 (payments made under deduction of tax before passing of Act imposing income tax for that year), in subsection (3) (payments subject to adjustment) after paragraph (*a*) insert—

"(*aa*) any payment for or in respect of a right in a design to which section 537B applies; and".

(8) In Schedule 19 (apportionment of income of close companies), in paragraph 10(4) (cessation or liquidation: debts taken into account although creditor is participator or associate), in paragraph (*c*) (payments for use of certain property) for the words from "tangible property" to "extend)" substitute—

"—

(i) tangible property,

(ii) copyright in a literary, dramatic, musical or artistic work within the meaning of Part I of the Copyright, Designs and Patents Act 1988 (or any similar right under the law of a country to which that Part does not extend), or

(iii) design right,".

(9) In Schedule 25 (taxation of UK-controlled foreign companies: exempt activities), in paragraph 9(1)(*a*) (investment business: holding of property) for "patents or copyrights" substitute "or intellectual property" and after that sub-paragraph insert—

"(1A) In sub-paragraph (1)(*a*) above "intellectual property" means patents, registered designs, copyright and design right (or any similar rights under the law of a country outside the United Kingdom).".

## SCHEDULE 8

Section 303(2)

### REPEALS

| Chapter | Short title | Extent of repeal |
|---|---|---|
| 1939 c 107 | Patents, Designs, Copyright and Trade Marks (Emergency) Act 1939 | In section 10(1), the definition of "copyright". |
| 1945 c 16 | Limitation (Enemies and War Prisoners) Act 1945 | In sections 2(1) and 4(*a*), the reference to section 10 of the Copyright Act 1911. |
| 1949 c 88 | Registered Designs Act 1949 | In section 3(2), the words "or original".<br>Section 5(5).<br>In section 11(2), the words "or original".<br>In section 14(3), the words "or the Isle of Man".<br>Section 32.<br>Section 33(2).<br>Section 37(1).<br>Section 38.<br>In section 44(1), the definitions of "copyright" and "Journal".<br>In section 45, paragraphs (1) and (2).<br>In section 46, paragraphs (1) and (2).<br>Section 48(1).<br>In Schedule 1, in paragraph 3(1), the words "in such manner as may be prescribed by rules of court".<br>Schedule 2. |
| 1956 c 74 | Copyright Act 1956 | The whole Act. |
| 1957 c 6 | Ghana Independence Act 1957 | In Schedule 2, paragraph 12. |
| 1957 c 60 | Federation of Malaya Independence Act 1957 | In Schedule 1, paragraphs 14 and 15. |
| 1958 c 44 | Dramatic and Musical Performers' Protection Act 1958 | The whole Act. |
| 1958 c 51 | Public Records Act 1958 | Section 11.<br>Schedule 3. |
| 1960 c 52 | Cyprus Independence Act 1960 | In the Schedule, paragraph 13. |

| Chapter | Short title | Extent of repeal |
|---|---|---|
| 1960 c 55 | Nigeria Independence Act 1960 | In Schedule 2, paragraphs 12 and 13. |
| 1961 c 1 | Tanganyika Independence Act 1961 | In Schedule 2, paragraphs 13 and 14. |
| 1961 c 16 | Sierra Leone Independence Act 1961 | In Schedule 3, paragraphs 13 and 14. |
| 1961 c 25 | Patents and Designs (Renewals, Extensions and Fees) Act 1961 | The whole Act. |
| 1962 c 40 | Jamaica Independence Act 1962 | In Schedule 2, paragraph 13. |
| 1962 c 54 | Trinidad and Tobago Independence Act 1962 | In Schedule 2, paragraph 13. |
| 1963 c 53 | Performers' Protection Act 1963 | The whole Act. |
| 1964 c 46 | Malawi Independence Act 1964 | In Schedule 2, paragraph 13. |
| 1964 c 65 | Zambia Independence Act 1964 | In Schedule 1, paragraph 9. |
| 1964 c 86 | Malta Independence Act 1964 | In Schedule 1, paragraph 11. |
| 1964 c 93 | Gambia Independence Act 1964 | In Schedule 2, paragraph 12. |
| 1966 c 24 | Lesotho Independence Act 1966 | In the Schedule, paragraph 9. |
| 1966 c 37 | Barbados Independence Act 1966 | In Schedule 2, paragraph 12. |
| 1967 c 80 | Criminal Justice Act 1967 | In Parts I and IV of Schedule 3, the entries relating to the Registered Designs Act 1949. |
| 1968 c 56 | Swaziland Independence Act 1968 | In the Schedule, paragraph 9. |
| 1968 c 67 | Medicines Act 1968 | In section 92(2)(*a*), the words from "or embodied" to "film".<br>Section 98. |
| 1968 c 68 | Design Copyright Act 1968 | The whole Act. |
| 1971 c 4 | Copyright (Amendment) Act 1971 | The whole Act. |
| 1971 c 23 | Courts Act 1971 | In Schedule 9, the entry relating to the Copyright Act 1956. |
| 1971 c 62 | Tribunals and Inquiries Act 1971 | In Schedule 1, paragraph 24. |
| 1972 c 32 | Performers' Protection Act 1972 | The whole Act. |
| 1975 c 24 | House of Commons Disqualification Act 1975 | In Part II of Schedule 1, the entry relating to the Performing Right Tribunal. |
| 1975 c 25 | Northern Ireland Assembly Disqualification Act 1975 | In Part II of Schedule 1, the entry relating to the Performing Right Tribunal. |
| 1977 c 37 | Patents Act 1977 | Section 14(4) and (8).<br>In section 28(3), paragraph (*b*) and the word "and" preceding it.<br>Section 28(5) to (9).<br>Section 49(3).<br>Sections 72(3).<br>Sections 84 and 85.<br>Section 88.<br>Section 104.<br>In section 105, the words "within the meaning of section 104 above".<br>Sections 114 and 115.<br>Section 123(2)(*k*).<br>In section 130(1), the definition of "patent agent".<br>In section 130(7), the words "88(6) and (7),".<br>In Schedule 5, paragraphs 1 and 2, in paragraph 3 the words "and 44(1)" and "in each case", and paragraphs 7 and 8. |

| Chapter | Short title | Extent of repeal |
|---|---|---|
| 1979 c 2 | Customs and Excise Management Act 1979 | In Schedule 4, the entry relating to the Copyright Act 1956. |
| 1980 c 21 | Competition Act 1980 | Section 14. |
| 1981 c 68 | Broadcasting Act 1981 | Section 20(9)(*a*). |
| 1982 c 35 | Copyright Act 1956 (Amendment) Act 1982 | The whole Act. |
| 1983 c 42 | Copyright (Amendment) Act 1983 | The whole Act. |
| 1984 c 46 | Cable and Broadcasting Act 1984 | Section 8(8).<br>Section 16(4) and (5).<br>Sections 22 to 24.<br>Section 35(2) and (3).<br>Sections 53 and 54.<br>In section 56(2), the definition of "the 1956 Act".<br>In Schedule 5, paragraphs 6, 7, 13 and 23. |
| 1985 c 21 | Films Act 1985 | Section 7(2). |
| 1985 c 41 | Copyright (Computer Software) Amendment Act 1985 | The whole Act. |
| 1985 c 61 | Administration of Justice Act 1985 | Section 60. |
| 1986 c 39 | Patents, Designs and Marks Act 1986 | In Schedule 2, paragraph 1(2)(*a*), in paragraph 1(2)(*k*) the words "subsection (1)(*j*) of section 396 and" and in paragraph 1(2)(*l*) the words "subsection (2)(i) of section 93". |
| 1988 c 1 | Income and Corporation Taxes Act 1988 | In Schedule 29, paragraph 5. |

# Index